The War in the Empty Air

The
WAR *in the*
EMPTY
AIR

Victims, Perpetrators, and Postwar Germans

Dagmar Barnouw

INDIANA UNIVERSITY PRESS

Bloomington and Indianapolis

This book is a publication of

Indiana University Press
601 North Morton Street
Bloomington, IN 47404-3797 USA

http://iupress.indiana.edu

Telephone orders 800-842-6796
Fax orders 812-855-7931
Orders by e-mail iuporder@indiana.edu

Library of Congress Cataloging-in-Publication Data

Barnouw, Dagmar.
  The war in the empty air: victims, perpetrators, and postwar
Germans / Dagmar Barnouw.
    p. cm.
  Includes bibliographical references and index.
  ISBN 0-253-34651-7 (cloth : alk. paper) 1. Memory—Social
aspects—Germany. 2. World War, 1939-1945—Germany—
Historiography. 3. Germany—History—1933-1945—
Historiography. 4. Photography in historiography. 5. National
characteristics, German. 6. History—Psychological aspects.
I. Title.
  DD256.48.B37 2005
  940.53'072'043—dc22
                                                2005011537
  1 2 3 4 5 10 09 08 07 06 05

To the memory of my mother

CONTENTS

PREFACE

The Loss of History in Postwar German Memory

In human-political terms, the concept of a guilt
beyond the crime and an innocence beyond
kindness and virtue is meaningless.

—HANNAH ARENDT TO KARL JASPERS, 17 AUGUST 1946

The War in the Air

For a saving grace, we didn't see our dead
Who rarely bothered coming home to die
But simply stayed away out there
In the clean war, the war in the air.

Seldom the ghosts came back bearing their tales
Of hitting the earth, the incompressible sea,
But stayed up there in the relative wind,
Shades fading in the mind,

Who had no graves but only epitaphs
Where never so many spoke for never so few:
Per ardua, said the partisans of Mars,
Per aspera, to the stars.

That was the good war, the war we won
As if there was no death, for goodness' sake.
With the help of the losers we left out there
In the air, in the empty air.

—HOWARD NEMEROW (*WAR STORIES* 1987)

Since the end of the Second World War, the politics of German memory
has been fraught with fears of being misunderstood—fears that have
grown and intensified over the last decades and have themselves become
a part of German postwar history. They are familiar fears, and when

asked about them ordinary Germans tend to shrug them off as a natural leftover from the Bad German past, a fact of life. Life, on the whole, has been relatively pleasant and reassuring for large numbers of Germans, as it has been for most populations in the West, once the all-consuming chaos of World War II ebbed. For the many millions of refugees, deportees, and late-returning POWs it took longer to get settled, but finally most West Germans, even those whose traumatic wartime experiences left them with harrowing memories, found their way back to a relative normality. Surprisingly soon, given the physical and emotional devastation, the unimaginable destruction caused by that war, the past retreated. As far as it concerned their own lives during the Third Reich, the past became shadowy, insubstantial, in the powerfully persuasive substantial presence of rebuilt cities and well-functioning political and social institutions that followed, as if logically, from the good, clean Allied victory.

In hindsight, it may seem both natural and strange that this normality had repressed the recent past so quickly and thoroughly; that forgetting had become so impenetrable—as it were, memory-resistant. This would have been natural in the case of extreme experiences, because the instability and fragility of memory processes allowed a protective shield to form between the acceptable present and the unacceptable past. Yet it seems also strange because not all German experiences during the Nazi regime were extreme, or troubling. In its early years, the Third Reich seemed a good place to many of the intended inhabitants of that National-socialist utopia, the working and lower middle classes—better at any rate than the Weimar Republic, particularly in its late stage. But memories of these earlier years too appear to have retreated into a past beyond remembrance. It is true, this utopia's pronounced exclusionary tendencies would soon show their true destructive, dystopian nature; and this change for the worse would have contributed to collectively forgetting the past experiences of those ordinary Germans who were not the designated victims of the Nazi regime's increasingly violent tactics.

If, looking back over sixty years, one sets aside for a moment those tactics and their terrible results, the most difficult to understand, the most strange, might seem the absence of German mourning for their dead killed in battle, in air raids, on the enforced treks from the East—as if, since they had not been permitted access to public memory, they could not be mourned. And like the dead, the loss of artifacts, created over many hundreds of years and destroyed in a few minutes by the huge storms of fire unleashed in the Allied air raids, was not mourned to keep them alive in memory. Their pitiful remnants were swept up in the clear-

ing away in preparation for rebuilding that started while the bombs were
still falling, the corpses still decomposing under the rubble. The Federal
Republic of Germany developed, as if naturally, into a stable and competent democratic technocracy boasting a high standard of living for a
remarkably large percentage of the population, content with a curiously
blank memory of the war years.

In East Germany, where life was neither pleasant nor reassuring for
all but a small part of the population, the past did not retreat that easily,
though the more "normal" continuity between past and present did not
really conceal the many gaps and distortions of the new Communist
state's historical memory. The designated heir to the battle against fascism during the Weimar Republic, the new state saw itself as predicated
on victory rather than defeat. German wartime memories were encouraged as long as they recorded the ideological and military victory of the
Red Army. Moscow was the holy site of present Communist power and
Stalingrad the holy site of past Russian suffering—as Auschwitz was the
holy site of Jewish suffering. In its selective focus on Nazi persecution of
Communism and Communists, East Germany's history was not "bad"
in the sense West Germany's history was thought to be, because it had
led to a Communist victory and, after the fires of war which in that case
replaced the fires of a revolution, to the foundation of a Communist
utopia, the German Democratic Republic.

If there was, on the whole, less forgetting of wartime experiences
than in the Federal Republic, there was also no or very little rebuilding,
and the ruins remained, everywhere and highly visible, as witnesses to
the physical destruction of the old Germany without which there would
not have been ideological rebirth into the new. The ruins, in East German fashion, served several purposes: they were also reminders of capitalist air war against Germany—one criminal capitalist aggressor against
another. The history ordinary East Germans were taught was a severely
restricted and distorted version of twentieth-century historical events
and developments, but it was not *their* "bad" past. It was not a history
for which they were responsible as long as they were, or pretended to be,
loyally supporting the Communist state. The issue was not whether they
knew "their" history but whether they embraced its ideologically correct version as it changed in time. Yet, ironically and sadly, it was the
East Germans' restricted and impoverished lives over almost five decades that really paid for the German "bad" past, the heavy debt of
collective guilt.

For ordinary West Germans, that elusively familiar silent majority
given a voice by politicians and public intellectuals, their "bad" history

has been synonymous with the moral-political obligation to remember their past selectively as pure Nazi Evil. Often evoked but never explained for fear that explanations might detract from its moral weight, this evil history has been close to them and also remote: an over and over repeated tale of relentless horror that has had no or little connection with their present. The "bad" past in need of remembering has not concerned their own experiences under the Nazi regime but solely the experiences of that regime's designated victims. If the memory-stories of the victims were shaped by the Evil of their extreme suffering, so should the memory stories of the Germans be shaped by the Evil of having contributed to that suffering. At the end of the war, ordinary Germans in their collectivity were expected to acknowledge their past active or passive complicity with Nazi criminality and commit it to memory, regardless how they remembered their feelings and actions during the Nazi period. Vanquished, they did as they were told and then they fell silent—a private silence, separating them from their memories. This separation has endured for almost six decades; and for many Germans, whether or not they "really" understood what had been asked of them or why, it made the war a terra incognita, inaccessible for want of information except the Evil of Nazi persecutions.

The purpose of this book is to argue that the nearly total exclusion from historical memory of German wartime experiences, among them large-scale air raids, mass deportations, and warfare involving millions of conscripts, has over the decades created a serious loss of historical reality. This loss is particularly damaging in that it has affected the historical memory of a technological war of huge and still insufficiently understood dimensions that was a part of the still insufficiently historicized Nazi period. My concern is not that Germans suffered too—all populations caught in this particularly terrible war suffered. The issue is the usefulness now, sixty years later, of an enduring hierarchy of suffering that has removed from historical memory the larger part of a war so familiarly and viciously destructive that it should have meant the end of all wars.

If German remembrance of their difficult experiences has been deemed inappropriate, in contemporary terms "offensive," because it might take away from the greater intensity, the "uniqueness," of other groups' suffering, this was understandable at the end of the war. The physical and psychological damage caused by the Nazi persecutions was so extreme that it had to appear "unique" and uniquely significant, beyond human measure, outside of human, that is, historical time. But this insistence on singularity over a long period of time would also have serious psychological and political implications that bear closer scrutiny. Claims for a unique and therefore supra-historical status of "Auschwitz" have drawn on the horrified inability to understand how what had happened could have happened—an existential displacement that, for the victors, carried immeasurable moral power. This power, inevitably admixed with political interests, has over the years had an enormous influence on questions of memory, identity and history in postwar Germany but also, and increasingly, in the United States. The good, clean war prosecuted by the Allies has been the absolutely just war to be invoked as justification for quite a few unjust wars in the postwar era, notably the preemptive strike against Iraq, with its dangerous insistence on an enduringly secure preeminence of American—by extension also Israeli—political and military power.

I am interested here in the political and psychological dynamics of this power because it has so far prevented a more comprehensive historical memory of the Second World War that would require a more consistent historization of the Nazi period, including a more critical comparative study of Allied warfare. In its end stage, the Second World War was fought on both sides "as if there was no death," no limits to the destruction of humans, combatants and civilians alike, no modern sense of the fragility and finiteness of life. In the end, that war had created its own "empty air," spaces of annihilation peopled with millions and millions of the anonymous dead. The huge and still growing construct of Holocaust memory-stories has been built up over many decades to undo in remembrance precisely this anonymity.

Sadly, the cultural centrality of Holocaust remembrance has contributed to the enduring anonymity of the other war dead and to the diminished memory of the other parts of the war. Connected with this issue is the question of the aftermath of that war in twentieth- and twenty-first-century political culture: what happens after dramatic regime and power changes? After traumatic cultural collapses resulting in massive redirection of group memories that leads to selective and exclusive histories? One of the consequences of WWII, the end of empire, has brought about potentially liberalizing population migrations and globalization, but in their wake also a notable increase of power for politics of identity that often has proved selectively unifying at the cost of greater political and cultural polarization. Based on the authority of remembered persecution and suffering, such political discourses of identity echo in certain instructive ways the memory discourses of the Holocaust. Their extraordinary cultural appeal lies in harnessing the power of memory to rescue the dead from anonymity and, speaking for them, make them speak for the causes of the living. In a series of case histories I will trace some of the interdependencies between a still growing presence of Holocaust memory discourses and absence of German memories of the recent past: how and why they forgot having forgotten. Taken together, these case histories will make it easier to look more realistically, namely from different angles, at the moral and political demands made on ordinary Germans over the last sixty years to remember the extreme experiences of others and to forget their own—demands that have hindered the building up of a more inclusive and differentiating historical memory. The introductory chapter, "The Uses of Remorse," identifies and analyzes the three core issues that will be explored in detail in the individual case histories: suspicion, power and impotence, memory and identity.

The War in the Empty Air

1 Historical Memory and the Uses of Remorse

Suspicion

The single most exploitable political commodity in the postwar era has been Nazi Evil. At the end of what was arguably the most destructive war in Western historical memory, Germans were confronted with the inescapable enormity of material and moral devastation and the expectation that they accept it as their responsibility. Collectively they had become "the German Question" announced on the title page of *Life*'s famous photo essay on the opening of the concentration camps. Like televised images later, these photo images would reach a large American viewership, penetrating into the private sphere of their homes. But photographs' presence there would be more permanent and thus more powerful. Connected with other photos sequentially, each moment frozen in the individual image would not supersede nor yield to the others; it would not easily release the appalled and fascinated viewer.

Widely distributed and looked at repeatedly, these photographs were meant to assure the permanent memory—"lest we forget"—of the unspeakable, unbelievable suffering of the victims and the cruelty of the perpetrators: how could "the Germans" have done it? Were they not all monsters? For a variety of reasons, assumptions of collective guilt and demands for collective remorse would not only endure but grow for over half a century. This period has seen enormous cultural and political changes, among them rapid globalization; but the notion of a uniquely German "unmastered," "uncompleted," unspeakably and inexhaustibly "bad past" has remained a politically potent issue—in important ways even more so now than in the first decades after the war.

The politics of suspicion since the end of WWII have drawn on profound doubts that "the Germans" will ever "truly" confront their "bad past"; that "they" have never been, will never become "truly" remorseful, and therefore can never be "truly" forgiven, readmitted to the comity of peoples, "redeemed" in normality. Morally powerful arguments, these doubts have drawn on semireligious, supra-historical yearnings for an enduring, uniquely meaningful status of the victims of Nazi persecutions: "the Holocaust" as the exclusive focus of German collective memory of the Second World War and the crucible of Western modernity. The desire, inevitable in this situation, for acknowledgment of guilt and signs of remorse and the suspicious accusations that the remorse of the guilty, the irredeemable *Tätergeneration* (generation of perpetrators), was not sincere were to increase and harden over the decades because German collective guilt had seemed, and therefore remained, irrefutable from the beginning.

This did not mean that the Germans felt collectively guilty but that it had become increasingly difficult to discuss this topic with any degree of openness, once the anxiously self-searching debates of German guilt in the immediate postwar years had come to an end. Curiously, over the years it seemed more and more impossible to look at the issues from different perspectives supported by different experiences and state these positions publicly. One of the reasons was the moral-political authority, from the beginning, of the assumption of collective guilt, which would reassert itself powerfully in the generational conflicts of the sixties and seventies.

This authority was largely responsible for focusing all public remembrance of the war on the victims of the Nazi regime, especially Jews, which made public control of memory more effective. The desire to direct collective memory has to be seen in connection with both spontaneously horrified and politically calculating reactions, on the American as well as the German side, to the extraordinary scale of Nazi criminality revealed at the end of the war.[1] In time this control would result in a near total lack of interest, both German and international, in the extreme war experiences of a large part of the German population. An important aspect of this development has been fear that memory discourses of German war experiences might be perceived as intentional parallelism suggesting comparability with the experiences and memories of the victims of the Nazi regime.

Such feared misperception would provoke strong accusations that Germans wanted to challenge the uniqueness of Nazi persecutions and thus question the cultural status of the Holocaust, "Auschwitz," as the all-devouring black hole of Western modernity. In postwar Germany, all public and private German memory discourses of WWII could only mean one thing, namely guilty attempts to avoid the responsibilities of an overwhelming German collective guilt. Such memories would then be automatically rejected as a priori irrelevant explanations or completely implausible excuses. In *comparison* (ironically an indispensable point of reference in principled arguments for incomparability) with the supra-historical experiences of the victims, the historical experiences of Germans were unreal, as if the events they remembered had never happened. The term "apologeticism" has worked like a spell over many decades, rejecting all German attempts to explain at least some aspects of the catastrophe, regardless whether or not their explanations were politically responsible and historically sound. The declared uniqueness of Nazi persecutions has meant claiming a supra-historical and thus supra-rational status for their remembrance, with the result that it is eo ipso impossible to pose rational questions. Attempts to better understand at least some aspects of these persecutions in historical terms have been notoriously suspect as immoral "apologeticist" assaults on the moral and political uniqueness of the Holocaust.

It is not surprising that accusations of apologeticism, Holocaust denial, and anti-Semitism, often leveled on the basis of little or no rationally accessible evidence, have played an important part in the steady growth of Holocaust memory discourses that claim a supra-historical remembrance for the historical experiences of the victims of the Nazi regime and historical forgetting for the wartime experiences of Germans. Since these claims are protected by politically powerful taboos, they present a threat for anyone who questions them. Once suspected of apologeticism, Holocaust denial, and anti-Semitism, the quester can no longer explain his/her intentions, much the less defend them. The fact alone of a "real" question expecting an explanatory rather than ritual answer suggests heresy and demands sincere remorse.

The familiar political potency of this demand was once more demonstrated in the fall of 2002 by the "highly offended" reaction of an American president and his advisors, eager to prosecute a preemptive war against Iraq, to the German chancellor's politically expedient critique of this enterprise in his election campaign. True, the situation had been complicated by a notoriously outspoken German minister of jus-

tice's critical remarks about Bush's aggressive political style and strategies: Bush's overeagerness to attack, the old-style social democrat had
said in an informal meeting with union bosses, reminded her of the
strategies used by other leaders, among them "Adolf Nazi." Inevitably
taken out of context, and considerably distorted, the minister's remarks
were politically irresponsible, given current pieties; but were they morally sinful? It seemed so, judging from the bitter complaints by the Bush
White House that a fatally combined "German anti-Americanism and
anti-Semitism" had "poisoned" the relations between the United States
and Germany.[2]

When the German chancellor, anxious not to appear "insensitive,"
fired several of his high-ranking officials and sent a letter of apology, his
words and acts were deemed insufficiently remorseful. The political and
economic importance of this moral rejection was promptly impressed
on the German chancellor by more flexible German business leaders,
and the foreign minister, Joschka Fischer, was sent to pledge, once again,
Germany's abiding moral and political loyalty. During an interview for
the PBS *NewsHour with Jim Lehrer* (October 31, 2002), Fischer shared
with American viewers his deep dismay about recent misunderstandings between two close friends and allies: "the Germans," he said, were
painfully aware of their "bad past" and "forever indebted to America"
to whom they "owed their second chance." He explicitly reassured his
interviewer that "they" would "never forget" their troubled past and
never endanger this special relationship—a promise that surely violated
one of the most important tenets of a modern secular democracy, its
sense of its own historicity: "forever" and "never" are alien to the modern understanding of historical time.[3]

Fischer's specialty has been successful navigation of politically treacherous, highly emotional situations. Learning how to deal smoothly with
the Greens, his own quarrelsome, opinionated party, has prepared him
to an extent for the slippery moral politics of American group sensitivities. He knows that he is expected to be sincerely invested in representing, by showing it, German remorse, and for this, too, he came well
prepared. A year earlier, on the same program, he had promised that his
social-democratic government would "forever" prevent anti-Semitism
from raising its ugly head again in Germany. On these occasions, TV
cameras hover over his expressive, mercurial face, intrigued by the visible paradox of a successful, competitive politician's sincere feelings of
inherited collective guilt and remorse.

More than half a century earlier, the cameras of the U.S. Army Signal Corps photographers were not so lucky. Searching for signs of re-

morse on the faces of the "German civilian population" forced to "view the atrocities" committed in "their" name by "their" criminal regime, they were sorely disappointed. What they found and documented were the notoriously "stony" faces of women and their small children, at that time the only civilians, showing horror and repulsion rather than sadness.[4] It was a lack of expression that signified to the American viewers of these photographs nothing but German collective criminal culpability and the absence of even a trace of redeeming remorse.

It is impossible to guess how many American viewers watching Fischer's performance on that serene PBS show really believed him, since fascination with supra-rational Nazi Evil seems to be alive and well even among the intellectual elite.[5] Fischer is first German and then human, if still of the morally inferior kind—precisely what enables him to speak in moral terms for *all* Germans. On the other hand, the majority of his audience would or should have been aware of the fact that allegations of a renascent German anti-Semitism could not but be politically useful to the Bush administration intent on evoking WWII, the most successful, indeed holy, war in American history, to justify invasion in Iraq. Like defeated, invaded, and/or liberated Germany and Japan, invaded Iraq would be an excellent candidate for moral-political cleansing by means of redemptive democratization. To have the German minister of justice make any kind of connection between Hitler's and Bush's politics of aggression in their strategies of distraction was indeed a great gift because it reaffirmed the need to extend WWII into Iraq: the evil of al Qaeda is linked with the still lurking evil of the Nazis, and both are linked with Iraq.[6]

Like Bush, a deeply religious politician with unquestioned moral certainties, the British prime minister Tony Blair made it a habit during the months building up to the invasion of Iraq to admonish his reluctant subjects to "remember the second World War when America and Great Britain rid Europe of Nazi Evil."[7] But beyond the personal religio-political convictions of these two energetic political visionaries, the Manichean scenario of absolute Right and Wrong, Good and Evil, has been the cultural and political matrix of that archetypically "just war," a simplifying vision that so far has resisted all necessary revisions. Among many other problems, Hitler's heritage has also contributed to an increasingly powerful process of political re-religionization, parallel to the growth of "the Holocaust," and the creation of a cultural climate that discourages secular skepticism and promotes affirming "spirituality."

Over the last decades, American culture has become attuned to the politics of suspicion—evils of the past brought into the daylight of the present and checked for usability—and addicted to demonstrations of remorse: the more sincere, it seems, the more remote the crimes. Bill Clinton's sincere apologies for American slavery were historically absurd, morally self-serving, and (up to a point) politically effective; and so, for similar reasons, were Bush's demands for the German chancellor's sincere apologies for German "anti-Americanism and anti-Semitism." There is some disagreement whether the cultural power of proliferating politics of identity concerning race, religion, gender, and sexual preference has in important ways drawn on the strategies of Holocaust memory discourses. However, authorized by their respective memories of previous persecution, all the groups involved in the politics of identity have been demanding collective remorse from collectively guilty perpetrators, deriving mutual benefit from observing each others' strategies in presenting their victimization. Fischer's performance of German remorse was effective: he had managed to suggest that he was speaking as a human being, not as a politician, certainly not where the issue was Germany's somehow supra-historically bad past.

But in this role, he was also asked to make promises that a politician cannot and should not be asked to make. He did so, because he was asked and, as a German, has been socialized into compliance in these matters—as if it had become his second nature. It is a moot question whether this makes his remorse less or more sincere; but there is a question that may be worth asking: has not the moral-political authority on which a widespread American expectation of collective German remorse has drawn over many decades, and which was reenergized by the collapse of the East Block, contributed to superpower certainties that might prove unhealthy for the body politic? How long can any group, especially one that has great power, survive so much righteousness?

It took such a notoriously independent and temperamental novelist and essayist as Martin Walser to break some of the taboos that have "protected" German collective memory, the source of collective remorse —a particularly provocative act since he chose the solemn occasion of his acceptance speech for the prestigious *Friedenspreis des deutschen Buchhandels*.[8] His writings over many decades have reflected his (as all important postwar German writers') preoccupation with the troubled German past and German responsibility not to forget it; but on this highly public occasion he lamented openly the monumentalization and ritualization of German guilt and shame. Voicing his frustration with the increasing cult of public remembrance of German collective guilt, he argued for a more broadly and reliably informed historical memory and the legitimacy, however partial and conditional, of individual Germans' private memories of their own experiences during the war.

The appeal was unusually emotional; but the highly offended reactions voiced in the German elite media across a broad political spectrum were predictable, demonstrating once more that public speech about this topic triggers a minefield of sensitivities that requires obedience to strict rules of self-censorship. Accusations came from powerful Jewish organizations such as the (Western-style) orthodox *Zentralrat der Juden in Deutschland,* but also from influential individual German intellectuals and politicians, many of whom had at first seemed to embrace Walser's complaints.[9] For about a week, their interestingly various reactions—a most welcome change—were published in the conservative *Die Welt;* but then they fell silent or changed their position. From the beginning, there had been the familiar general anxiety about international political irritation threatening economic relations, for instance internationally connected print and broadcast media's fears of an American boycott. Owned by a multinational concern, *Die Welt* habitually has journalists sign a clause forbidding all openly critical remarks about America or Israel, to avoid everything that might be interpreted as anti-Americanism or anti-Semitism and damage business.[10] There is the nice irony that the Right had been historically less stern and suspicious than the Left where it concerned a morally correct German remembrance and remorse. After all, the Left has always seen itself as intrinsically, as it were, genetically antifascist and therefore more sensitive to Nazi Evil; but the increasingly dominant model of power as symbiosis of moral-political-economic issues, notably also where it concerns the fuzzy but potent allegations of anti-Semitism, has brought with it some intriguing changes.

Like Grass and the majority of other (West) German writers and intellectuals, Walser had for many decades placed "Auschwitz" in the center of Western modernity,[11] but references to his past impeccable conduct concerning the issue of collective guilt did not protect him against strong suspicions that his intentions in breaking the taboo would of course have been evil: morally sinful rather than socially awkward. Given the by now hardened, meta-historical status of public remembrance, can one even ask how this situation has come about? Does not enduring insistence on a uniqueness of Auschwitz a priori prohibit all comparison and differentiation, all consideration of political and cultural developments in time? Each new outbreak of yet another heated memory-debate in Germany has caused the Western press to declare their ironical amazement that the politics of memory could be so explosive and tenacious: how much self-laceration can Germans be humanly expected to take, even though it seems to come to them naturally after so many decades of practice?

It is generally acknowledged that the hypercautious anticipation of potentially negative reactions to even the most cautiously gradual normalization of memory discourses—a more sober and critical *way* of thinking, speaking, and writing *about* the difficult past, not the (in any case impossible) normalization of that *past itself*—has been typical for the intellectual, cultural, and political climate in postwar Germany. An ironically puzzled perspective on the taboo-protected thoroughness of German politics of memory is undoubtedly much easier from the outside, where internalization of these taboos is not an issue. There is, however, also the hypocrisy of this outside perspective, pointing to both the silliness of and the need for such internalization: that is how the Germans are—that is how they should be. Who would we be, where would we put the limits of the civilized world, without the gold standard of Nazi Evil?

The extraordinarily messy war in Iraq is a good case in point. The Bush administration's astonishing and, to the nonbeliever, troubling arrogance of power has been derived from the extraordinary events of September 11, 2001. Their apocalyptic effect on a great majority of Americans has released the utopianist energies of the United States as the morally, politically, and economically superior *novus ordo seclorum* that would sanctify an ever more expanding "war" against terror. It is not by accident that in his eagerly embraced role as commander-in chief George W. Bush has habitually used references to Nazi Evil, from the "axis of evil" to the justness and goodness of the Second World War. Visiting Auschwitz on the first day of his first trip abroad after the fall of Baghdad, he invoked the murder of six million Jews to legitimate his "war on terror," referring to the gas ovens as "a sobering reminder of evil and the need for people to resist evil." He ended his trip in Qatar with a visit to the troops, and the young American soldiers applauded ecstatically when their president told them "Because of you, a great evil has been ended."[12] It was the summer of 2003, and they had won a clean, just war. All these references are meant to emphasize the religio-political importance of the Bush administration's mission to remove the evil of Saddam Hussein and replace it with the absolute good of (American) democracy, no matter the cost, notably considerable "collateral damage" to the Iraqi civilian population.

There was no problem with the enormous damage done to the German civilian population by Allied firebombing in WWII since all Germans were evil Nazis, down to the babies, and in desperate need of purification—done most thoroughly by fire. By definition, German civilians, at the end of the war overwhelmingly women and children, could not have been *relatively* innocent or victimized, no matter what they had actually done and what was done to them. In view of the scale and method of Nazi persecutions, innocence and victimhood had become synonymous and absolute: a powerful symbiosis that categorically and enduringly excluded all Germans. It has proved useful over the decades in selling U.S. military intervention,[13] because this absolutism has made WWII an irresistible comparison and point of reference—the "Mother" of all just wars—also for the unprecedented preemptive strike against Iraq.

If a shared religious view of the world has shrunk the political imagination of the leaders of "the Coalition" against Iraq to Manichean simplifications, demoralized American Democrats have been afraid to oppose the Republican president's dangerously single-minded determination to root out evil whatever the consequences. They assumed that after September 11 a divinely inspired, decisive leader would be so desirable to a majority of Americans across the political spectrum as to threaten their own political power if they stood in his way. That fear also made it difficult for them to appreciate why large German populations weary of war and ideological politics were unwilling to join "the Willing" in their hot pursuit of "the Enemy."

The German chancellor's political response to the German electorate's mood was deemed sinfully expedient, beyond mere politics, not only by Republicans: it "betrayed" the special relationship between postwar Germany and the United States by refusing to accept as an article of faith that invading Iraq was the right thing to do since it would be done in self-defense. Ironically, the "heinous" comparison drawn by that hapless official (whom Schröder had inherited and was glad to get rid of on this occasion) contained an element of truth.

Hitler's rhetoric and strategies of aggression are of course not really comparable to Bush's aggressive eagerness to involve the whole world in the coalition's absolutely just war against the evil of Saddam Hussein and beyond. But there are some instructive echoes: the real dangers inherent in religionized politics that prevent diplomacy, the willingness to negotiate opposing positions rather than "take them out" by force without considering the serious consequences for the already profoundly compromised psycho-political stability of the Middle East. The more heated and single-minded Bush's forcing his will on the United Nations to enlarge the congregation of the "Willing," the greater became the general willingness to tolerate physical destruction brought about by U.S. weapons of "shocking and awful" destruction. Starting out as an at best unimpressive, not even fully legitimized, president, the proverbially most powerful man in the world seized this power by becoming a decisive, determined leader admired for being untroubled by the hesitations and doubts associated with political thoughtfulness.[14]

In his rise to power, Bush was helped by fundamentalist Christians and American Jews concerned about upholding Israel's divine right to the land of Palestine, "undiminished and undivided"—a religious concept of Land and Security set against Nazi Evil that in part explains the Bush administration's habitual comparisons of the War against Terror with WWII.[15] The religious dimension of an evil Nazi past and German collective remorse came about partly in reaction to the extraordinary, "unspeakable" nature of Nazi persecutions revealed at the end of the war; the Allies then used it as a moral-political tool for German denazification and reeducation.

Given the confusing terms of these large and complex goals, the simplistically demonizing perspective on insufficiently understood extreme experiences proved mostly unsuccessful. Over time, however, it was to assume an ever more powerful cultural influence on postwar interdependencies of German national and international politics and German (collective) memory, and it encouraged mythification, rather than sober historiography, of that terrible, all-too-real war. Arguably, it was its supra-historical Nazi Evil, asserted by the victorious Americans and easily internalized by the vanquished Germans, that made the war appear enigmatically alluring and repulsive, beyond human time, place, and comprehension. The ever-increasing cultural importance of the Holocaust as an ever-growing complex of survivors' personal memory stories further criminalized the German war experience.[16]

Over time, the taboos on memory stories of that experience have become more rather than less prohibitive, to the point where it seems almost impossible now to even raise the question to what extent mutual political expectations and prejudices have played a role in this process. It is as if the Holocaust, unchanging, had always existed outside and beyond temporal human affairs, deriving from its permanent singularity its never-to-be questioned authority. But the war, the persecutions, were manmade; they happened and have been remembered in human time; their significance does not transcend historical inquiry—though it is true that we still know little about the nature of extreme situations and even less about their memory. This means that the temporality of past memory discourses needs to be explored more thoroughly, that is, historically. The same is true for the political uses to which these memories have been put and from which by now they seem to be almost inseparable.

At the proverbial end of the day there will have to be a cultural political consensus that "now is a good time" to start asking whether it is indeed useful to go on upholding German *Betroffenheit,* the notorious collective bad conscience about the bad German past that more often than not has resulted in self-censorship where the history of German memory is concerned. Arguments in support of the strategies of such *Betroffenheit* draw on an unquestionable moral authority to demand German acknowledgment of guilt and shame, of remorse. But limiting the German experience of WWII to German collective responsibility and guilt for the deeds of their criminal regime has contributed to forgetting the historical reality of a total, highly technological war that was extraordinarily destructive in the experience of many different groups.

The attempt to retrieve and record more aspects of that historical experience has to include the millions of Germans who were not the designated enemy groups, the official victims of the Nazi regime, but also not guilty for the crimes of that regime in any real, not to speak of legal, sense. If anything, such attempt will lead to a better understanding of the ways in which enforced memory control, forgetting as well as remembrance, can be and has been used politically. The enduring, seemingly self-evident primacy of a moral authority associated with the victim status has largely obscured the politicized uses of remorse in the postwar period, and with it important questions concerning the responsibility of power in the United States, in Israel, and in Germany.

The topic of this book is the persistent near-impossibility of discussing rationally the German experience of that war: its shadowy past presence in German memory that has provoked the notorious bitterly hostile, intertwined debates and controversies over a morally and then politically correct collective remembrance of collective guilt. Whether or not hindsight makes it possible to arrive at a better understanding of what was said, was not said, was not allowed to be said, it is easier to recognize the powerful effect of taboos if they are seen in their temporality, in the course of time passing. German postwar political culture has developed a peculiarly inverse relation between a growing temporal distance from the war as a complex of historical events and an increasingly intense, as it were supra-temporal, presence of German collective guilt. We need to explore the impact of different groups' private and public memories of WWII on the different cultural and political "presents" of the postwar period—how they were used or misused, whether they were seen as useful, useless, or damaging.

Many of these remembered events are no longer fully accessible; this is true for all things past, but particularly for the experiences of extreme situations that profoundly influence memory processes. Six decades after the events, a sober, comparative investigation of traumatic memories is important also because it is still rejected as "provocative" or "offensive" where it concerns the victims of Nazi persecutions. Their extreme experiences called for coherent, in themselves meaningful, memory stories that a modern secular historiography based on the principles of temporality and accident could not deliver.[17] Yet affirmation of the limits of historiography where it concerns the Holocaust had consequences not only in German postwar culture but also in the United States, among other things in divisive memories of victimization.

Given the current preoccupation with an omnipresent threat of terrorism, mistrust in sober historical research and representation discouraged critical comparisons between different kinds of politicized group terrorism, yet comparisons between political Zionism and fundamentalist Islam would be particularly instructive and important. In both cases, Manichean memory discourses of radical evil and absolute victimization have led to a rejection of historical differentiation—not unlike in the German memory debates—and have formed one of the most important reasons for the persistent political crisis in the Middle East. The aggressive redundancy of these discourses—the sameness of the bitter memory debates in Germany and the inexorably repeated accusations and suspicions at the core of the conflict between Israel and the Arabs that is now shared by the United States—might reveal, if momentarily, their in fact absurdly "irrational" nature.

Power and Impotence

Assumptions of a German collective responsibility, that is, guilt for all events of WWII, have intensified during the last decades rather than diminished. Collective memory of victims of Nazi persecution has become increasingly ritualized, and so has the expectation that collective silence about German experiences of WWII will endure into an indefinite future. Cultural acceptance of selective and exclusive memory discourses where victims are concerned has generally led to an increase in power for groups whose current politics of identity draw on the collective memory of previous persecution—a power with built-in moral authority within the larger community even though it may be privately questioned or resented. In Germany, where this scenario is played out most literally in the relations between Jewish Germans and what are now officially called "non-Jewish Germans," it has led to rather curious power constellations, a good case in point being the "Friedman affair" that kept the media happily preoccupied for six weeks in the summer of 2003.[18]

Michel Friedman, colorful, unconventional vice president of the conservative, orthodox *Zentralrat der Juden in Deutschland* and lovingly hated moderator of a highly successful TV show, was found in possession of an illegal amount of cocaine, which he took in the presence of several East European prostitutes who had been brought to Germany illegally by a *Menschenhändlerbande* (slave-trading ring). It was probably not so much the rather minor drug issue as the ominous if speculative associations with *Menschenhandel* that caused the pleasurable excitement among the public. Friedman was sentenced and fined for possession and consumption and, now *vorbestraft* (a convicted felon), he resigned from his official positions and from his role as host of the TV show. The prosecution's allegedly aggressive gathering of evidence led to complaints of anti-Semitism in the media, particularly in the papers that habitually monitor the conduct of non-Jewish Germans toward Jewish Germans; but thankfully the affair did not blossom into yet another large-scale anti-Semitism debate.[19] Part of the reason for its "understated" resolution may have been Friedman's long-time expensive but sensible lawyer who, for his own reasons, decided not to challenge the prosecution. Friedman took it like a lamb; he dutifully showed remorse and in the end even begged for forgiveness for his (sinful) transgressions. It was a definitely "unseemly" scene in the eyes of many of his former irritated and fascinated viewers, who would have hoped for a noisier exit; but TV is bigger and more seductive than (almost) anything else, and Friedman wanted to keep the door open for a comeback.

The temperamental, clever moderator was feared by his interviewees, especially non-Jewish German politicians, for his arrogantly aggressive, relentlessly judgmental style. In turns accusatory, sentimental, witty, heavily moralizing, exotically self-important, Friedman was as provocative as he was entertaining. Under the current circumstances, his stunning infatuation with power combined with his unpredictability could be treacherous and dangerous; and it provided a great spectacle for his audience watching him tormenting his public victims from the safe privacy of their livingrooms, where they could say what they really thought of him. One of his favorite topics was the neurotic Jewish-German relations, and he shocked (and no doubt also delighted) his piously philo-

Semitic German viewers with his shrewd cynical observations on German and Jewish variations of human nature, claiming an "honesty"
that would have been impossibly offensive had it come from a non-
Jewish German.

Friedman is not only Jewish but a *Musterjude* (model Jew), and this
fact is the single most interesting aspect of the Friedman affair. The term
was coined by Rafael Seligmann in his picaresque novel *Der Musterjude*
(1997), whose protagonist, Moishe Bernstein, is a hyper-clever, hyper-
sexed, hyper-corrupt, hyper-successful, and hapless journalist, an "anti-
Semitic" incarnation of both Jewish "self-love" and "self-hatred." As
an editor, he brilliantly uses the deepest of German fears, to be accused
of anti-Semitism, to increase the circulation of his paper, only to be fired
by the paper's real owners for having alienated an international advertising business exclusively interested in the German present, the better
the more immoral. While the paper is happily hunting alleged anti-
Semites, creating a series of juicy anti-anti-Semitism episodes feeding on
the bad German past and dramatically increasing its readership, all the
big advertisers withdraw their business, which is the real money for
this, for any, paper.

In certain ways, the connections between Bernstein and Friedman
are quite obvious, and Seligmann, who shares with Friedman the political agenda of relentlessly seeking out and combating German anti-
Semitism (and other nasty German "isms"), has been a strong Jewish
voice in the print media for reminding the Germans, in no uncertain
terms, of their moral obligations to always be remindful of their bad
past. At the end, Moishe learns that his father may have been German,
perhaps even a Nazi; his mother never knew, does not remember, and he
is not even so sure she is Jewish. But when his German girlfriend argues
that his non-Jewish mother could no longer oppose their relationship,
Moishe accuses her and "all the other Germans," that it is they who
"make him a Jew, their *Musterjude!*"[20] Not unexpectedly, everything is
the Germans' fault; and the picaresque protagonist is really a tragic
antihero, the *Musterjude* as *Musterkind* (model child) trying so hard to
please everybody and being punished for it.

The highly serious topic of enduring collective German anti-Semitism has been the central topic of Seligmann's writing,[21] and it was quite
in character that he was "the first prominent German Jew" to ask for
Friedman's resignation from his position in the *Zentralrat*. In an article
for the illustrated paper *Stern*, he harshly reproached the TV moderator
for his lack of seriousness and maturity demanded by this position.
Friedman, Seligmann pointed out, is not Dreyfuss, the victim of an anti-

Semitic intrigue, but a "Jongleur der Moral" (juggler of morals) who had to have reckoned with his fall. Playing the "Jewish Robespierre," the "incarnation of virtue, and its guillotine," he should not be surprised "that others are hoping for his fall."[22] Friedman, in Seligmann's scenario, had cheapened the source of his power, the authority of the memory of Jewish persecution. But like many others, Jewish and non-Jewish Germans alike, Seligmann also thinks that the Germans do indeed need their *Musterjuden* to tell them the nasty truth about their real feelings about Jews—a truth artfully constructed by the clue-holding analyst for the clueless analysand.

In an intriguingly open, self-contradictory article on the Friedman affair, Harald Martenstein remarks that relations between Jewish and non-Jewish Germans are "still not normal," as already indicated by the politically correct "verbal monster *nichtjüdische Deutsche.*"[23] He quotes from a more conciliatory essay in *Die Zeit* by another "prominent Jew," Salomon Korn, shortly before the Friedman news broke, in which he explained that non-Jewish Germans who get on Jewish Germans' nerves by mistaking them for Israelis are "clueless rather than malicious" and suggested that saying something wrong was better than not speaking to each other at all. Transferring this sentiment to the Friedman affair, Martenstein advocates going beyond a minority's anti-Semitic delight with the Friedman case and another minority's anti-anti-Semitic conspiracy theories, and recognizing prejudices on both the German Jewish and the German gentile side: "It irritates Jewish Germans to be constantly confused with Israelis; it irritates non-Jewish Germans to be constantly confused with Nazis. In each case, so the prejudice, the racist and Anti-Semite emerges if one digs deep enough. There is a basic mistrust. Perhaps a kind of anti-German racism, why not."

This seems a curious parity between two very different German "prejudice" problems and the kinds of irritation caused by them. Non-Jewish Germans may be confusing Jewish Germans with Israelis simply because a considerable number of them immigrated from Israel, some of them recently, and may have retained some speech or social habits, or, as in the case of Friedman and Seligmann, have tended to be inexorably critical of German-Jewish relations. But such confusion by no means signifies a negative attitude toward Israel in general and Israelis in particular. On the contrary, the perspective of a large majority of Germans on the state and its citizens has been reliably positive despite the constant criticism of their always suspect relations with Jews in the present —too little love; too much love—and lingering bad past. They are used to it. Moreover, as *Musterdeutsche* they are easily persuaded that they deserve it; and it was only very recently that they have begun criticizing Israel for its objectively destructive conduct in the Middle East, which earned them accusations of anti-Semitism in the elite press. Confusing individual Jewish Germans with Israelis has no negative connotations—or does it? an interesting possibility—whereas confusing all non-Jewish Germans with Nazis does have—no ambiguities here. Though time-honored by now, this equation is actually a serious insult for which references to the historical Nazi persecution of Jews are no excuse.

Martenstein also juxtaposes a non-Jewish prejudicial assumption of Israeli racism with an Israeli prejudicial assumption of non-Jewish anti-Semitism and seems to think that Israeli anti-German racism would be ok; not so, of course, gentile anti-Semitism. He knows that for most Germans the accusation of anti-Semitism is deadly serious; for this reason they prefer silence, at least in public, in tricky situations, such as the Friedman affair where they might be asked about their dislike of Friedman: is it because of his arrogance and self-inflation or the fact that he is a Jew? This is where the *Musterjude* comes in—the highly useful phenomenon in Martenstein's scenario of "öffentliche [public] Jews" such as Broder, Wolffsohn, Friedman, Seligmann, and so on. (In America, and in more innocent times, Hannah Arendt was very critical of what she called "professional Jews.") They are called on to comment critically on Jewish topics and on other Jewish intellectuals, and in general to test the limits of political correctness.

These "specialists" have the right "aura" and therefore simply cannot be accused of being racists or anti-Semites, which, in turn, empowers them to be provocative and insulting—to the non-Jewish Germans whose modern identity, in Martenstein's view, calls for more than a touch of masochism. *Musterjuden,* the "first intellectual product of German-Jewish postwar history," are an important part of it. Friedman drew on his aura for his *Moral-Bonus* that empowered him to question his interviewees more aggressively and insultingly than a non-Jewish German could have done. Martenstein is fascinated by Friedman's playing power games with the audience, pushing them to the point where he seems to be asking them: can you still stand it (me), or is it true that what you like best is Klezmer music and your Jews dead?

Despite Martenstein's relatively open discussion of the German-Jewish neurosis—a fairly rare openness made possible, no doubt, by the "exciting" Friedman case—he does not seem to see any problems with this strangely unequal relationship of the two groups. The *Moral-Bonus* supported by millions of dead Jews inevitably creates a *Moral-Malus* for the Germans, who, unlike Jews, do not carry *Opfer-genes* (victim genes) but dutifully remember "forever" their bad history—as Jews remember forever their persecution, the bad histories of other peoples. It does indeed seem "crazy," as Martenstein puts it, that one has to be Friedman with his special aura to be a usefully aggressive critic in Germany, feared by all the evasive, cowardly non-Jewish German politicians. Yet this "craziness" also appears perfectly normal in contemporary Germany, and it may actual have a damaging effect on the social and cultural politics of a twenty-first-century multiethnic, globalizing technological mass democracy. Is it not precisely the provinciality of Friedman's self-styled, self-important identity that seeks to intimidate and silence others rather than encourage them to talk back? The issue, then, is not the usefulness of critical questions that can be posed only by German *Musterjuden* but their *power* to pose them and the *impotence* of contemporary *Mustergermans* to consider and answer them rationally, on their own terms, and without fear.

The German *Moral-Malus* is based on the diminished power of a group that is collectively and publicly held responsible for collectively remembered previous persecutions, regardless of its members' differing private, individual memories of the time when they happened. The more secure this scenario, the less the division between collectively innocent victims and collectively guilty perpetrators will be challenged by requests for explanation: *whose* was and is, and for what *reasons,* the political and moral power to deny the war generation of women, men, and children their diverse complex historical reality? their place in the historical memory of this extraordinary war? This question has been crucially important to German history and historiography in the postwar era; it has also been persistently provocative to the point of being silenced since it suggests a possible simultaneity, and then validity, of different groups' different memory discourses.

The cultural-political agenda for all German discourses of remembrance since the end of WWII has been an increasingly exclusive focus on the Jewish victims of the Nazi regime. Intensified since the mid-sixties, the notorious German collective inability to mourn their victims in order to "master their (criminal) past" has been a potent political issue in postwar Germany. Seen from a less politicized, historically comparative perspective, the expectations over a period of almost sixty years that all Germans mourn spontaneously and remember collectively the victims, and only the victims, of the Nazi regime might seem unusual, even questionable. Such intensely public and permanent memory of past victimization tends to be focused on the painful past of one's own group —the Holocaust as a construct of memory discourses being a prime example. However, the expectations directed at the Germans could draw on the extraordinary violence of Nazi persecution, particularly in the case of Jews, that has created, also for the larger world, an absolute moral authority of Jewish memory of victimization in its historical importance for the survival of Jewish identity.

Understandably, if not always usefully, this authority has had a profound influence on German historical memory. As chairman of the *Zentralratder Juden in Deutschland,* Ignatz Bubis in his speech on the occasion of the sixtieth anniversary of *Kristallnacht* attacked Martin Walser's critical remarks on controlling German public memory as an attempt to "repress history and erase memories." In the view of the influential *Zentralrat* for whom Bubis was speaking here, Walser's critique not only linked him with the intense anti-Semitism of the radical Right but amounted to a denial of the Holocaust. The accusations were extreme and insulting; above all they were clearly absurd both in the terms of Walser's peace prize speech and of his well-known, long-standing position on the issue of Germany's troubling history. But Bubis's invocation of the central power of memory as "the mysterium of redemption" in the heart of Jewish history still carried a near-absolute moral-political authority in Germany that could easily silence critics. Any normally unbiased person listening to Walser's speech would have understood that he had not pleaded for German forgetting of Jewish suffering but for a less exclusive not-forgetting that would also admit fluid, ambiguous, even questionable private memories and not automatically defer to preauthorized public politics of memory.

The issue here, mentioned neither by Walser, who was speaking for himself, nor by Bubis, who was speaking for his group, is a broadly diffused German internalization of claims to a unique victimization of Jews, beyond historical understanding and historical time, that call for a unique German guilty and shameful collective memory to keep such claims alive and powerful "forever." This scenario was politically and psychologically understandable, even inevitable, in the immediate postwar era. But during the last six decades the world has undergone dramatic changes. For one, the troubles of a Jewish state in Palestine, built on the foundation myth of "Auschwitz," have been detrimental not only for the Middle East but globally. Yet Israel, whatever its problematic politics, has had the unquestioning support of the great majority of American Jews because there has been the largely unquestioned assumption that Jews have suffered more, and more significantly, than all other groups in the history of this planet. The security needs of a Jewish state will then have to be given highest consideration in accordance with the highest victim status that bestows on them greater moral-political authority than on all other groups.

Ever more common accusations of anti-Semitism for a broad spectrum of offensive and then religiously sinful, rather than socially inappropriate, behavior draw on this empowering authority. In the United States, these accusations are used in the same generalizing way as "racism," but they appear to be politically and economically more dangerous and are therefore more feared, more powerful; in Germany they have contributed to the enduring taboos on historical memory, including the threat of prison sentences for publicly made statements that could be interpreted as Holocaust denial.[24]

The power of previous suffering has been most irresistible where it concerned demands for German remorse since postwar Germans have been carrying a greater burden of collective guilt toward previous victims than all other groups. As the moral strength of a collective superior victim status tends to produce general cultural-political claims to power, the moral weakness of collective guilt produces declarations of cultural-political impotence—made in the name of those whose collective guilt presumably prevents them from speaking for themselves about their historical experiences and memories.

Since the end of WWII, this impotence has been intensified by the politicization of the question of German guilt, which had immediately become the question of German identity posed by *Life* in its May 1945 issue. To this day, ordinary Germans have not been able to challenge publicly the assumptions repeated by German politicians and public intellectuals of an enduring German collective guilt. The greater the moral certainty of those who speak about the collective guilt of others, the more easily others can be commanded to feel shame, the more powerful become the voices of these self-appointed judges, and the more secure they feel in their group judgment. Since they distinguish themselves from ordinary Germans, they feel called upon to judge them. And since they are certain of the righteousness of their judgment, they can never themselves be judged to be like "them," participating in "their" burden of collective guilt. The collectively impotent because collectively indicted Germans, then, have to face not only the powerful (Jewish) victims but the here even more powerful (German) prosecutorial advocates of their guilt—not the least because these have become ever more conformist in their use of the power of the mass media.

It would have been impossible for Auschwitz to become so central in German postwar culture without this politicized self-righteousness concerning the alleged criminality of all others. This resounding conformity of the discourses of suspicion and accusation enabled by the enforced silence of the Germans in their potentially multivocal difference needs to be questioned, and so do the divisive self-interest politics of identity characteristic of many groups in Western societies. Collective memory discourses of previous victimization tend to draw on a totalizing concept of power relations that cannot but compromise historical understanding of a past complex actuality.

Looked at realistically, the politics of identity, as they are currently practiced by previously persecuted or disadvantaged groups, prefer the certainty of culturally preauthorized moral claims over the uncertain negotiations of political, social, and economic conflicts of interest. If current positions of power can invoke the authority of immorally imposed past impotence, it is in their (understandable if not automatically justified) interest to evoke it as enduring, total, and homogenous: removed from historical time and historiographical differentiation. Hannah Arendt's early critique of the strategies of Zionist identity politics in Palestine (1944–48) was particularly provocative because it made transparent political strategies that invoked a general and absolute authority of past suffering where they really meant specific contemporary conflicts of interest. She understood perfectly well the literal vitality of these interests in the immediate postwar years, the issue of Jewish survival; but she still thought it accessible to rational analysis and discussion.

Today, this rationality is more needed than ever, since Israel's politics in the Middle East have been drawing precisely on this intertwinement of power and impotence. "Auschwitz" as the foundation myth of the new Jewish State, the uniquely significant story of its origin, has caused exactly the problems Arendt and others foresaw sixty years ago. As client of a superpower, Israel would be a disproportionately powerful state in Palestine, and its combined theocratic and technocratic energies would prove an enduring source of conflict because they were bound to encourage rather than check the politics of religio-political redemption.

The divine promise of the "land without people" to the "people without land" meant reclaiming the undiminished whole of Palestine as the permanent property of the "chosen people." Claiming the uniqueness and absolute authority of Jewish suffering, Auschwitz would make it de facto impossible that the new Jewish state would see itself as one nation among others, namely share with them an open-ended, unpredictable future shaped by accidents and contingencies, by concessions, compromises, and responsibilities. The two pillars of "lest we forget" and "never again" would ensure that this new political foundation would remain forever the exclusively Jewish state of 1948—despite the rapid, radical social and political changes of the last half century that seem to both stretch and condense the experience of time. Ironically, because of its enforced, enduring impotence, German collective memory inhibited a clear and decisive critique of Israel's long-time political and social oppression of impotent Palestinians: in addition to their collective responsibility for the criminal acts of the Nazi regime, Germans could then also be seen as co-responsible for Israel's destabilizing politics in the Middle East.

Memory and Identity

Nothing separates more inexorably than does time. Contemporaries to late modernity, we are grounded in historicity but also future-bound in ways that promise release from the cultural authority of history as an overwhelmingly intricate, elusive complex of connections between past and future. There is no co-temporality with the past, not even in the imagination; the past is a different planet, light years away and difficult to know. Connections are made and judged from the future side of the past: inevitably, it is we, the living, who decide what and how we see when we look back. Yet the promises of release are also a threat. The modern open-endedness, the secular uncertainties of history, have been arrested, as it were, in a growing number of selective group histories insisting on their respective redemptive certainties. It seems to be getting harder for the dead to talk back to the living; if they do, it is by permission and on the terms of the living, who draw on the past for justification of their own questionable deeds in the present.

The living prefer the awesome inarticulate innocence of the dead, purged of the ambiguities, the muddle of historical agency. The more respectful Western cultures have become of difference, the more bigoted they appear toward temporal difference, namely the more reluctant to engage with the cognitive distances and differences created and marked by the passage of time. Oddly, in the interest of a desirable moral-political identity—democratic, compassionate, and globally powerful—we have become a culture of hindsight judgment and self-righteousness. We too easily accuse others of sexism, racism, anti-Semitism; worse, we are ourselves too easily cowed by such accusations because we tend to mistake the discourses of public memory, of which they are a part, for the real thing, the often not fully understood past events on which these discourses draw. One might say that temporal discrimination is the only remaining ideologically founded and protected discrimination in Western culture, making us seem less and less inclined to bring to the past patient and soberly critical questions. It seems that the more we have

opened ourselves to cultural pluralism, the more restricted our historical imagination has become where it concerns the particularities of the
past, beyond the generalizing, abstracting scenarios of colonizer and
colonized, victimizer and victim, exploiter and exploited. And the more
restricted the historical imagination, the more strained appear the relations between private and public memory, because the controlling narratives of public memory thrive on disregard for historical differentiation.

In Western modernity, the clearest example of a public memory that
has censored, or simply overridden, a plurality of fragmented, unstable
private memories is the notorious assumption of an enduringly unmastered, unredeemed German past. Instructively, it was the ongoing public
debates of the meanings of that past that have been most instrumental
in upholding the censorship of private memories that do not fit the
dominant model of public memory. Silence has been an important aspect of the tension between private and public memory, so much so that
the fact of the silence itself has become unspeakable, taboo. Over a
period of almost six decades, this tension has led to a growing separation between private and public discourse of all issues concerning the
recent German past—a familiar separation largely responsible for the
equally familiar redundancy, circularity, and ritualization of the politics
of not-forgetting that have defined postwar German political culture.

The explosive growth of Holocaust memory stories in recent decades is in important ways linked to a current Western preoccupation
with multiculturism that supports multiple, often mutually exclusive,
monological public memories and histories of identity on the basis of
former persecution. Taking Holocaust discourses for their model, they
share the tendency to exclude what might disrupt their respective preestablished coherence. In general, constructs of public memory, no matter
how various in substance, extend the sameness of their control over
private memories of the past into the future. Public memory preserves,
by preauthorizing them, only those private memories that will affirm its
resistance to transformation in time. Thus it can promise the enduring
collective identity of those who remember in the collective memory of
their persecution as Jews, African Americans, Hispanics, Native Americans, gays, and so on, as long as this memory can activate sufficient
remorse to support public remembrance. Normally fluid and incoherent
private memories, in contrast, undermine such identity in that they alert
to the separations, the changes created by the passage of time. The fundamental conflict, then, between public and private memory derives
from the hindsight perspective of public memory that seeks to deny the
temporal, processual nature of memory and identity.

Yet, like private memory, public memory draws on the extraordinary emotional and, in a broader sense, moral energy of the plea "remember me" to claim cultural significance for the politics of remembrance. Pleading to be allowed to remain, for a time, in another person's memory that reaches back into a shared past is a poignantly tentative affirmation of the desire not to be forgotten. "Do not forget me," in contrast, connotes a demand in the form of a prohibition, whether welcomed or feared, that commands future remembrance of a person who will then no longer be present. Since the end of WWII, Germans as a group have been sternly warned, and warned themselves, "do not forget them!" They have rarely been asked, as individuals, "remember us."

Depending on the context in which the two words "remember me" are spoken, they can signify a number of quite commonplace communications. Differently emphasized reminders of previous contacts, they can refer to past closeness, distance, promises, threats. It is precisely the range of connotation that enlarges the emotional pull of that phrase, because it anchors, against the threat or the reality of absence, the desire for a continued presence in the familiar life-world shared with others. Responsible for the centrality of memory in cultural and individual consciousness, this desire connects public and private memory. And it releases the emotional energy that public memory needs for its construction: the anxiety of changes in time that lead to feared or mourned absence.

The plea "remember me," made by one person to another, expresses the perhaps primary, most urgent human need: to be allowed to emerge again, in remembrance, out of the shadows of absence. Since human consciousness is predicated on the awareness of death, a final absence, much of human culture has been driven by the craving for prolonged, renewed presence. Thus pleas for remembrance have had a powerful hold over the imagination, individual and collective, and never more so, it seems, than in the twentieth century with its mass destruction of human life. This may explain the curiously pure appeal of remembrance no matter how impure its uses.

Since the end of WWII, there has been an unspoken agreement in the West that autobiographical memory stories of Holocaust survivors, because of their extreme traumatic nature, could not and should not be expected to be collaborated. They could lay claim to a singularly truthful interpretation of the past, despite—or because of—the fact that the normally selective and temporally fluid sequence of past events in memory questions the value of memory stories as historical evidence. The issue here is not distortions of the truth in the sense of lying but the conceiving and then constructing of stories that fit a preconceived, above all meaningful, interpretation of a traumatic past. The Eichmann trial with its deliberate, highly controlled choreography of a large number of individual memory stories took these acts of constructing one significant step further. The stories recited by eyewitnesses *became* their memories; the surviving victims *were* the authorized delegates of the Holocaust, embodying, as it were, the a priori *unquestionable* facts.[25] This hyperfacticity of the victim status has repressed all other war experiences, excluding them from public remembrance and contributing to significant losses—through enforced forgetting—of the historical reality of WWII and its consequences.

Arguably, this repression has been largely responsible for the enduring summary equation of Germans and Nazis attaching to the war generation in Germany and, if fuzzily but not therefore less potent, to all Germans in the United States. Repressing the traumatic memories of the war generation has substantively contributed to the myth of the *Tätergeneration,* making that whole war generation collectively suspect of having actively participated in the most heinous criminal acts of their regime, Nazi Evil. The political uses of suspicion have been reinvigorated and expanded over the last decades, demonstrating a historically meaningless but morally and politically effective desire to impose on all Germans, alive or dead, the status of *Täter*—curiously parallel to the supra- or trans-temporal status of Auschwitz. In one way or the other, the many controversies about the still "unredeemed" German past have drawn on this desire, making good use of the mythical *Täter* in their lamentations about an insufficient, incomplete, at any rate unsatisfactory German collective memory. They signify a regress to the beginnings of the debate of German collective guilt at the end of the war, a politically ambiguous, morally certain, and therefore highly important concern of U.S. occupational politics in the chaotic aftermath of their absolute victory over the Nazi regime.

It ought to be possible now, six decades later, to look at the collective memory of WWII in its relation to individual memories of extreme situations from the multiple perspectives of both the victims of Nazi persecution and the victims of Hitler's war—a war that Germans in their large majority had not wanted but feared. One could for instance ask, how does cultural rejection of a perceived unjust, dishonorable war or affirmation of a perceived just, honorable war influence or control the collective remembrance of that war experience? What are the interdependencies in these different cases between collective (public) and individual (private) memories? A particularly clear example would be the apparent congruence of public and private memories associated with D-

Day in the United States and their divergence in Germany. D-Day has been emblematic for the contrast between absolute military, political, moral victory on one side and defeat on the other.

German public monological memory of an unjust war ending in total defeat and criminalizing the whole civilian population and the whole (mostly conscript) army has for over half a century prevented multivocal private war memories of German soldiers and civilians from becoming a part of German postwar culture. The collective memory of the Vietnam war, perceived by a majority of American citizens as unjust and unsuccessful, was at first also shaped by cultural rejection, but because of the different scale of injustice and defeat, private memories were differently affected.

Instructively, the Vietnam War Memorial in Washington with its emphasis on individual dead soldiers—their names visible and accessible to their families and friends—has supported the individuality of that war experience and thereby the importance of individual memory stories. These memories would eventually become the stuff of verbal and photographic documentaries, of fiction films and novels. Even more suggestive, the peculiar appeal of that memorial seems to be based on its ability to elicit the spontaneous and changing processes of private memory since it seems to be designed to be changing in time, even to retreat into partial forgetting. In a curiously moving way, it acknowledges that the people who come to it to trace the names of their dead will change in time; and their acts of remembrance will change and finally stop because they will die and will themselves be absent, in need of remembrance.

That public monument to the memory of the dead, who gave their lives for the greater good of their country, is also a monument to the temporality of memory and remembrance: unusual but fitting in view of the nature of that war and of the public response to it. In contrast, the increasingly monumentalized, ritualized memory discourses of the Holocaust could be said to share some aspects of Hitler's pet project of a huge second Arc de Triomphe to be built above Napoleon's. Into the granite walls of this monument of inhuman proportions he would have had chiseled the names of all the soldiers killed in WWI. They would have been the treasure of *his* dead, their public memory reserved for his political uses, and preserved forever because, invisible and untouchable, they would have been removed from the feared transformations of historical time and historical memory. So would the public memory of millions of Jews killed by the Nazi regime be preserved forever as the source of the powerful moral authority of the survivors? It is in the nature of the past to be at the disposal of the future and of the dead to be at the disposal of the living—for better or worse.[26]

WWII has become the archetypal war in both the American and the German imagination: the just war, the clean war "we won" in the U.S.; the criminal, dirty war "they lost" in Germany.[27] The subtext to all the postwar debates of German political identity has been the kind of public memory permitted to Germans. May it include past extreme situations experienced by German civilians and soldiers? Or is such inclusion a priori suspect because it might suggest a comparison with atrocities committed by the Nazi regime? And indeed, in the last half century there have been very few accounts, whether documentary or fictional, of the war experience of common soldiers, of civilians' experience of air raids and deportations from the East, of large-scale destruction and chaos. These were individual experiences that would have resulted in memories shaped by the need to deal in some ways with extreme trauma, but they were suppressed by the collective memory of a criminal war. And they never came to the surface in the heated and redundant memory debates starting in full force in the late eighties, when reunification recast the difficult question of national identity. Since then, the debates have flared up repeatedly, driven by the mass media across the political spectrum and increasingly also by publishing houses interested in the economic advantages of safely choreographed "hot" controversy. All the more surprising, then, are some recent attempts to give German wartime experiences a voice. The first and tentative one was W. G. Sebald's *Luftkrieg und Literatur* (1999), based on a series of lectures in poetics at Zurich University in 1997 that circled around the question why Allied bombing, with its wholesale destruction of German cities and German civilians, had left almost no traces in German postwar literature. The ensuing debates included the usual warnings that Sebald's focus on Allied destruction could be seen as apologeticism—one of the shibboleths of postwar memory discourses, almost as dangerous as anti-Semitism since it allegedly suggests a comparative perspective on German and Jewish suffering and victim status meant to ease the burden of German guilt. Still, Sebald's question "*why* this almost total silence?" intrigued many readers. Reminding his German audiences of the degree and kind of physical and moral devastation caused by the Allied air war, Sebald argued that the taboo-protected silence surrounding it had its source in German shame—a motivation he applauded rather than criticized, thereby defusing the message of his in some cases strikingly effective descriptions of the results of air war.[28]

The text credited with opening German wartime experiences to discussion is Günter Grass's docu-fictional novel *Im Krebsgang* (2002; *Crab Walk*, 2003) about a Russian submarine's 1945 sinking of a ship carrying mainly German women and children refugees, which resulted in the loss of almost ten thousand lives. The Nobel Prize winner's novel provoked few reservations in Germany and hardly any in the United States, a very small controversy, and quickly became a huge commercial success in Germany. Half a year later, Jörg Friedrich's *Der Brand Deutschland im Bombenkrieg 1940–45*, the first comprehensive historical documentation of Germany's destruction by Allied air raids intended for a general readership, created more controversy. Yet even though the majority of the British reactions were negative, some of them aggressively so, and the book has so far been tacitly "banned" from publication in the United Kingdom and has not yet come out in the United States, it did get some intelligently perceptive reviews in England.[29]

In its skillfully narrated immediacy, Friedrich's detailed documentation of total air war against German civilians appears unemotional, but whether remembering or just imagining the horror, readers will feel affected by it. Friedrich did not include photographs of the devastation to aid the memory of its trauma, though he must have been familiar with the photo-documentation of air raid destruction and drawn on it to describe the superhuman, inhumanly harnessed elemental power of firebombing. There would have been several reasons for the decision not to reproduce this documentation together with the printed text; one of them would have been that discussions of the meanings of these photographs had been censored over a period of many decades. Even if it had been possible to agree on what the images he chose actually showed, their picturing horrible destruction of German cities and civilians would still have carried the stigma of an implied inherent German desire to compare or counterbalance their suffering with that of the "real" victims of the Nazi regime.

The absence of these images gave more power to verbal descriptive documentation, because its message was clearly mediated by the author, who explicitly abstained from censoring it. In late 2003 Friedrich published a book of powerful photographs of WWII with brief captions but without a coherent text, *Brandstätten* (places of fire), that provoked some controversy in Germany about the provenance of the photographs and their sometimes eerie openness to multiple interpretations.

The more powerful the documentation of German wartime experiences, the more insistent the arguments "they asked for it."[30] They started at the end of the war and have continued till today. A nicely

comical example was the conversation between Charlie Rose and Joschka Fischer broadcast on PBS July 15, 2003, which started with Fischer's
familiar protestations "we Germans will never forget what you did for
us," and then listing liberation, democratization, the Cold War, unification. It was a list that soothed the American nationalist Rose, who at
that point also liked the preemptive strike against Iraq and disliked
Germany's lack of willingness to join it. Among other reassurances of
enduring German loyalty was Fischer's assertion, most curious in view
of the huge commercial success of Friedrich's *Der Brand* in the fall of
2002, that recent German publications on Allied air raids had had no
impact at all on German audiences. Rose had asked whether they had
not been bad for the time-honored American-German friendship, but
Fischer claimed that the topic had never been important, had been discussed only in private, and that anyway "all German experiences started
with the Nazi's criminal acts against Jews." It does sound strange, but
this is what he said. Did he mean to say that the Germans, "asking for
it," had all been exquisitely desensitized by these acts and never noticed,
much less remembered, the bombs falling on them from the empty air?

Given the context of the entrenched politics of German collective
memory, Friedrich's descriptions were much more disturbing than Grass's
mannered, temporally layered narration of the catastrophe of so many
women and children perishing in the black icy waters of the Baltic Sea.
Despite the, in parts, virtuoso evocations of the chaos aboard and in the
water, and the panic of the drowning, the powerfully amoral force of
these events is in danger of being dissipated, obscured in the discursive
layering that supplies too many and too various moral messages. From
the *Tin Drum* on, all of Grass's novels have been concerned with the
troubled German past, and they all have been similarly flawed. Still,
once Grass had cautiously felt his way back, like a crab, to the awe of
this promptly forgotten scene of senseless dying—two and a half million
civilians, almost all of them women, children, and old people, died on
that forced exodus from the East in 1945–46—he stayed with it long
enough to admit it to historical memory.[31]

In his more straightforward, accessible way, the documentarist Friedrich has allowed German civilians to speak about their traumatic experiences in their own voices, without interrupting them with the familiar
admonitions not to compare their sufferings with those of Nazi victims.
Ordered to forever forget their own war experiences in order to never
forget the experiences of their victims, Germans had hardly found comparing experiences to be an issue for them. But it had been an issue for
German politicians and public intellectuals, who from the beginning

have contributed to the sharp division between public and private memory. For the sake of an absolutely, religiously just war, a great political asset then and now, the victors expected them to embrace the politics of memory and remorse, and they complied, for their own political reasons. On the way—inevitably, given the long duration of their powerfully symbiotic moral-political authority—the pieties of remorse, though by no means weakened, have occasionally shown some cracks, even moments of darkly comical absurdity. In support of an argument against the usefulness of an enduring politics of suspicion, I will seek out these moments because they best reveal the cultural-political dynamics of the uses of remorse and with them the need for a better informed historical perspective on the German past.

Allowing the German experience to be remembered historically will not, as is often feared, "make the Germans want to forget" the victims of the Nazi regime. If they have done anything collectively over the last six decades, they have internalized not-forgetting. Their felt obligation to do so will be recognized for a while longer because of the nature and scope of that particular historical mass persecution. But it is true that eventually their remembrance will change, and so will their remorse. More importantly, the passage of time may even diminish the political usefulness of German guilt and shame. Will they always remember? Will they never forget? Can they ever forget? How could they ever forget? I hope that I will be able to persuade my readers that these and other morally sanctioned speculations have been all too politically powerful and exploitable in the postwar era: they have done enough harm in their disregard for the temporality of human affairs that calls for a more inclusive, more self-revising historical memory.

2 "Their Monstrous Past"

German Wartime Fictions

In 1945, when Germans were confronted with the now visible material and moral devastation left behind by the violence of war and Nazi persecutions, the immediate past seemed monstrous, and trying to accept responsibility for it a near impossible task. The German Question, how a civilized people could have committed such acts of unspeakable, unbelievable cruelty, was not meant to be answered. An irrefutable, total accusation, it established the assumption of collective guilt and demand for collective remorse that were to endure into the next century, creating and upholding the moral-political issue of a uniquely unmastered or uncompleted past that would stay with all Germans forever.

At the end of the war, with most of the men killed or held in POW camps, the German civilian population consisted of women and children. They were ordered to view the atrocities committed in their name by their criminal regime and were photographed looking from up close at piles or long lines of corpses by U.S. Army Signal Corps photographers whose job was to document the Germans' criminal culpability and remorse. But the women's notoriously "stony" faces showed horror and repulsion rather than sadness and shame; and the children, in shock, recoiled from the terrible sights and smells. Obviously, they did not know how to react to what they saw, and they did not understand what was asked of them.[1] They were ordinary women who together with their children had just barely survived a total war of hitherto unknown dimensions, and when the victors asked the notorious question, "How could you have done it?" they would answer, "We did not know anything about it," which confirmed the victors' certainty that "they must all have known."

Whether they did or did not know is still a politically important but psychologically moot question because it failed, from the beginning, to address the different ways of knowing and of remembering. Instead it imposed an enduring sameness of guilt—they all knew everything and did not do anything—and of memory—they will now all remember, and in the same way, that they did know and did not act. The resulting conflicts between private and public memory made it difficult to remember spontaneously, though over a period of six decades Germans have been abundantly reminded of their responsibility for the Nazi regime and its atrocities and have been unfailingly pious in their public rituals of collective remembrance.

The general cultural collapse at the end of the war meant that a "normal" temporally constructed identity sustained by a "normally" selective and fluid complex of memories was dramatically redirected. What the evidence forced Germans to believe and thereby accept as their responsibility contradicted in most cases their memories of what they had known at the time when the events occurred. The burden of responsibility seemed overwhelming precisely because it denied them authority over their past, their memories, their historical identity: collectively guilty, they had become collectively *unmündig*, minors without a voice.[2] Moreover, the new German collective memory of having participated in the most brutal acts of victimization was constructed to endure because of the nature of that victimization and of the Allies' absolute moral and military victory. This new collective memory that supported German collective guilt, though embraced by many Germans in the immediate postwar period because they wanted to understand what had happened and atone for it, remained alien but inescapable, removed from the normal gradual changes in time.[3]

The new collective memory produced a collective German bad conscience that arguably contributed to West Germany's remarkably undisturbed democratic development: having "learned their lesson," the citizens of the *Bundesrepublik* made their new state a stable political presence in postwar Europe. Yet the nature of the lesson and the way in which it was taught have also been responsible for the often deceptively smooth symbiosis of political and moral arguments in German postwar culture that has created its own considerable problems. Where the history of Germany's "uncompleted" past is concerned, the inclination to impose taboos has always been stronger than the willingness to invite questions. Whenever history became an issue, it was in the context of an, in somebody's view, (un)desirable politics of history, the most notorious example being the Historians' Dispute of the late 1980s about historiographical approaches to the Holocaust.[4] Fragmented and uncertain, German historiography of the recent past has reflected quite accurately a general cultural and political inability to deal with the historical reality of Nazi aggression, particularly the persecution of Jews.

Since the end of the war it has been difficult to approach these events in relational, historical terms, that is, as phenomena whose current cultural significance would not be exempt from changing, like all things, in time. Soberly critical inquiry into the historical events that were later subsumed into the increasingly ritualized, monumentalized Holocaust has been suspect as sinful revisionism that would diminish their political and cultural uniqueness—curious in view of the fact that all historiography worth its salt draws on new research that would revise, at least to some degree, the old orthodoxy. The Historians' Dispute had little to do with questions of historiographic methodology and everything to do with the political uses of memory and remembrance in postwar Germany. A political controversy rather than scholarly debate, it was ended by moral-political *fiat* rather than professional consensus—the German president's declaration, "Auschwitz remains unique. It was perpetrated by Germans in the name of Germany. This truth is immutable and will not be forgotten."[5]

The Holocaust commemorations of 1995 were to confirm his verdict; so too, in the 1990s and into the new millennium, were many other similar disputes and controversies. All of them have drawn on the intense politicization of German cultural memory that goes deeper than the usual political affiliations and interests, though the Left has seen itself as Germany's conscience in this matter, even more so after reunification and the discrediting of communism. Unless they are rigorously focused on collective guilt and remembrance of the victims of the Nazi regime, discussions of recent German history tend to provoke politically overheated mutual suspicions and accusations. The Right is then seen as prettifying German history for political gains, the Left as imposing on all Germans a politically opportune singular significance of Auschwitz. Self-appointed *preceptor Germaniae,* the social philosopher Habermas started the Historians' Dispute but then simply refused to differentiate between different historiographical positions: disagreeing on principle with all historians on the Right, he assumed that they would all be the same. All of them would look for the wrong evidence in that "unredeemed" past, whereas he, speaking for the Left, would look for the only true evidence: the signs of collective guilt and lack of remorse. This huge and harmful simplification has contributed to the fact that after more than half a century there is still no psychologically realistic attempt at understanding the very real difficulties of individual memory caused by the never clarified concept of collective guilt and collective atonement through public remembrance. The increasing fetishization of Auschwitz is the result not so much of questionable historiographical method as of the unquestioned politics of historical memory.

One of the most prolific defenders of the uniqueness of Jewish victimization, Saul Friedlander, has consistently argued for retaining a transhistorical remoteness or, the other side of the coin, an ahistorical immediacy of Auschwitz. He has rejected "historicization" because it would mean "reinserting the Nazi phenomenon into normal historical narrative," which to him equals "minimizing or abolishing what still makes it appear as singular."[6] In all his writing, Friedlander has emphasized an unquestioned and enduring centrality, for cultural modernity, of the collective remembrance of Auschwitz. He sees no problems with privileging memory and poetic discourse over historiography, since in his view "no amount of factual information" will "resolve" the issue of a "centrality or noncentrality" of Jewish persecution in Western culture.[7]

In his "Plea for a Historicization of National Socialism" (1985) and in an exchange of letters, the historian Martin Broszat argued with Friedlander that representation of the entangled German-Jewish past required a history that was not exclusively shaped, as was collective remembrance, by the perspective of extreme victimization during the final stage of the Nazi regime.[8] But Friedlander has been adamant that in the case of Auschwitz historicization would mean an unacceptable "normalization" of the monstrous past created by the Germans: there had to be an enduring "total dissonance" between past apocalypse and present normality.[9] And indeed, since the end of the war, narratives of victimization have commanded complete belief, no matter how consistent or how contradictory, how clear or how confused, how concrete or how formulaic, how believable or how unbelievable they are. They have been accepted on their own terms of reference, which, certainly for German readers, listeners, or viewers, has made them different in kind from all other discourses.

Born out of experiences beyond civilized imagination for which all Germans were held accountable, these accounts of memory were rarely questioned as to the veracity and validity of the stories they told. Archetypal stories of victimization, they are complete by virtue of their own authority; by definition they cannot and need not be corroborated. Acceptance of such complete authority of remembered persecution has called for the essential primacy of poetic over historical discourse where the Holocaust is concerned. In this scenario, supported by many Holocaust scholars, all historiographical representation of the Nazi period not firmly anchored in the transhistorical uniqueness of Auschwitz is eo ipso a suspect position that reflects the collective hypersubjectivity regarding mass victimization that, explosive and exploitable, has also contributed significantly to the politics of memory and history in postwar Germany.[10]

Public remembrance of Jewish victimization has been remarkably static and exclusive in German postwar culture, despite the fact that the lives of millions of non-Jews were prematurely ended or painfully disrupted and changed by the experience of a total war that they had feared above all else. If recalled, their memories, too, would make present normality seem strange. But these memories have been individual and fragile, not the certified group memories of the Nazis' official victims; more importantly: recalled into different presents during the past half century of (relative) normality, they have not remained the same. Their authority has been partial and temporary, to be questioned and in need of corroboration. Separating the fully authorized narrative of the persecution of Jews so radically from an only partly authorized "normal" history of the period has prevented us from looking at the German-Jewish catastrophe as part of a complex, contradictory, and insufficiently understood historical experience. Normally the past is recalled under the conditions of the present, and since its recalling is provoked and shaped by that present, it is, in each instant of recalling, no longer the same past. Precisely this insight, central to the modern concept of cultural historicity, has been suppressed in German postwar culture with its emphasis on "honest confrontation," generation after generation, with past Jewish persecution. This emphasis has disregarded the fact that the past is a creation of historical time, fluid, porous, and multilayered. Events in the present can be confronted. The past can and must be revisited, but not without critical acknowledgment that these visits, departing for the past from different presents, will not leave it unchanged.

In its open perspectivism and multivocalism, fictional discourse differs from the largely monological discourse of remembrance, but also from historical discourse with its critically shared and controlled processes of establishing evidence. There is a different relation between representation and knowledge in each case, and fictional discourse is characterized by the fact that it withholds both affirmation and negation. In principle, that could create more space for exploring different positions in different visits to the past, different returns to different presents, including areas where psychologically painful and politically divisive aspects of individual and collective memory are concerned. Fictional discourse may clarify, but also obscure, issues; it may help understanding, but also create misunderstandings: it is the reader's role and privilege to negotiate them. However, the uncompleted, unmastered German past that has been present, at least as a subtext, in all of postwar fiction seems on the whole to have defeated that privilege: the potential of fictional discourse for nonassertive accommodation of many different voices has here been severely restricted.

As in historiography, fictional representation of the Nazi period and its aftermath has met with formidable obstacles, not least because these went largely unexplored. Ordinarily the different status of truth statements in fictional discourse opens up, for both author and reader, a variety of interpretative choices in relation to a shared life-world. But here the cultural context of collective memory and guilt has proved, on the whole, too massive to allow for such flexibility. Many of the novels dealing with the German Question are curiously reluctant to ask questions; they inhibit critical dialogue, even where they seem to invite it. George Steiner, speaking here for many professional and nonprofessional readers, unwittingly confirmed this in his 1964 review of Günter Grass's *Dog Years* (*Hundejahre,* 1963), the third novel in what is now called the Danzig Trilogy:[11] he praised especially Grass's "bawling voice" that had managed "to drown the siren-song of smooth oblivion, to make the Germans as no writer did before face up to their monstrous past."[12] Grass's "enormous success" with *The Tin Drum* (*Die Blechtrommel,* 1959)—300,000 copies sold in Germany, more than 60,000 in France, almost 200,000 in the United States—was therefore highly important to Steiner and, he suggested, to every civilized reader in the Western world.[13] The issue was not partial, provisional illumination of an extraordinarily difficult and painful past, but total confrontation.

But what were the reasons for Grass's success that put "German literature back on the market"?[14] Steiner seems to overlook the fact that the boom enjoyed by what he calls the Grass "industry" would seem to undermine his assertion that Germans did not want to remember—unless Grass had been devilishly clever in forcing them. But how? and much more importantly: who were "they"? Clearly, Steiner did not give Grass's readers a second thought as long as "they" were made to "face up to their monstrous past." His argument here is exuberantly eloquent, conceptually contradictory, and instructively cliché-ridden. Thus he acknowledges the problems with Grass's self-consciously tortuous prose but lauds him for throttling "the falsehood and cant out of the old words, trying to cleanse them with laughter and impropriety so as to make them new." More, this forceful prose managed to counteract the "arrogant obscurities of German philosophic speech." Steiner, whose general observations on Grass's style apply to both *Dog Years* and *The Tin Drum,* is clearly referring to Martin Heidegger, notorious for his hermetic poetic-philosophical style and his temporary association with the Nazi regime. Yet the mostly Jewish, Hegelian-Marxian intellectuals of the Frankfurt School share this indeed culturally arrogant verbal obscurantism and so, in the thick, sprawling wordiness of his fiction, does Grass.

Steiner himself admits Grass's "uncontrolled prolixity, his leviathan sentences and word inventories," and concedes that "in the end . . . his obsessed exuberance undermines the shape and reality of the work."[15] But where the "monstrous" German past is concerned, such reservations do not seem to matter, and Steiner concludes his review with the familiar judgment that Grass's readers more than deserved what they got: he "has rubbed the noses of his readers in the great filth, in the vomit of their time. Like no other writer, he has mocked and subverted the bland oblivion, the self-acquittal which underlie Germany's material resurgence. Much of what is active conscience in the Germany of Krupp and the Munich beer halls lies in this man's ribald keeping."[16] It was a question of separating the sheep from the goats, "us" from "them": many German reviews of *The Tin Drum* in 1959 shared Steiner's celebratory appropriation of Grass's position and his righteous distaste for the morally dimwitted.[17]

The Tin Drum is a richly grotesque variation on the arch-German *Bildungsroman.*[18] Its commercial and critical success in forcing confrontation with the past was predicated on approaching it through the allegorical figure of the little monster Oskar Matzerath with his glass-shattering drum, who literally refuses to grow up by stopping to grow at the age of three. Oskar's senses have the peculiar sharpness but also the narrowness of a young child's perception, as is shown in the ways in which he sees, feels, and smells around him the *kleinbürgerlich* (petit-bourgeois) Germany during the Nazi era. His observation of the attacks on Jewish businesses, *Kristallnacht,* in 1938 is sharply focused but restricted to a small area, for instance in the ruined shop of Sigismund Markus. Markus was important to Oskar because he had supplied him with the original (magical) toy drum that gave him the power of self-assertion. But the discovery of his lifeless body is narrated through a consciousness so flooded with sensations that the shock of finding the

corpse seems minimal, certainly not overwhelming. For Oskar everything is equally interesting and surprising, be it the opportunity to loot
some spare drums or the results of the brutal behavior of storm troop-
ers. Contemporary readers reacted to this jarring narrative perspective
and the intermingling of images and references from biblical texts, fairy
tales, and descriptions of Nazi violence with fascination and revulsion—
as intended by Oskar's creator.

A more openly sinister version of Peter Pan, Oskar is a highly unreliable narrator of his picaresque story, as is his author, younger by a few
years and sharing with him part of that story. Oskar is an intricately
composite, deliberately ambiguous and confusing character, and Grass's
proverbial logorrhea and meandering narration further complicate the
matter. Is Oskar, in his own grotesque way, a Jesus figure? or is he the
anti-Christ?[19] Is he or is he not responsible for the deaths of his mother,
his uncle, and his father (who suffocated trying to swallow the Nazi
Party badge that he thought safely hidden from the Russians but that
was found—maliciously?—by nosy Oskar)? Is he or is he not the real
father of his father's son by his second wife? He seems to think that he is
guilty on all counts. Whose past is represented by him and his exotically
petit-bourgeois family, depicted with so much gusto and familiarity by
Grass?

It seems doubtful that the readers who made *The Tin Drum* such a
success acknowledged that past as theirs; certainly not the (intellectual)
critics: they knew, had always known better. Oskar is the artist son who
exorcizes his Nazi father by (perhaps) killing him at the age of twenty-
one and then giving up his drum (his art), promising to grow up after
all and become a responsible member of society, the conclusion of all
Bildungsromane. However, after a short-lived attempt in the late 1940s
at replacing the artist's life with that of the stonemason, he returns to
art, his drum, and thereby, on a higher level, his childhood.[20] This return appears connected to the 1948 currency reform and the beginning
of West Germany's return to "normality," a politically stable, democratic, bourgeois technocracy. But, earning good money with his records
even while he is in a mental institution, Oskar has and has not withdrawn from West Germany's economic miracle, achieved mainly by the
parents' generation: mothers, many of them war widows, even more
than fathers.

The anarchic, darkly comical figure of Oskar, who refuses to grow
up, is the perfect allegory of Adorno's Freudian-Marxian theory of fascism: all Germans were Nazis, and the price they all had to pay for their
monstrous regression was acceptance of collective guilt in confronta-

tion with their monstrous past. They did as they were told. But what did such obedient acceptance say about *their* memories of that past? Grass, though roughly half a generation older than the student generation of 1968, shared in some important ways that cohort's self-definition by absolute distance from their parents and, consequently, their forceful insistence that the parents acknowledge their guilt and thereby redeem the past for the children. *Local Anaesthetic* (*Örtlich betäubt* 1969), expanding the *Schuldthema* (theme of guilt) of the Danzig Trilogy, is set in West Berlin in 1967, shortly before the eruption of student demonstrations. The protagonist, a high-school history teacher about Grass's age, manages to prevent his favorite pupil from burning his dog on Kurfürstendamm to protest the Vietnam war by showing him pictures of people who died in fires. But dreams, flashbacks, and memories reveal his own violent reactions to his cultural and political environment when he was a teenager. The novel's unifying theme is perennial violence and pain as the key to history, the individual's and the group's, and the violence and pain was somehow all the parents' fault—though the teacher could be, and in some ways acts like, a father in his relation to his pupil, who is old enough to participate in the students' uprising.[21]

The parents' greatest failure in their relation to their children, largely unavoidable under the circumstances, had been to protect them from the terrible memories of the war, in fact, from having to become adults. Rebuilding at a frantic pace, creating that seemingly instantaneous "economic miracle," they created what looks from hindsight like a curious suspension of time. It was as if their normal temporality had been ruptured in the physical and political collapse of their country. This rebuilding effort was all the more remarkable because so many men—the fathers of the student generation of 1968—had been either killed in the war or physically and emotionally damaged, often severely; millions had spent years as POWs after the war, the longest and most difficult in Russia, from where very few would return, and almost none of them whole. An important part of this rupture was a mass mutilation, as it were, of families: the absence of fathers both conspicuous and taken for granted. (When I came to America as a young woman in the early sixties, I was struck by the fact that there were no amputees in the streets, that everybody seemed to have a father, and that these fathers seemed different, more fatherly, more indispensable.)

As the dark times demanded, the women had been extraordinarily resourceful, courageous mothers during the war years and in the immediate postwar period, when life continued to be hard and dangerous. But though they and their children survived, often against all odds, alone without the men lost or broken in the war, the men's absence as fathers profoundly affected the children's passage into adulthood in that it gave them a diminished, distorted concept of family that then also concerned the women as mothers.[22] For the children, the parents could never have been different people: younger, more hopeful, less certain, less lucky as survivors, more vulnerable. Whatever their lives—or deaths —had been during and after the war, their identity was frozen, defined by their knowing involvement with the criminal acts of the Nazi regime then and their denial now of having known about them. Projecting their parents back into a past largely unacknowledged by the parents themselves and unknown to the children, they refused to understand both their parents' and their own temporality. But any more or less successful passage into adulthood involves at least a tentative understanding of the temporal instability of identity. Failing in that respect, the children also did not understand that the ambiguities of guilt and atonement had their source in the changing symbiosis of past and present.[23] For the parents, the expectation that they accept their identity as monstrously guilty Germans became both more concrete and more impossible the more unbelievably horrible the victimization: the victims (*Opfer*) were so clearly nothing but victims, which would make the parents so clearly nothing but perpetrators (*Täter*).

Born in Danzig in 1927, Grass focused the *Schuldthema* of the Danzig Trilogy on the persecution of Jews and Poles. The two come together in the character of the Jew Fajngold, who represents millions of murdered Jews, bringing with him his large invisible family who died in Treblinka. Like many Poles in 1945, he has come to Danzig to take over the homes and businesses of Germans forced to leave the eastern provinces where their families had lived for many centuries. Fajngold is happy with the well-run Matzerath food store, explaining its advantages in great detail to his dead family. Without consulting with his dead wife, he proposes that he help Matzerath's pretty young widow and her children (perhaps half-brothers, perhaps father and son) to stay in Danzig and that he give her a share in the business; but she wants to leave the past behind and go west. Fajngold and the Poles have an inalienable right to their new properties. Germans of their generation will never be able to pay their moral debt to them, especially not to Fajngold and his dead family; nor will their children. How could they even begin to explain to them what they thought had been *their* past without seeming to deny the past of the victims?

Across the generational distance, the children responded precisely to the extraordinary violence of Jewish victimization, and it made their demands on the parents all the more forcefully absolute: *they* were the true victims of their parents' inevitably wrong memories; speaking about the past, the parents could not but indict themselves. Ironically, given their general anti-Americanism during the Vietnam War, the children's perspective on their parents was in certain instructive ways similar to that of the (mostly) young American soldiers in 1945: in their double role as liberators and invaders, they had penetrated Germany, revealed all her horrible secrets, and turned the whole country into evidence against itself. Both shared a self-righteous innocence that may seem seductive in hindsight as the Manichean opposite of Evil; it was terrible for the parents, no matter what they had done and felt during the war. Like travelers on another planet, in a totally different time and space, the children, the soldiers, saw certain things overly clearly, and others not at all: they *did* see stony-faced monsters refusing to acknowledge their guilt and show remorse. Much of postwar (West) German fiction shares the righteous obscurities of their innocence, which has arguably hindered rather than helped the process of knowing more about the past, let alone understanding it.[24]

In the early 1950s, Wolfgang Koeppen published three novels that were unusually sensitive to the changing symbiosis of past and present and the temporal, unstable nature of memory: *Tauben im Gras* (1951; *Pigeons on the Grass,* 1988) analyzes one day in Munich in the early spring of 1951; *Das Treibhaus* (1953; *The Hothouse,* 2002) describes two days and two nights in Bonn in the spring of 1953; *Der Tod in Rom* (1954; *Death in Rome,* 1956) takes the reader through two and a half days in May of 1954. Intent on witnessing and anamnesis, the undoing of forgetting, the three novels employ an explicit interplay between different strata of time and memory. The relation between an immediate postwar past and present is mirrored in the short space between the time of the novel and the time of its contemporary reader. In *Pigeons on the Grass,* Munich is still the setting for pantomimes of power relations between the German "have-nots" and the American "haves," focused on the instant gratification offered by cigarettes, liquor, chocolate, coffee.

Need in its most naked black-market form is already a memory, but one that is right underneath the surface of the present, not yet transfigured: a level of memory easily accessible to the characters acting in the *now* of the fictional world and to (contemporary) readers in the, as it were, adjacent future of their life-world. In the preface to the second edition (1956) of the novel, Koeppen explained that his intention had been to show the anarchy and chaos of the immediate postwar years as symbiotically linked to the restorative, affirmative 1950s. A growing attitude of tolerance toward economic corruption and inequality, toward social-political ruthlessness and forgetfulness, is traced back to missed opportunities for German renewal after the fires of war and persecution. In order to argue that "undoing the forgetting" of these difficult years might have helped to undo the cultural-political shortsightedness of the still young Federal Republic, Koeppen rooted anamnesis at greater temporal depth, in a period more remote from the reader's present and yet more painfully entangled with it, the past reality of war and persecution. His elaborate orchestration of temporal interdependencies supports a surreally sharp critique of postwar developments in West Germany that is predicated on the acknowledgment that Hitler, repressed, demonized, or domesticated, has remained with us.[25]

Koeppen's protagonists are not able to use this insight constructively; they are either stunted or destroyed by it. In *Pigeons on the Grass*, Philipp, a writer and observer like his author, is helplessly caught up in the confusions of his present, which he cannot really relate to the past. The result is silence and noise: he is unable to find a language in which he could tell others what he sees and clarify his perceptions for himself. The same is true for the protagonists of *Death in Rome*, the sons in their ineffective confrontation with their fathers, who either murdered or condoned murder. Terrified by the past, the sons reject it so totally as to do themselves harm, without helping their fathers, who still seem untouched by the meanings of their past acts. Committing suicide, the politician Keetenheuve in *The Hothouse* withdraws into the ultimate silence, too desperately intent on escaping from the corruption and complications of the politics of rearmament.

The search for a connecting language, a shared system of reference, is the subtext to *Pigeons on the Grass* and the author's comment on the characters' despair of meaning. Men and women in their social and political relations and actions appear like pigeons on the grass; if there are patterns, they cannot be recognized. The young American soldier Richard is struck by the fact that he cannot fathom the people he meets in Munich. They appear to him in some inexplicable way distorted, caught in a sick lack of balance between hustling and inertia. The reader sees the confusion with the eyes of an outsider, but she also sees the inside through Philipp, the author's delegate witness. His perspective is contrasted with that of the "great" poet Edwin, a combination of Thomas Mann and T. S. Eliot. Celebrating European *Geist* (mind, spirit) as the future of freedom, Edwin is successful, dignified, and futile. He

dismissively quotes Gertrude Stein: "Pigeons on the grass alas," rejecting her and other *Zivilisationsgeister* (mere intellectuals) with their emphasis on man's contingency, that is, his lack of connection with the
divine origin and meaningful order in which Edwin believes. Every pi-
geon knows its home in the hands of God, he declares, while his audience has gone to sleep.

Koeppen is not like Edwin: he is in some ways close to Philipp, who
shares Edwin's futility; he is close to Keetenheuve in *The Hothouse*,
who is too imaginatively apprehensive to be a competent politician, and
also to the young composer Siegfried Pfaffrath in *Death in Rome,* son
of the fellow traveler Friedrich Wilhelm and nephew of the murderous
SS general Judejahn. Pfaffrath decides to delight in the beauties of the
world rather than allow himself to be hurt by the challenge to remember. In his 1962 acceptance speech for the Büchner Prize, Koeppen spoke
of the writer as naturally involved in the struggle against the abuse of
power, violence, the coercion of mass culture—a struggle that would
naturally make him an outsider.[26] In his view, all art is responsible to
society; in his experience, society can defeat the artist. Born in 1906,
Koeppen saw his generation of writers as the truly defeated, the lost
generation that had suffered too intensely through too many speechless
years. Yet while admitting these doubts and reservations, he insisted on
the enduring importance of the artist's social-political role and function.[27] "Who but the writer should play the role of Cassandra in our
society?" he had asked in a 1961 interview; and in 1971 he referred to
his books as manifestos against war and oppression: "As a human being
I feel powerless; not so as a writer." Yet on this occasion he also spoke
of the problems with communicating the disturbing implications of a
West German postwar reality in a period of rapid, "unheard-of" technological development and mass communication.[28]

In stark contrast to Grass's *Tin Drum,* Koeppen's novels did not
reach many readers, though he has always had a substantial number of
sympathetic, even admiring, reviewers from across the political spectrum.[29] Almost all these "professional readers" assumed that his novels
would have difficulties with a general educated readership. Krämer-
Badoni titled his perceptive 1952 review of *Pigeons on the Grass* "They
will Cry 'Crucify Him!'"[30] mainly on account of the novel's relentless
pessimism regarding a German *Wiedergeburt* (rebirth) or meaningful
restoration. And Koeppen's consistently modernist narrative strategies
did not help, even though, in contrast to Grass's work, their meanings
were always accessible. Actually (and predictably), "they," the readers
of *The Tin Drum,* neglected rather than crucified Koeppen. *Pigeons on*

the Grass had two editions and sold 6,500 copies in 1951—a figure that, given the circumstances of that time and the fact that Koeppen was an unknown author, was not all that low. However, paperback editions of 1956 and 1966 did not do much better. When the novel was included in the highly successful Bibliothek Suhrkamp in 1974, at a time of heightened sensitivity to the danger of forgetting the "uncompleted past," it sold no more than 5,000 copies, though it was generally acclaimed as one of the most important postwar novels. The 1953 *Hothouse,* thought to be a roman à clef about the world of Bonn, did better, selling 12,000 copies; but the 1954 *Death in Rome,* which dealt most explicitly and harshly with the problem of cultural memory and generational conflict, sold only 6,000.[31]

The intensely personal but historically reflected perspective that guided Koeppen's conceptual and narrative strategies left no doubt about his skepticism with regard to a "completion" of the German past and the finding of a meaningful order in history. But Koeppen has also made it clear that such order, even if possible, could never be found by him. All the poet can do is consider history a cultural challenge rather than a given. Here, I think, is the most formidable obstacle to a fuller acceptance of his novels, even for sympathetic critics impressed by their dark beauty of loss, resignation, elegiac withdrawal, despair, negation, significant silence.[32] When Koeppen won the prestigious Büchner Prize in 1962, Walter Jens in his *laudatio* ranked him as perhaps the greatest prose writer in postwar Germany, an ever more perceptive sophisticated verbal gourmet of sounds, tastes, smells, shapes, and shadows of the past in the present.[33] Helmut Heissenbüttel in a 1968 *Merkur* essay, "Wolfgang Koeppen-Kommentar," proclaimed him to be at the frontiers of language, wrestling, in Wittgensteinian fashion, with that which cannot be (fully) articulated, the complexities of the self, the real reality. Koeppen may have allowed his characters to indulge in such beauty of futility in order to show the quality of their failure. Yet his narrative strategies have been informed by his intention to warn of the temptations of this failure, because it would sap the energy needed to keep the past open for the present.

When *Death in Rome* came out in English translation in 1961, a lonely reviewer wrote in *Library Journal* that "this modern *Goetterdaemmerung* . . . should have been published in this country much sooner; however, its appearance during the Eichmann trial does seem timely."[34] In contrast to Siegfried Lenz's *Deutschstunde* (1968; *The German Lesson,* 1972), a bestseller in the Federal Republic and well received in the United States, *Death in Rome* found few readers in Germany and fewer in America, precisely because it was and had been so timely. The ghosts from the past that Koeppen visits on his readers are not the picturesque goblins of *The German Lesson;* they clearly pose threats, and their claims to be heeded are unambiguous.

The German Lesson was published in the midst of a lively cultural debate on the issues of guilt, memory, and remembrance that had begun in the mid-1960s as a political disruption of the status quo by the sons turning ostensibly against the generation of the economically successful fathers. The millions of fathers killed as young men in a cruel war were forgotten, lost in the past like the war itself, already unimaginable to the sons who had never known them. The political, if not the personal, energy of this disruption was soon dissipated. *The German Lesson* was so successful because Lenz was much less clear about the significance of the past for the present than Koeppen, and readers, professional and general, were much freer to read into or out of his text positions with which they agreed or disagreed.

Like Oskar Matzerath, Lenz's protagonist Siggi Jepsen is not an adult, and he is a highly unreliable narrator. His search for the unmastered past is intimately connected with his father, the petit-bourgeois policeman Jepsen, with the artist Nansen (based on the Expressionist painter Emil Nolde), and with the relation between Nansen's devotion to the demands of his art and Jepsen's devotion to the demands of his duty. Despite the prohibition of his paintings by the Nazis, which Jepsen tries to enforce with obsessive zeal, Nansen's artistic credo shares (as Nolde's did) certain aspects of Nazi ideology, most clearly a significant rootedness in the landscape of *Heimat*. In the view of one critic, the great success of the book depended on its readers' failure to understand Nansen's/Nolde's ambiguity; they simply "identified as the positive features of *The German Lesson* its story of a family divided under Nazism and its evocative descriptions of familiar North German landscapes and of what they take to be re-creations of the spirit of Nolde's vision of this landscape." This assumption makes it possible to insist simultaneously on Lenz's clear insight into Nansen/Nolde's "basic ambiguity" or "inner dualism" and on the inability of the readers of a best-selling novel to follow him.[35]

But why would all these readers have been unable to follow Lenz's by no means difficult narrative strategies? Many other reviews of the novel attributed its success, rightly, to the fact that Lenz approached the problems of the uncompleted past in ways that made them more accessible, something that Koeppen's novels with their specific temporal complexities and general cultural anxieties had not managed to do. On the occasion of the American edition of *The German Lesson* in the spring of 1972, Michael Hamburger reviewed the book for the broad educated readership of *Saturday Review* (March) under the title "A Third Reich with No Demons," meaning a discussion of the German "monstrous past" that enabled the readers to see beyond the monsters. Hamburger's reading did much for the reception of the novel in the United States; yet it still seems to me that the effectiveness, the pleasure, of the book was predicated precisely on the *presence* of demons, if of the manipulable, domesticated kind.

Lenz presented to his readers a very clear construct of Nansen-Nolde's "inner dualism" and of Jepsen's obsessive belief in duty that made him the perfect petit-bourgeois tool of the criminal regime; it turned out to be highly successful and much too simple. It would have been more difficult, (probably) less successful, but more useful to show how important social-psychological needs and desires were shared by the supporters of the Nazi regime and its opponents; how Jepsen's inarticulate, abstract concept of duty, dangerous to himself and others, was rooted in the same search for metaphysical order that had entangled the artist Nansen. But the demoniacally sparkling buttons and clasps of Jepsen's uniform and the demons that live under the artist's old blue cape resist such sober analysis. These demons may be fun, but they do not tell us how Jepsen and Nansen got caught in the dualisms of their author's making, nor how the son Siggi will be able to disentangle himself. The monstrous German past may have become more accessible; the challenge of the uncompleted past has become both more remote and more exploitable.

————

The monstrous past emerged again in the mid-1980s, this time as an intergenerational conflict about the uniqueness of Auschwitz in the center of the evil singularity of the German past. The darkness and bitterness of that past, unresolved, enduring, surged up powerfully in the politicized confrontations of the Historians' Dispute that seemed to bear out the urgency of Koeppen's warning. He had posed the question of a radically evil German past in *Pigeons on the Grass* and *Death in Rome,* but deferred it in a manner that might suggest, more than four decades later, a way to circumvent the permanent stalemate in which many of today's political invocations of Nazi (German) Evil are mired. In Koeppen's lucid analyses of memory as the complex temporal shaping of past experience, the notion of a singularly tormenting past appears in conditional terms: if Hitler remains with the Germans in any significant way, then only because they will finally be able to accept into their present the challenge of his different meanings in the past—Broszat's plea for a historicization of the Nazi period.

The controversy in the early 1990s about Christa Wolf's involvement with the East German *Stasi* (state security service) more than three decades earlier reads like a tragi-comical epilogue to the Historians' Dispute, as does the whole issue of a collective responsibility of East German intellectuals for the repressive cultural policies of the regime from which they also derived their power.[36] Like those of Grass and Lenz, Wolf's attempts at dealing with the memory of the past have been highly successful with large readerships, because, like them, she kept her distance, where Koeppen came too close for comfort. Wolf was helped here by the official East German position that the victory of Communism had made the German Question irrelevant; the fascist part of the German past was completed and forgettable. This allowed her and other East German writers to pose arguments for not forgetting in the different, as it were more innocent, terms of "moral memory." The great interest in East German literature outside the Eastern Bloc was based partly on that fact as well as on the curiosity about life in that (for West Germans) so near yet so radically unfamiliar Communist utopia.[37] Unlike intellectuals in the *Bundesrepublik,* intellectuals in the *Deutsche Demokratische Republik* did not have to affirm at all times their profound *Betroffenheit* (emotional-moral concern) about the meanings of the monstrous Nazi past for the democratic present. They could worry, if in all manner of intriguingly secretive ways, about the meanings of the socialist present for their individual futures; they could write openly about their private memories and be all the more relevant. Wolf's best text remains *In Search of Christa T.,* in which she at least stated the conflicts between the demands of social and individual memory and identity, allowing them to remain unresolved because irrevocably private.

Kindheitsmuster (1976; *A Model Childhood,* 1980) and *Kassandra* (1983) were more problematic in this respect. Wolf had in the meantime become a best-selling author in the West, not least because of the mainstreaming of feminism.[38] Increasingly she presented herself abroad as the conscience of her country, but managed all the same to avoid open dissent and to hold on to her "travel cadre" status and other Eastern privileges. Intellectuals safely ensconced in the West could not possibly blame her for that; but it *was* a dilemma and it *did* blur her awareness of the actual limitations of the East German perspective, a blurring that inevitably extended to her private vision, which became more self-centered the more it claimed larger social and political relevance. The "moral memory" she advocates in *Kindheitsmuster* is not convincingly realized, because the novel's intricately temporal and geographical search for the Nazi past remains essentially concerned with her own writerly identity. In the spring of 1971 Wolf traveled with her brother, husband, and youngest daughter to the places of her childhood in what is now Poland, writing the book in 1972 to 1975. These three time spaces are interwoven: the past of childhood, the past of the journey, and the on-going present of the writing process. The narration shifts constantly between Nelly, who inhabits the childhood space and whose voice is rendered mainly in narrated monologue, and the adult author in search of her childhood. Alternating between third-, second-, and first-person narration, she creates an erratic interior monologue interspersed with sententious reflections on narration and memory.

In the end, Nelly merges into the identity of the author, who then states that this composite "I" is now in need of being narrated differently. Does she refer here to the *Grenzen des Sagbaren* (limits of what can be articulated)? or the need for a sequel to expand the theme of memory and identity? The novel is ostensibly finished, but the reader is left, in its last sentences, with a list of questions touching on this theme that are self-centered to the point of coyness.[39] Has the child (book) hidden in her "come forth" or retreated to a "deeper, more inaccessible hiding place? Has memory done its duty? Or has it proven—by the act of misleading—that it's impossible to escape the mortal sin of our time: the desire not to come to grips with oneself?" She does not know; as she says in the concluding ambiguous sentence: "Sure of finding myself once again in the world of solid bodies upon awakening, I shall abandon myself to the experience of dreaming. I shall not revolt against the limits of the expressible."

Wolf seems to be saying here that she will have to respect the *Grenzen des Sagbaren* where it concerns the crucially important questions of memory and identity; that as a contemporary to the late twentieth century she will have to succumb to the desire not to confront herself in her relation to the uncompleted, unmasterable past because that past is monstrous to the point of unspeakable. Yet her preoccupation with these limits—a neo-Romantic position privileging instantaneously revealed and then complete meaning over the secular processes of partial, provisional meaning—has little to do with any of the real, that is, social and political, questions posed by that past. In the modern situation of acknowledged human temporality and historicity, understanding the German past is not different in kind from understanding other pasts: *all* of them are "uncompleted" in that they rely on critical historical research that will yield some useful information, some insight, but never full knowledge, at least not before the end of human time.

Since its subject is temporality, the inexorable succession of pasts and presents into the future, modern historiography is the most literal example of postlapsarian knowledge. It evolves in processes of establishing and reestablishing plausibility and does not intend to arrive at complete, unchanging truth. Wolf's desire for higher, complete meaning in all her work, but particularly where the German past is concerned, has shielded her and her admiring readers from modern epistemological self-restriction: not the Manichean scenario of knowing everything or nothing, but the relativism of knowing more in time (as long as there is a critical community of inquiry). In her own view, Wolf's straining against the *Grenzen des Sagbaren* in this novel about the difficulties of dealing with the German past—in one way or another *the* enduring topic for West German writers—is intimately connected with the unquestioned, unchanging cultural significance of her "labor of writing," *Schreibarbeit*.

Instructively, her use of this term in this context invokes the collective labor of remembering and mourning, *Erinnerungssarbeit* and *Trauerarbeit,* prescribed by the psychoanalysts Alexander and Margarete Mitscherlich for the collectively guilty (West) Germans whose illness they had diagnosed as a collective "inability to mourn" the victims of the Nazi regime. Psychologically vague but culturally influential, the arguments of *The Inability to Mourn: Principles of Collective Behavior* (1975; *Die Unfähigkeit zu trauern,* 1967) were based on the Mitscherlichs' Freudian model of regressive repression that abstracted and reduced the complex political-psychological reality at the end of the war, when Germans had to accept both the newly visible enormity of Nazi atrocities *and* the burden of their own collective responsibility for these acts.

For the student generation of 1968, *Erinnerungssarbeit* and *Trauerarbeit* quickly became buzz words, a "must," since these terms supported their self-declared moral authority vis-à-vis the *Tätergeneration* of their parents. For Wolf, *Schreibarbeit* and *Erinnerungssarbeit* have meant the importance and assertion of her own writerly identity, which she articulated in increasingly stilted, self-conscious language. This purple prose suggests a flawed performance for some, for others the artist's profound *Sprachskepsis,* namely significant mistrust in the ability of language to express what cannot be expressed fully: her writerly struggle with the past.[40] Before the fall of the Wall, Wolf's work was given a substantial benefit of doubt as to the cultural value of this struggle since she had engaged in it and demonstrated her *Betroffenheit* voluntarily— in contrast to West German writers for whom such demonstrations have been obligatory and whom critics have easily accused of immorality and irresponsibility where they found them wanting in this respect.[41]

Kassandra, another search for the writer's significant identity, this time from an antiwar, antitechnology, rigidly feminist position, also suffers from this self-indulgent writerly self-reflection. In the five lectures on the "presuppositions" of *Kassandra* at Frankfurt University in May 1982—a rather pompous affair given the slightness of her novel—Wolf presented the familiar simplistic arguments against the logocentrism, dualism, domineering systemicity, and violent objectification of Western (Greek) patriarchy.[42] The attractiveness of these arguments, especially to certain feminist groups, came from this summary critique, the subtext of Cassandra-Wolf's reflections on her cultural role as seer, *vates,* poet, to which she attributes her heroic desire to remain a witness beyond the end of human time.[43] Speaking for victims and against victimization in such totalizing, supra-historical terms, she can rely on her absolute writerly authority in the by now hallowed tradition of Holocaust discourses: no questions allowed; no reservations, qualifications, differentiations; no research and potential new evidence; no knowledge that changes with time.

The Cassandra of Greek myth was not a victim; she wanted the gift of prophecy but was not willing to pay the price, to sleep with Apollo. Brilliantly, he did not withdraw the gift, but punished her by adding to it the condition that she would not be believed. Wolf could have done much with the implications of that modern dilemma: there is no prophecy in modernity because the future, as ever more complex interdependencies of contingencies and choices, is truly unpredictable. What Cassandra sees is *her* vision, which may not be shared by others. Is it really *their* fault that they cannot believe her? Might it not be the quality of her witnessing, of her rigidly one-sided monological discourse of victimization? Whatever repressive properties can be found in Greek culture from the hindsight of several millennia, that culture has also produced the enormous achievement of conceptually organized discourse that enables the participants to persuade and be persuaded by the power of superior rational argumentation, not the violence of superior physical strength.[44]

A persuasive argument is dialogical; it has to be constructed in a way that enables the person to whom it is addressed to reconstruct it critically and to her intellectual satisfaction. Wolf's Cassandra is never made to understand that she has to be convincing. Like her author, she speaks with the preestablished authority of prophecy and expects to be listened to, though she knows from experience that, speaking the way she does, she will not be believed. At no point in the narration of her conscientious suffering for womankind, for humanity, does she ever consider intelligibly the implications of her position: does she want to be partially right in her warnings that others could consider but also question; or does she want to insist self-righteously on the whole and only truth of her vision? Assuming too easily the authority to speak for others, Wolf has shown little imagination for the difference of other people. The myth of Cassandra is of course a complex of stories interwoven in many temporal and cultural layers—an interweaving that scholars have traced painstakingly but that is hard to disentangle to the point where it makes sense in its own terms. The same is true of the stories of the Trojan War. Apollo, god of the light of reason so much disliked by Wolf, does play an important part; but so does Athena, the goddess of wisdom.[45] Wolf—and this is her privilege—took from this complexly composite story what she could use for her own much simpler, predictable narrative; to claim for it general cultural significance is another matter.

Here is the link to Wolf's panicked reaction to the critical discussion of her *Stasi* involvement. The existence of her *Stasi* file was seen by many critics as regrettable but unimportant, since the information obtained from her thirty years earlier was harmless and her involvement due mostly to political naiveté and the young writer's ambition.[46] The real harm was done by Wolf's playing simultaneously to East and West, her success in giving both sides what they wanted. It was a strategy that over the decades dulled her cultural-political sensitivities and among other things allowed her to claim equal victim status with the exiles of the 1930s and 1940s and equal significance for East German and Weimar literary culture.[47] This moral and intellectual hubris predictably caused much consternation among West German intellectuals, but it also demonstrated that they shared with Wolf the belief in an, as it were, preauthorized higher moral and *geistig* status of "the writer,"[48] especially when drawing on it to deny it to others. Such authority soothed their own identity problems as intellectuals in a Western mass democracy and technocracy that, involved in its own politics of self-interest, expected them to be the conscience of the nation, namely to figure out how to cope with the uncompleted German past. Wolf, an East German writer, seemed to have accepted that task voluntarily, nobly, altruistically; they had given her too much credit and now they asked too much back.[49]

Perhaps the most curious aspect of this instructive tempest in a tea-pot was West German intellectuals' reluctance to accept, along with the banality, also the obscurity of the alleged "betrayal." Their "profound disappointment" at the *Stasi* revelations echoes their reactions to the uncompleted Nazi past, which they have held up to others whose pub-lic (not to mention private) memories of their collective guilt have al-ways seemed unsatisfactory in that they did not, after all, yield enough mourning, remorse, moral certainty. The political and moral muddle after the fall of the Wall half a century after the end of the Second World War might be a useful occasion to consider more soberly the obscuri-ties, the moral gray zones, the avoidable and unavoidable compromises, conflicts, and ambiguities of the German Question—its all-too-human mix of closeness and remoteness.

3 Censored Memories

"Are the Germans Victims or Perpetrators?"

The Manichean divide of German postwar memory has drawn a sharp line between memories of guilt that were to become the public memory discourses of WWII and memories of painful losses that were to be excluded not only from public remembrance but also from historical memory. For a brief time, in the mid-eighties, there seemed to be some cautious development toward a more explicitly historical discussion of the Nazi period, best summed up in the historian Martin Broszat's "Plea for a Historicization of National Socialism" (1985).[1] But by the mid-nineties, the new political realities of reunification and of the growing conflict between the Arab world and the United States, in which Israel played an important role, had reenergized suspicion of German wartime memories and reemphasized the need for an enduring German identity of guilt and remorse.

A year before the collapse of the Berlin Wall, in the fall of 1988, President Richard von Weizsäcker had ended the heated and highly public dispute among opposing groups of West German historians about the historiography of the recent past by declaring: "Auschwitz remains unique. It was perpetrated by Germans in the name of Germany. This truth is immutable and will not be forgotten."[2] The Historians' Dispute broke out in the summer of 1986, and from the beginning it had little to do with methodological questions of historiography and everything to do with the political uses of memory in postwar Germany. An issue of general cultural concern in Germany and to a degree also in the United States,[3] the *Historikerstreit* was to become the arch-model for the many bitter memory controversies in the next two decades in part because it was so clearly and successfully media-driven: the high-serious drama of professional German Bad Conscience was performed to the great fascination, the applause, and the displeasure of different audiences on two opposing stages, the left-liberal *Die Zeit* and the (politically) conservative *FAZ*.

From hindsight, this performance looks like a dress rehearsal for the politicized correctness of German remembrance in its symbiotic relation to German *Kollektivschuld* that became again the focus of attention in the next decade, ostensibly to counteract any reawakening of German national consciousness and desire for national power. One of the results of this renewed attention was an intensified fear that, if permitted, the wartime memories of many millions of German civilians would be primarily focused on loss—the experience of air raids, large-scale expulsion (*Vertreibung*), the loss of husbands, sons, brothers in a brutal war that most of them had not wanted and into which they were thrown as conscripted canon fodder—and detract from the burden of their shared guilt, their having to make amends for their past.

This renewed desire for a clear separation of loss and guilt in remembering the war has imposed an indefinite deferral of all attempts to deal with memory processes in ways that would allow for more differentiation and contextualization. German war experiences differed greatly, despite the fact that at the end stage of that indeed "total" war death seemed to be all-present and all-powerful, touching almost every family. The war hit hardest in the eastern areas and in urban centers. More than 16 million Germans were forced to leave their homes in the former German territories of Czechoslovakia, Poland, and Russia, where their families had lived for centuries. Millions of them died or were killed on the trek from the East, the overwhelming majority women and children. Urban populations suffered more than rural populations from air raids, and then from hunger and cold in the immediate postwar era. The treatment of German POWs was particularly brutal in the Soviet Union, from where a tiny percentage (about 5%) returned, and then late and often badly damaged both physically and emotionally.[4] There was also a broad spectrum of attitudes toward the criminal Nazi regime; more importantly, these attitudes changed over time as the war became more total and the true nature of the regime began to reveal itself. It was these changes in which the historian Broszat was explicitly interested when he pleaded for a historicization of the Nazi period.[5]

These changes would have shaped individual Germans' feelings of shame and guilt toward their recent past, and with them memories of loss and pain. Like all memories, theirs too were an unstable, if familiar, complex of layered, shifting, contradictory, sometimes obscure, other times overly clear images and meanings—the more unreliable, the more traumatic the remembered events. For the first six decades after the war, the general instability of memory was hardly an issue since Germans, collectively encouraged to forget their own war experiences and focus on the experiences of their regime's, *their,* victims, had indeed done so. They seemed to have largely forgotten what had happened to them; and so had their children. But in recent years, notably since the publication of Günter Grass's docu-fictional novel *Im Krebsgang* (*Crab Walk*) in the spring of 2002 and later that same year Jörg Friedrich's antiwar documentary *Der Brand,* there has been more openly expressed interest in retrieving German memories of the war.[6] One of the explanations for this phenomenon has been the aging of the generation of *Kriegskinder,* many of whom now seem less preoccupied with the burden of inherited collective guilt and increasingly curious about their families' actual war experiences.

Since their own feelings of guilt and responsibility for the troubled German past have in most cases been vicarious, they are in a better position to explore it more freely than their parents had wished or had been able to do. It is meaningless to speak of an innocent "generation of *Kriegskinder,*" as it is meaningless, if more harmful, to speak of a guilty "generation of *Täter.*" In the first case it depends on individuals' psychological and moral involvement with memories of the war; in the second case it depends on individuals' actual conduct during the war. But differentiations have not been a priority where it concerns the "bad German past": the denunciatory concept of "the generation of *Täter*" is still alive and well. More troubling is the public resistance coming not only from Jewish-German organizations and their speakers, but also from a large group of non-Jewish German politicians and public intellectuals against the growing interest of *Kriegskinder* in reconstructing for themselves a less one-dimensional past. Such past would differ from the "bad German past" in that it would include the private wartime memories of their parents and other individual Germans with all their contradictions, lacunae, and moral gray zones—uncertainties to which their own (in most cases) fragmented memories would contribute. Perceived as a serious, even dangerous, break with entrenched habits of forgetting, this interest has rekindled and newly energized the old arguments first made at the end of the war, that memories of German war losses would diminish both the memories of their regime's victims and the weight of German guilt by relieving, at least partially, German collective bad conscience with the assertion "we suffered too."

The question of allowing German memories of WWII a visible and audible cultural presence has rapidly become a strongly polarizing issue because of fears that the cultural presence of these memories could or would obscure the clear divide between *Opfer* (victims) and *Täter* (perpetrators) needed to keep in check an always suspected, "fated" reemergence of anti-Semitic feelings allegedly still dormant in German culture. The nature and scale of Nazi persecution of Jews may seem to support the plausibility of this scenario, even though the utopianist anti-Semitism of the Third Reich differed radically from previous versions of political anti-Semitism. Despite the concrete racialist violence of Nazi persecutions, the regime relied on generalizing and abstracting notions of Jews as agents of modernity in evoking the ills of the Weimar *Systemzeit* to be healed by the Third Reich, among them the very real difficulties of technological globalization experienced by the working and lower-middle classes.

The history of Jews in Germany is an extraordinary success story in the eighteenth, nineteenth, and into the twentieth centuries, due to the efforts of Jewish and non-Jewish Germans alike.[7] However, the predominantly post-Holocaust perspective on German-Jewish history has gravely distorted the past realities of Jewish life in Germany: all Jews everywhere, but particularly in Germany, have always been persecuted and always in the same ways.[8] A good case in point was the enthusiastic German reception of Daniel Goldhagen's irrational argument of an inherently German murderous anti-Semitism in his *Hitler's Willing Executioners* (1996) that nicely excluded the grandchildren of the *Täter-generation:* some higher power had cleansed their German genetic heritage, and it was now almost as good as that of Americans.

Jewish fear of reemerging German anti-Semitism has been respected and internalized by Germany's well-intentioned political and intellectual elites to the point where it could never be discussed in rational historical terms, even less so after the events of September 11, 2001, when Muslim anti-Semitism seemed to be increasing in Europe and a highly generalized, fuzzy concept of anti-Semitism was automatically linked with anti-Americanism.[9] For most contemporary Germans, the issue has not been the fear of anti-Semitism itself but of being *accused* of anti-Semitism: a fear that more than anything else has lent itself to political exploitation. The imprecise concept of anti-Semitism allowing for different meanings in different historical situations has considerably enlarged this fear since it has stretched and thereby made more powerful the imagination of anti-anti-Semitism. By putting the connective *oder* (or) between the word "*Opfer*" and the word "*Täter*," the question currently much debated in Germany, "Sind die Deutschen Opfer oder Täter?" has been perceived as fudging the familiar divide between *Opfer* and *Täter*—a serious issue since it might put into question the claims made by the Nazi regime's official *Opfer* to a unique, supra-historical victim status.

A guest at several recent German panel discussions of this question, I pointed out that the Germans *are* neither victims nor perpetrators, but that a large number of them *had been* victims of WWII and a small number *had been* perpetrators. Oddly, in this context, the word *Opfer* itself seemed to connote a hierarchical significance, uniqueness of suffering. Notwithstanding all the good intentions of panelists and audience, the discussions always went back to a pervasive German collective guilt that could not be debated in neutral historical terms for fear of offending the sanctity of the Nazis' official victims. Similarly, since the word *Täter* used in this context connotes the purest evil, any connection with *Opfer*, be it in the form of a question, is heresy since it disturbs the accepted belief in a world divided into Good and Evil, friends and foes.

Right after the war, Hannah Arendt discussed with Karl Jaspers the political and cultural consequences of Nazi persecutions and pointed out that the innocence of the victims was as "inhuman" as Nazi culpability: "No human being can be as innocent as all Jews were in the face of the gas oven (the most revolting profiteer as innocent as a newborn child, because no crime matches such punishment). In human-political terms, the concept of a guilt beyond the crime and an innocence beyond kindness and virtue is meaningless." If the Germans are burdened with hundreds of thousands who can no longer be punished adequately within a legal system, "we Jews are burdened with millions of innocents who make every Jew today feel like innocence incarnate."[10] Arendt wanted Jews to see themselves as a people among other peoples and as historical agents, co-responsible for current and historical political events of which they were a part. Right after the war, in close temporal proximity to the horrifying persecutions, claiming such agency and historical co-responsibility must have seemed very wrong, blasphemous to many Jews —as did her book on the Eichmann trial almost twenty years later. But that does not detract from the psycho-social and political shrewdness of her observations then and later.

Another four decades later, historical developments have proved her right. The perceived meta-historical, meta-political dimension of Nazi persecutions, resulting in the absolute guilt of the people enacting them, the *Täter*, and the absolute innocence of the people on whom they were perpetrated, the *Opfer*, has to this day encouraged political exploitation rather than historical understanding of the Nazi period—very much so in the case of Israel's problematic politics, as predicted by Arendt in uncanny detail.[11] For Germans who had survived the war without becoming *Täter* in the stricter meaning of the word, absolute guilt became a collective unmovable burden. In the late sixties, when their children found themselves confronted with it, the very fact that most of their parents had not been "real" *Täter,* not *active* victimizers, was turned into accusations of their collective *passivity* in the face of Nazi criminality, which assigned them all to the status of *Täter,* the generation of *Täter.* From now on, this collective accusation could always be invoked, whenever it seemed to benefit the dynamics of a specific political situation. Conveniently lumped together with the equally stretchable concepts of remorse, anti-Semitism, and Holocaust denial,[12] it has proved to be nonnegotiable because nonspecific.

Feeling guilt and showing remorse are the most basic and most mysterious emotions because they are both intensely private and emphatically social. Perhaps more than any other emotion, they draw on the reality principle of other people since they are needed, and then demanded, to create and uphold social stability. At the same time, they are indispensable for the development of the individual's consciousness, which is connected with his social conscience since it concerns the individual's understanding of the status of his own morality in the larger context of others' morality: How (well) do I understand the consequences of what I have done? Acknowledging my guilt and showing remorse, where am I with other people, at any given time and in any given situation?

In one of a series of *Spiegel* interviews on "Hitler und die Deutschen" in the summer of 2001, Joachim Fest was asked why the shadow cast by Hitler has become longer since his suicide so many decades ago. He thought that Hitler, "one of the incarnations of evil, though not the only one," has played a special role in a secularized world where evil is no longer represented by the devil.[13] In the late sixties, while Fest was working on his Hitler biography (1973), he was a consultant for Albert Speer, Hitler's well-educated, upper-middle-class architect, in whom he and other historians (such as Hugh Trevor-Roper) saw the key to understanding the puzzle of National-socialism, the collaboration of the elites with Nazism. More than thirty years later, the Nazi phenomenon is still an enigma for Fest (he thinks for historians in general) and Speer still important to its solution. Working with Speer on his memoir, a text that instructively reflects Speer's spontaneous openness to Hitler's fascination with religio-political symbolism, Fest became convinced of his unreserved condemnation of the Nazi regime, but not of his really understanding the meaning of his own failures. Speer may have felt guilt; but he did not seem to know what guilt really was. He was sincere in showing remorse, but he never had a clear concept of what he was reproached with, what he was guilty of.

Fest may have expected too much from Speer's capacity to understand his particular version of German guilt. The German political, intellectual, and professional elites, left and right alike, many of them morally principled, did not seriously try to resist the Nazis when their rise was still resistible; nor did the officers' caste. Many reasons for this failure have been debated for many decades, and they probably will not go away in the near future, particularly the much lamented traditional German lack of a political civil society that would keep in check the rise of political religions such as National-socialism. Few individuals had the strength to resist a criminal regime without such a, as it were, naturally civil society.[14] And the lack of it has also made it more difficult for Germans in their collectivity to develop an adequate understanding of their guilt; even if their individual remorse about the results of Nazi criminality may have been (and still be) sincere.

The difficulties of German guilt—and in that they are shared by the relatively few active *Täter* like Speer and by the tens of millions of passive *Täter* of the collective guilt scenario—have to do with this enduring enigma of the Nazi phenomenon: How did it happen? How can we be guilty if we do not even now understand how it happened? What exactly is our guilt? These questions cannot be answered without allowing the Germans full access to their memories of the Nazi period and permission to bracket, for the sake of understanding, the polarizing question "victims or perpetrators." Moreover, their memories need to be retrieved in discourses of their own that are in certain important ways outside of, parallel to, the memory discourses of the Holocaust. Since the latter have been at the center of postwar German culture, even more so after reunification, this is a difficult enterprise, not only because it will be a priori suspect, but also because there are no models for it in the history of the *Bundesrepublik*.

How can these relatively few and still uncertain discourses of German wartime memory relate to the monumental construct of Holocaust memory discourses? The Berlin *Holocaust-Mahnmal,* in size and design the most challenging architectural project of the new capital, will be consecrated on May 8, 2005, the sixtieth anniversary of Germany's unconditional surrender. This enormous field in the middle of a twenty-first-century European metropolis, planted with nothing but 2,751 light

gray concrete steles, is meant to protect "forever" the remembrance of
Jewish victimization and keep all other memories out. Despite an often
bitterly divided debate, over more than a decade, on whether it should
be built or not, it is for many German politicians and intellectuals a fitting allegory of the *Berliner Republic* whose foundation myth is "Auschwitz."

The German novelist and essayist Peter Schneider remembers how
the student revolutionaries of 1968, his generation, had "simply ban-
ished from their version of history all stories about Germans that did
not fit in with the picture of the 'generation of perpetrators.' It was the
frantic attempt of those born after the war to shake off the shackles that
bound them to the guilty generation and regain their innocence by iden-
tifying with the victims of Nazism."[15] Like all these socially concerned
students, he never discussed the actual wartime experiences of his parents because they were the generation of perpetrators: "we never said a
word about the Germans who were expelled. The same taboo applied
to the civilians who were burned to death in the German cities; it applied to Stalin's resettlement of the Volga Germans; to those Germans
who were interned after the end of the war in the Sachsenhausen concentration camp, often for arbitrary reasons; to the deportation to Sibe-
ria of the opponents of the forced merger between the German Social
Democratic and Communist parties in the Soviet zone to form the East
German Socialist Unity Party; and to the victims of the mass rapes during and after the fall of Berlin."[16]

Over time, Schneider would develop a remarkably balanced perspective on postwar German culture: his generation's difficulties in dealing with the complexities and contradictions of the parents' past were
"powerful reasons" for their instinctive avoidance of these "forbidden
topics." The avoidance was typical for the "1968 generation" with its
moralizing self-righteousness and rigid ideological utopianism. But it was
also shared by many other Germans who were not, as were Schneider
and his activist comrades, determined to extinguish the parents' bad
past by superimposing a good future of their own creation. It did not
take a Marxian lack of political realism to never talk about the experiences of the parent's generation other than to denounce and reject them.
For most Germans of the children's generation, whatever their view of
the future, the past was as bad as it was abstract; it had no depth, no
challenges, no mysteries. There needed to be a forgetting so deep that
nothing that had been forgotten could ever be retrieved.

Contrary to the (instructively misleading) title of his *New York
Times* essay, "The Germans Also Suffered," Schneider is not interested

in German suffering but in the exclusion of German wartime experiences from the Western collective memory of WWII. More inclusiveness in this matter has been his concern for some time. Given the enduringly treacherous aspects of German-Jewish relations, his writing about this topic has been surprisingly thoughtful, if a bit too optimistic in hoping that people—individuals and groups—will "really" learn from their mistakes. In the concluding passage of his essay he tries not only to assuage fears about restituting their memories to the Germans but to see this process as promise for a better German understanding of, what else, their collective responsibility and guilt.

> Probably it is only possible now, after the realization of the terrible things that the Germans did to other nations, to remember the extent to which they themselves became the victims of the war they unleashed. That this is happening now seems to me to be a gain. It turns out that the belated recollection of suffering both endured and culpably inflicted in no sense arouses desires for revenge and revanchism in the children and grandchildren of the generation of perpetrators. Rather it opens their eyes to and enhances their understanding of the destruction that the Nazi Germans brought upon other nations.

This uplifting conclusion is clearly meant to placate and reassure: a political gesture that promises more than is (hopefully) necessary or possible. For the time being, it should be good enough that many individual Germans can make use of a now seemingly greater political tolerance for remembering and talking about their own and their families' war experiences—an opening which will indeed in most cases not "arouse desires for revenge and revanchism."

Yet it is true that this opening will probably result in more differentiating, critical perspectives on the end stage of WWII, the too easily sanctified "just war." More historical information about what actually happened and is largely forgotten will become of greater cultural interest; the "forbidden topics" on Schneider's list will become subjects of public discussion. To expect of the Germans another round of enhanced understanding of Nazi Evil for which they would still be held collectively responsible seems both unimaginative and impractical, unless such efforts at understanding go beyond enhanced German remorse. What is needed now and in the near future is more broadly distributed information about the prehistory of WWII in its connection with WWI, and a more detailed historical account of the end stage of WWII and the immediate postwar period. The enduringly narrow post-Holocaust perspective on German guilt and the ensuing fixation on German remorse, though understandable in the first decades after the war, has led, among other things, to the huge buildup and increasing cultural centrality of the Holocaust, whose exclusive monumentalism has created its own considerable problems.

If there could be a more open, rational discussion of the reasons why their memories are feared—suspicions of anti-Semitism, revanchism, Holocaust denial—the generation of *Kriegskinder* could use their reactivated memories of what was done to them and their families for a better understanding of the end-stage of a total war of indeed unimaginable destructive power. If there are fears that their remembering more about their wartime experiences might disturb the neat split between good and evil associated with that "absolutely just" war, one might want to point out that such past unquestioned justness has been a highly useful tool in American politics to justify wars of aggression in the postwar era. World War II was a justified war, and fighting it was a credit to the United States in the 1940s; it also was a terrible war in the experience of many different populations.

Greater openness to German memory discourses means new and therefore unpredictable questions. The controversies surrounding these questions are fed by apprehensions and assumptions: how are the Germans going to behave, once they have greater freedom, granted or taken, to remember. There was a great deal of American indignation about Germany's reaction to the preemptive strike against Iraq: how could the Germans, of all people, not join the "coalition of the willing" in the defense of America against the "Axis of Evil"? Was it not a war that, in view of the enemy's massed weapons of mass destruction that would destroy us all momentarily, could be compared only to the just and good WWII?

A guest on a National Public Radio panel on international reactions to the imminent war (the war broke out later that same day, March 19, 2003), I was repeatedly asked by callers how I could justify Germany's "immoral" lack of loyalty and, by implication, of remorse: was it not the duty of the Germans to make amends by joining? Several times connections were made between German anti-Semitism and anti-Americanism, and my pointing out that 70 percent of the U.S. population was against the preemptive strike was to no avail. This fact must also have been overlooked or misinterpreted in the Democrats' irresponsible vote to empower the president to go to war. Once it had started with a "successful" demonstration of technological "shock and awe," and once "our young men and women" were in harm's way, the attitude changed—a common change of heart rather than mind in such situations. But ill conceived and prosecuted, the war proved to be highly destructive, also to the United States, and public opinion changed. Six-teen bloody months later, on September 28, 2004, Dick Cheney, in a speech preparing for the presidential debate on September 30, spoke about the need to persevere at any cost in the all-out fight against Ter-rorist Evil, as the Americans had persevered so magnificently fighting Nazi Evil in WWII. Never a word that the rise of terrorism would have to be related in some way to previous American conduct, nor that Nazi Evil was a belated motivation for the American involvement in WWII .

It would be nicely ironical if attempts to justify with that "just war" current destructive U.S. enterprises in accelerated democratization and oil production had contributed to a more critical questioning of Amer-ica's actions in WWII. A recently released film by the documentarian Errol Morris, *The Fog of War*—which, surprisingly given its message, immediately got the 2004 Academy Award for best documentary film— is a feature-length interview with the eighty-five-year-old former secre-tary of defense Robert S. McNamara. A "history lesson or moral travel-ogue," the film shows the old politician "staring out at the camera and into himself while he talks about the hundred and sixty million people who died in wars during his lifetime."[17] The main motivation for Mor-ris in making this film, he said in an NPR radio interview,[18] was his desire "to go back to the past and try to understand it;" it was not to "attribute guilt and to judge." He points out that his interviews are "investigative": "If I let people talk without interrupting I learn much more." There is the issue of McNamara's apologies for his conduct dur-ing the Vietnam War, still the traumatic dark spot on the American notoriously clean conscience. It is a trauma that also explains the desire for apologies among some men and women who protested the war and, rather naively, refuse to be tainted by it, though all of us were, even if almost all of us did protest. Asked whether he had asked McNamara to apologize, Morris tells his moralizing interviewer: "I suppressed the de-sire to ask him." Extracting apologies now was much less important to him than McNamara's creating the Pentagon Papers that have enabled more access to the past.

Most of all, Morris has been "interested in learning more" about how the people he interviews "see the world," the documentarian's most difficult challenge since it includes different viewers' perceptions. His invention, a visual device, the *Interrotron,* allows the person inter-viewed by Morris and viewed by the film's audience to look at the cam-era as if he had eye contact with the interviewer—eye contact that ex-tends to the film's viewers. The Interrotron has been partly responsible for the peculiar intensity and intimacy of Morris's conversational interviews that, surprisingly, can be shared: as if we, the viewers, were listening and looking in on a real conversation into which we might be drawn any moment, to state our reactions.[19] This visual illusion of inclusion has long been important to the success of Morris's work; but it is so particularly here, where the questions about culpability and accountability asked of McNamara are very difficult to answer; "the hardest of them come from McNamara himself."[20]

McNamara does not apologize in the interview, but he says, "We all make mistakes." Surprisingly, his acknowledgements that some of his mistakes were enormously costly include also the decisions he made as a young man in the Pacific theater of WWII that resulted in the mass destruction of Japanese cities by fire: firebombs raining on Tokyo's wooden houses from the high-flying B-29 bombers of the American Twentieth Air Force, with the death toll of at least 87,000 civilians in one night. Sixty-seven Japanese cities were destroyed in the spring of 1945, 345,000 civilians burned to death, and the war against Japan was practically won, long before Hiroshima. McNamara, then an air force colonel and the hawkish General Curtis LeMay's chief statistician, seems close to tears remembering the inferno: "I was part of a mechanism that in fact recommended it." He also remembers LeMay's observation that both of them would be prosecuted as war criminals if the Allies did not win the war. And he quotes LeMay's question that has stayed with him: "What makes it immoral if you lose and moral if you win?"—for many centuries the crucial, often unanswered and unanswerable, question in warfare.

The journalist Roger Angell, at that time the editor of a G.I. air force weekly in the Pacific theater of war, was particularly impressed and moved by the interview, not only by what McNamara said but also by how he said it. Angell, like McNamara, could remember a world in which such a war had been literally unimaginable. But for most people alive now, the nature and scale of this war makes it still unimaginable, also for those who experienced it. Paradoxically, this may have made it easier rather than harder to unleash more, and also more sophisticated and destructive, technological power, from the nuclear mushroom spreading over Hiroshima to the "shock and awe" pinpointing of annihilation in Iraq. Collectively demonized, Japanese and German survivors of WWII have not been able to remind the victors of what happens to the vanquished in this kind of war. The issue now, sixty years later, is not that most Japanese or Germans were sufficiently human to also have suffered in that war or that other nations have also been culpable. Rather, the past reality of suffering and culpability has to be looked at in the larger context of the ideological wars of the twentieth century. Without this context, the specifically German, or Japanese, or British, or American culpability for the suffering of large populations cannot be really understood. The most harmful aspect of the current confusions, anxieties, and suspicions surrounding German-Jewish debates of the "victim or perpetrator" question has arguably been its astonishing provinciality.

––––––

The question "Sind die Deutschen Opfer oder Täter?" has been discussed endlessly in the media, on panels, on talk shows, at conferences. The more an increasing number of ordinary Germans, among them members of the professional, political, and intellectual elites, participate in these discussions, the more difficult it seems to agree unanimously that Germans could never, under no circumstances, have been war victims. Curiously, this lack of unanimity has provoked anxieties that even suggesting a past, temporary victimization of certain German populations at the end-stage of WWII might be perceived as anti-Semitic. Is it not true that the Germans could never have been *Opfer* since they could never have been as innocent as their regime's official victims? That they are actually all *Täter* since they have been held collectively responsible for that regime's acts of extreme victimization? Or, to take the argument one step further: Do they not *have to be Täter* since they *cannot be Opfer*? Is it not impossible for them to ever have been *Opfer* since they were and still are remembered as *Täter* by the *Opfer* and those who speak for them? Since they have never been innocent as long as there have been the real *Opfer,* who have been the real, that is, pure and enduring innocents?

In this scenario, the *Opfer/Täter* divide has to remain forever the same, as has the uniqueness of Auschwitz and fated anti-Semitism. For the memory discourses of many Jews, this uniqueness and fatedness had to be true forever, and so far it has been true. But the memory discourses permitted the Germans were different and, moreover, they changed in time. The victors' concern at the end of the war had been not to diminish in any way the official victims' memories of their persecution by allowing German memories of war and violence access to cultural awareness and then historical memory. The concern now, six decades later—and the current U.S. administration and Israel have a considerable stake in that—is not to diminish the still growing *status* of the official victims of the Nazi regime, the still accumulating power of Jewish memory discourses.

Insistence on the enduring purity of the victim status has arguably contributed to the frequently impure politics of memory over the decades, as Peter Novick has argued and documented incisively in *The Holocaust in American Life*.[21] But rational arguments do not seem to be welcome as long as there is apprehension that once Germans are permitted to voice their individual memories of the war they might get carried away and do the unspeakable, namely claim the *status* of victim. The current moral-political excitement about the purity and power of the official victim status is one thing; the historical fact that millions of German civilians, and also millions of common soldiers, had been victims of that most terrible war in Western history, is another. Yet for most of them, their victimization in the extreme situations of a total war of novel destructive potential was *then:* in the past.

The *present Opfer/Täter* controversy, as it is played out in the media, is not about that historically documented but largely forgotten victimization of Germans but about their alleged claims to the victim status *now,* no matter how little evidence of such claims there is. Such claims are feared because they would mean undermining the familiar scenario of Good and Evil established by the Allies as victors in the just WWII. Not only has this scenario granted a near absolute moral authority to the status of victim, but it has also sustained that status over the decades as a desirable political, cultural, and economic commodity. It is obvious and also understandable that among those who command this commodity now, few would be willing to discuss it and, even less, share it. Fear of possible changes in the victim status has caused an overuse of allegations of anti-Semitism and the refusal to look at the situation as a normal, if significant, conflict of interest.

Recent tentative changes allowing Germans to explore their own memories of the war will not be embraced easily by those who want to uphold the status quo of German-Jewish relations that for a long time have been centered on a uniquely significant and powerful Jewish victim status. From a different perspective informed by different interests, this status quo appears too rigidly defined by expectations of a permanent sameness of German guilt and remorse that, like the Jewish victim status, is supra-historical. When Bundespräsident Weizsäcker declared in 1988 the "uniqueness" of Auschwitz as "immutable" and enduring "truth," his concern was not the temporal historical memory of a secular society. Such memory of Nazi criminality would last for a time, not forever; moreover, lasting for a time, it would probably also be changing in time with new historical research and changing political interests. The immutable truth of a uniqueness of Auschwitz cannot be a part of historical memory because modern historiography does not deal in truth but in plausibility and does not think principled incomparability a viable concept. The main issue here is the denial of temporality and partial comparability where it concerns the Jewish Holocaust. Many of the self-appointed guardians of the official Jewish victim status, Jewish Germans and non-Jewish Germans alike, have refused to distinguish between past victimization and present victim status. Moreover, in their desire to preserve its status quo, they have adopted a mentality and strategy of preemptive strike against an allegedly reemerging German anti-Semitism that, so their argument, would diminish, with the current victim status, also the historical victimization of Jews.

There is no convincing evidence for this scenario; but for a significant part of the German elites, the Holocaust has increasingly become a *Zivilreligion*.[22] Centered on the radical, supra-historical evil of Nazi persecutions, this *Zivilreligion* by definition discourages rational discourse and critical questions, if it does not reject them outright as "offensive." The only correct way to deal with the memory stories of Holocaust survivors is total empathy and unquestioning recording as acts of religious devotion. This has meant a radical alteration of the role of evidence. The powerful cultural status of the Holocaust as a gigantic religious, suprahistorical allegory for victimization makes the search for historical evidence largely irrelevant. Worse, the historian asking critical questions and judging the survivors' memory stories as to their historical relevance may be accused of diminishing and disrespecting the memory of the victims of the Holocaust, which may be seen as proof of anti-Semitism and Holocaust denial. Following currently valid historical research protocols in this area of inquiry, the historian becomes the heretic who has offended a significant Jewish group identity founded on the memory discourses of the Holocaust. It seems irrelevant in this context that without the questions and judgments of a critical community of historiographical inquiry, no secular historical record and memory of the persecution of particular groups in a particular time and place could be constructed. Secularism, the precondition for (relatively) equal access to information, knowledge, and rationality, has been increasingly on the defensive when dealing with the *Zivilreligion* of the Holocaust.

The centrality in German postwar culture of the Holocaust or Auschwitz—in contrast to the historical record and memory of Nazi criminality—has contributed to and enforced the selective and exclusive nature of postwar German memory. The result has been a diminished perception and then loss of historical reality that has arguably contributed to a partial re-religionizing of German culture and politics. Like many religions, the *Zivilreligion* of the Holocaust has become an institution seeking to maintain and, if possible, increase its power. Its believers, in defending the unique significance and dignity of the Holocaust, strike out against perceived "nonbelievers," "infidels," because they see themselves as more sincerely, profoundly, and remorsefully influenced by the nature and scale of Jewish suffering. In the perspective of their ideological certainty, everybody else's attitude in this matter needs dramatic improvement.

The believers' convictions carry considerable power, which over the decades has protected the purity of their faith in the absolute uniqueness of Jewish suffering and the absolute evil of anti-Semitism. By definition, they are more compassionate, empathetic, moral, and responsible than the nonbelievers; and nobody in the current muddle of German-Jewish relations will be naïve enough to ask about their real feelings in that matter. What counts is their power to accuse others of not having the right feelings; not "keeping the faith." In order to get this message across, the believers have demonstrated a stunning verbal aggressiveness, hurling an array of negative adjectives such as "unspeakable" (*unsäglich*), "infamous" (*infam*), "revolting" (*widerwärtig*), "monstrous" (*ungeheuerlich*), "heinous" (*fürchterlich*), and "mortifying" (*furchtbar peinlich*), against every perceived breach of the elaborate etiquette of Holocaust piety and anti-anti-Semitism. Potential offenders are routinely and sternly warned of excommunication from civil society—a curious threat since the attacks on them are so uncivilized.

These always accusatory, moralizing commentaries and analyses are mostly published in the influential, previously left-progressive papers such as *Die Sueddeutsche, Die Zeit,* and *Frankfurter Rundschau,* and, since another anti-Semitism controversy involving Walser in the summer of 2002, also more frequently in the center-conservative *Frankfurter Allgemeine.* All of them are now publishing for online consumption large collections of articles under the special rubric *Dossiers* to keep their readers informed on and entertained by the many *Kontroversen* or *Affairen* that deal with the politicized, interconnected issues of postwar German memory, the Holocaust, and anti-Semitism. Revitalized and refashioned by the newly framed question of permissible or nonpermissible German wartime memories, these issues have provoked a heavy-handed, generalizing pedagogical fervor, particularly also among a younger generation of journalists and historians, that can be both comical and irritating in its redundancy.[23]

Ordinary Germans, shrugging their shoulders, accept it with some degree of stoicism as "typically German." From their more differentiating, if mostly cautious, perspective, they do not seem to think of themselves as typically German. Yet precisely their sensible lack of ideology in these matters makes them typically German in the eyes of their relentless teachers, who, untypically enlightened, cannot but distance themselves from "them," the inevitably bigoted silent majority of "the Germans." This might become a problem for the teachers. Officially required to use the absurd term "non-Jewish Germans" when speaking of Germans collectively, their attempts to distance themselves from the less enlightened in the matter of correct German-Jewish relations could be compromised by their own correctness. Are they not themselves members of all those unenlightened "non-Jewish Germans," in distinction to "Jewish Germans"? How could they distinguish themselves and other believers from the masses of nonbelievers in the matter of Holocaust piety?

The expression "non-Jewish Germans," meant to combat once and for all the always suspected German desire to distinguish (*ausgrenzen*) Jews from Germans, seems to achieve exactly the opposite, in that it shows so clearly the extraordinary strain in German-Jewish relations. Why should the, in proportion to the Jewish minority, huge German majority that by now includes many other ethnic groups be referred to as "non-Jewish Germans" unless Jews are thought to have the authority to define what is German? Some of the more radical Jewish Germans might want to do just that, have in fact done it in their denunciations of an inherent unchanging all-German anti-Semitism. But so far they have been a tiny minority within their own often fractious group.

The politics of this renaming makes asking "who is typically German" a moot question, which is too bad, because Jews living in Germany have shown tendencies to become, for better or worse, "typically German," in the Berlin of the Weimar Republic as well as in the brand-new *Berlin Republic*. And this, next to the considerable privileges for Jews living in contemporary Germany, is one of the reasons for what Peter Laufer has recently called *Exodus into Berlin*.[24] It seems that the deadly serious *Tragikomoedie* of morals about who controls whom has become a more primitive but also more treacherous version of the sixty year-old German Question. In the current situation of rising Muslim anti-Semitism in many European countries, all the more dangerous because partly justified by America's and Israel's political and military aggression, the German government has been most anxious to assert the country's position of unambiguous anti-anti-Semitism, no matter the cost to its non-Jewish citizens. Not to speak of the Jews who like to live in Berlin but do not approve of the holiness of "the Holocaust" and the groundless, politicized panic about reemerging German anti-Semitism,[25] and who do not feel the need to be protected in that way.

The "Declaration of the *Bundestag* on the Fight against Anti-Semitism" of December 11, 2003, was passed unanimously by all parties following a *Bundestagsdebatte* on this issue. It is a troubling document in its open proposal of restricted free speech, not only in view of the realities of Jewish-German life in contemporary Germany. Three of its seven paragraphs state Germany's duty to "fight against anti-Semitic thought, speech and acts," calling on every non-Jewish German "to engage in this fight individually." Paragraph 4 expresses "great concern" about "anti-Semitic resentments still noticeable not only in marginal groups but also in the society at large" and prohibits, under punishment of "excommunication from a democratic community of value," the "use of stereotypes and Nazi propaganda props."

This amazing threat of excommunication also applies to "verbal exclusion" or "denial of citizenship" of Jewish-Germans by using the term "Germans" instead of the officially approved "non-Jewish Germans," and to all attempts at a "relativization" of the murder of European Jews.[26] "Relativization" is commonly known as a synonym for "historicization" in arguments for a supra-historical status of the historical murder of European Jews. It is to be hoped that this set of regulations and threats will not lead to even greater limitations of free speech, namely removing even more from the public sphere honest, critical discussion of the difficult relations between Jews and Germans. Oddly, these regulations and threats of excommunication are expected to stem what is feared to be a "flood" of German wartime memories accused of "relativizing" the persecution of Jews just by looking for a more pluralistic historical context for their own experiences.[27]

The *Bundestag* declaration against anti-Semitism restricts free speech in an absolutist, regressive manner that, seen from the outside, seems both frightening and silly, and above all counterproductive. To be fair, the fact itself of passing such a declaration at this time is connected with the *Hohmann Affäre,* which in turn is connected with the current focus on the rise of anti-Semitism in Europe. Despite its obvious source in the problematic self-interest politics of the State of Israel in the Middle East and of the United States worldwide, this mostly Muslim anti-Semitism has also reactivated fears of an enduring indigenous German variety. In early December 2003, the European Jewish Congress (EJC) made public the controversial and so far classified "Report on Anti-Semitism" commissioned by the EU. It was the result of a study carried out by the influential *Berliner Zentrum für Antisemitismus-Forschung,* headed by

Wolfgang Benz. The report had found an atmosphere of latent anti-Semitism in Europe since September 11, 2001, and used remarkably forceful language: a "new wave of anti-Semitism is sweeping across Europe; many are speaking of the worst anti-Semitic wave since 1945." It was kept back by a special EU commission for questions of race and hostility to foreigners, because it had found growing anti-Semitism particularly among Muslim and pro-Palestinian groups, and the time span of the study, May to June 2002, was seen to be nonrepresentative. It was a time of high tension, made worse by Israel's particularly brutal attacks on Palestinian refugee camps.

For German politicians, suspected German anti-Semitism is synonymous with critique of Israel and thereby anti-Americanism. While anti-Americanism may temporarily have supported some German politicians' election strategies, in the long run, as all politicians know and fear, it is damaging to big business, which in the age of globalization is the most important factor in the power calculations of all Western political parties. German political and economic anxiousness contributed largely to the latest full-scale *Antisemitismus-Debatte* or *Hohmann Affäre* in the fall of 2003 that, in turn, triggered the unanimous *Bundestag* declaration on anti-Semitism. Martin Hohmann, a conservative (CDU) *Bundestagsabgeordneter* from a small town in Hessia, had argued in a speech he made in his hometown before a small local audience celebrating the anniversary of reunification, *Tag der deutschen Einheit*, October 3, that Jews, too, could be "*seen* as perpetrators" in certain historical situations, his example being powerful Jewish members of the Communist party in early Soviet Russia. The aim of his meandering speech was ostensibly to put a different spin on the *Täter/Opfer* dichotomy, a topic of great interest to his constituency.

For a reasonably unspooked reader, he had not claimed, as the media alleged almost unanimously, that Jews *were* a *Tätervolk;* but he did question the enduring collective equation of Germans with evil *Täter* and of Jews with innocent *Opfer*. It is difficult to guess in this highly politicized situation of inflated self-righteousness what might have been seen and/or presented as the more offensive crime: Hohmann's clumsy denial of German collective guilt or his even more awkward pointing to Jewish historical agency. The most intriguing aspect of this farce had to be that literally nobody took note of the provincial event for almost a month. Then an American net surfer came across some information about the speech and, "highly offended," informed the German elite media, which rapidly blew up the offense to gigantic proportions. In a few days, newspapers, radio, and television were flooded with hundreds of reports and condemning comments.

Everybody who was anybody, Jewish and non-Jewish Germans alike, wanted the world to know that they were all correctly offended to the core of their political hearts by the alleged anti-Semitic remarks—a criminal offense if found true. Hohmann's party, traditionally less excitable in such situations, at first tried to resist the immediate and urgent calls coming from the Left for him to resign from his party position and to be stripped of his MP immunity. He apologized several times, evidently without sufficient show of remorse; and within days the CDU gave in. The widely publicized, distorting, and exaggerating controversy about his—and then German—reemerging anti-Semitism had become too hot for comfort, and there were explicit fears of how this would play in the multinational business world: "we cannot afford this; how would we look in New York; in London, in Los Angeles?"[28]

The *Frankfurter Rundschau* reported on November 4, 2003, that the chair of the Central Council of Jews in Germany, Paul Spiegel, had demanded Hohmann's expulsion from the CDU. Hohmann's blunder was for Spiegel "the worst case of anti-Semitism that I have experienced in the last decade." The Central Council decided to bring a charge against Hohmann, and the Fulda Office of the Prosecutor started investigations after an unnamed Bonn citizen had denounced Hohmann for *Volksverhetzung*—a nicely concrete archaic term for "hate speech." Hohmann's crime was summed up in the *Dialog* rubric of the *Feuilleton* of *Frankfurter Rundschau* that deals with German-Jewish issues: Ulrich Speck, an expert on these issues who tends to err on the side of Holocaust piety, agreed with a reader's complaint about repeated claims made by the paper that Hohmann had referred to the Jews as "Tätervolk" when he had said just the opposite. Hohmann, Speck conceded, had indeed said that "neither 'the Jews' nor 'the Germans' were a 'Tätervolk.'" But introducing the "Tätervolk" question comparatively, he had given it a degree of plausibility before refuting it. Even more importantly, any suggestion of a link between Germans and Jews in the matter of "Tätervolk" was "infam" since it violated the "irrefutable victim status" of Jews.

It was a ridiculously contorted argument, echoing the haplessness of Hohmann's speech. But for Speck, as for many other public intellectuals, this status remains unique, supra-historical, extending from the present into an indefinite past and future. It is a hallowed space into which no German and no rational argument will ever be allowed. Hannah Arendt had thought such supra-temporal victim status problematic already at the end of the war precisely because it transcended the realm of history and the political, which for her meant rational speech. The enduring absolute authority of this status, whose invocation will automatically silence all critical questions regardless of their potential historical and political relevance, has been the most serious obstacle to all attempts at a halfway reasonable discussion of German-Jewish relations. Moreover, this authority seems to have become even more absolute since the events of September 11, 2001, and America's and Israel's reactions to them that caused even more conflicts with the Arab world and a notable increase in Muslim anti-Semitism.

A *Frankfurter Rundschau* report on German anti-Semitism, "Has Anti-Semitism Become Mainstream?" on the occasion of the *Bundestagsdebatte* preceding the formal declaration against anti-Semitism began with the presumably shocking statements: "Two out of three Germans are annoyed that 'the Germans are still reproached today for the crimes committed against the Jews.' Has anti-Semitism become mainstream? Is something exploding that has been controlled, if with difficulties, for a long time? Something thought unspeakable in public and therefore, and only therefore, overlooked? Is anti-Semitism on the rise again among Germans?"[29]

The point of reference for the writer of the report is the *Tätervolk-Vergleiche* (comparisons) between Germans and Jews that arguably triggered the *Bundestagsdebatte*. In the writer's perspective, a case of such open and therefore criminal anti-Semitism would not require the usual journalistic ethics to get it right, namely mention that Hohmann had explicitly rejected the term "Tätervolk" for both Germans and Jews. Hohmann did implicitly relate the past wartime *Opfer* status of Jews to that of Germans by saying that many Germans had also suffered during the war, but he did not question the permanent and therefore higher *Opfer* status of Jews, reminding his listeners repeatedly of the horror of Nazi persecutions. These reminders may very well have been perfunctory, not deeply felt; but that has been true for many discourses about the bad German past bound by strict observation of the hierarchy of suffering.

The media's collective elaborately anti-anti-Semitic exegesis of Hohmann's confusing, redundant, meandering text, which most of the commentators had never seen, much less read, but of which they had all heard and which they therefore knew was anti-Semitic, was absurd. Yet, as with the emperor's new clothes, nobody dared to say or write that while the affair was going on. As always, "ordinary Germans" were glad when it was over and forgot it quickly. When I asked friends in Germany about the affair in early January 2004, they had put it firmly behind them, hoping for a quiet, affair-less interim; and when the Fulda Office of the Prosecutor announced on February 5, 2004, that the expelled CDU *Bundestagsabgeordnete* Hohmann had been found not guilty of hate speech, insult, and defamation in his speech of October 3, the excitement and the denunciations seemed already in the remote past.

Hohmann, the prosecutor's statement said, "had not intended to identify himself with national-socialist ideology; there had been no denial of the Holocaust and its uniqueness."[30] Would it have been a felony to question the uniqueness of the Holocaust? Did Hohmann deserve to be expelled? And was it for moral or for political reasons? Or is it naïve to ask? Or naïve not to ask? I read the announcement on that day at the airport in Frankfurt, on my way to a panel "Sind die Deutschen ein Volk der Opfer oder der Täter?" I was groggy from the overnight flight and had to laugh out loud—no longer an embarrassment because I might have been laughing into a cell phone. After all, we live in a brave new world, unimaginably different from the time of the Great Wars; and my historian colleagues on that panel assured me that they could barely remember the affair, but that there would of course be many more. Strangely, I thought, they do not seem to mind their new identity as non-Jewish Germans, nor the other restrictions of free speech listed in that *Bundestag* declaration intended to counteract the evil of Hohmann's unspeakable offense.

As long as the Hohmann affair was an all-consuming media event, apprehensiveness about reenergized German anti-Semitism was tightly linked to the increasingly sinister figure of that hapless CDU politician. After some attempts to resist formidable pressure from Jewish-German groups and SPD and Green politicians, his party dropped him as quickly and visibly as possible. But the issue of anti-Semitism could and would not be dropped that easily. The author of the report on German anti-Semitism quotes from a long-term academic study that found a somewhat reassuring low 14.6 percent of the German population anti-Semitic, without specifying how the pollsters arrived at their finding. To begin with: How did they define anti-Semitism? Does being irritated by enduring German collective guilt for Nazi crimes equal anti-Semitism? It seems so: a "frightening" 69.9 percent of the population exhibit "sekundären Antisemitismus" since 69.9 percent of the subjects of the study said "yes" to the question "Are you annoyed that Germans are still reproached collectively for the crimes committed against Jews by the Nazi regime?"

Given the ways in which the Germans have been reproached in the elite press for decades by public intellectuals and politicians who presume to speak for them, their irritation seems quite understandable and distinctly remote from anti-Semitism, even of a mushy secondary degree. Besides, 65.4 percent of the population are pleased by the increasing number of Jews living in Germany.[31] But here the anti-Semitism experts are not so easily persuaded: invoking *das Volk,* they are apprehensive that the climate of opinion created over the years by strictly prohibiting public anti-Semitic statements may have caused the "regression of manifest anti-Semitism from a political ideology to a private mass prejudice."

As the Hohmann affair shows, there is anti-Semitism in politics, but no political anti-Semitism. The political elites always know better because they know themselves to be constitutionally unable to become infected with any kind of anti-Semitism, even of the secondary sort, no matter how diffuse the concept. Most importantly, however, they know how to avoid being accused of anti-Semitism by being the first to accuse others—with the Hohmann affair, the CDU has finally learned the advantages of that strategy. *Das Volk,* however, is another matter. The director of the study is "not sure anymore for how long the political elites will be able to determine the norms of anti-Semitism." Curiously, he does not seem to be aware of the fact that by now *das Volk* includes a large part of the political, professional, and intellectual elites across the political spectrum, who increasingly, if still only privately, deplore such generalized and politicized accusations of anti-Semitism.

The alleged rise of German anti-Semitism—a situation fundamentally different from that of demonstrably rising anti-Semitism in France or England, with their large Muslim populations—is linked with the new interest in German wartime memories that allegedly threaten to undermine the unique, because highest, Jewish *Opfer* status by suggesting that Germans, too, could have been *Opfer* and not only *Täter.* This perceived threat provoked renewed assertions that Jewish suffering has been worse and more significant than anybody else's, especially all German suffering. From a perspective outside the messy and treacherous German-Jewish entanglement, it seems faintly absurd for any group to insist that "our suffering is more significant, and then better, than yours," especially where it concerns WWII, which surely created enough suffering to go around. But from their group's perspective, many Jewish-German intellectuals have thought it important to insist on a permanent uniqueness of Jewish suffering, that is, an existential *incommensurability* of the Jewish experience, beyond all human understanding, the ultimate "Other," the stuff of myth rather than history.

In this scenario, non-Jewish persons, particularly non-Jewish Germans, can by definition have no intellectual and emotional access to this suffering other than accept its centrality to Western culture, remember it, erect monuments to it, and remorsefully mourn it. Recent cultural-political developments in Germany perceived to be possible threats to the status quo of unique Jewish suffering—reunification in the early nineties, the political architecture, literal and figurative, of the Berlin Republic at the turn of the millennium, and a new interest in German wartime memories since 2002—increased the desire for an absolutely clear and permanent distinction between *Opfer* and *Täter.* For Moshe Zuckermann, Martin Walser became a "prominent representative" of the "deutsche Tätergeneration" after Ignatz Bubis had referred to Walser's peace prize speech of October 1998 as reflecting right radicalism and Holocaust denial. Agreeing with Bubis, Zuckermann asserted that Walser as *Täter* could not expect any "normal" discussion of his arguments, but only their total rejection.[32]

Bubis saw in Walser's pleas for historical differentiation a shocking lack of respect for the dead and surviving *Opfer* of the Holocaust. Walser had committed the "unspeakable" offense of questioning the permanent collective memory-story of the victim status of Jews, which is the worldwide remembrance of an *Opfer* status that has dominated all other memory discourses of victimization.[33] According to Bubis, Walser wanted the Holocaust to "disappear in the orcus of history," a rather odd reproach in view not only of Walser's oral and written statements on the significance of Auschwitz for all Germans,[34] but also the voluminous detailed historical documentation of the persecution of Jews. But speaking for the *Zentralrat der Juden in Deutschland* and on that particular occasion, Bubis did not want to share either Jewish history or memory with that of other peoples. Rather, he once more admonished all non-Jewish Germans to confront their shameful history and adhere to the permanent sharp distinction between *Täter* and *Opfer* that Walser had (allegedly) fudged.

Zuckermann emphasized particularly this issue, claiming that Walser's experiences as "exemplary representative of the generation of *Täter*" were radically different from that of the Holocaust survivor Bubis. Walser seemed to have no clue, Zuckermann complained, that there can be, must be, no "symmetry," no relation between these two experiences and between the memories of Jews and Germans (GK, 9–10). The experiences of Holocaust survivors and their memories are infinitely removed from, infinitely more significant than, those of the *Tätergeneration;* there can be no real communication between Germans of that generation, no matter what their experiences had been, and Jewish Holocaust survivors. The crucial issue for Zuckermann in all his arguments is the preservation of a permanently unique significance and dignity of the Jewish victim status. He rejected the "vicious" suggestion made by the well-known SPD politician Klaus von Dohnanyi (whose father Hans von Dohnanyi had died in the KZ Flossenburg in 1945) that Jewish *Mitbürger* (fellow citizens) might ask themselves individually "whether their conduct would have been so much more courageous than that of most other Germans if after 1933 'only' the mentally handicapped, homosexuals and the Roma had been sent to the death camps."[35]

Zuckermann thought this "apologeticist relativization" a profoundly immoral denial of the absolutely clear distinction between historical victims and perpetrators: "When the historical *Opfer* are subjected to the abstract interchangeability of the *Opfer-Täter*-roles, the feeling of shame, the consciousness of guilt and the tormenting memories become mere psychic luxuries" (GK, 26–27). Zuckermann is afraid of an existential turning point in German discourses of their bad past, for which they are collectively responsible but about which they will then no longer feel guilty, for him a disastrous change in the status quo of the Jewish *Opfer* status.

The point made by Dohnanyi was actually quite different, and implicitly even more subversive regarding the status quo of the Jewish victim status. He was talking about contemporary Jewish Germans living in a secular society in which such questions would be permissible because the historicity of Nazi criminality, and then of the persecution of Jews, could be taken for granted. He argued from the present, which he shared with the victims of the historical persecutions (or their children), at a time when they could look at these events as having happened in the past when they were victims. That was then; it was now that they were asked to put themselves momentarily in the place of the Germans as it was then. At the time when Dohnanyi asked Jewish Germans to momentarily change their perspective, they were no longer victims in a concrete, namely co-temporary sense, though by German-Jewish cultural and political consent, their official victim status had been made permanent.

It is impossible to say whether either Zuckermann or Dohnanyi saw the implications of this scenario. But it is arguable that this shifting of time and perspective could, however subtly, question the preauthorized power of the official victim status. For sixty years, the Germans have been challenged to "confront their shameful past honestly" by putting themselves in the place of "their" victims. That challenge had no regard for their wartime experiences—a regard that might have helped them to relate to, and then better understand, the experiences of the Nazis' official victims. Then and now, the issue has not been understanding but the acknowledgment of its impossibility: the by definition absolutely incomprehensible nature of Jewish suffering.

This paradox has been the substance of German postwar collective memory as collective remorse. In the beginning of the twenty-first century it ought to be possible to engage in acts of historical imagination in which both groups, different kinds of *Opfer* and of non-*Opfer*, would try to relate their past wartime experiences so that they can become the stuff of a historiography of the Nazi period that is aware of that period's historicity as well as its own, now. Even though Zuckermann and others may condemn such "promiscuity" as the sinful "new signs" of "relativization" and "historicization" (GK, 110), there ought to be the beginning of a general cultural consensus that such historical relationism is necessary for the humanity of both Jews and Germans.

In reality, such consensus may be long in the future. As the conflict in the Middle East has been fed by Israel's preoccupation with its security, invoking past suffering and victimization, the Arab world has seized on the current suffering and victimization of Palestinians as (partial) justification of their anti-Semitism—a deadly dynamic that cannot but harden Jewish insistence on the overriding significance and acknowledgement of their official victim status. Accusations of German anti-Semitism are on the rise parallel to the rise of Muslim anti-Semitic complaints, and this does not help to clarify what (exactly) is meant by contemporary accusations of German anti-Semitism. The originally left-liberal weekly *Die Zeit* has since reunification seen itself as the voice of conscience for the new Germany, and it published a series of essays on the occasion of the Hohmann affair to attack an allegedly growing anti-Semitism in Germany, especially among the Right. In his column on German-Jewish relations in *Die Zeit*, Richard Herzinger castigated the CDU in general and Hohmann in particular for subconscious, *dumpfe* (dimwitted) clichés regarding Jews and a politics of *Entlastung*, relieving the Germans of the burden of their guilt.[36]

Herzinger, who had called immediately for Hohmann's expulsion, argues that it is

> the task of the democratic parties to define clearly where the reinterpretations for the purpose of supporting a new national self-confidence have their limit. This limit is where Jews are held responsible for the fact that Germany will have to go on paying for the National-socialist crime of the century. Even if the new, more refined anti-Semitism, more sophisticated than the old one, no longer claims "it is all the Jews' fault" but that "it is

all our fault, as well as the Jews." Unfortunately, as a mordant essayist observed, there are many Germans who to this day have not forgiven the Jews for Auschwitz.

Here as in his other commentaries on German collective guilt, Herzinger's comments are a predictable symptom of the psychological-political dynamics of an impossibly pure Jewish innocence and victim status that Hannah Arendt foresaw and feared sixty years ago. Its allegory "Auschwitz" has long since meant much more and much less than the historical events, namely the monumental, still growing construct of memory discourses that supports, among other things, also the highly profitable business of "the Holocaust," which Arendt would have hated passionately then, as do many Jews now.

The "mordant" paradox that "many Germans to this day have not forgiven the Jews for Auschwitz" might simply mean that many Germans, old and young, are to this day appalled by what happened in Auschwitz and other killing places of WWII, including burning German cities. Their enduring sense that they should go on *feeling* guilty is a composite of spontaneous and of prescribed internalized reactions, and as difficult to define as is "true remorse." For many Germans the plentiful reminders over many decades of an absolute Jewish innocence that presupposes acknowledgement of their absolute guilt have become more difficult to endure: over time, they have demonstrated so clearly that nothing can be done with such absolute guilt and innocence that would make sense in human or political terms. Hohmann's awkward, unintelligent approach to a very real problem could have been criticized much more productively. It did not warrant Herzinger's and other "teachers'" automatic turning on him and the Germans the heavy gun of "Nationalsocialist crime of the century" with its connotations of unique criminal anti-Semitism and enduring collective guilt.

Ordinary Germans, they are not worth his ire and they do not deserve it, since they cannot argue back. In most cases they would not want to and, more importantly, they would not be allowed to. It is true, Germans are on the whole reluctant to speak their mind when confronted with these questions, afraid of being misunderstood and wrongly accused. What is much needed is more open discussion of these issues, though not in the private sphere where the discussants are largely like-minded. It would be good to have such conversations among people who have different opinions and explanations regarding German guilt in a kind of protected environment where the word "anti-Semitism" would be shelved for the duration and mutual accusations would be left behind when the discussants part. In the last two years I have experienced more occasions like this on panels and at conferences in Germany that I thought surprisingly successful precisely because of the diversity of the participants, mostly a mix of academic and general audiences. But there have been very few such open discussions that brought together Jewish and non-Jewish Germans because the *Täter* and *Opfer* dichotomy has again become too overpowering and has silenced attempts at a shared discourse about the aftermath of the persecutions.

In a long essay in *Der Spiegel,* "Lieber Täter als Opfer,"[37] Henryk M. Broder argued on the occasion of the still fresh *Hohmann Affäre* that Jews attempting to combat rising German anti-Semitism should stop presenting themselves as victims. Though they have been victims historically, they have used their victimization as a strategy to "appease" non-Jews—a strategy that, Broder claims, has resulted in "completely absurd contortions." Broder's essay is partly satirical, but his accusations, no matter how self-contradictory, are meant for real. As in Seligmann's *Musterjude,* all the indeed "absurd contortions" are the Germans' fault. Broder has the Israeli minister, visiting Germany to negotiate software and weapon deals, hasten on arrival "to get to Dachau, Sachsenhausen, or Buchenwald to lay down a wreath and write into the guest book 'Nie wieder Holocaust.'" Visiting Israel, his counterpart, the German minister, is "on arrival dragged to Yad Vashem to declare that the Holocaust must never happen again." These, he points out, are "highly embarrassing, tasteless, and meaningless rituals that have nothing to do with reality."

But what, for him, is reality? Arguably, the Israeli minister is not appeasing the Germans with his perfunctory visit to Dachau, but reminding them of their very bad past and therefore their enduring responsibility to give him a good deal, especially on the weapons, and refrain from specifying that they not be used against Palestinian civilians. The German minister's declaration is equally motivated by the politics of economics, namely trying to prevent Israel from complaining about German lack of remorse and potentially ruin some business deals lined up in New York or Los Angeles. Broder prides himself on his realistic assessments of the German-Jewish mess: no unctuous moralizing from him. But his scenario has the nonspecified German minister be "dragged" to Yad Vashem, where in reality he would be eager to go there for a photo opportunity. That would be in his, in Germany's, self-interest, as it is in the Israeli minister's and Israel's self-interest to keep up the rituals of Jewish remembrance of suffering and German remorse.

Since Broder's satirical argument is his principled preference for *Täter* over *Opfer* because they not only "have more fun but also a longer life expectancy" (citing Leni Riefenstahl and other evil Nazis), he just juxtaposes the German minister's passivity with the Israeli minister's hyperactivity without paying any attention to their real self-interest politics. His abstracting satirical strategies and exaggerating rhetoric do little but obfuscate the, for him obviously very important, issue of the Jewish *Opfer* status and do not save him from the notorious self-righteousness and redundancies of most public *Opfer/Täter* debates.[38] In the end, he cannot do without the familiar invocation of the age-old persecution of Jews: "It is more than enough to have been the whipping-boy for 2000 years"—a rather selective summary of the history Jews have shared with other peoples over millennia. It makes it easier to admonish Jews to "be *Täter* from now on; and happy about it. Anyone who messes with us will regret it."

Whatever Broder's threat means, it is too much honor for Hohmann, though it is instructive. He advises the *Zentralrat* to use its political power rather than seek recourse from the legal system: threaten the CDU with severing all connections with them unless they kick out their sinful party member Hohmann. Does the *Zentralrat* have this political power? Most importantly: Does it speak for a significant majority of Jewish Germans? Is the source of its political power more than the moral claims to an enduring Jewish victim status and German remorse?[39]

Like his listeners, Hohmann was irritated by the political uses of German absolute guilt in relation to Jewish absolute innocence. His argument—that, like all other peoples, Jews as a group have been agents in history who might have caused problems for others—would have been self-evident in a normal situation but not, as the politician Hohmann should have known, in the current minefield of German-Jewish sensitivities. It would have been good if he had managed to speak more directly about certain serious problems with the official Jewish victim status that presupposes an, in political terms, impossibly pure collective Jewish innocence. But he seems to have been lacking in the political intelligence and verbal skills required by this explosive topic; and he was hampered by the fact that he, like his listeners, had internalized the powerful taboos protecting that victim status and therefore had difficulties speaking about this issue more freely and clearly.

His motivations were of course not pure, but neither were those of his critics, Jewish and non-Jewish Germans alike. However, they spoke fluently in the moral-political clichés established over many decades. His arguments came as a stutter, disconnected, redundant, reformulated, reorganized. He knew that he was on treacherous ground, and his awkwardness would have been caused, to a certain extent, by his apprehensiveness and unreflected irritation. His critics, rushing to declare their absolute contempt for this momentarily most eligible anti-Semite, politicized and misrepresented rather than misunderstood his clumsily presented arguments. If, according to generally stated German relief, the actual Hohmann affair is already safely in the past, there remains the larger and enduring cultural-political threat of rising anti-Semitism in Germany: Hohmann's irritation put him into that "frightening" 69.9 percent of the population that exhibited "sekundären Antisemitismus" by saying "yes" to the question "Are you annoyed that Germans are still reproached collectively for the crimes committed against Jews by the Nazi regime?"

What exactly is meant by "sekundärer Antisemitismus"? In the summer of 2002, at a panel discussion, "Zur aktuellen Rehabilitierung des Antisemitismus durch Walser und Möllemann u.a.," on the occasion of the second (largely fictitious and scurrilous) anti-Semitism controversy involving Walser and the editor of *FAZ,* the issue of secondary anti-Semitism was clearly an important item.[40] The panel had been arranged by several Jewish research institutes that had formed a closer alliance after the events of September 11. This partly explains the panel's interest in a "diffusen Antisemitismus" expressed in the language and conduct of non-Jewish Germans that Jewish Germans, as one of the speaker argued, could feel as an "irritation of their self-perception."[41] Möllemann and Walser, so the assertion went, were working on a rehabilitation of anti-Semitism, supported by e-mails and letters to the editor, "sent eagerly by the *deutsches Volk.*"

Micha Brumlik (Fritz-Bauer-Institut), a Jewish historian and harshly critical commentator on German-Jewish relations, proposed a more "analytical" attempt to define anti-Semitism, namely a "binary code" of "permitted and prohibited" at the core of contemporary anti-Semitism that cancelled out the argument of "free speech." In contrast to his later remarks on Hohmann's "heinous" anti-Semitism, Speck's report on the panel discussion was quite sensible, if too condescending to the audience, the *Volk,* always suspected of wrong consciousness and wrong emotions. He asked for the criteria needed to distinguish between legitimate and illegitimate references to the basic democratic right of free speech, pointing out the need to produce evidence for individual cases of anti-Semitism—issues that Brumlik has notoriously disregarded. Another panel member made what Speck thought an interesting distinction between primary and secondary anti-Semitism: attribution of "primary anti-Semitism" in the case of Holocaust denial[42] and "secondary anti-Semitism" in cases of admitted but unreflected guilt for the Holocaust. The latter was applicable to both Walser and Möllemann, who do not deny their (or German) guilt but have worked through the issue of responsibility in an "intellectually perverse way."

These echoes of the Mitscherlichs' rigidly Freudian "inability to mourn" sound strange forty years later, in the summer of 2002; but members of the panel expressed fears that this—in their view still dangerous—"secondary anti-Semitism" would be "legitimized" in the near future. In the fall of 2003, with the increasingly difficult and confusing situations in Afghanistan, Iraq, and Palestine threatening to fudge clear distinctions between perpetrator and victim in the conflict between the Arab world and the West, Hohmann's "secondary anti-Semitism" would be seen as reason enough to reassert at all cost the overriding importance of the purity of the Jewish victim status. Was it useful to do so?

Instructively, Hohmann did not choose to refer to the aggressive military and political strategies of the State of Israel when arguing that certain Jewish leaders and their followers could be seen as historical agents, *Täter.* German *Betroffenheit,* an enduring guilty awareness of the horrors of Nazi persecutions, has over the years upheld German reluctance to openly criticize Israel's conduct in the Middle East—a reluctance generally internalized and expected, in Germany and in the United States.[43] For Wolfgang Benz, the influential anti-Semitism czar, relations between Germany and Israel reflect a profound, lamentable ambivalence in contemporary German political culture. Finding both *Ausgrenzung* (exclusion) and *Zuwendung* (closeness) in German attitudes toward Jews, he sees everywhere the threat of virtual and real anti-Semitism.[44] He cannot discuss his fears rationally with the Germans as his political and moral equals, but feels compelled to speak for them and about them: relentlessly "insensitive," they still have not learned how to deal correctly with Jews in Germany and with Israel.

Admired for his moral-political position of certainty in the always emotionally heated matter of German anti-Semitism, Benz has eagerly embraced his responsibility to stamp out the lingering influence of their bad past on the Germans. The behavioral regulations controlling non-Jewish Germans in their relations with Jewish Germans passed by the Bundestag in December 2003 were partly informed by arguments previously made by Benz. He has been consistently lecturing the Germans to watch their language carefully when talking to or about Jews, insisting that it is highly, even dangerously, inappropriate to use the term "jüdische Mitbürger" (Jewish fellow citizen) since all Jews are, or are most welcome to be, German citizens. Never mind the old, familiar meaning of the term "Mitbürger," invoking a community of *Bürger,* denoted in the preposition "mit" (with). In Benz's Manichean scenario the (in this case perfectly innocent) prefix "mit" could create noxious "relativization" of the citizen status of Jews—an "unspeakable" transgression in view of the historical stripping of German Jews of their citizenship by the *Nürnberger Gesetze* of the thirties.

Benz's moralizing anxiety of ambiguity denies language its communicative relational complexity. We don't speak to each other in words but in sentences; doing so, we have a basic trust that we will be understood more or less according to our intentions. If we did not mean to make an anti-Semitic statement, reasonably open-minded people who heard (or read) our statement would not have thought that we did. But in his capacity as chief guardian of a correct German attitude toward the bad German past, namely awareness of the always threatening evil of anti-Semitism, Benz thinks that the official victim status of Jews requires a discourse that excludes all possible misunderstanding. Paradisiacally pure, that victim status claims the same purity for its discourse—a by no means uncommon phenomenon, given the lively politics of identity on the basis of memory discourses of previous victimization as they are played out in the West. In the American utopianist culture of "politically correct" speech, which is frequently (and comically) close to Orwellian *newspeak,* Jews have to share the purity of the discourse of their victimization with a growing number of other groups. This plurality of victimizations on the basis of religious belief, gender, race, ethnicity, disability, sexual preference, and so on has itself produced different shades of purity. Regrettably, there are no such refractions in Germany, though it might be good for both the Jewish-German and the non-Jewish-German psyche—if only to get rid of the latter.

Speaking for and about Jews in Germany and invoking for all of them the same authority of the same enduring victim status, Benz does not have to be concerned with that plurality. If Germans are well-intentioned, they should be aware of the fact that referring to Jews living in Germany simply as Jews might be understood as, might indeed be, an anti-Semitic offense. Dispensing advice on the etiquette of dealing ethically with a bad political conscience, Benz thinks that Germans never ought to speak of Germans and Jews but use instead the correct terms "Jewish Germans" and "non-Jewish Germans." He is very insistent on this issue because there has been much privately expressed puzzlement about it: why should the large majority of gentiles living in Germany, which now includes many other ethnicities and religions, be defined by the tiny Jewish minority? But "the Germans" in their relation to Jews

need a firm hand. Benz sums up the difficulties of "the German position" six decades after the historical events that for him defined, once
and for all and exclusively, their bad past: "Talking about Jews in Germany, the majority of Germans are rather anxious, insensitive, thoughtless—but full of good will. They are afraid to make mistakes, intent on
showing empathy (or trying to hide resentment) and avoiding, if possible, to say something wrong." Is it just my untrained ear, that I feel
myself cringing before so much pedagogical moral certainty?

Benz's arguments here and in his many statements over the years on
the sorry state of German collective moral-political conscience are as
forcefully prescriptive as they are contradictory. Germans are wrong
to be so clumsily apprehensive (*beklommen*) in their behavior toward
Jews because they can never be sure whether they will not be misunderstood; Germans should be absolutely sure to get it right so that they
cannot be misunderstood; if what they say *is* misunderstood, it can always be understood as an expression of anti-Semitism; can indeed *be*
anti-Semitism. And anti-Semitism, as every German knows, is a seriously dangerous matter because it always leads to accusations. Perhaps
because of his semi-religious intensity and purity of belief in German
collective guilt, Benz appears remarkably reluctant to recognize the fact
of temporality: the enormous political and cultural changes since the
end of the war brought about by the passage of time. Habitually speaking of and for "the Germans," he seems to think that they all have
somehow continued to be contemporaries to the Nazi period, still persuaded by Nazi exclusion of German Jews as *Fremde* (strangers).

Everywhere in Germany he sees prejudicial stereotyping of the Jew
as *der Fremde*. At the same time, he is curiously unaware of his own
relentless stereotyping of Germans, who owe their enduring "false consciousness" to the "long-lasting effects of Nazi Propaganda." For him
the German bad past has remained tenaciously present, the *nunc stans*
of a supra-historical evil that the Germans, whatever their ages, experiences, and circumstances, cannot escape. They still live with the collective responsibility, and thus guilt, for Nazi persecution of Jews. Discrimination against Jews by the Nazi regime began with the definition
of Jews as *Fremde,* and today's Germans continue this tradition of discrimination in their inability to control their desire for *Ausgrenzung*
whenever they are dealing with Jews. Benz even asserts that the foundation of the State of Israel has caused the Germans to justify their *Ausgrenzung* of Jews with the Jewish Homeland in Palestine: they maintain
that Israel, not Germany, is the home of Jews, their native country.

Benz's anecdotal evidence for this attitude is one of the many controversies that have dotted German postwar political culture, in this case a local mini-affair involving Ignatz Bubis and a member of the Rostock city council who lamentably asked the chair of the *Zentralrat derJuden in Deutschland* whether his homeland was Israel. Asked in a public space and, in Benz's words, in a "sensibilisierte" political situation, this evidently audible question was deemed highly inappropriate and caused the "impertinent" person who had posed it to resign immediately from the city council. In Benz's view, this resignation was not only justified but inevitable: the offense had been so great as to require the immediate removal of the offender from his office. He is disappointed that this act of acknowledging and atoning for the offense did not diminish the "traditional, wide-spread prejudice of the Jew as stranger." Some Germans who had witnessed the event had not even made the connection between the resignation and the "highly insensitive" question, which *must* have been motivated by some degree of anti-Semitism. The combination of Benz's own extravagantly exquisite sensitivity to the most delicate nuances of anti-Semitism and his considerable cultural and political influence as director of the Berlin *Zentrum für Antisemitismus-Forschung* is by no means unproblematic. No critical questions can be asked about his authoritarian anti-anti-Semitism, since he is only defending the purity of the Jewish victim status.

The moral of the anecdote about the hapless council-man is: "Anti-Semitism is not allowed to be publicly expressed in the *Bundesrepublik;* this prohibition is self-evident and one of the achievements of the political culture in Germany after Auschwitz. Persons who break this taboo lose their professional and social standing (*Amt und Ansehen*)." The anti-anti-Semitic power game can be a big deal for the person accused of anti-Semitism. The clue to correct, that is, safe, behavior in public spaces is attention to the protean phenomenon of "Sensibilisierung," that is, to anticipate *Betroffenheit* and complaints of being *offended.* The best way to not risk the loss of *Amt und Ansehen* is to publicly profess staunch anti-anti-Semitism. There actually may be no other way for the duration, since the most aggressive and damaging accusations of morally-politically reprehensible anti-Semitism often rely on a remarkably opaque understanding of the offense—it could be anything, even appearing to be insufficiently *betroffen* when talking in public about the Nazi past.[45] It can also be the innocent assumption that Ignatz Bubis had come to Germany from Israel because this is where many of the Jewish Germans who are politically active in Jewish organizations in Germany have indeed come from.

For Benz, only declared anti-anti-Semites are exempt from the suspicion that deep down they have to be anti-Semites—a scenario that goes back to the end of the war, when only officially declared Good Germans were not Bad Germans. For this reason everyone else's speech needs to be controlled by strict rules, at least in public places. As inquisitors go, the Germans could of course be worse off. Despite Benz's principled *praeceptor Germaniae* stance in the matter of anti-Semitism, he reassures them that "Sanktionen" for not conforming to anti-anti-Semitic sensibilities, if it happens in private or "small" public places, will not be enforced. As he had warned the Germans before: the same behavior in public spaces will inexorably lead to the loss of one's professional position and one's standing in the community. But anti-Semitic prejudices uttered "in front of a smaller public, or at the *Stammtisch* (pub), on the occasion of daily social contacts, and then casually" are not to be treated as felonies, though they *are* sinful.

There is a mind-boggling disconnect, both comical and frightening, between Benz's absolutist fervor for stern punishment of what in each respective public situation could be considered a criminal expression of anti-Semitism and his pragmatic concession that suspected casual transgressions in the semi-privacy of offices and pubs would/could not be prosecuted. Who has the authority to decide what is a large or small public occasion? What is casual? And the multi-million-dollar question: What exactly is, passes for, anti-Semitism? The mention of *Stammtisch* is quite revealing since it evokes the enduring massive, unthinking solidarity of existentially anti-Semitic beer-drinkers signifying the eternal sameness of German bigoted unwillingness to "confront" their past. Beer—not wine—suggests the proverbial *Dumpfheit* (torpidity) of all Germans arrested in the *Dunstkreist* (miasma) of anti-Semitism.[46]

Unfortunately, it does not help much to ridicule the absurdity of Benz's and others' anti-anti-Semitic accusations in view of postwar Germany's longtime serious attempts at making amends for the past, which is not an easy task in a situation controlled by the powerful politics of self-interest hidden behind the pieties of the Holocaust. In their conceptual obfuscation and verbal aggressiveness, these accusations are frightening because of their irrational disregard for social and political reality. One would think that these guardians of German bad conscience would know that very few Germans could have escaped internalizing the strict taboos imposed by the many decades of focusing exclusively on Holocaust memories. There simply is not that much left to say about that topic at the *Stammtisch*. The harmful divide between public and private opinion goes much deeper than casual conversations around the water cooler or at the bar of the favorite pub.

Yet there is, has been for many decades, the same suspect *Stamm-tisch* scenario of the Germans raising their mugs of beer and casually muttering anti-Semitic (now also anti-immigrant) slurs because they have never been, indeed cannot be, adequately punished, and the guardians of their bad conscience can never be quite sure that they have learned their lesson. This conundrum is at the heart of the enduring German Question, which has always been a German-Jewish question: absolute guilt requires the absolute punishment of all the perpetrators in order to maintain the absolute innocence of all the victims, which requires the relentlessness of ideological paranoia. The sixty-year-old German Question—What were/are they really thinking? Did they/do they really feel remorse? Will they always feel (the same) remorse?—has never lost its seductive power for the guardians, Jewish and not Jewish. Even as less grandiosely sinister versions of the grand inquisitor, these guardians have over the years done a lot of harm by narrowing access to the past and thereby hindering a better understanding of the conflicts of the present, notably also the role of Israel in the troubled Middle East and beyond.

Why did the Germans allow them to do it? In the summer of 2002, Joe Klein complained about contemporary Germany's "ferocious bland-ness" in a semi-satirical essay in the *Guardian,* "How Germany Was Suffocated." He lists but does not explain the symptoms of an unusu-ally high enforcement of political correctness regarding the bad German past. There is for him "something crashingly Teutonic about the mania to become the precise opposite of Hitler's Reich" with the result that public life "has the congealed quality of a Bavarian *Kartoffelsuppe.*" He asks "has Germany become too nice for its own good? Has it con-sensualized itself into a coma?"[47] He should have been given the col-lected fire-and-brimstone sermons of Benz and other "concerned" pub-lic intellectuals, which also would have told him about Germany's policy regarding free speech in public places. Germany's flat past, the sameness of Nazi Evil, and bland present, the sameness of *Opfer* and *Täter,* is just the other side of anti-anti-Semitic paranoia. I doubt that Joe Klein could have published this text in the *New York Times* or the *New Yorker,* both of them provincially partisan in things Jewish, in contrast to the cosmopolitan *Guardian.*

Klein is rightly critical of the Germans' reluctance to take risks, rightly makes fun of their exquisite "sensitivity to anti-Semitic nuance," and is intrigued rather than shocked by the less sensitive Jürgen Mölle-mann, "a former paratrooper who has been known to skydive into po-litical rallies [and] who recently said that Ariel Sharon's government in

Israel and certain members of the German-Jewish establishment—he named one in particular, a journalist named Michael Friedman—were bringing anti-Semitism upon themselves by their extreme behavior." Whatever Möllemann actually said, the issue here is not that the war criminal Sharon and the overly aggressive Friedman deserved anti-Semitic sentiments but that it should be possible for Jews and gentiles alike to openly criticize Jews for their conduct, if warranted, and not be accused of anti-Semitism. Klein clearly thinks that the Germans have lived long enough under the protective shield of their bad past and need to wake up to the real world. Politically he likes the Greens, though they are now too established, and the Free Democrats (the Yellows), the preferred party of the Greens' children, many of them entrepreneurs. When he talks with these young businesspeople about politics, they tell him that they will have to vote for the CDU because Möllemann made the Free Democrats an impossible choice: "We can't encourage even the appearance of anti-Semitism. We learned in school that we were responsible for the past. Literally responsible. If you ever said, 'Hey, I'm just 15, I'm not responsible for anything,' you'd have some serious trouble on your hands. I think that's part of why we're so nervous about asserting ourselves." When Klein had these conversations with young Germans, they did not know yet that the enfant terrible Möllemann would be ousted from the FDP and soon after die in a somewhat mysterious jumping accident. It did not help them much; there would be Hohmann and others; there is still Israel's bad politics protected by the bad German past; and there is still that past itself.[48]

Klein would have enjoyed seeing Benz painfully embarrassed by official congratulations extended to Ignatz Bubis in his role as chair of the *Zentralrat* after the prime minister of Israel—"Your President, Herr Bubis"—had made a "moving" speech before the *Bundestag* on the occasion of his state visit. This, one might think, minor faux pas made the deeply offended Benz draw the necessary "conclusions as to the degree and widespread diffusion of internalized resentment of 'the Jew as Stranger.'" He had observed yet another anti-Semitic sentiment uttered in public, another indication of the *Ausgrenzung* of Jews: the offending speaker(s) evidently did not know Bubis' biography.[49] Suggesting (again) that Bubis had come to Germany from Israel disregarded or questioned the sacrosanct status of a Jewish-German Holocaust survivor, the most potent moral-political transgression in postwar Germany. The welfare of Israel has always been highly important to postwar Germany, Benz reminds his readers, because it has meant a possible, if partial, atonement for unforgivable German sins. But there have also been "opposite reactions, namely new reservations against Jews, that can be connected with the existence of Israel. Not all Germans react with shame and mourning . . . to the heritage of National-socialism. Horror also triggers aggression, and the offensive reaction has stimulated a new anti-Semitism that developed not despite but because of Auschwitz." "Self-pitying Germans"—a staple accusation in anti-anti-Semitic sermons— have the nerve to ask how long Israel will receive reparations, and this "mobilization of traditional resentments and prejudices is responsible for keeping alive the familiar ordinary anti-Semitism."

Dutifully, the academic anti-Semitism expert Benz also concedes that reliable social research has found a steady decline of anti-Semitism in political and cultural attitudes toward Jews. Yet reunification has also meant "contamination" of West Germans with remnants of the official anti-Zionism of the former German Democratic Republic, where, as Benz argues, "the construction of the *Feindbild*" of a worldwide Jewish conspiracy had undermined "all interest in the reality of the state of Israel." What does he think Germans could learn from this "reality" of oppression and aggression? It is true that the Holocaust never became a *Zivilreligion*, was not even an issue in the GDR; their "martyrs" were communist intellectuals and politicians. In the GDR they were revered for their opposition, active or passive, to the Nazi regime; less so in the *Bundesrepublik*. In both states, for a variety of reasons that differed in East and West Germany, communist victims of the Nazi regime did not share the purity of the Jewish victim status. Political actors in a (Western) historical context shaped by human decisions, accidents, and contingencies, they *were* potentially dangerous opponents of the Nazi regime.

In contrast, Jewish history shaped by assumptions of eternal anti-Semitism and fated persecution has exempted "the chosen people" from historical agency—a situation deplored by Hannah Arendt at the end of the war, when the full disclosure of the nature of Nazi persecutions made this exemption most painfully clear.[50] If Nazi ideology constructed Jews as dangerously pure enemies, it also created powerfully pure victims. As long as the GDR existed, left-liberal West German intellectuals who saw themselves as continuing the antifascist left position of the Weimar Republic were on the whole quite uncritical of GDR cultural politics; and what Benz now criticizes as GDR state anti-Zionism was hardly an issue for them. Their genteel Marxism discredited after the implosion of the East Block, some of the influential leftist newspapers, notably *Sueddeutsche Zeitung, Frankfurter Rundschau,* and *Die Zeit,* found their new mission in an intensified focus on the cultural centrality of the Holocaust and a strongly anti-anti-Semitic stance, ostensibly to ensure the correctness of German collective memory and remorse. But if this stance ever made sense, it certainly does not now in a situation of rising Arab anti-Semitism fuelled by the general destructive dynamics of extremism but also by the destructive anti-Arab politics of the United States and Israel.

In a report on a European Union conference against anti-Semitism provoked by fears of its rise in Europe in the spring of 2004, Richard Herzinger complained that the participants of that conference were well-intentioned but unrealistic.[51] He criticized the "equation anti-Semitism = racism = fear of foreigners on which the EU bases its humanitarian pathos and the distinction between perpetrators and victims, Good and Evil," because today's "anti-Semitic violence is supported mainly by Arab and Turkish Muslims who themselves suffer from racism and fear of foreigners. And anti-Semitism in general is different from racism." Herzinger is right when he points out that hatred of Jews is not limited to racism. But when he claims that anti-Semitism sees "the Jew" abstractly as a "chiffre for Western liberal civilization," he disregards the concrete grievances of many Arabs against the United States and Israel. His scenario is a better fit for National-socialist ideological anti-Semitism than for the rising ideological religious anti-Semitism of the Arab world. It in fact prevents him from understanding the role of Israel in this process: Jews who do not criticize Israel can be seen as racists by Arabs—a perspective that he finds irrational but that his argument has in part acknowledged.

The purpose of his self-contradictory commentary is not to look at the indeed dangerous and troubling situation realistically but to admonish "the official Europe" to not leave the battle against anti-Semitism to the Jews. Most of the participants at the conference had been rabbis, interspersed with some Christian clergy pleading for Jewish-Muslim-Christian reconciliation; Joschka Fischer, who during the Hohmann affair had called for a conference on anti-Semitism for his own moral-political reasons, was the lone brilliant guest star. Anti-Semitism, so Herzinger's warning, should no longer be seen as partially understandable transgression of oppressed minorities but "as a threat of the first order for the European process of unification and the values on which it is based." However, this will only work if the real oppression of these minorities, notably the Palestinians, is acknowledged and dealt with and if Israel—representing the values of the West in Herzinger's scenario—is willing to see itself as one nation among others and therefore open to criticism of its politics by other nations and especially the European Union.[52]

The publication and reception of Günter Grass's *Im Krebsgang* (2002; *Crab Walk*, 2003) has been an important event in what is still in many ways German postwar culture. The many admiring readers of that docu-fiction on the whole disregarded the overwrought cautionary ending—in the words of the *Spiegel*'s intelligently laudatory review a superfluous, noisily pedagogical finale that damaged the finely interwoven narration of facts and fictions.[53] Grass clearly was apprehensive about the explosive emotions set free by his skilled and powerful description of so many women, so many children, drowning in the icy black waves of the Baltic—a part of the German experience of the horrors of that war that was given here a rare firm and persuasive voice. Was his fear of the readers' enthusiastic reactions to his novel justified? Would the Germans, waving Grass's new book, now all be rushing to claim the victim status? He must have feared something like this, and it may partly explain his explicit political reservations against the plan proposed in 2002 by the association of deportees, the *Bund der Vertriebenen* (BdV), for establishing a *Zentrum gegen Vertreibung,* a central institute for the comparative research of large-scale expulsions and distribution of information.

Grass had over many decades been an outspoken, even aggressive critic of German repression of the past and with it their responsibility for Nazi criminality. Perhaps more importantly, he had been, from the beginning, a fervent supporter of Polish-German reconciliation and, partly for that reason, one of the few political-intellectual critics of reunification. He may have been particularly sensitive to the strong, in some cases implacable, Polish objections to the idea of the *Zentrum,* at least to its allegorical location in Berlin that might make it appear too much of a "national project" and provoke the mistrust of the neighboring countries. Accordingly, the Germans were admonished not to balance their suffering against the suffering of others, but to think of their troubled past.[54] But such balancing is clearly not the issue here; Germany's explicitly remorseful *Polenpolitik* (reparations, economic aid, cultural exchanges, etc.) has been focused on Polish suffering and the need for German-Polish reconciliation for decades and broadly supported by the BdV.

Politicians who have welcomed the plan come from across the political spectrum, among them Innenminister Otto Schily (SPD). Despite his declared sympathies for the losses of the *Vertriebenen,* one commentator argued against the *Zentrum* for curiously contorted reasons: he disapproved on principle of separate monuments for different victim groups such as Jews, Gypsies, physically and mentally handicapped people, and homosexuals, maintaining at the same time that these would concern Nazi victims and express German guilt, whereas the *Vertriebenen* would erect a monument to themselves.[55] Asserting German collective guilt, this argument also denies to the *Vertriebenen* any experience of victimization. More important in this context, it assumes a German majority insensible to the particular historical experiences of the *Vertriebenen* for whom and with whom they would build this monument and with whom they would mourn their historical losses of family, traditions, landscapes, cities, that in important ways they all share—as Germans and as Europeans.

There are some Polish intellectuals who acknowledge political changes toward greater openness in the *Bund der Vertriebenen,* Adam Michnik among them, though they still have misgivings about building the *Zentrum* in Berlin, preferring Breslau as a European rather than national location. An old German, now a Polish, city, Breslau has been since the end of the war a city of *Vertriebene,* and its choice for building the *Zentrum gegen Vertreibung* would, in the Polish intellectuals' eyes, send a good symbolic message.[56] But such a message would focus attention on Polish victimization, whereas the *Zentrum* wants to work with a broader European perspective that would allow including the little-known German experience of large-scale *Vertreibung.* The disagreement was mainly between politicians and public intellectuals on both sides of the argument, enlarged and energized by the media. There is some anecdotal evidence of informal reconciliation between Poles, Czechs, and Germans, but the many incidents where Czechs and Poles brutally killed German civilians because they were Germans, regardless of their attitude toward the Nazi regime, have gone largely unexplored because Germans could never have been victims, nor could Poles and Czechs be perpetrators.[57]

If Grass and the other signatories of the statement against the proposed *Zentrum* feared that the Germans allowed to remember their own wartime experiences would overthrow the official hierarchy of suffering, this fear was more a part of their own political agenda. Besides, given the enormity of that war's destructive impact on so many human lives, the need to still hold on to a distinct hierarchy of suffering—our (Polish) suffering is better than yours—is dismaying. And so is the suspicion that the Germans who have obediently flattened and folded away their own memories for all these years would now immediately forget their moral obligation to respect the superiority of the Jews' (and next to them the Poles') official victim status. Many older Germans, not only among the *Vertriebenen,* would welcome a historical narrative of the Second World War sufficiently spacious to accommodate German extreme experiences too. But this will not happen as long as the issue of their memories continues to be so highly politicized. There was a terse announcement in the English Version of *FAZ* of September 25, 2003, "German-Polish ties lauded":

> The leaders of Poland and Germany have declared that their two countries' relations are excellent, despite the ongoing controversy over plans by a private group to build a memorial in Berlin commemorating the expulsion of some 12 million ethnic Germans from present-day Poland and other parts of eastern Europe at the end of World War II. Chancellor Gerhard Schröder, welcoming Polish Prime Minister Leszek Miller to this city in Germany's Ruhr region on Monday for the sixth annual bilateral consultation meeting, said Germany shared Poland's concern that the memorial could stir up fresh resentments over a closed chapter of history.[58]

The most incendiary aspect of the planned *Zentrum gegen Vertreibung,* one that has provoked the most heated objections from Germany's neighbors to the East, especially Poles and Czechs, concerns their fear that the Germans would now want to go beyond recognition for their suffering to explicitly replacing the role of the *Täter* with that of the *Opfer.*[59] Polish fears in this respect seem to have been connected more with the debate on strategic air raids on German cities triggered by the commercial success of Jörg Friedrich's documentary *Der Brand Deutschland im Bombenkrieg 1940–45* than the even greater commercial success of Grass's *Im Krebsgang.* Expectedly, there were complaints coming from Polish and Czech intellectuals that any suspicion of a change from the status of perpetrator to that of victim would compromise a reconciliation that in their eyes is still fragile after many decades of German attempts to bring it about by making amends, among other things a great deal of economic aid and reconstruction.

German public intellectuals and politicians have been, on the whole, too eager to assuage Polish and Czech fears in this respect instead of openly discussing them. It seems plausible to ask in this case why there is so much resistance to share some memory-space to accommodate the experiences of large German populations that unquestionably *were* victims of that war. But in contrast to the official victim groups, which include, at least in the German perspective, Poles and Czechs, they do not see themselves as victims *now* and in many cases still feel, if not the elusively "true" collective remorse, some kind of responsibility for the criminal acts of their regime—a responsibility that would exclude claims to an enduring official victim status. There is more than one reason for Polish and Czech resistance to admitting German wartime experiences to a larger, shared historical memory of the war, and these reasons may differ dramatically with different individuals and groups; but there is one aspect that they all share. As the political scientist Herfried Münkler has pointed out, the Polish and Czech critics of the *Zentrum gegen Vertreibung* have demonstrated a keen sense for the currency of the victim status, namely political advantages that make it more difficult for those without this status to compete.[60]

The fear of eroding the power of the victim status is one of its built-in dynamics, which causes individual victims to disappear behind the political imperative inherent in the *Opfer* status or behind an imposed role as *Täter*. Münkler refers here to a particular group of *Vertriebene* from Czechoslovakia, the *Sudetendeutsche,* who had lived in this area for many centuries. At the end of the war they suffered mass expropriation and expulsion and, less known, frequent torture and large-scale killing of civilians, mostly women and children, regardless of their political sympathies and affiliations. Czech politicians have tended to present all *Sudetendeutsche* as politically conservative and therefore almost all of them Nazis, which made it easier to disregard the troubling record of Czech atrocities at the end of the war. It is true that the supporters of their cause in postwar Germany were mainly the conservative parties, CDU and CSU, but that does not mean that they had all been Nazis. On the whole, their politics as a group have been remarkably responsible over the years. Over time, like all the other millions of refugees and deportees, they accepted their losses without much political friction.

Their losses were in most cases not shared by their liberal critics, who would remind "these people" habitually of their "successful integration" in the *Bundesrepublik* without ever asking them about their feelings in that matter. It was particularly the *Sudetendeutschen* who cultivated their old customs; but their love of folk costumes, folkdances, and folksongs was not only ridiculed but also suspected as revanchist by German public intellectuals and SPD politicians who would have eagerly applauded such celebration of "native culture" in all other contexts, European and non-European. For fear of Nazi associations and offending their neighbors to the East, they thought they needed to be particularly rigorous in their judgment of any connections with a lost *Heimat* (homeland) that this group might have wished to maintain emotionally and enact culturally, particularly in their dances and songs. As always, the critics felt comfortable speaking *for* others without knowing much about them, and of course without authorization. Much of the debate on the desirability or undesirability of the *Zentrum gegen Vertreibung* rehashes their suspicions and prejudices.

Münkler's both enterprising and cautious approach to the cultural phenomenon of the victim status makes for a rather meandering argument: it is difficult to figure out not only his own position in this matter but also the general direction of his analysis of others' politics—a difficulty characteristic of many of the commentaries on this issue, also from the Polish side.[61] Pointing out that *Sudetendeutsche* social-democrats who did not support Hitler's politics of expansion were nevertheless forced to leave their *Heimat* in the spring of 1945, Münkler also accepts this as inevitable collateral damage (*Kollektivhaftung*) in wartime. But what does that mean for the debate pro and contra the *Zentrum gegen Vertreibung*? Is it impossible to admit the experiences of groups like the *Sudetendeutschen* and the Germans expelled from formerly German, now Polish, territories to the historical memory of WWII because they might then try to claim—or be perceived to claim—the victim status, and with it the bonus or currency attached to this status?

It is true, it would be a huge number of claimants, since more than sixteen million civilians were forced to leave their homes and more than two million of them lost their lives on the trek from the East. Münkler seems to believe that the dynamics of the victim status make these mass claims as automatic as unstoppable. If the wartime experiences of individuals and groups are thought to have political currency, they are counted against each other, regardless of their own wishes: "In this case the economics of political morality do not make any exception, not even where there are reservations against the currency of the victim status, because all individual victims, no matter how many of them, had also collectively been members of the *Täternation*."

This scenario of the powerful currency of the victim status may seem too stark and too simplistic but, conforming to the politics of identity on the basis of previous persecution, it is relatively transparent, presenting things as they (more or less) are. Münkler points out rightly that the power of that currency can be dangerous, since any enduring victim status means privileges as well as threats—see Serbs and Israelis. Still, the internationalization from a European perspective suggested by the planners of the *Zentrum* would permit a historical memory to be shared by previous enemies, both of them previous victims of war and violence, that could become a powerful counteragent to victimization. Moreover, some of the proponents of the *Zentrum* explicitly wanted to draw on the transcultural issue of shared suffering rather than the moral-political currency, and then hierarchy, of the victim status. Yet,

Münkler may be right when he warns that it might be difficult to control the uses of the victim status so that it can be translated into shared memories of suffering.

Is he apprehensive about allowing more open and rational debates of the victim status? Such debates seem to me the only way to explain and analyze, with the uses of the victim status, also the uses of remorse. But even if they were permitted, the temptation not to remove all taboos would probably be considerable: Would it not still be unspeakable to point out that previous disadvantages preserved in each group's collective memory, if they converted previously powerless victims into privileged holders of the victim status, could be expected to strengthen that group's self-interested determination to make the best use of their privileges by pushing aside the interests of other groups? Granting the millions of Germans driven from their homes at the end of WWII the same powerful currency of the victim status now available to Poles and Czechs would contribute to the already polarizing politics of self-interest where it concerns the uses of previous victimization. Nevertheless, Münkler's argument, despite its contradictions and lacunae, is helpful in that it admits the political, social, and economic desirability of the victim status—an admission that, perhaps more than well-intentioned humanitarian impulses, might eventually lead to a new perspective on the entrenched German-Jewish memory-and-remorse debates.

The victim can present claims and behave in ways not allowed to non-victims, since there is a direct connection between the political and moral privileges of the victim status. Anybody with that status would be interested not only in retaining it but also in not having to share it, since the greater the number of persons sharing in the victim status, the smaller the political and moral bonus. Would Poles and Czechs, then, claiming in unison the privilege of their victim status in the case of the controversial *Zentrum*, see it as their moral-political advantage or disadvantage if German Jews joined them in trying to block it? If that happened on a larger scale, would there be a hierarchy of the victim status and would not—at least in the view of German politicians and public intellectuals—the Jewish victim status be the highest?

In the United States, where more and more various groups are claiming the political and moral privileges of the victim status, each seeks to grow its own racial or ethnic group, sharing the victim status within the respective group to enlarge its political importance and impact. In competing with other victim-groups for resources and political power, they all try to discourage an equality of victim status, arguing instead from the position of a hierarchy of suffering that traditionally has put Holocaust memory first, followed by African-American memory of slavery. In the context of U.S. domestic political strategies, the hierarchy issue becomes more messy because of the varying size and/or financial influence of political constituencies. A good example is the fast-growing political influence of Hispanic populations: their alleged previous political persecution by the United States is nebulous, and their victim status seems somewhat speculative; but their rapidly increasing numbers send a powerful message supporting (almost) equal victim status with American blacks, namely equal share in preference programs in the areas of employment and education. Looking at the victim status in the concrete terms of its bargaining power—for the last decades an extraordinarily important cultural and political issue in the West—may put in perspective the resistance to the *Zentrum gegen Vertreibung* despite all the reassurances of its proponents to document and study the history of expulsion in a comparative European context.

Münkler's approach to the controversial issue encourages this "mundane" and very necessary perspective. But in the end he coats his analysis of the advantages of the victim status with warnings that the *Zentrum gegen Vertreibung* might be misused by the *Vertriebenen* to clamor for their own victim status and its privileges and that if granted that bonus, they might use it "irresponsibly." Like many German public intellectuals and, even more so, politicians, he fears the possibility that his motivations might be "misunderstood," namely perceived to encourage Germans to embrace the status of *Opfer* and reject their customary status of *Täter.* The suggestion of "irresponsible" conduct on the part of *Vertriebene,* for instance reclaiming the property they lost when expelled by the Czechs or Poles from places where their families had lived for centuries, also suggests that the Germans, regardless of their war experiences, would never be granted the status of *Opfer.* To be really powerful, the *Opfer's* moral-political privileges had to be reserved for the official *Opfer* of the Nazi regime. In the politically and culturally polarized postwar situation with its absolute distinction between *Opfer* and *Täter,* this has meant that whoever cannot be officially recognized as *Opfer* has to be a *Täter*—an unfortunate expansion of the Allies' (American) distinction at the end of the war between a very small group of "Good Germans" and huge group of "Bad Germans."[62]

"Are the Germans victims or perpetrators?" is at best a rhetorical question that does not expect an answer; at worst it is an accusation: "How can Germans be anything but perpetrators?" The accusation can be evaded by reaffirming one's own *Betroffenheit* and enlightened distance from the *dumpfes Volk.* If the question is debated in public, it is often not clear to the participants that at issue is the current *Opfer status,* not past victimization; and politicized memory *discourses,* not memory in the sense of spontaneous anamnesis, the retrieving of the now historical past. Fudging of these differences has also obscured the fact that victim status and memory discourses are interdependent with present political and cultural conditions: what are the current politics of power and self-interest? Since the end of WWII, German self-perception has always been politically controlled and directed, if to different degrees. The current situation is characterized by a collective German self-perception of non-victims in the sense of not-included-in-the-victim-status, and therefore more easily confronted with suspicions of the perpetrator status, which then can also lead to accusations of anti-Semitism, Holocaust denial, and other culturally undesirable attitudes—accusations that are often arbitrary, emotional, and irrational and therefore irrefutable in rational discourse or debate.

The real argument, then, should concern the justification of the juxtaposition itself of *Opfer* and *Täter,* since the issue is *Opfer* status in contrast to *Täter* conduct, that is, asymmetric oppositions. Highly politicized from its inception, the moral, political, and economic power of the official *Opfer* status has always depended on being balanced by the assumption of the largest possible *Generation der Täter* or, even better, *Volk der Täter.* Since it was desirable for the moral bonus of the *Opfer* status to grow rather than to shrink over time—hence the astonishing growth of the Holocaust as a construct of memory discourses of the historical events—the moral deficit of collective German criminality had to increase in size and virulence, at least virtually, over time—hence the power of the increasingly abstracted, ritualized concept of the Germans as *Täter:* even though very few of them had acted criminally, they "must all have known" of the crimes of their regime and been inactive; their collective criminality was their collective passivity. The dynamics of this interdependency have been both obvious to many observers and rigorously excluded from public discourse; to speak about them openly would break massive taboos and provoke feared accusations of anti-Semitism and Holocaust denial. Both accusations have been used much more liberally in recent decades; all critique of Jews, individuals and groups, can be seen as anti-Semitic, especially also the politics of Israel. The accusation of Holocaust denial has expanded beyond questioning the historical actuality and evidence of Nazi persecutions of Jews to questioning the uniqueness of Auschwitz.[63]

Taboos are notoriously effective in hiding the strategies of power, especially where they concern the power of previous impotence. Such strategies are more clearly visible and therefore more open to comparison where they concern not one but several and diverse groups with *Opfer* status engaged in the power politics of identity on the basis of memory discourses of previous persecution. Competing for resources and recognition, they have arguably learned from the highly successful strategies of Holocaust memory discourses. Though in many ways a problematic, divisive presence in American politics, it is precisely the plurality of these politics of identity that makes it possible to talk, if cautiously, about the dynamics of the power politics and self-interest politics connected with the moral bonus of the *Opfer* status. Different groups' politics of identity and memory are dependent on the various cultural and political contingencies of the present—the larger community's respective politics of power and self-interest at any given time and place.

In the United States, the growing number of groups practicing the politics of identity and their explicit accommodation in U.S. politics as a whole is a relatively recent phenomenon and reflects the enormous cultural and political changes of the last half century, especially since the Vietnam War. In Germany, like other European nations a fast-moving technocratic, globalizing mass democracy, the politics of identity and memory have remained remarkably unchanged where it concerns their uses of collective remorse. German *Betroffenheit,* an enduring guilty awareness of the horrors of Nazi persecutions, may have seemed highly satisfactory to the United States in general and American Jews in particular, and to the State of Israel. It has been problematic for ordinary Germans' perception of the domestic and foreign politics of their country, since the expectations controlling *Betroffenheit* have not only excluded the traumatic German experiences of the horrors of WWII in general but explicitly forbidden attention to this trauma as "offensive" "apologeticist" relativization of the official victims' suffering.

In the summer of 2001, *Spiegel* tested the waters with a series of remarkably sensible articles on "Hitler und die Deutschen," among them an essay by Bernhard Schlink on the danger and the necessity of dealing with the Holocaust. He thinks the insistence on an incomparable uniqueness of the Holocaust "almost as fatal as *banalisierende* comparisons. After a while, we do not engage any longer with what is unique, incomparable and past, and the moral pathos with which we talk about it does not take us anywhere." Like Peter Schneider a now self-critical member of the generation of 1968, Schlink points out that what they learned from the past were concerns of morality rather than institutions; they blamed their parents' generation for their own moral failure rather than the failure of their inherited institutions.[64] Schlink states here once more what by now seems self-evident but has seldom been seriously reflected for fear of apologeticism: to be effective, individual morality needs the support of functioning social and political institutions. At issue is a larger concept of community of which the individual is a viable part. Precisely this community based on mutual critical trust rather than the unilateral conformism of solidarity has been perceived as dangerous by all utopianist totalitarian regimes—National-socialist *Gleichschaltung* being a good case in point. Schlink, who had shared the one-sided, rigid moral perspective of the generation of 1968, needed a learning process during the next decade to arrive at this insight; whereas the sociologist Dahrendorf, half a generation older, had learned already by the end of the 1960s that freedom can be guaranteed only by institutions.[65] Precisely this understanding of the importance of functioning institutions—the importance of their absence—enables also a more balanced attitude to the troubled German past. Schlink's novel *Der Vorleser* (1995; *The Reader*) became an international bestseller also because it explores the question of German guilt as an issue of the quality of individual judgment at the core of a society's concept and practice of justice. Like Grass's *Im Krebsgang, Der Vorleser* was attacked in the spring of 2002 for a "new lack of concern about the past," "throwing off the burden of the past" (*Entlastung*), "cleaning up the past."[66] The events of September 11, 2001, may have had something to do with the fervor of these renewed rejections and accusations; and Schlink's *Spiegel* essay was published in the summer of 2001, a temporarily more innocent period. What Schlink said here is, in a quiet way, much more radical than even his extraordinary story of the relationship between a young German of his generation and a female KZ guard, the most shockingly subhuman being imaginable in the Western imagination because excluded from a Western concept of justice.[67]

A judge by profession, Schlink listened attentively to both sides. With this most rare double perspective on the bitterly entangled German-Jewish past, more perceptive than an outsider's view could ever be, Schlink had been present to each side. He pointed out that a past, whether collective or individual, can be traumatic not only if it is barred from remembrance but also if it is forced into remembrance. Removing the trauma requires both remembrance and forgetting; and this holds true for both sides, the *Opfer* and their descendants and the *Täter* and their descendants. Schlink is not interested in an *Opfer/Täter* dichotomy, but proposes that both groups can be involved in their own processes of remembering and forgetting. Acknowledging the enduringly difficult relations between both sides, he also acknowledges that the side of the *Opfer* is entitled to respect from the other side for their particularly difficult past. However, the claims made by one side on the other should not be absolute, unquestioned, but open to processes of dialogue and negotiation guided by civilized conventions such as mutual consideration and tact. It is important that Schlink uses "tact" in the context of the heavily moralized and politicized issue of German-Jewish relations: Tact, as Siegfried Kracauer argued in *History: Last Things before the Last* (1969), is an important aspect of the secular anteroom of history because it enables a critical community of historical inquiry based on the concept of historical truth as a process of procuring and trusting evidence. The historians involved in this process have to negotiate many different versions of historical truth to arrive, temporarily, at the most plausible one, and, ideally, they do so with tact, that is, an awareness of and consideration for the positions, the truths of others.[68] Invoking "tact," Schlink suggested a more civilized debate of German-Jewish relations in the literal sense of being guided by a civility based on a shared understanding that both sides have a right to their own discourses of the past and that these will have to be negotiated tactfully—if they want to learn from each other. Not an admonition; just a suggestion.

4 The War in the Empty Air

A Moral History of Destruction

The publication in the *New Yorker* of W. G. Sebald's "A Natural History of Destruction" in November 2002 provoked several letters to the editor declaring as immoral any sympathy for German wartime experiences.[1] One reader was "shocked and offended" by the text "with its implicit suggestion that the Allied bombing of German cities was distinguished by ruthless aggression. It was only toward the end that Sebald fully brought home the point that the Germans were themselves responsible for this suffering." Another found suggestions of "Nazi rhetoric" in Sebald's description of air raids, quoting as evidence the phrase "wholesale annihilation" and asserting that "Hamburg, Dresden and Berlin will be forever trumped by Auschwitz, Sobibor and Buchenwald, a fact that may explain why Germans have continued to show penitence in public for the horrors that they visited on others but have chosen to regret in more secluded ways the sufferings that others brought on them."

The advice, then, is to refrain "forever" from speaking in public about memories of a war that for millions of Germans had literally meant "wholesale annihilation." Publishing articles and books dealing with this topic will be forever offensive and therefore taboo. These letters reflect the opinion of a majority of American Jews and also a large number of educated non-Jewish Americans: the German experience of this extraordinarily destructive, brutal war should remain forever erased from German individual and collective memory, long since replaced by the greatness of American victory in the "good war," the "clean war," the most successful war in American history. Relatively few Americans have looked at WWII with some degree of skepticism as the "war we won, as if there was no death, for goodness' sake, with the help of the losers we left out there in the air, in the empty air."[2]

In the same vein—he "paused immediately" when he read Sebald's phrase "wholesale annihilation"—Christopher Hitchens reflected on German reactions to the near-total destruction of their cities at the end-stage of WWII in a review essay for the *Atlantic Monthly* entitled "The Wartime Toll on Germany. W. G. Sebald wrote of the pain of belonging to a nation that, in Thomas Mann's words, 'cannot show its face.'"[3] Hitchens's meandering argumentation, both censorial and inconclusive, comes back again and again to that "pain," which is for him the most fascinating aspect of Sebald's argument. Sebald's essay is not quite that self-centered, but equally inconclusive, touching on some of the most difficult moral-political questions in German postwar culture but never really attempting to clarify, much less connect, them. This lack of conceptual coherence is in part due to the fact that the published text is the English translation of a series of lectures on poetics, *Luftkrieg und Literatur*, that Sebald gave at Zürich University in December 1997 and then allowed to be published in 1999 under the same title and with very few alterations.[4] They had aroused a good deal of interest because of their taboo-protected topic, the scale and manner of Allied air raids on Germany's cities, especially firebombing—an apocalyptic destruction that *Life* had documented for (approving) American audiences in a powerful photo-essay, "The Battered Face of Germany" (June 4, 1945).

Pointing out that there had always been silence about the true degree of the material and moral destruction and that it had become something like "a shameful family secret," Sebald lamented the fact that almost nothing had been written about these huge and crucially important events.[5] The reactions to his statements were mixed. Some critics applauded his breaking the silence: even if there had been more published accounts than Sebald seemed to know or wish to acknowledge, their number was remarkably low in view of the cultural and political importance of the events.[6] There were also the familiar arguments warning of apologeticism: Sebald's own relatively few but effective, sharply naturalistic descriptions of the horrors of large-scale air raids interspersed with many quotes from a variety of eyewitness statements might be misunderstood as keeping a record of comparative suffering. One critic claimed, rather extravagantly, that "the silence was hiding a shame more precious than all literature."[7] Significantly, critics on both sides of the argument agreed that the few existing accounts of these catastrophic events had not found many readers. For a variety of interlocked reasons, Germans had somehow agreed that they would not remember, certainly not talk about, their experiences of air raids. The burden of collective guilt and shame imposed by the Allies on the Germans at the end of the war succeeded in repressing all collective and individual German psychic trauma of overwhelming physical destruction: declared enduringly unspeakable, it seemed to have disappeared. Arguably, it was the radical disappearance of German memories of that terrible war that prevented the traumas caused by it from receding over time.

Sebald regretted particularly the lack of literary descriptions of these horrendous events, since he thought a "synoptic and artificial view" was necessary to complement eyewitness accounts whose general verbal "normality" in the face of the most extraordinary visual and auditory impressions made them less "authentic" representations of the terrible sights, sounds, and smells they referred to.[8] He claims authenticity for his own description of the results of a series of attacks by the RAF and the U.S. Eighth Army Air Force on Hamburg during the hot summer of 1943. The goal of Operation Gomorrah had been to burn the whole city to the ground, and, as Sebald recounts, during one raid on July 27 ten thousand tons of high-explosive and incendiary bombs were dropped on many densely populated residential areas, all of which he lists by name to clearly locate and thus recall more powerfully the disastrous events. Drawing on eyewitness accounts, he invokes the raids' "now familiar sequence": windows and doors would have been "torn from their frames and smashed" by high-explosive bombs weighing four thousand pounds; then firebombs weighing up to fifteen kilograms would have ignited attic floors and upper stories. Within a few minutes, Sebald writes, "huge fires" were burning all over the target area of about twenty square kilometers, and they connected so rapidly that after only fifteen minutes the whole airspace was an all-encompassing "sea of flames." Five more minutes and an unimaginably strong firestorm arose: reaching up two thousand meters, the fire "snatched oxygen to itself so violently" that the air currents became a hurricane, "resonating like mighty organs with all their stops pulled out at once."

Burning like this for three hours, the storm "lifted gables and roofs from buildings, flung rafters and entire advertising billboards through the air, tore trees from the ground and drove human beings before it like living torches." The flames "rolled like a tidal wave" through the streets at over 150 kilometers an hour and "spun across open squares in strange rhythms like rolling cylinders of fire." Fleeing from the oven-like air raid shelters, people "sank, with grotesque contortions, in the thick bubbles thrown up by the melting asphalt. No one knows with certainty how many lost their lives that night, or how many went mad

before they died." The smoke rose to a height of eight thousand meters, and the heat, which the bomber pilots said they could feel in their
planes, went on rising from the smoldering rubble. The destruction of
large residential districts was total, and horribly disfigured corpses lay
everywhere:

> Bluish little phosphorous flames still flickered around many of them; oth-
> ers had been roasted brown or purple and reduced to a third of their
> normal size. They lay doubled up in pools of their own melted fat which
> had sometimes already congealed. . . . Elsewhere, clumps of flesh and
> bone or whole heaps of bodies had cooked in the water gushing from
> bursting boilers. Other victims had been charred so badly and reduced to
> ashes by the heat, which had risen to a thousand degrees or more, that the
> remains of families consisting of several people could be carried away in a
> single laundry basket.[9]

This passage, intended to make present the enormously powerful
energy of fire, was included in the excerpt that was published in the
New Yorker and offended readers who thought that the horrible death
by fire of German civilians, at that point overwhelmingly women and
children, was not worthy of being described in such detail.[10] If they had
read the text with a few less moral blinders, they would have noticed
the statement one page before this passage. In the context of discussing
the strategies of Allied bombing, Sebald said here that "in contrast to
the mainly passive reaction of the Germans to the loss of their cities,
which they perceived as an inescapable calamity, the program of destruction directed primarily against a civilian population was vigorously
debated from the first in Great Britain. The ambivalence was even more
pronounced after Germany's unconditional surrender." And in the concluding paragraphs, Sebald also explicitly acknowledges that Germans
today know "that we actually provoked the annihilation of the cities in
which we once lived" and that Göring's Luftwaffe would have wiped
out London by the same method that wiped out Hamburg and so many
other German cities had it had the technical resources. He also mentions explicitly that "the real pioneering achievements" in air war—
Guernica, Warsaw, Belgrade, Rotterdam—were the work of the Germans, and that in August 1942 the city of Stalingrad, "then swollen
(like Dresden later)[11] by an influx of refugees, was under assault from
hundreds of bombers." During this raid alone, which "caused elation
among the German troops stationed on the opposite bank [of the
Wolga], forty thousand people lost their lives"—the last words of the
New Yorker text. It is to be assumed that a good number of Sebald's
readers were also offended by the parallel drawn here between Stalin-

grad and Dresden. They might want to reflect on the moral inversion of war: killing becomes a virtue on both sides; and mass destruction develops its own self-feeding, seemingly irresistible dynamics.

There is, on occasion, a cold fire in Sebald's synoptic artistic anamnesis: he rewrites what others saw to make it literally more impressive by settling the images of destruction in the mind so memorably that they could not be easily overlooked and forgotten. In their enameled precision, some of these descriptions are reminiscent of passages in Ernst Jünger's war diaries. But where Jünger was fascinated by the esthetics of terror, Sebald, less "brilliant" verbally and less ambivalent about the horrors of warfare in general and this war in particular, was motivated by the writer's moral imperative of anamnesis. If he complained about the scarcity of literary texts dealing with the topic of Germany's physical destruction, he was even more dismayed by what he saw as a general German inability to engage in anamnesis: the recalling, at least in private memory, of past moral and physical devastation.[12] This is the core argument of these lectures. His conclusion was that the Germans' reluctance to remember and then relive the fiery apocalypse of Allied bombing could only mean that they had never really tried to remember and then relive the suffering of their regime's victims for which they were collectively responsible.

Importantly, the writer's moral imperative of anamnesis did not extend to the actual (possibly remembered) past experiences of air raids. Searching for the right words to invoke the overwhelming force of fire, as in the passage from which I quoted, Sebald was less concerned with its concrete traumatic impact on Germans as individuals and as groups than with the stylistic and moral quality of their witnessing. Had it been more "authentic," they themselves might have found the right words. It is true, eyewitness stories, especially in the case of traumatic events, are in most cases not as effective and in that sense true to the experience of the witness as are later, well-written accounts culled from them. Yet it is also worth noting that Sebald applied this demanding concept of authenticity in the case of German eyewitness stories of extreme experiences where he was reverently accepting of the often formulaic and ritualized eyewitness stories of Holocaust survivors. Here he respected not only these stories' personal importance to the survivors but, most importantly, the general cultural relevance of the recorded experiences—a respect that German eyewitness stories, if they were told at all, have never been granted. This culturally sanctioned a priori lack of interest in historical German experiences of extreme situations may have made it easier for Sebald to blame the Germans collectively for not remembering the past actuality of air raids and to overlook himself the connection between the impotent silences of German forgetting and the powerful voices of Holocaust anamnesis.

Past German losses on the battlefields, in air raids, and in mass expulsions did not interest Sebald because they seemed to him irrelevant in relation to the remembered past losses of Holocaust victims. His concern, then, was not particular problems of perception and representation in the case of traumatic German war experiences but rather a general moral imperative of anamnesis attaching to the war as the time and space of the victimization of Jews. A historian of German literature and himself a creative writer living and teaching in England, Sebald had been invited to give a series of lectures on a topic of his choice at the university of Zürich, as had other writers before him. He chose a topic he thought oddly neglected by German writers and literary critics, a topic that had indeed been removed from public German remembrance by taboos. But Sebald himself, living and teaching in England for decades, seems to have been unaware of the fact that his well-received docu-fictional novels tracing the damaged lives of Holocaust survivors, *The Emigrants* and *The Rings of Saturn*, had bestowed on him a moral authority, especially in the United States, that made it easier for him to write about the terror of air raids that many of his German readers had survived but, prevented from speaking about it, largely forgotten. He recreated the apocalyptic scenes from others' memories and descriptions, giving them a hyper-naturalistic intensity that to a degree revived, if momentarily, the experience of that terror. Himself untouched by the war, these significant moments of poetic anamnesis became *his* imagined sublimely terrifying reality, the more fearfully real, the less tainted by any inchoate, inauthentic eyewitness stories of ordinary Germans, who at some point might have welcomed forgetting in order to be able to see a future for their children.[13]

Luftkrieg und Literatur did draw attention to the indeed surprising gap in the articulated individual and public memory of Germany's mass destruction by air raids. Yet, breaking a taboo, Sebald also justified it. Any empathetic articulation of such memories (in contrast to "objective" descriptions of the events that caused the trauma) would have been inappropriate in view of the memories of Holocaust survivors. More significant in the terms of Sebald's perspective, German losses were eo ipso unreal in comparison to the reality of their victims' losses because of a quintessentially German insensitivity to violence and destruction. In his view, this insensitivity had caused their general acceptance of mass destruction and therefore their desire to forget their own losses as quickly and fully as possible. Unwilling to remember even their own horrible *Luftkrieg* experiences, Germans could not but resist remembering the experiences of what for Sebald have always been the only *authentic* victims of that war. Given that German inability to perceive the temporal layers of their own past, they would of course not be interested in the archeology of these victims' pasts and futures lost to the Holocaust. Whoever they were and whatever they had done or not done, the German people had been much too intent on surviving in the dark times of their bad past; and later they wanted too much to live normally in the present, forfeiting the grandiose scale, the sublime pain of their own moral and physical destruction. Hitchens's review (probably because he read only the excerpt and the letters in the *New Yorker*) is too narrowly focused on this morally "interesting" pain, misunderstanding and simplifying Sebald's argument.

It was arguably Sebald's concentration on the literariness of anamnesis—his recalling the sublimely condensed, literally meta-physical power of fire—that detracted him from the terrifying but banal experiences of ordinary Germans caught in the extreme dynamics of modern hyper-technological warfare. The archeology of loss in his docu-fictional prose reconstructions of the damaged lives of Holocaust victims is shaped by a nineteenth-century sensibility of melancholic anamnesis: the careful, reverent gathering and bringing back in poetic memory of what was thought or feared to be lost. Sebald's subjects are almost all irreversibly traumatized, existentially exiled Holocaust survivors and, in that, archetypical victims in the manner of Jean Améry, whose relentless concentration on recalling his experience of Nazi torture Sebald deeply admired as a significant gesture of absolute resistance to a re-emerging German normalcy.[14] *The Natural History of Destruction* includes the translation of Sebald's worshipful essay on Améry's inability to leave behind the Holocaust. After Améry reflected on and wrote about it for many decades, this experience would eventually drive him to take his own life, as he had always known and said it would do.[15]

Asked about his literary strategies in *Die Ausgewanderten* (1992; *The Emigrants*, 1996), the book that established him in the United States, Sebald said that his medium was prose, not the novel, but that history needed "Metaphorisierung" to become "empathetically accessible."[16] He was not interested in "pure" fiction, but the narration of fictionalized facts, which he seemed to think a better place for keeping past real facts safe than historiography would be. Yet, as in his most memorable descriptive passages in "Air War and Literature," it was precisely this self-consciously "innocent" poetic fact-fiction relation that enabled him to appropriate the personal and physical facts that he wanted to "rescue" through anamnesis. The characters in these narratives are as much or more *his* construct in reconstruction than *their* reconstructed selves; he is and remains their author, an unmistakable if shadowy presence. In the beginning of *The Emigrants*, Sebald gives a good example of such imaginative reconstruction. When he could not learn anything useful about his former teacher Paul Bereyter by talking to the villagers who had been familiar with him for a long time but never really known him, he began to imagine how Bereyter had lived, sleeping in the open on his balcony in the summer, skating on the fish ponds in the winter, and, finally "stretched out on the track" waiting for the train to kill him—he, too, a victim of his memories of the Holocaust:

> As I pictured him, he had taken off his spectacles and put them on the ballast stones by his side. The gleaming bands of steel, the crossbars of the sleepers, the spruce trees on the hillside above the village of Altstädten, the arc of the mountains he knew so well, were a blur before his short-sighted eyes, smudged out in the gathering dusk. At the last, as the thunderous sound approached, all he saw was a darkening greyness and, in the midst of it, needle-sharp, the snow-white silhouettes of three mountains: the Kratzer, the Trettach and the Himmelsschrofen. Such endeavors to imagine his life and death did not, as I had to admit, bring me any closer to Paul, except, at best, for brief emotional moments of the kind that seemed presumptuous to me. It is in order to avoid this sort of wrongful trespass that I have written down what I know of Paul Bereyter.[17]

When Sebald complained about literary texts' "self-imposed silence" on the topic of air raids, he included in this absence also "other areas of discourse, from family conversations to historical writings." Surprised that there had not yet been "a comprehensive or even an exploratory study of the subject" by historians, he mentioned as a notable exception a chapter in Jörg Friedrich's *Das Gesetz des Krieges* (1993; the law of war) that "looks more closely at the evolution and consequences of Allied strategies of destruction. Characteristically, however, his remarks have not aroused anything like the interest they deserve." Sebald thinks this a "scandalous deficiency, which has become ever clearer to me over the years" and "reminded me that I had grown up with the feeling that something was being kept from me." The area where he was born in 1944 and where he grew up, the northern outskirts of the Alps, was left almost untouched by the war, and yet he felt "as if I were its child . . . , as if those horrors I did not experience cast a shadow over me, and one from which I shall never entirely emerge."[18]

I wonder what Sebald would have thought of Jörg Friedrich's later book *Der Brand* (2002), whether its intense focus on every physical and moral aspect of the firestorms caused by the Allies' strategies of "moral bombing" would not have been too much for him: too much detailed information about the devastating attacks on German cities that still continued in April of 1945, when Germany had long lost the war; too much mourning of the human and cultural losses. It was definitely too much for Hitchens, whose review essay also includes, if fleetingly, Friedrich's *Der Brand* and Grass' *Im Krebsgang* (2002). Hitchens's rigid, uninformed reservations against both books point to the enduring difficulties for a majority of Jewish and non-Jewish American intellectuals to deal halfway rationally with their feelings about a possible change in the cultural status quo of Nazi Evil. Not that Hitchens would see it in these terms; the reassuring metaphysics of Nazi Evil will probably remain his negative gold standard "forever." Now living in the United States, writing for American journals, and being part of the culturally influential New York Jewish intellectual scene, he has an uneasy sense of something changing. In order to reaffirm the status quo, he reads into Sebald's more open and conflicted text a central, dominating German sense of "inescapable calamity." He does not engage with Grass's and Friedrich's much more substantial and important texts, nor with their reception, because this would mean a great variety of contemporary German, British, and American reactions to what for him is still the neatly Manichean German Question as it was posed six decades ago, at the end of the war.

Instructively, Hitchens approaches Sebald's arguments through the perspective of Thomas Mann's ambiguous and contorted evocations of Germany's collapse in *Doctor Faustus*. He envisions Mann arguing with himself "in what must have been exceedingly dark nights of the soul, by balancing his horror of a German defeat against his loathing for a German victory."[19] Hitchens's account is too easily impressed by the unspeakable and unanswerable dimension of that fictitious balancing act that Mann assigned to his narrator and chronicler, Zeitblom. Oddly, he seems to assume that Zeitblom is speaking directly for his creator, to whom "the horror of a German defeat" was actually not that important. Important was the chance to punish, as severely as possible, the collectively evil Germans who had robbed him of his German readership.[20]

Thomas Mann, like Hitchens, was not interested in the fate of many millions of ordinary Germans who in their majority had not voted for Hitler, had not welcomed the war, and had demonstrably changed their attitude toward the Nazi regime as it changed for the worse. But since they did not actively resist the regime as it was becoming more aggressively totalitarian, they were all tainted by it, all of them guilty. If Mann regretted the nearly complete destruction of German cities and historical cultural objects, it was only because he feared it might somehow reflect negatively on the worldwide importance of his work. Since the end of WWI, he had seen himself as *praeceptor Germaniae,* with a unique status in German high culture because as the Great *Dichter* he could claim an a priori higher and deeper insight. The 1929 Nobel Prize in Literature, the first for a German writer after WWI, was for him preeminently the confirmation of his *German* greatness, putting him on the same level with Goethe. It was not by accident that he would later attempt to deal with Nazi Evil by writing a negation of Goethe's *Faust.* Largely uninformed about German intellectual and cultural history, Hitchens does not seem to be aware of these connections, which might have helped him to be less fascinated by Thomas Mann's ruminations on Nazi Evil and more critical of its powerful and obscuring politicization in the postwar era.

"Typically" and neo-romantically German, the status of the *Dichter* had been an anachronism in the period between the two World Wars, a time of enormous scientific and technological development that required not so much the inspired profundity of a *Dichter* but the informed social and political imagination of highly intelligent and talented writers such as Robert Musil in his *Man without Qualities* (1932ff) and Alfred Döblin in his *Berlin Alexanderplatz* (1927). A throwback to the pre-WWI period, Mann's well-told, conceptually simplistic *Bildungsroman, The Magic Mountain* (1928), did not make more accessible the cultural and political problems of that brilliantly and dangerously modern Weimar Republic. Nor was Mann's negative *Bildungsroman, Doctor Faustus,* in any way helpful to sort out the indeed impossibly difficult and painful German Question. It is true, its composer protagonist, the most *German* creative genius, on his fated descent into the fiery abyss of Hell, was obviously an allegory of Germany's collective punishment for Nazi Evil by fire rushing from the skies. Writing in a more coherently, intelligibly complex culture not yet spooked by Germanness and Greatness, Goethe knew that pure negation, Faust's free fall into Hell to pay for his sinful contract with the Devil, would not do in a secular drama. There would have to be possibilities of other endings. Weimar culture, however, with all its shiny libertinisms and artfully choreographed chaos, was not secular. Its artists and intellectuals, like the masses, pined for redemption through German Greatness, even though it came in different shapes.[21] They might have met in the movies; but for the most part, the intellectuals, Jews and non-Jews alike, did not want to know anything about "the Volk" and its difficulties during the Weimar period and thus were ill prepared for the Nazis' resistible rise to power.

Hitchens is interested only in the stark and finally barren conflict between the desire for and the fear of Germany's destruction. Sebald often expresses his dislike of "the Germans" but does not, as do Thomas Mann and Hitchens, condemn them collectively. He would not say with Thomas Mann (quoted and italicized by Hitchens) *"whatever lived as German stands now as an abomination and the epitome of evil . . . a nation that cannot show its face."* In fact, Hitchens suggests that Sebald might be too accepting of the Germans' "vague feelings of shared guilt." He "paused immediately" at Sebald's expression "war of annihilation." And he "winced a bit at the way in which he mourns the Luftwaffe crew slightly more than he regrets the 'raid' on Norwich." This, he reassures his reader, is not "for any insular or tribal reasons" on his part. It is for fear of fudging the crucial distinction made by Heinrich Böll in a letter left for his sons, in which he told them that they would "always be able to tell everything about another German by noticing whether this fellow citizen, in conversation, described April 1945 as 'the defeat' or as 'the liberation.' Thomas Mann and Victor Klemperer were quite decided on this point and they did write about—and in the latter case endure—the very calamity that Sebald says is somehow unmentionable."[22] Sebald actually wrote "inescapable calamity" and meant something else.

Many ordinary Germans would have experienced the American invasion in the spring of 1945 as both defeat and liberation, though from the official American perspective everything that made the invasion possible was literally "liberating" and could not have had any other meaning for all Americans and all Germans. The neatest evidence for the American military-moral certainty of their power to invade as liberators (a disastrously seductive power to this day) was the captions on the photographs of their war tools as cultic objects signifying that most just of all just wars in history. In their great variety of form and function, their ships, submarines, tanks, guns, air planes, bombs were all given the descriptive adjective "liberating."[23]

Such literalness, almost nostalgically, calls up more innocent times. At the end of the war, the German population was under the unquestioned, total rule of the victors, as is common for the totally vanquished. They were women and young children; all the teenaged boys and girls, conscripted to defend the fatherland in a "last effort" by working with anti-aircraft guns or in the defense industry, were still gone. Still, living with their children in the rubble created by the victors' military and moral power, many of them did feel liberated, at least in certain ways and for a certain time. During the notoriously, magically beautiful hot summer of 1945 their constant fears of death and mutilation receded. They had feared for their men at the front, and for themselves and their children in the bomb shelters. Now they were waiting for their men and their teenaged children to come back, which in many cases took a long time or never happened.[24] One of the saddest aspects of this terrible war has been the anonymous, unmourned death of many millions of German soldiers of all ages who had not wanted it. Even their photos displayed on the walls of my friends' living rooms seemed strangely small and faded, as if they were not meant to be looked at, had never been looked at. It seemed to me, growing up among women without men, that for the women who had survived the war with their children, these men, unmentioned, had always been superfluous, dispensable. Remembering them would have been a luxury they could not afford; for their children they were, had become neutral ghosts, strangers.

These fathers never knew how during that magical summer, after the guns had fallen silent, their families lived in the cities that stank of death, with tens of thousands of corpses still buried under the rubble, sickening their hungry and thirsty children for whom there was neither milk nor water. One of my very few memories of this summer is the blinding heat, the ever-present sticky, smelly, stiff sweat from the different layers of clothes we had to wear walking endless kilometers because this was the only way we could carry them; the everlasting thirst, much worse than the hunger, and our blistered feet, because there seemed to be no water left on earth. There was nothing to wash with, nothing to drink; the heat was silent; our mouths were too dry to complain; long lines of women and young children stumbling silently, unseeing, from nowhere to nowhere, on the open road and in the rubble of destroyed cities.

Sebald disapproves of the Germans' not looking at, not talking about the destruction. Their "quasi-natural reflex, engendered by feelings of shame and a wish to defy the victors, was to keep quiet and look the other way." He quotes a Swedish reporter writing in the autumn of 1946 from what was left of Hamburg, that traveling on a train "through the lunar landscape between Hasselbrook and Landwehr," "perhaps the most horrifying expanse of ruins in the whole of Europe, he did not see a single living soul. The train, writes Dagerman, was crammed full, like all trains in Germany, but no one looked out of the windows, and he was identified as a foreigner himself *because* he looked out."[25] Obviously the Germans were familiar with the view, and the Swedish journalist was not. But the obvious won't do for Sebald, intent on being the first to see and recognize the monstrous scale and truth of a destruction ultimately justified by the monstrous German past. About Janet Flanner's description of Cologne, "in the rubble and loneliness of complete physical defeat. Through its clogged streets trickles what is left of its life, a dwindled population in black and with bundles—the silent German people appropriate to the silent city," he comments: "That silence, that reserve, that instinctive looking away are the reasons why we know so little of what the Germans thought and observed in the five years between 1942 and 1947. The ruins where they lived were the terra incognita of the war."[26]

Was Sebald really interested in finding out more about it? Solly Zuckerman points out in his autobiography *From Apes to Warlords* (1978), a book consulted by Sebald, that Sir Arthur Harris, commander-in-chief of Bomber Command and responsible for, among others, the annihilation bombing of Dresden and Pforzheim, liked destruction for its own sake. Sebald extrapolates from this statement that the "war in the air was pure and undisguised. Its continuation in the face of all reason suggests that . . . the victims of war are not sacrifices made as the means to an end of any kind, but in the most precise sense are both the means and the end in themselves."[27] As far as it concerns the dynamics of extreme situations, there is some truth in this dense argument. But the notorious "Bomber" Harris, executing Churchill's strategies of "moral bombing" long after Germany was defeated, was also motivated by the desire to assert the omnipotence of Bomber Command. There were no limits to its power in "the war in the empty air." Sebald does not look at the moral dimension of Harris's responsibility for the consequences of his acts; he looks at him as part of the *phenomenon* of total warfare: "pure and undisguised." Solly Zuckerman's perspective was not quite that pure; there was his professional interest in the effects of area bombing and his visit to the "ravaged" city of Cologne—an impression so overwhelming that a report on the destroyed city tentatively titled "On the Natural History of Destruction" remained unwritten: "My first view of Cologne cried out for a more eloquent piece than I could ever have written."[28] In the 1980s, asked by Sebald about his decision not to write the report, Zuckerman said that "he could no longer remember in detail what he had wanted to say at the time. All that remained in his mind was the image of the blackened cathedral rising from the stony desert around it, and the memory of a severed finger that he had found on a heap of rubble."[29]

These mental images conclude Sebald's first chapter, which contains his most powerful descriptive passages, indeed a sublime "natural history" of heretofore unknown forces of destruction: mountains, tidal waves of fire, a hurricane of flames. How could they be remembered? As images of "incredibly" powerful natural forces? As allegories of war? Of inescapable punishment? Of the illusionary "never again"? Peter Schneider in his review of *Luftkrieg und Literatur* has high praise for Sebald's brilliantly sharp descriptions of the monstrous transformation of human bodies under the firestorm of Operation Gomorrah, from which he quotes the same passage I chose. But in the end, expressing slight impatience with Sebald's lamentations about the few literary texts on this topic, he asks whether this "natural history of destruction" could be dealt with in the form of the novel. Sebald himself did not write a story or a novel about air raids, but an essay—and, one should add here, a poetically condensed rather than exploratory essay.[30]

Sebald is not interested in the people who experienced these horrors and have had to live with the trauma they left behind. He is interested in the hyper-physical effects of this kind of destruction: the ruins of the Cathedral and the severed finger, the shrunk purple corpses, the congealed fat of the bodies cured by fire; the surreally clear, incomprehensible mass transformation. As to the ruins as the terra incognita of the war: they need not have remained unknown, if more people had looked more closely at the women and their children living in the ruins. One who did was Albert Richard Behnke, a captain in the U.S. Medical Corps, who researched the effects of severe malnutrition in postwar Germany and among whose papers I found a cache of U.S. Army Signal Corps photos showing the abysmal living conditions of civilians in the devastated cities. Where other American officers ordered from Army Pictorial Services photographs of planes (including handsome young aviators), tanks, battle scenes, and the destruction of German industrial and military installations, Behnke collected photos of hungry children. He also acquired photos showing women trying to live with their children as normally as possible: a tin with flowers in a hastily thrown together wooden shack in the midst of piles of rubble; washing clothes in the street in Nürnberg—magically, that city still had water for which women stood in line for hours (April 24, 1945); a mother and her children in the damp and cramped but orderly cellar of a destroyed house, eighteen feet under ground, where they had lived for two years (September 19, 1945).[31]

These photos and the people who took them and who looked at them are an important part of the German Question: who were these silent German women with their silent children? They would have talked to the soldiers who took their pictures; they "spoke" to the physician Behnke. Hitchens, fixated on the all-pervasive Nazi Evil, is on principle against looking more closely. Sebald's looking is selective and ultimately focused on the awesome technological unleashing of the natural forces of fire, the sublime horror beyond any moral imagination and responsibility because the Germans had abdicated all morality and responsibility. In some cases he does look. But then he complains that the people who looked before him, and whose accounts he needed to consult for information, had not looked closely enough to notice the vermin on the corpses, the stench.[32] Hitchens is suspicious of Sebald because of his focus on the phenomenon of "annihilation"; and this suspicion stays with him. But he need not worry; Sebald never empathizes; he never links the phenomenon to the past actuality of its human experience; he would never have looked twice at these Army Signal Corps photos.

Hitchens's "calamity" refers not to the German's allegedly passive acceptance of Germany's destruction but to the dilemma, as he saw it, for a German intellectual such as Thomas Mann who did and did not welcome the destruction, viewed from the safe distance of exile in Los Angeles. He finds the same dilemma in Victor Klemperer's diaries. Married to a gentile and therefore spared deportation till the very last stages of the war, Klemperer had recorded his feelings about the bombings of Dresden in the diaries he kept during the war at great risk to himself and his supportive wife. Published much later (*I Will Bear Witness,* 1998 and 1999) but then promptly received as a "holy" text in Germany (and, if not quite so fervently, in the United States), they are for Hitchens an absolute moral authority and guide to the German war experience, as they are also to one of the critical reviewers of Jörg Friedrich's *Der Brand* (2002). In an article in *Die Zeit,* Volker Ullrich refers to the same "authorities" as Hitchens, drawing on *Doktor Faustus* and Klemperer's diaries and putting the latter in the same context, namely the firebombing of Dresden on February 13–14, 1945, that saved Klemperer's life but cost the lives of tens of thousands German women and children.[33] Ullrich agrees with Thomas Mann, who said in a radio message from Los Angeles to German listeners that he accepted the complete destruction of his beautiful native Lübeck: "I am thinking of Coventry and I have no objections against the lesson that everything has to be paid for." The "horrible" attack on Dresden in February 1945 is for Ullrich justified by the fact that it also meant "the hour of salvation" for Victor Klemperer.[34] It seems remarkably easy for him, as for Hitchens, to speak *for* millions of other Germans, who might have had some doubts in the matter. But they were all collectively guilty since they had all supported a racist regime, some of them passively; the majority actively—as Ullrich knows for certain.[35]

Dresden in February of 1945 was particularly vulnerable because it was crammed full with refugees, women and children who had fled their homes in the eastern provinces from the advancing Russian army and just barely survived the trek west, on which eventually more than two million of them lost their lives, partly because of brutal attacks on them by the Russian army. Yes, the German army had treated the Russian civilian population brutally too; but this does not make less memorable the mass killing of German women and children in that terrible winter of 1945, which is Grass's topic in *Im Krebsgang*. I remember my mother frantic to find my sister in one of the overcrowded Dresden hospitals; somehow she had learned that the child had been run over by one of the many oxen-drawn refugee carts on her way home from school, and she wanted to get her out of the hospital as quickly as possible because she knew that hospitals had become increasingly frequent targets for air raids. Dresden was a hospital city; there were many of them, and they all had "hospital" written in huge letters on their roofs—my mother had told me about the writing on the roofs, and many decades later I would see it on photographs and remembered her saying so. But the regime had in many cases just ordered to mark buildings that way whether or not they were hospitals, and so the Allied bombers had long since stopped honoring this protected status. In the end when the air raids became worse and worse, they seemed to seek out the buildings that claimed it, rightly or wrongly.

This past Dresden, with its real milling crowds of anxious and exhausted women and children on the verge of panic, was neither Hitchens's nor Ullrich's concern. They used it as an abstract weight—condemning these women and children to perish in the air raids—to balance German guilt with the salvation of a small group of innocent victims of the Nazi regime. The survival of Klemperer and his wife was highly important, but was it automatically more just than the survival of other groups less absolutely innocent? Ullrich does not even consider this question since the answer seems so self-evident; Hitchens raises it implicitly, circling around it. But on the whole he shares Ullrich's and many other German intellectuals' absolute disdain for the "wretched" German civilians tainted by Nazism then—why should they *not* have perished?—and the anonymous mass of ordinary Germans, *das dumpfe Volk*, tainted by reactionary conservatism now. For both Hitchens and Ullrich, the partial serialization of *Der Brand* in the mass-circulation *Bildzeitung* puts its author into a large if fuzzy "right" camp. That makes it much easier for Hitchens to just reject the book's argument, which he knows only from negative reviews, and for Ullrich to emphasize its potentially dangerous "revisionist" aspects. Yet Ullrich, despite his ideological blinders, is a perceptive reader of *Der Brand,* able to appreciate the book's historiographical and literary achievement. At the same time, he also repeatedly suspects and then accuses Friedrich of the dreaded *Aufrechnung,* attempts to equate the horrors of the Holocaust with the terrible experiences of German civilians during the end-stage of the war.[36]

Suspicion and accusation have long been characteristic for Ullrich's and other progressive intellectuals' political strategies. In the spring of 1996, when Daniel Goldhagen's denunciatory *Hitler's Willing Executioners* had just come out in the United States and not yet been translated into German, it was already hectically marketed by the German publisher. Expecting huge sales, he published in the *Börsenblatt des deutschen Buchhandels* an open letter from Goldhagen to all German booksellers, warning them to put all their efforts into selling his book so as not to appear to be lacking in *Betroffenheit* about their very bad past. It was in this situation that Ullrich was persuaded to write a positive review of that profoundly flawed book in *Die Zeit* (April 12, 1996) that made it impossible to pass it over in silence since all the media were now rushing to signal their awareness of this highly important event.

Instructively, the almost unanimously negative reactions to the book by credible historians seemed to stimulate even more the enormous public interest in it, especially among young Germans, the grandchildren generation, eager to "honestly confront" their bad past without obligations.[37] Ullrich's declared purpose in writing this review was to counteract what he called a general German desire to get rid of their bad past fifty years after the end of the war and "freely enjoy their new 'normality'": "And now here is that brilliant *Harvard-Dozent* and teaches us that we are not done by a long shot with the most horrible chapter of our past. We will learn much about the historical consciousness of this *Republik* from the reception of this provocative, troubling book."[38] All "we" have learned is that the grandchildren generation tends to be almost as lacking in historical information and imagination as their media-savvy idol Goldhagen.

Unlike Ullrich, Hitchens does not have to deal with a "bad past"; and "normality," even if desired by Germans, is for him nothing special. However, the moral dilemma of burning Dresden and of who deserves to survive *is* something special as Hitchens describes his own "indescribable" fascination reading Klemperer's diary entries on the event:

He registered every premonition, both of the aerial destruction of Germany and of the simultaneous extirpation of the Jews, an extirpation that became more frenzied and more cold-blooded as the Hitler regime imploded. Klemperer clearly desired that the latter calamity might be forestalled but without the necessity for the former. In a reckoning so ironic and fateful that even Faustus himself might have gasped at it, he and his wife were saved by the immolation of Dresden, on February 13 and 14, 1945, beginning just a few hours after they had been informed that all remaining Jewish spouses must report for deportation, which they both understood to be the end. The now overworked word "holocaust" means literally "destruction by fire": the old Klemperer couple escaped the holocaust in one sense by passing through it in another. On the smoldering morrow they took advantage of the utter havoc, removed Victor's yellow star, and set off on foot toward survival and, ultimately, liberation.[39]

There is a certain irony in the fact that Sebald included Klemperer in the group of eyewitnesses to air raids whom he finds lacking in verbal expressiveness: "Even Victor Klemperer's diary entry on the fall of Dresden remains within the bounds of verbal convention." Sebald suggests here that nobody observing the all-encompassing conflagration of Dresden could have "escaped with an undisturbed mind," and thus they could not be expected to find the language suitable to produce an "authentic" recording of their experiences.[40]

Ultimately, only the official victims of the Nazi regime count in Hitchens's selective perspective on the war. Despite blaming the Germans for having forgotten their own apocalyptic catastrophe and (to quote Ullrich's much repeated complaint) wishing to "freely enjoy their new 'normality,'" Sebald is less exclusive: now and then he allows German civilians a place among the past victims of WWII, if in rather general terms. Hitchens has an issue with precisely that inclusion, but confronting Sebald with German evil a la *Doctor Faustus* does not make things any clearer, though it may make for a more fascinating dilemma. There are a few short passages in his text when he seems to consider the reality of other lives. Reading Sebald on the death of a German pilot, the same age as his father, whose plane had crashed in a field not far from his house during an air raid on Norwich, Hitchens remembers growing up in and around British air bases and playing on disused airfields. The war was for him—about Sebald's age—and his cohort "a cause for pride and excitement" that made them eager to listen to their fathers' war stories. And then he has an unexpectedly perceptive comment: "What must it be like to have this in one's immediate past, yet with no cause for affirmation, let alone celebration."

He does not extend this thought to suggest that it might be all right for Germans now to remember with sadness the millions of dead German soldiers, young and old, who lost their lives for less than nothing in a dishonorable war most of them had feared. Yet he does ask why his German contemporaries should have to "feel inhibited about discussing the erasure of great cities and churches and monuments in their country, to say nothing of the killing of numberless civilians? There are many British people who feel that needless harm was done, and cruelly inflicted; and the unveiling in London a decade ago of a statue to Air Chief Marshal Arthur 'Bomber' Harris, the architect of the air campaign against Germany, was attended by some forceful protests in print and on the streets."[41] There were actually very few and mild protests. Hitchens's particular reservations about Sebald's text and his uninformed dismissal of *Der Brand* do not suggest that he would really be willing to have his German contemporaries discuss freely the past mass destruction of Germany—nor would many other British intellectuals. Despite a number of cautiously favorable reviews, reactions to *Der Brand* in England were on the whole negative, and there were "some forceful protests" against an English translation (which does not exist to date)— because of, not despite, the fact that the book is one of the most powerful antiwar documentaries.

The German protest against the celebratory statue of Bomber Harris came mainly from the inhabitants of Pforzheim, once a pretty, quiet, medium-sized town in Baden-Württemberg that was leveled in one horrendous air raid on February 23, 1945, lasting nineteen minutes and killing about twenty thousand inhabitants. The town had gone largely untouched because, like Dresden, it had no war-related importance. But Harris wanted to demonstrate the effectiveness of area bombing and show off once more what Bomber Command could do, especially with old timbered buildings crammed full with people burning so beautifully in the narrow streets. By that time, many officers in the RAF, and also his immediate superior, Sir Charles Portal, favored precision bombing. It was too late; the powerfully obscure dynamics of mass destruction had to run their course. Richard Overy points out that it was only Great Britain and the United States who used area bombing against the industrial centers and densely populated areas of their enemies and yet claimed the moral and political superiority of their modern democracies over the outdated ideological militarisms of their enemies, Germany and Japan. His explanation for this "paradox" is the combination of a Western uncritical acceptance of modern warfare in the wake of WWI, notably Germany's bombardment of targets in Great Britain in 1916–17, and the particular strategic circumstances of Great Britain and the United States during the first years of WWII.[42]

General Hugh Trenchard, commander of the Allied Independent Force of Bombers, had argued in 1917 that systematic area bombing of densely populated areas, resulting in high civilian losses, would destroy the morale of the population. They would therefore be more important for victory than even substantial industrial and infrastructure damages. Issues of morality and the law of war—erasing the distinction between combatants and civilians—were easily bracketed after the 1917 German attacks on London; and the overriding concern in the British debates was military effectiveness. Instructively, the new concept of unlimited air war was not presented as revenge since England had attacked Germany from the beginning of WWI; it was, rather, "the beauty of the coming war," as Lord Fisher would put it in 1919. The new war in the air was characterized by the absence of obstacles: no crossing of mountains, rivers, forests, deserts. It was a quintessentially modern minimalism. Waging war in the empty air, one could just fly high above and removed from everything, unhindered, drop tons of bombs, and never look back. Only in Great Britain and the United States was the doctrine of air war focused so exclusively on bombing. The 1935 War Manual of the RAF defined the bomb as the main weapon of the air force; and both U.S. and British pilots saw themselves as harbingers of the new modern total war that had totally dispensed with the distinction between combatants and noncombatants.[43]

Instructively, given the concrete consequences of this doctrine, the air war strategies described before the Munich agreement in the 1938 RAF War Manual called for area bombing of densely settled areas such as the industrially vital *Ruhrgebiet*. They would result in large numbers of civilian dead as part of the goal to demoralize the civilian population to the point of the nation's collapse. Anything that might contribute to weaken decisively the "national efforts" of the enemy was seen as a strategically worthwhile measure. But random attacks on enemy civilian populations were not, since they "do not do justice to the principle of concentration." This principle was shared by the U.S. Air Force during WWII and into the Cold War, the notorious carpet bombings of the Vietnam War being a particularly brutal example. When the war broke out in 1939, both British and U.S. pilots were conditioned to look at modern warfare as "total war" and at civilian populations as "the enemy," to be destroyed by any means. The theories of total war were masked by an abstract or metaphorical discourse—hitting systems, the nerve center, heart, brain, veins, and so on—to turn the attention away from the extreme damage done to the hundreds of thousands of real bodies this kind of warfare would surely create. Bomber Harris used habitually the metaphor of exterminating insects, vermin, when talking about the civilian victims of his "moral bombing." But there was also the, on the surface, more "innocent" contemporary enthusiasm for modern "rationalization" and "national efficiency," the pseudoscientific calculation that area bombing, no matter how destructive, would avoid even bigger losses of human life—foreshadowing arguments made in favor of the terrible decision to drop atomic bombs on Hiroshima and Nagasaki.[44]

In the course of 1943, Harris justified his systematic attacks on German cities in letters to the Air Ministry, asking for the officials' open admission that the task of his air force was to "extinguish German cities and their inhabitants." He made suggestions how the ministry should describe the goal of these extermination attacks, namely make it absolutely clear that the mass killing of German civilians was done intentionally for political reasons and should not be seen as incidental to the destruction of industrial or military targets. The total destruction of Germany's infrastructure, the creation of a refugee problem of a heretofore unknown magnitude, the demoralizing experience of ever more brutal air attacks, were the Bomber Command's explicitly stated and accepted goals. This was too frank for the Air Ministry, even in late October of 1943, and Harris was told that the devastation should not be presented publicly as an end in itself but as an inevitable side effect (our more polished "collateral damage") of a comprehensive attack on the enemy's ability to wage war. Harris would not be subdued that easily: he thought this distinction "purely academic" and asserted that British public opinion would accept the real intent of area bombing without consideration for "the sentimental humanitarian scruples of an insignificant minority."[45]

He was right, as far as the British press was concerned; and he would be right long into the future. The city of Pforzheim thought the erection of Harris's statue to the memory of his heroic acts of extermination half a century after the city's devastation a cruelly superfluous reminder of the moral inversion in wartime: not only does mass killing not count as a crime, it becomes a cultural and political value for the victor. Their appeals in Bonn and London were defeated.[46] As for Hitchens, his putting himself in the place of Germans was indeed momentary: immediately after mentioning the protests against the statue to Harris he expresses his deep unease with the phrase "war of annihilation" occurring in Sebald's "evocative paragraphs" about the airfields. In his Manichean scenario of WWII, the concept of "annihilation" went exclusively with the vanquished. By definition, it could never have been used in the case of the victors, who as liberators would have caused only "collateral damage" to civilian populations, and as invaders would have been justified in punishing all Germans because they were all Nazis. In any case, it was the victors who would have the military and political power to write the moral history of mass destruction.

Hitchens's jumble of fragmented, contradictory thoughts, presented with the familiar gestures of disdain and moral certainty, reflects his difficulties with any shift in the interpretive conventions that have controlled German historical memory and thereby diminished historical reality. Any attempt to modify this control would have to be rejected as heretical revisionism. His essay reflects an enduring and troubling psychological and social distance to all German wartime experiences. It is true, his erratic argumentation may have mimicked what he might have thought his ambivalence about some aspects of the German Question in its relation to the mass destruction of German cities. But it in no way obscured his opinion that German wartime experiences do not deserve to be remembered; much less become a legitimate part of the history of this war. Precisely this exclusion motivated the military historian Jörg Friedrich to write his disturbing, remarkably effective antiwar documentary *Der Brand:* he wanted to reacquaint ordinary Germans with *their* still largely hidden part of the Second World War.[47] The book came out in the fall of 2002, preceded by Grass's *Im Krebsgang* in the early spring and a brief, grotesque interlude of yet another anti-Semitism flare-up involving Walser and a powerful Jewish German literary critic in the summer. Curiously, that affair might indirectly have helped Friedrich's breaking of a taboo with his dramatic reclaiming for the larger historical memory of WWII also the German experience of British and U.S. air raids. Lighting up the denunciatory politics of anti-Semitism, the episode may have suggested to Friedrich's potential readers, especially after Grass's *Im Krebsgang,* that there had been for a long time too much censorship of historical memory and too much forgetting of German wartime experiences.[48]

The most important marketing strategy to get access to a large number of readers who did not know the scholarly historian Friedrich, where they had known the Nobel Prize winner Grass, was serializing excerpts of *Der Brand* in the mass-circulation daily *Bildzeitung*—a strategy invariably denounced in negative reviews of the book. A pleasantly neutral review in the *Economist,* "Another taboo broken. A German historian describes German civilian suffering in the last world war," also kindly attributes to the Germans a more consistently bad conscience than is probably realistic: "For decades after the second world war, Germans could not bring themselves to talk about their own wartime suffering. Their burden of guilt was simply too great. But more than half a century later, the old taboos are gradually being broken." The Germans had a lot of help remembering that burden and forgetting their own wartime experiences, though many of them were and still are horrified by the extent of the Nazi regime's criminality. Known for its general level-headedness, the *Economist* seems quite sanguine about the gradual changes in German attitudes, pointing out that the fifty-eight-year-old Friedrich, "like most Germans of his generation" had originally looked at the bombing as "'the right response to the crimes of the Third Reich.' But he changed his mind"—precisely what Good Germans should never do.

Friedrich's quoted statements that the air raids were "'the biggest catastrophe on German soil since the Thirty Years War'" and that "'apart from the firebombing of Dresden and Hamburg, it is barely registered in the official German collective memory'" elicit the comment that

> it is still rare for a German to take a public look at the second world war from a German perspective. But things are changing. Earlier this year, Günter Grass, a Nobel prize winner, caused a tidal wave of agonized German heart-searching with his novel "Krebsgang". . . . "Never," says the Old Man, Grass' *alter ego* in the book, "should we have kept silent about all that suffering simply because our own guilt was overpowering and our professions of regret paramount for all those years, for we abandoned the suppressed reality to the right-wingers."[49]

It took time and the changes that come with it; and then it took looking more closely at the evidence.

Most of the British reviews were not that understanding, though some of them were fair.[50] Most of them mentioned German suffering—positively, negatively, neutrally—but Friedrich's focus is not on the suffering caused by air raids but on detailed and precise recalling of and then reconstructing *sensory perceptions* of air raids. In a short concluding "Editorial," he stated that much has been written about air war, but for a long time nothing about its "Leideform." This neologism refers neither to a *general* German suffering from air war, nor to traumatic *individual* experiences of air raids. Friedrich is interested, rather, in the *particular* shape of the shared experience of being firebombed. The peculiarly terrifying passivity of waiting for the manmade bombs to drop is linked to the inherent inability to escape the superhuman natural forces of fire unleashed by them: their programmed *and* uncontrollable power to annihilate everything in their way.

Over the last half century, individual cities have published chron-
icles listing the dead and witness reports describing the air raids. But
given the chaos wrought by the air war against the German civilian
population, these records only rarely meet scholarly standards and have
to be used with caution. Friedrich calls for "a public project" to evalu-
ate critically all the existing records, since to this day we lack even a
reliable estimate of the number of air raid fatalities. The official German
figures tend to be on the low side to avoid any suggestion of *Aufrechnung*.[51] There is also the question of evaluation: the (in relation to their
populations) very high numbers of dead recorded for Pforzheim and
Swinemünde, both of them small towns, put their bombardments among
the "great tragedies of the Second World War," but they do not appear
as such in the historiography of the Second World War, whereas cities
like Hamburg and Dresden do. Another important project would be
to record the remembered experiences of the still living survivors of
air raids, members of the *Erlebnisgeneration*—a term used to qualify
Tätergeneration.

Der Brand is a detailed chronicle and in part stunningly powerful
narrative account of all the particular physical and mental aspects of air
raids on German cities; and in that it is a general indictment of all air
raids at any time, in any place, Pforzheim 1945 as well as Baghdad
2003. In a curiously provocative, troubling sense, it is precisely the extraordinary attention to the detailed historical particularities of extreme
destruction that makes Friedrich's documentary so relevant for understanding the general nature of warfare. His highly specific discussion of
the modern technology of an air war much "improved" in the latter half
of WWII to become more and more deadly is then applicable to the
dynamics of other extreme situations in warfare. Friedrich is a remarkably skilled but on the whole *sachlich* (matter-of-fact), even distant,
narrator of this antiwar documentary. The chapters have lapidary titles
naming places, events, concepts, objects; and each of them has an introductory summary, which is densely conceptualized and carefully formu-
lated. These summaries define the meanings of what is going to be documented, creating a kind of meta-documentary discourse that attempts
to be as complete as possible because the documentation itself, a mixture of many, mostly unidentified, voices and Friedrich's narration, is by
its very nature incomplete. The first chapter, "Waffe" (weapon), is also
the most strictly object-focused. Unprefaced, it goes straight to the description of the air raid as a complex entity comprising human skills
and activities and sophisticated technology: "Der Zielanflug" (destina-
tion), "Brandingenieure" (fire engineers), "der schwere [heavy] Bomber,"
"Radar," "Die Crew." The summary clarifies that "the bomb does not

find its way to the target but the target is what the bomb can find," creating an existential uncertainty for the human beings waiting to become that target. It is the unbearably nerve-wracking, disorienting civilian experience of waiting for the bombs to drop.

Moreover, "live" bombs are not self-contained but interactive, in the literal sense of "alive" objects; they are modern technological black magic meant to be as deadly as possible. The extreme destruction wrought by the bomb is caused not by the tonnage of the explosives but by the "self-multiplying" damage done by the mixture of explosives and firebombs, *Brandmunition.* It took the combination of two scientific disciplines to achieve this self-multiplication, resulting in raging firestorms of heretofore unknown proportions. Over a period of three years, engineers trained in firefighting and electrophysicists developed the systems that would locate and then target particularly incendiary settlement structures to start the fires. But on its way to the target the plane itself, pumped full with gasoline and bombs, is the most sensitive target. Pursued by *Flakkanonen* (anti-aircraft guns) and *Abfangjägern* (small, agile anti-aircraft planes), the crews charged with the task of mass killing are almost exclusively concerned with their own survival. War as the paradoxical symbiosis of death and survival has found its most striking allegorical representation in the war in the air when bombers are dropping mass death on civilians, and their crews performing beyond their known limits to get out of the way of death, to survive, at least momentarily, in the empty air. Many did not; 55,000 British airmen died in their burning bombers, a death no less gruesome and cruel than that of their German victims.[52]

Like Friedrich, the historian Lothar Kettenacker is critical of Churchill's extremely destructive, ultimately futile air war strategy against the German civilian population, which was also very costly for Britain. But he is also more dispassionate in considering Churchill's composite motivations, his dilemma increased by the fact that the RAF would be such a perfect tool. Churchill's precarious political beginnings had given him a strong sense of the necessity of an all-out success of his strategies, namely the near-total destruction of the enemy, which for him more than for others also meant the civilian population. He pursued that goal with an extraordinary single-mindedness supported by his peculiarly volatile, aggressive temperament and, as it were, archaic warlord mentality, which increased mightily in the course of the war. There was also his desire, caused partly by Great Britain's military weakness in the early forties, to impress and please Stalin. The air war against Germany, its industrial centers and civilian populations, was seen by Churchill as

England's real contribution to the fight of the "United Nations" against the Third Reich, but Stalin did not appreciate it as such. The same day the Soviet Union was attacked by the Nazi regime, June 22, 1941, the prime minister offered "the Russian people" an alliance with Great Britain in a radio address; and on July 7 he promised "all the help allowed us by time, the geography, and our increasing resources."

It took almost a year to finalize the formal alliance on May 26, 1942, especially the mutual obligation not to make peace treaties with either Hitler or a succeeding government—an agreement that would prevent the British government from entering into negotiations with the German resistance, which might have meant preventing the loss of millions of lives, German and non-German, in the end-stage of the war. Never satisfied, Stalin wanted what Churchill could not give him, tanks, aircraft, and troops, at least twenty-five to thirty divisions to relieve the pressure on the Russian Army. In the spring of 1942, Churchill went to Moscow to explain his concept of air war to Stalin, emphasizing the importance of increasing the brutality of the attacks on the civilian population: ever more cities to be bombed by ever more planes carrying ever more heavy bombs (four tons). If necessary, so Churchill's promise went, every house in almost every town would be destroyed by fire. The protocol of that conversation mentions that "Mr. Stalin," despite his disappointment by not getting more help on the ground, "smiled and said that would not be bad."[53] The results of Churchill's air war came close to this promise, and Mr. Stalin, so successful in his persuading Roosevelt and then Truman to approve the mass expulsions of all German populations from the East, had plenty of reasons to smile.

Focused on the vivid documentation of this extraordinary and in its last stages grotesquely unnecessary destruction, Friedrich admits to being distressed by the surreal brutality of Churchill's air war. He tries to communicate the pity of the terrible harm done to so many German people, their cultural objects, and the documents of their cultural history by one powerful political leader. To this day, Churchill has been revered as a "savior" by the Allies and by a large British majority precisely because of his profound lack of moral scruples where it concerned the fight against "Nazi Germany," meaning largely the German civilian population. Implicitly, Friedrich's account suggests Churchill's criminality in fighting his air war against Hitler without any thoughts given to the literal transformation of Germany's cities into mountains of rubble. He is careful not to suggest that Churchill would have or should have been prosecuted as a war criminal—a possibility that, unlike McNamara, Churchill would never have considered. His alliance with Stalin was, as he said, his "Faustian pact with the devil" in order to defeat Hitler. The air war, as he fought it, was an important, curiously fitting part of this pact: the combined finely tuned technological control and hugely powerful elemental fury of the firestorms.

The justification for his merciless strategies of "moral bombing," much repeated but fictitious, was Churchill's stated goal to undermine by any means the morale of the German civilian population, their will to hold out to the bitter end. In reality, the bombing went on long after it had become clear to everybody that Germany was defeated. With roads, railroads, bridges largely destroyed, electricity and communication broadly interrupted and no longer functioning air defense, without weapons, ammunition, food supplies, water, medical supplies and services, the civilian population, women frantic to find protection for their children from the bombers, from hunger, from cold, from infection, simply went on living or dying with the air raids to the bitter end.

The firebombing of Dresden in early 1945 was complicated not only by the large influx of women and children refugees from the East but also by dangerous epidemics, among them typhoid and polio. There had been a severe diphtheria and scarlet fever epidemic in Dresden the year before, sending my two younger sisters and me to an overcrowded hospital for many weeks. I was the first one to go; I remember a fiery dryness in my throat and my mother sitting on my bed crying, waiting for the ambulance. I had never seen her cry before and remember it as a part of being sent off by myself in the ambulance, an extension of the quarantined hospital. One after the other, we were all delivered to the same high-ceilinged hall crammed full with hundreds of small beds, and I remember the persistent sharp smell of disinfectants that in my fever-ish perception pierced the dark fuzzy drone of complaints about hurting throats, headaches and earaches, and violent thirst—always thirst, and the strictly rationed, deliriously smooth and cool sips of water.

Most of the children had very high fever, and there seemed to be no medication to bring it down. As the fever followed its unpredictable course, we were temporarily removed from the big hall when it got worse. There also was no medication for pain; I remember the fact of pain but not what it was like, only sharp burning in the throat and endlessly throbbing earaches. I spent what seemed to me an eternity in a small remote room upstairs from the big hall, reached after a maze of narrow corridors through which the nurses seemed to be hurrying day and night with trays of tinkling instruments and what we hoped were carafes of water. There was one other child in this room, a young girl whose face had been hurt in an air raid and who had a glass eye, which

I feared. We were deadly bored whenever the fever let up a bit, without anything to amuse us and nobody allowed to visit us, and she forced me to go on telling her stories for what seemed to me hours by threatening to take out her glass eye whenever I stopped. Every time she rolled it toward me like a malevolent marble I panicked, fearful that it was somehow alive. My mother often said that my vivid imagination was fed by my general fearfulness, and she would call me her *Hasenherz* (heart of a little rabbit), which I liked because it sounded small and soft and nothing big and hard would be expected of me. Since the child's face, in parts roughly stitched together, looked itself frightening, the removal of the glass eye should not have been such a big scare, my mother pointed out later. But she conceded that it might have been, given the combination of a *Hasenherz* and high fever.

I remember mostly the thirst, the isolation, and fear, which I could not talk about since the notoriously overworked nurses barely had time to give us the intensely desired sips of water. Once we were over the worst, we were wrapped up and walked to one of the tall windows so that our mothers could get a glimpse of us and we of them. From high above I saw her, tiny, waving to me and calling, but I could not hear her. I thought it inevitable then that I would never be with her again, and the feeling, it seems to me, was not fear but resignation. By then I had been taken back to the big hall where all the other children were, and that was all the security allowed to me from now on. Though her bed was not far from mine, I was no longer afraid of the girl's glass eye; and where I had first pitied her for the absence of her mother—I never knew whether she had survived the air raid that had destroyed her little girl's face—I now thought we were in the same situation, motherless. The destruction of her face and the loss of her eye I must have accepted with the child's sense of fatality. What had been meant to reassure the mothers, recognizing us in the windows, standing there, alive, must have very much unsettled me: seeing my tiny mother and not hearing her must have made the distance between us seem insurmountable, my loss of her almost certain.

But we all got home, one after the after, shaky and looking, our mother said, like little ghosts. Being the first to go and come back, not having really seen but only felt my bony arms and legs and prominent ribs under the big hospital shirt, and familiar with the encompassing cloudy weakness, I was surprised that my mother cried when she saw me, as she would do twice again a few weeks later when my sisters came home, one after the other. I did not know then that for her the challenge of getting us reasonably well again was almost impossible and that she was terribly afraid she would be helpless to help us. There is a photograph of us three little ghosts taken in the fall of 1944, which our mother had sent to her parents in Berlin and retrieved when she dissolved their household in the sixties; it had survived the air raids in Berlin in a suitcase in their basement. But notwithstanding our appearance and my mother's worries about our recovery, once we were all home, the fearful memories receded, changing into games and stories that also brought out the more comical aspects of our encounters with nurses and other children in the hospital.

Many decades later I suddenly remembered a book that our clever mother had found in some Dresden bookstore even in 1944, the story of a middle-class family like ours but in peacetime, with three little girls who had all been seriously ill and, like us, came back from the hospital one after the other and for a time enjoyed special privileges. In our case, they were larger portions of any food our mother could find; in theirs, very special delicacies and toys. But in both cases, the first little ghost had to give them up when the next little ghost came home and demanded special attention. It was, as I remember it, a very shrewd and funny book about using the power of suffering. It would have served our mother and us ex-sufferers well because it set up a scenario in which we could look at ourselves as both pitiable and laughable. My mother was no longer alive when I remembered this book, and I have never been able to recall the title or the names of our fictional counterparts. After the war we never talked about what happened during the war, as if out of my mother's fear that we could still be consumed by its fires and then its darkness. But I do remember the laughter, even as the situation grew more and more desperate. I also remember asking my mother on the day I had somehow, somewhere heard about Roosevelt's death whether the war would now end sooner. We were outside, and in my memory this day in mid-April is steel gray and cold, probably because my mother said that she did not know and that there might be more destruction before the end. Looking around me, I think on a street like ours, among ruins of houses and of big trees, I found this incomprehensible; but how could I not believe her.

In his memoirs, Churchill put a different, more gallant spin on the responses of a civilian population to the chaos on the home front largely created by his ever accelerating air war. He acknowledged that he had been wrong to think the Germans could be broken by massive air raids; they had shown surprising endurance caused by well-organized rescue efforts, strict police surveillance, and the discipline and courage typical of the Germans.[54] To a more realistic observer, the women's discipline and courage in those situations would have seemed mixed with increas-

ing despair, physical exhaustion, and mental numbness. On some level
beyond political and military explanation, the exotic brutality of Churchill's air war seems even more difficult to comprehend today than in
the immediate postwar era. In contrast, the U.S. air war appears to
Friedrich not so obviously driven by personal obsession with political
power, more controlled by professionals thinking in terms of function-
ality rather than pure destruction. Were the results less terrible for the
civilian population? On some level, Friedrich seems to think so; perhaps because he does not find here, at least not to such a degree, the
trans-moral, self-fulfilling will to destroy that he finds so appalling in
Churchill and Arthur Harris, his chief of Bomber Command.

Many observers have described how, once unleashed, the furies of
the bomber war could no longer be called back. Destruction on this
scale, especially by fires of this surreal size and force, would develop its
own uncontrollable "natural" dynamics. Yet they were still the result of
the inhuman strategies of air war against a civilian population. This is
what Friedrich wants to document and clarify: WWII as the total war
started by the Nazi regime meant a collective identification of the civilian population with its leadership that called for collective punishment.
These women and children fully deserved the destruction by air raids,
despite the fact that the German population had never been asked by
their leadership whether they wanted this war. "*Bekanntlich* (as everybody knows)," Kettenacker writes, "there was absolutely no *Kriegs-
begeisterung* (enthusiasm for the war) in 1939, only disconcerted silence and questions."[55]

Hans Mommsen, one of the best-known historians of the Nazi period, defends Friedrich's arguments against accusations that they show
or might trigger "revisionist tendencies"—accusations responsible for
the mostly critical reception of the book in Great Britain; so far there
has been no reception in the United States. For Mommsen, the book's
importance lies in its detailed representation of the debacle's full horror,
"near incomprehensible in its whole scope, as it resulted from the ever
more systematically carried-out air raids in combination with an ever
more weakened, in the end non-existent air defense."[56] He also deals
with critics' complaints that Friedrich's powerful representation of "moral [area] bombing" targeting civilian populations signified an irresponsible attempt to put the experience of *Bombenkrieg* alongside the Holocaust instead of reminding his readers of the vast differences in the scale
and method of the Nazis' destruction of human life.

Churchill himself, as Mommsen and others point out, repeatedly
used the term "extermination," *Ausrottung,* when speaking about German civilians. The concept of creating spaces completely emptied of

human life, whole cities turned into moonscapes mirroring the empty air in which they waged their limitless war, played an important role in British war strategies. "Massacres" was indeed the right term for the large number of particularly brutal attacks so late in the war on almost undefended spaces without any military value and the disastrous consequences for the mostly defenseless civilian populations.[57] Friedrich shows the unscrupulous escalation in the choice of weapons and strategies on both sides. The brutalization of warfare in WWII that started with Hitler was almost limitless, and area bombing has to be understood in this context. Once it was technically perfected, area bombing separated itself from the more narrow military goals. It could then be seen as the so far unrealized Allied "second front" and was also temporarily Great Britain's only effective weapon against the Axis powers. But these contingencies, Mommsen thinks, should not obscure the "truly horrifying" relentless focus on making more and more perfect a destructive technology of such unheard-of power, directed more and more exclusively at civilian targets. It was a technology that culminated in the creation of self-multiplying firestorms, eliminating human agency like rescue teams and firefighting squads through the use of delayed detonators.[58]

"Strategie," Friedrich's second chapter, has two sections: "Der Weg in das Moral Bombing," tracing the development of that concept, which includes also the German attacks on Warschau and Rotterdam; and "Der Weg zum Rhein," dealing with the bombardments of France and then Germany by the American and British invading armies. In the first part Friedrich briefly introduces the description of the phenomenon of the firestorm in a 1927 article in *Berliner Illustrierte Zeitung* by a WWI pilot and inspector of the Royal German *Fliegertruppe,* an Oberstleutnant Siegert: "If you succeed in creating more sources of a fire than can be extinguished simultaneously by existent fire-fighting squads, you have started the sources of catastrophe."[59] Friedrich distinguishes air raids in connection with military activities on the ground that, though not always essential to the war effort, were caused by the war (*kriegsbedingt*),[60] from the pure, self-justified devastation, *Resteverwüstungen,* undertaken by Harris's Bomber Command: "His intentions pretended to be coordinated with the last military battles, but they were not. They had no purpose. Why burn down Pforzheim in the night of February 24, 1945 by creating a fire-zone of 4.5 squarekilometers and killing 20 000 people? For the exact execution of this raid Masterbomber Swales was posthumously awarded the Victoria cross." Every third person died in Pforzheim, every seventh in Nagasaki.[61]

The firestorms that destroyed Pforzheim, Hamburg, Kassel, Dresden, and a dozen of other places could not be fully staged before September 1944; they could only be initiated, encouraged. Friedrich sees at work here "the symbiosis of a raging human desire to destroy with nature's vulcanism. Atmospheric reactions transferred to the fire ammunition an unprecedented, untameable rage of aggression [the attack on Hamburg, July 1943]. The British welcomed this combined force and fury as a divine judgment and immediately tried to find its mathematical equation. They did not succeed because there were too many variables and unknown quantities."[62] But eventually they would figure it out. Pforzheim was particularly attractive to Harris because it was small, had no defense industry, and had so far escaped serious bombing. Its narrow streets and old timbered houses were crammed full with refugees and their possessions fleeing the air raids still expected in larger, already heavily damaged cities. There was no fire protection, and Masterbomber Swales could execute his bombardment under laboratory conditions.[63]

The "Präzisionsvernichtung" (annihilation) of Dresden and Darmstadt in February 1945 was also highly successful. Every tenth person died in Darmstadt because the firestorm had sealed many basement exits, causing high rates of death by heat and gas; neither city had bunkers. Dresden's population was dramatically increased by the influx of refugees, from 640,000 citizens to possibly one million, with both groups contributing to the more than 40,000 fatalities of the "double blow" air raid of February 13–14.[64] Harris had selected for Dresden the double attack strategy that had worked so well in Duisburg, Cologne, and Saarbrücken. Given the heavy weight of gasoline, the Bomber Command planes could not carry more than 877 tons of bombs, the same amount used for one attack on the smaller city of Darmstadt. But the "double blow" would achieve more than double the amount of destruction and killing: the first attack drove everyone into the shelters; the second attack hit them when, relieved and exhausted, they emerged from them. Cellars do not provide shelter against firestorms for more than two hours; whoever returns to them a short time after the first attack will not leave them alive.

But it did not help to be outside, like the hundreds of thousands of refugees with their oxen-drawn carts in the Dresden *Grosser Garten,* or the tens of thousands of bombed-out fleeing from their burning houses and hospitals to the banks of the Elbe. The Masterbomber had taken care to really hit the big square of the park and the banks of the river Elbe, the two possible spaces for people to flee to during the second attack.[65] And, promptly following the "double blow," the American daylight raid had sections of the feared Mustang fighters flying low and gunning the riverbanks and the *Grosser Garten* area, killing the survivors of the firestorms of the first two attacks, panicked women, children, animals rushing around in their futile search for shelter; patients in their hospital pajamas lined up in long rows on the ground and abandoned to the raging fiery skies.[66] An ordinary hellish scenario of total air war.

If the success of the Hamburg mission in July 1943 that so delighted the Bomber Command had been partly the result of a rare atmospheric condition, the attacks on Dresden, Darmstadt, and many other cities were the result of technological experiments completed only in September of 1944. Plans for an all-out Allied attack on a German city, possibly Berlin, went back to the summer of 1944. It was conceived as a supernaturally strong "Donnerschlag" (thunder bolt), a "colossal massacre" expected to produce more than 100,000 dead. The plan was itself the more moderate version of Churchill's plans at the time to subject sixty German cities to gas and bacterial attacks.[67]

Friedrich's argument in the case of all these late bombardments draws attention to the interdependencies of the timing of disastrous air raids and the time taken by technological developments. But though he finds Harris's prosecution of Churchill's air war morally repugnant, his main concern is the inevitable immorality of decision making in the extreme situation of a total war, regardless of the psychology of individual leaders. When the friend-enemy split has become such a powerful obsession, and killing the perceived enemy the ultimate political-military virtue, the race for developing ever and ever more effective killing machines becomes obsessive. The bomb aimer of a Lancaster (635 Squadron) remembered looking down at the tidal waves of fire during the second attack, which had taken the population of Dresden by surprise since the sirens were no longer working: "It was the only time I ever felt sorry for the Germans. . . . But my sorrow lasted only for a few seconds; the job was to hit the enemy and to hit him very hard." The enemy were women and children, and he had done his job well.[68] Once the Bomber Command had the technological resources to unleash unearthly fire storms without having to rely on the support of random atmospheric conditions, they would obsessively repeat and, if possible, perfect, the massacres by fire falling from and rising to the sky.

The seduction of having the controllable means to mimic the self-multiplying and then uncontrollably powerful symbiosis of technological and natural forces was irresistible. Friedrich's antiwar documentation of the results of total warfare derives its particular power from precisely this aspect of WWII air war. Critics rejecting *Der Brand* as revisionist also tend to trivialize the issue of suppressing and largely forgetting the German experience of air raids. They think nothing of the fact that the unveiling of a statue to Air Chief Marshal Arthur "Bomber" Harris in London provoked almost no public protest in Great Britain and even less in Germany. Ever since the war, Harris had been the darling of the much loved Queen Mum and was admired by a majority of his countrymen. Few of them, it seems, were willing to question the official narrative of WWII: it was safer to embrace in remembrance the general Goodness of victory than to consider the terrifying details of defeat.

The will of "the German population" to fight and resist to the bitter end was not broken by the increasing terror of air raids because it had never existed. At first incremental, the force of the attacks and number of fatalities grew dramatically from 1943 on, exponentially in the last two years of the war, when it was clear that Germany was defeated. The Allies' adoption of "moral bombing" in 1942, erasing the separation line between front and homeland, would have dawned slowly on German civilians who from then on lived under the conditions of total war, open to mass destruction as "the Nazi enemy." At the Casablanca conference in January 1943, the combined chiefs of staff agreed on the demand for Germany's unconditional surrender, which would be achieved by the "increasing destruction and paralysis of the German military, industrial, and economic system" and the "systematic undermining," by means of increasing air raids, of the German people's "will to fight to the point of a decisive weakening of their capability for armed resistance."[69] There was no need to be apprehensive: "the Germans," overwhelmingly women with small children, were exhausted to the point of numbness by the air war waged against them. They had in many cases disapproved of the war forced on them by the Nazi regime and were of no mind to offer any resistance.

In the penultimate chapter, "Wir," Friedrich documents the growing exhaustion that in the end destroyed the sense of community that many people had experienced in the earlier years of the air war. The desire to demonstrate "gute Haltung," composure, consideration, and efficiency in the face of attacks that unleashed raging fires on increasingly helpless civilians worked as long as there was still a sense of possible action. Friedrich quotes a report of an attack in July 1942, when the number of dead was 337, the *Flak* had shot down twenty-nine bombers, and the citizens of Hamburg were disappointed because they had expected better protection: "all of Hamburg showed solidarity; everyone helped to pull people out from under the rubble, moved furniture out of endangered apartments, sprayed water, threw sand, tore down barracks and fences, the notorious fire bridges. Women and girls showed their willingness to tackle any task, no matter how hard or unfamiliar."[70] In late 1943 the situation looks quite different: the dark mood of depression, the hundreds of thousands of homeless in Berlin after the last attacks, which are getting worse and worse. Official statements still praise the "gute Haltung" and "discipline" of air raid survivors, *Ausgebombte*. But Friedrich, summarizing witness reports, comments that this "discipline" hides a "Trance": "Rescue activities, at first energetic, are on the decrease; people no longer help each other to pull out people buried under the rubble, much less to remove furniture."

Only *Hitlerjungen* were still eager to help: "They throw themselves into battling the fires, hold out for 24 hours, are blackened like negroes, have neither slept nor eaten a real meal. They are unsurpassed as dispatch-runners and lose their lives working anti-aircraft cannons. There are still 120,000 children in Berlin who could not be evacuated because there is no room for them; the schools have closed; ten thousands of pupils are loitering in the streets and join bands." The only men left in Berlin are *Ostarbeiter* and prisoners; the women are falling apart, even the party is concerned about the increasing nervousness of women no longer able to bear the sounds of air war, the insistent wailing of sirens and ominous hisses of bombs about to crash into houses. Even professional radio announcers show stress, stumbling over words; everyone is compulsively talking about air war.[71] The chapter concludes with reports of the general sentiment in Hamburg: "'The Brits should come now and make an end of it.'" The 197th of 213 air raids takes place on March 11, 1945. Ten thousand bombs are dropped, killing ninety-seven persons. In the sharp whistling sound made by their rushing from the sky, a middle-class Hamburg woman says: "if only it hit me. I have nothing left, no purpose in this world. I have given them all my children, my husband has been killed at the front; and now all these sacrifices are in vain. That is the worst."[72] The issue for Friedrich is not the suffering of the German civilian population but the Allies' responsibility for having stripped them of their civilian status in order to expose them to the extreme destructiveness of a new kind of air war. At the end of this war, not even the victors should have been able to claim innocence; if they claimed it with a vengeance, it was to protect it once and for all from all critical questions.

Mass killing by air raids eventually required mass graves—a kind of burial for *Bombenopfer* that Hitler had strictly forbidden in February 1944 to distinguish his war of annihilation from that of the Allies: German civilians were entitled in death to the dignity of their own graves, in contrast to the enemies of the Third Reich. But by the end of the year, the grotesque promise of this entitlement had become a moot question; the ever more intensive annihilation bombing had made mass burial for German *Bombenopfer* a common practice. Six thousand victims of an air raid on the tiny medieval town of Heilbronn on December 4 were buried with the help of a big dredger: 3,500 corpses to a deep ditch in layers of ten to fourteen. The same machine was sent eleven weeks later by the mayor of Heilbronn to the city of Pforzheim, which had accepted the army's help in taking care of 20,000 corpses with flamethrowers. This kind of burial corresponds logically with the annihilation killing of "moral bombing": collective denial of the right to live meant denial of the right to an individual death.[73] The thousand children that were stacked into the Heilbronn mass grave, all of them under ten, had not been bombed for punishment. Bomber Harris, Friedrich writes, "did not impute their guilt in any way. Churchill only insisted that they could not claim any rights. They would have had these rights in WWI; no longer in WWII. Hitler, Churchill, and Roosevelt had taken them away."[74] That was their just treatment as Nazi Germans.

Occasional attempts at revenge in the last year of the war came in the form of lynching Allied pilots, especially the notorious *Tiefflieger,* who made a sport of randomly killing women and children from their low-flying planes. They were young, skilled pilots used to killing, and loving the excitement of shooting from up close at the Nazi enemy. Friedrich has an account of eight downed American pilots who were taken to a POW camp in Oberursel, a small medieval town close to Frankfurt by three *Luftwaffe* pilots. On their way through a village, a route necessitated by air raid damage, they were attacked by a crowd wielding sticks and shovels; outnumbered, the guards did not intervene. An air raid stopped the villagers, but six of the men were already dead. The two survivors fled and were caught by a policeman, who escorted them to the safety of the POW camp. In the last year of the war, more than a hundred Allied pilots were lynched, sometimes with the help of German soldiers. But policemen and soldiers also managed to protect them from civilians enraged by their own defenselessness under the killing skies.[75]

Zero hour for the second attack on Dresden on February 13–14, 1945, was 1:30 A.M. When the master bomber arrived at 1:28 A.M., he found a violent firestorm raging in the center of the city and huge clouds of smoke over large areas that made it impossible to clearly identify aiming points. The deputy master bomber, arriving two minutes later, agreed to concentrate the main force of the second bombing on areas not so far affected by the first attack. Afterward, the bomb-aimer of Wing Commander Le Good's crew wrote in his logbook: "13/14th February, 1945, Dresden. Nil defenses, six red target indicators and four 500-pound H.E. bombs carried; smoke from the first attack prevented marking aiming point." His Australian wing commander noted, "Clear over target, practically the whole town in flames. No flak."[76]

The most striking, most important aspect of Friedrich's argument is its focus on the nearly absolute military and political defenselessness of the German civilian population at the end-stage of WWII. It came with the use of a new incendiary technology based on a new concept of human superfluity. The controlled unleashing of uncontrollable firestorms with the intent to kill large numbers of German civilians and reduce to ashes most German cities signified a qualitative change in warfare. Together with the firebombing in Japan, it prepared for the decision to use the atomic bomb. The same decision would have been made by Hitler had he had the resources to do so; but he did not. And so the person who did make this decision would be the American president Truman. His memory has remained curiously blameless even though the reasons for his extraordinary act seem as problematic today as they were six decades ago. Started by the Nazi regime and then helped along by the Allies, WWII would introduce new, heretofore unimaginable methods of mass destruction. The Allies' victory was absolute, and it made them collectively innocent; yet their leaders, too, had made terribly wrong decisions. Stripping the whole German civilian population of its civilian status was one of them, and it was aggravated by adding the burden of collective guilt. The perfection of their own innocence could be maintained only if all Germans were declared guilty.

Friedrich has been accused of establishing, at least by implication, a parallel between the Allied air war against German civilians and the Holocaust in his powerful narrative of firebombing—a parallel that could only mean hyper-apologeticism. Over the last half century, this accusation has become the most powerful cliché in arguments for an enduring uniqueness of the Holocaust; and it was to be expected in the case of a book such as *Der Brand*. Reasonably unprejudiced readers would understand that Friedrich is interested neither in upholding nor in questioning a by now greatly politicized hierarchy of suffering. A military historian, he wanted to clarify some of the terrifying radical changes in modern warfare made during WWII of which both the Allied air war and the Nazi regime's "final solution" are a part. Allied fire-bombing was intended to result in spectacularly cruel and gruesome mass killings that fit terms such as "annihilation" or "massacre."

For Friedrich, the extreme scale and strategies of Allied mass de-structions are on a level that is still partly incomprehensible, and in that aspect similar to the scale and strategies of National-socialist persecu-tions. The issue for him was not, as it was for Sebald, the relative pau-city of their documentation, even less a competitive comparison of the degree and significance of suffering. It was, rather, the particular feroc-ity of Allied air raids and the problem of their political and military immorality. Like the Holocaust, if in a different way, they raise seri-ous questions about our common humanity. Friedrich may be skeptical about arguments supporting a uniqueness of the Holocaust; many his-torians are, though the enduring political power of such supra-histori-cal and supra-rational singularity is undeniable. If Friedrich has put his discussion of firebombing on a level of historical significance and seri-ousness parallel to that of Nazi warfare, it was precisely because he has always been deeply aware of the horrors unleashed by the Nazi regime. But they have had a central place in postwar Western cultural conscious-ness for almost sixty years, whereas much of WWII is still largely terra incognita; worse, *terra prohibita*.

It was to be expected that the sharpest criticism of *Der Brand* would focus on its larger political implications. For a critic such as Volker Ullrich the arguments in chapter "Ich" dealing with the topics "Die Sensorik," "Die Emotion," and "Das Erleben" (experience) are the most directly accessible and impressive since they explore the reactions of *individuals* to the extreme experience of bombing.[77] Yet in Friedrich's account, the documentation of individual reactions is by no means em-pathetic, neither in this nor in other chapters. The summary of chapter "Ich" prepares his reader for the observer's position of distance:

> The physical pressure of the bombardment is absorbed individually. Nerves and vessels are gauged by the moment of detonation. The real attack changes the inner realities of the *Ich* (self). It falls out of the time-frame of its inner clock, sweeps up the occurrences and stays behind the course of the attack. The *Ich*-time shrinks and actions are no longer informed by the conditions of reality. A psychic filter reduces the duration of the shocks transmitted by the scenario of the attack. The perception of warfare by fire is momentarily numbed and will stay in the mind.[78]

Friedrich lists rather than describes the effects of the attack on all the senses, starting with the feeling of horror when the roar of the falling bomb is heard. The nose registers burning and the smell of gases, the skin the rising temperature and air rushing by, the increasing glow, the wind that carries it.

"The *Ich* is normally active in war; it demonstrates strength, skills and courage transferred to the group. The corps is not a body; it does not succeed as a body but as a cohesive unit." But the target of the bombardment is the individual body; here the "war is not fought but absorbed." Individual senses endure the attacks individually, that is, differently; thus deaf persons have an advantage because their hearing cannot be attacked.[79] The sense of time, too, changes with extreme fear and horror, and Friedrich describes these changes matter-of-factly, using reports of survivors. This matter-of-factness, the observational distance, distinguishes his account from most Holocaust memory-stories, even though the extreme experiences of isolation and being at the mercy of an overwhelming malevolent force may seem in some sense similar. But, again, the issue is not a similarity and then comparability of suffering but the documentation of a particular *Leideform*, the shape of specifically painful passivity.

There is a cool, precise description of the gathering of pieces of corpses carried away in buckets by the families of the dead. Photographs of these buckets are neither part of the iconography of WWII nor do they appear in the families' photo albums; but the image, Friedrich remarks, cannot be erased from a memory that "overflows with unforgettable visual scenes preserved by the *Erlebnis-Ich* in a local anaesthesia." He refers to the findings of postwar psychotherapy that emotional paralysis warded off the experiences of *Bombenkrieg*: "civilians endured a *Leidensdruck* (pressure, weight of suffering) thought impossible. It does not seem as if the numbness had later receded." There have been references to this numbness in documentary and literary texts of the postwar years, and also to the apparent emotional coldness in turning away from the vast destruction to rapid rebuilding: "It would have made no sense to look back at the head of Medusa. For that it is too close."[80]

If "Ich" examines the mass attacks on humans dispassionately, as objects rather than subjects of physical and psychological study, the following and concluding chapter, "Stein," deals with destroyed buildings, sculptures, archival materials, and books as if they were alive, conscious creations of a now terribly damaged high culture. The most important difference is their mobility (mobile works of art, archival materials, and books can flee to the safety of special places such as caves, mines, or tunnels built into rocks) or their immobility (small and big houses, palaces, churches, official buildings, libraries, museums, large sculptures, and large painted glass windows cannot flee and will be destroyed). The move of objects housed in museums started on a large scale in early 1944: 75 percent of the forty million volumes held in Germany's scholarly libraries were moved. The archival materials, close to Friedrich's heart since he has worked with them all his life, did not fare that well: about 50 percent were moved, and about 80 percent of the remaining half was destroyed by fire. The bombs thrown at buildings and large immobile objects become one with the matter of the city, stone, wood, and interiors, and their destructive power becomes even greater in this symbiosis. Needless to mention that the Allied air war created the biggest, most spectacular burning of books and archival documents of all (historical) time.

The München *Bayerische Staatsbibliothek*—half of the city was destroyed in seventy-three attacks, thirty of them in the winter and spring of 1945—lost half a million books during the night of March 10, 1943, when Bomber Command dropped seventy thousand firebombs. The attack started at midnight, and parts of the monumental building of wood, stone, and glass went up in huge flames, helped by a strong wind from the southwest. By 2 P.M. one thousand people had gathered to help rescue the books, incunabula, and archival documents. Friedrich's narration invokes their moving hurriedly among the huge erratic flames eerily lighting up the early morning sky, bent over stacks of books and papers in the attempt to protect them against armies of sparks rushing at them in the turbulent air. In the adjacent *Universitätskirche,* the saved books were piling up like a mountain range. Known for its magnificent holdings, the *Staatsbibliothek* sustained its greatest losses in the area of classics, art history, theology, non-European geography, and cultural history. Four months later, the State and University library of Hamburg lost 625,000 volumes.

If Friedrich shows any emotion, it is in this chapter: mourning the destruction of a large part of Germany's now defenseless culture, he mourns the impotence of the vanquished. It is an impotence that does not release them from whatever responsibility they might have had for preventing the Nazis' rise to power. Friedrich wants to impress on his readers the terrible, humanly shameful pity of total warfare with its radical moral inversion when death and destruction reign supreme: "47% of Potsdam's historical buildings, the work of Schlüter, Schinkel, and Knobeldorff, was destroyed in the evening hours of April 14, 1945. It took Bomber Command 500 planes and 1700 tons of bombs. It was its last big attack, with an imposing target and the result of 5000 dead, more than in all of Germany during the years 1940 and 1941." The attack erased whole streets of buildings admired for their restrained classic beauty because the material of which they were built, stone, had been shaped to teach beauty, form, proportion, and purpose. The bomb, too, Friedrich writes, "was an educator passing judgment on power and impotence. The impotent vanquished are defenseless, without the possibility of an appeal. . . . The victor cannot be indicted in the name of religion, human rights or morals because he *is* the religion, the rights and morals. Iustus iudex ultionis. . . . Potsdam was destroyed to erase Prussian militarism from history."[81] England had often been in alliance with Prussian militarism, but that was not the issue at the end of the war. England's enemy was National-socialism, Hitler's Third Reich, a utopianist ideology that made the very idea of negotiation impossible and demanded cleansing by total destruction. It demanded the erasure from German cultural memory of historical Nürnberg and Potsdam, to be replaced by deterrent images and stories of aggressive Prussian militarism and German fascism.[82]

Many *Kriegskinder,* I among them, cannot (or do not want to) remember much of the war. Fitfully reminded by others' memories, they may look at their own memory fragments as something long left behind in the past where forgotten things belong; to be retrieved reluctantly and uncertainly now and then, for private use only. It seems to me that any coherent memories would, in some sense, do damage to the meanings of that past as long as there has not been a general critical recognition of the still pervasive unreflected ignorance and suspicion of German war experiences. Like all pasts, this one would have needed to be questioned expertly, and that means tentatively, from a variety of perspectives. But in the postwar era it has been judged in a more intrusively literal sense than other pasts. The enduring perception of German evil has caused the memory of WWII to be uncommonly abstract and incomplete, and its history uncommonly selective.

When in the early nineties I started to research different documentary perspectives on Germany's chaotic collapse, I wanted to test my findings in a just finished book on the shapes of objectivity in historiography and photography. My question was, what happens to the verbal and photographic documentary in a situation of extreme cultural and political crisis when conventions of perception are profoundly disrupted —a crisis for which the Germany of 1945 seemed a good example.[83] As far as I knew then, the Germany project had nothing to do with the fact that the house in which I had lived as a child was in Dresden and had been destroyed by Allied bombs in the winter of 1945. It could have been another city; another year; it could have not happened at all. I had long since become an American with a comfortably porous identity, and when I happened to visit Dresden in the early eighties, I did not even try to find what I assumed was still there: the ruin of our house. Almost a decade after reunification, when my American husband wanted to see Dresden and insisted on finding the house, we looked for it. We found the street, with its few substantial old villas and new buildings and many empty lots that had recently been cleared to be built on again, ours among them. The street did not tell me anything I had not known all along: that my childhood had vanished like the houses and trees. I know a few facts, quite horrifying in retrospect though nothing to scare me now; but I have almost no visual memories because, like many other families, ours almost never talked about the war as far as it concerned us. And it is true, looked at from the outside, (West) German postwar culture appears curiously smooth and flat because there has been little interest in the uneven, incoherent layeredness of its history. Whether accepted by individual Germans or not, the overriding public remembrance of German collective criminality during the Nazi period, and of collective guilt in the aftermath, have resulted in the sameness of a deceptively perfect present. It has been closed to, protected from disruption by more differentiating memories of German wartime experiences.

Once the seal of this protective present is broken, there may indeed be arguments for a greater sharing of the *historical* victim status. Rightly or wrongly, some Germans might want to be seen as former victims of the war, especially in its end-stage; and such aspirations may be perceived by other groups as politically and morally unacceptable. The project of a *Zentrum gegen Vertreibung* (for the research of large-scale expulsions) was first presented by the association of refugees and deportees (BdV) in 2000 and immediately provoked heated debates pro and contra. Its most controversial aspects have been its location in Berlin and a planned "Requiem-Rotunde" for the 16.5 million refugees and deportees from the previously German Eastern Provinces, Czechoslovakia, Ungarn, and Poland, in their majority women and children, of which 2.5 million did not survive the ordeal. In the summer of 2003, the *Zentrum* was still being debated by German politicians and public intellectuals across the political spectrum—high-ranking SPD and CDU officials shared in supporting or rejecting the plan, though SPD and Green politicians have been on the whole more negative and willing to consider blocking the project. A statement of July 14, 2003, warning that the *Zentrum* as "a mainly national project would provoke the suspicions of our neighbors and cannot be in the common interest of our countries," was signed by politicians, historians, and artists from Germany, Poland, and the Czech Republic, among others the Czech vice-ministerpresident, two previous Polish foreign ministers, the president of the *Bundestag* (SPD), his predecessor (CDU), the former German foreign minister and the Nobel laureate Günter Grass. The statement warned of attempts to settle accounts of suffering and called for a European *Zentrum* that would not focus on the *Vertreibung* of German populations. At this point the *Bundesregierung* was still sympathetic to the project as proposed by the BdV, whose supporters stated that they, too, were interested in a European perspective, pointing to their plans for the research and documentation of other groups' *Vertreibungen*. But several German historians expressed fears of "Renationalisierung," and a Polish expert for the history of *Vertreibungen* warned of a "regress in relation to the developments of the last decade" if a *Zentrum* focused on German suffering were to be established. And by the early fall of 2003, the *Bundesregierung* had decided that this was not the right moment to appear regressive. There was a terse news item about the official German-Polish position, emphasizing the two countries' "excellent" relations "despite the ongoing controversy" over plans for a memorial of the millions of Germans expelled from present-day Poland and other parts of eastern Europe at the end of World War II: "Germany shares Poland's concern that the memorial could stir up fresh resentments over a closed chapter of history."[84]

But is it closed? Günter Grass, who was born in Danzig, the son of German-Polish parents, and who in his novels has always reimagined that magical, multiethnic city on the Baltic, published his docu-fictional novel *Im Krebsgang* in the spring of 2002 (*Crab Walk*, 2003).[85] The center of the novel is the description of the sinking by a Soviet submarine of a German ship vastly overloaded with German refugees and wounded soldiers on January 30, 1945. Leaving from Gotenhafen, close to Danzig, in the direction of Kiel, the *Wilhelm Gustloff* was torpedoed the same evening and became one of the greatest disasters in marine history, with almost 10,000 lives lost in the icy Baltic Sea, most of them women and children, and few survivors.[86] The great commercial success of *Im Krebsgang* in the spring of 2002 can be attributed to Grass's realistic, virtuoso descriptions of the sinking ship, the fearful chaos of women and children, panicked and shrieking for help, flailing helplessly in the huge black waves; and then the even more terrible silence of their mass drowning. It was a focus on German wartime experiences new to German audiences almost six decades after the end of the war, and they responded to Grass's narrative of that dramatic, tragic scene. Arguably, they were less interested in the surrounding baroque, meandering stories with which Grass, as has been his pedagogical habit for half a century, tried to diffuse his German readers' feelings of loss—of people, of cities, of sacral and secular buildings, artifacts, land- and seascapes, memories.

In signing the statement against the project of a center for the research and documentation of *Vertreibung,* Grass may have been apprehensive about accusations that he put German suffering on the same level as the suffering of Nazi victims. For this reason, too, he created the elaborate narrative frame of the description of the disaster, complete with a young right-radical who collects information about the sinking of the *Wilhelm Gustloff* for a neo-Nazi Web site and debates the question of Germans as *Täter* and/or *Opfer* on the Internet with a young Jew named David (like the Jewish assassin who shot the Nazi official after whom the ship was named), whom he eventually kills. In addition to this Manichean scenario there is the voice of a mysterious character, a kind of alternate narrator resembling Grass, who presides over the moral conundrums of German memory. He is the one who expresses regrets that preoccupation with German guilt and remorse has led to neglecting the past experiences of Germans—"so much suffering"—to the point where only the radical right would pay attention to them. His question "why only now?" (a question much quoted in the reviews) may imply his wanting to know "To whom does memory belong?" And what is the meaning and the cost of its repression?

Asking these questions, one perceptive reviewer pointed out that Grass's topic is an enduringly sensitive one and that, though flexible, clever, and surprisingly sober, the construction of his novel leaves intact the security of a "literary snail-shell"—a "Schneckenhaus," which in German means the archetypically safe place sought out by the timid.[87] Having ventured out to describe the sinking of the *Wilhelm Gustloff,* Grass thought that he needed to get back into this safe place again. The *Spiegel's* intelligently laudatory review ends with a similar reservation. Grass has gone too far with the contorted, highly self-conscious construction of his ending that has the young neo-Nazi kill the young Jew, who turns out to not have been Jewish but just borrowing this seductively loaded identity. Where does that leave the reader who wants to make sense of the novel and not just be "moved to tears" by the sinking of the *Gustloff,* as the influential Jewish-German literary critic Reich-Ranicki professed to have been—tears that probably contributed to the enormous commercial success of the book. The *Spiegel* review asks sensibly, did Grass give any thought to the possible reactions his conceit might have triggered? In Germany? Perhaps even a worldwide uproar if it had suited some influential group's current politics of previous victimization? Did not Grass damage a sophisticated web of different narrative strands in having the novel end with both sets of parents before a mellow family judge, consoling each other with regretful stories of their (German) pedagogical mistakes? Most importantly, does not this awkward moral allegory detract from the powerful historical reality of the sinking of that ship on January 30, 1945?[88]

American reviews seemed more accepting of the "intricately woven generational saga" and even of German wartime "suffering."[89] This attitude is reassuring, but it also obscures some of the more important political and moral issues raised by the novel. Alan Riding in his interview with Grass in Lübeck, the first German city to be bombed in WWII, states them more clearly. He quotes Grass's linking the strong opposition among young Germans to the war in Iraq and to the bombing of Iraqi cities with memories of the "'air raids on German cities, the feeling of impotence and terror. Somehow the memory has been passed down to the younger generation.'" Addressing other "long-buried wartime memories," that of *Vertreibung* and flight, and the sinking of the *Gustloff*, Grass appears to Riding "most interested in the impact of a distant memory on attitudes today. And he warns here of the dangers posed by repressed memory": "One of the many reasons why I wrote this book was to take the subject away from the extreme right. They said the tragedy of the *Gustloff* was a war crime. It wasn't. It was terrible, but it was a result of war, a terrible result of war. It was not a planned act." There is nothing subversive here; and Grass's stated desire to take the topic away from the extreme right is downright orthodox. But not so his belief "that the Allied bombing of German cities was criminal because it had no military objectives." Referring to the earlier German air raids, he said: "What we started came back to us. But both are war crimes;" and he explicitly "welcomed Mr. Friedrich's book about the Allied bombing."[90]

Why, then, Grass's negative attitude toward the *Zentrum gegen Vertreibung* and the cautiousness of his narrative strategies set against the daring of his docu-fictional account of the *Gustloff* disaster? While the new interest in remembering German wartime experiences has provoked renewed German political anxieties about allegations of anti-Semitism, it has done little to stimulate a greater cultural interest in the plurality and variety of these memories. On the contrary, the anxieties have caused more self-protective generalizations. It is true, some Germans, individuals and groups, who have recently become interested in their memories and in sharing them may also have become interested in constructing, and then claiming, some sort of morally and politically valid victim status that might even entail reclaiming lost property.

This, understandably, is a frightening prospect to any German government. In contrast to African-American reparation demands for slavery, it is not the ensuing concrete organizational and financial difficulties of such claims (which could in any case be easily be defeated in the courts), but the moral-political difficulties with Germany's eastern neighbors, especially Poles and Czechs. The very fact that some Germans have dared to make such claims has set off urgent, emotional protests and complaints made by the Polish government because in their view such claims, no matter their small number and uncertain legal status, reflect badly on the enduring certainty of German remorse, arguably one of the most stabilizing factors in postwar European politics and of considerable material interest to Poland.

It is by no means clear how many Germans who now speak more openly about their memories would actually be interested in such feared recidivist perspective on the German "bad past." What seems clear is the desire of many Germans of that generation to feel free to share the pleasures and pains of recovering, at least partly, the events and the emotions of their *Kriegskindheit*. They will do that in many different ways and on many different levels of social intelligence and imagination. It should be historians who sort out the meanings of such memories—not politicians or public intellectuals upholding a rock-solid Nazi Evil frozen in time. They will have to decide what is useful for the temporal process of the historical memory of the Nazi period at any given time—now, ten, thirty, hundred years from now.

The issue of German wartime memories has been "controversial" because it has been perceived as a supra-historical threat, parallel to the supra-historical suffering of the Poles as Nazi Germany's victims. Sadly, this fear has resulted in apprehensive assumptions and suspicions rather than relatively open-minded interest. Many ordinary, generally well-intentioned Germans have been increasingly irritated by the never-ending, never-changing official pronouncements about a collective "German memory" of their collective bad past when referring to the memories of many millions of individuals. Both too familiar and too distancing, these generalizations may in the past have been seen as a kind of usefully abstracting appeasement. But this by now automatic reminder of the Germans' enduring collective bad conscience vis-à-vis their bad past has always been a highly useful tool for the exercise of political power. Its large ahistorical abstractions and generalizations have been an excellent protection against critical questions that would not have been shielded so well if confronted by a multifaceted composite of admittedly unstable and contradictory memories. In some form these memories have existed all along; and occasionally their very instability has also enabled them to bring up new questions and encourage new alliances.

The summer of 2004 ushered in the celebration of the sixtieth anniversary of the end of WWII in 2005 with connected memorial events such as the sixtieth anniversary of the Polish uprising in Warsaw against the German occupation in July 1944 and the liberation of Paris in August. The German press made much of a speech by Ralph Giordano delivered in Berlin on the occasion of the Polish uprising. A Holocaust survivor, Giordano has for many years written on the topics of German guilt and insufficient remorse, lamenting an overriding, all-German desire for *Entlastung* (de-burdening) that would fudge a clear separation between victims and perpetrators.[91] No wonder, then, that he criticized as *unzulässig* (inadmissible, intolerable) Friedrich's focus on Bomber Command's air war against the German civilian population, given the suffering of Jewish victims that trumped all other suffering. Like many other critics of *Der Brand,* Giordano feels that the book has served as affirmation of a German victim status in which "all too many Germans feel most comfortable." He fears that Evil will now go by the name of Bomber Harris and not Adolf Hitler, and this fear compromises his hopeful question whether there "might finally be a generation that mourns the German victims of air war and Vertreibung without relieving the aggressors of their responsibility." Friedrich, his friend whose earlier historical work he admires, has crossed a "threshold of pain" when he draws "comparisons between bomber fleets and *Einsatztruppen,* . . . between the dead of the air war and exterminated (*ausgerottete*) Jews."[92]

Friedrich's concern is not muddled comparison but clear definition: under the conditions of total warfare, German civilians killed by "moral bombing" *were* exterminated. His intention is to make present as a new phenomenon the historical reality of total warfare during WWII to which both Nazi *and* Allied aggression had contributed. Representing it as factually as possible, Friedrich suggested, if implicitly, a shared responsibility, German and Allied, for the horrors of WWII: Hitler's trumping them in evil acts does not automatically relieve Churchill or Roosevelt from responsibility for their problematic decisions. This is the real provocation of his book and indeed a serious issue. It is not enough to permit Germans to mourn their dead sixty years after the war; they need to be given full access to this war's historical reality so that they can really mourn all its victims. This also holds true for all the other regimes and populations involved in this war, notably the British and the Americans (who would so "willingly" and wrongly invade Iraq in the spring of 2003, appealing to the Good, Just WWII). Any serious antiwar argument has to question the goodness of the winners and the badness of the losers. The nasty young Nazi soldier in Spielberg's *Saving Private Ryan* may have made the movie even more commercially successful than its sensationalist representation of warfare, but it also made meaningless Spielberg's claiming for it the status of an antiwar film to justify the lucrative visual hyper-realism of the brutality of war.

Giordano's position has been much more exclusive: the Good Allied war against the Bad Germans. It came as something of a shock when, at the end of his official speech celebrating the Warsaw uprising, he asked Poles and Czechs to acknowledge their human rights violations against German civilians sixty years ago. He also explicitly defended the president of the *Bund der Vertriebenen* (BdV), Erika Steinbach, much disliked by the Poles and Czechs as the strong supporter of the "Stiftung *Zentrum gegen Vertreibung*." In this Giordano was no doubt motivated by the fact that the *Stiftung* had awarded him the prestigious 2003 *Franz-Werfel-Menschenrechtspreis* for his long-time activism for human rights.[93] Still, he presented as a "necessary epilogue" to his public narration of the historic uprising of the Poles the remembrance of German civilians expelled, mistreated, tortured, and randomly killed by Czechs and Poles. He also mentioned here that he had been pressured by persons with whom he felt "profoundly connected" to cancel his anniversary speech since the event had been arranged by the BdV in cooperation with the *Bundeszentrale für politische Bildung* (education). Addressing "especially my Polish friends," Giordano embarked on a remarkably passionate plaidoyer for recognizing the historical suffering of German *Vertriebene* and the achievements of the BdV president Steinbach working on their behalf. It was no longer possible for any feeling and thinking person to "relativize" the suffering of Germans by claiming that they had "brought it on themselves": "I will not be ashamed of my grief over German suffering, my ability to feel compassion and distress!"—a promise enthusiastically applauded by the audience.

Invoking his authority as a Holocaust survivor ("mit der Legitimation eines Überlebenden des Holocaust"), Giordano asked the Polish and Czech critics of his position "not to shrink back from their own history where it had been darkened by criminal deeds and violations of human rights." His statement that expulsion was always terrifying echoed one of the central theses of the BdV. It would have to be provocative in the current situation of Polish misgivings about a new cultural and political interest in the experiences of German civilians at the end of the war. But Giordano also praised changes in the current leadership of the BdV, notably a new empathy for the large-scale victimization by the Nazi regime that had preceded the mass expulsions of German civilians. His own history as a Holocaust survivor had taught him a heightened sensitivity to all aspects of suffering.[94] His concluding promise, "I will resist anybody who denies Steinbach's good intentions," seems, under the circumstances, an extraordinary affirmation. But there was also his caveat: his new openness to the goals of the BdV depended on their good behavior. If they wanted his future cooperation, it had to "be clear to them that chronologically and causally German suffering came after Hitler and Auschwitz." The *Spiegel* report of the event underlined its hopeful aspects: "Giordano has never before gone that far in his defense of Steinbach. The audience thanked him and rose applauding. Few remained in their seats."

The BdV has always acknowledged the obvious "chronology and causality" of victimization, but it might also have been somewhat wary of the influence on German wartime memories of the powerful postwar politics of remorse. Giordano's reservations make sense where they concern Polish fears of potential reclamation of land and property lost through *Vertreibung* of all Germans from all previously German areas in the East and all settlements abroad as agreed on by the victors at the conferences of Teheran, Yalta, and Potsdam. But German historical memory of the experience of expulsion is another matter; and here Giordano's invocation of his moral-political authority as Holocaust survivor in his relations with both non-Jewish Germans and Poles seems not entirely unproblematic. By now it ought to be possible to remember and discuss openly and on their own terms the experiences of German civilians at the end of the war, regardless of certain groups' political interests and politicized moral pieties. Only then can there be a more spontaneous and critical discussion among women and men about their and their families' past war experiences—that is, speaking with a shared authority that admits to particular self-interests and a general instability of memory.

If more than sixteen million Germans lost their homes where they had settled for centuries and became *Vertriebene* and refugees, this "has to be understood as part of the Second World War that drove ca 50 Million people from their native land and triggered the up to now largest *Vertreibung* in the history of the world."[95] But so was the Nazis' final solution a part of this war. The official absolute justness of this indeed justified war has made it vulnerable to being invoked whenever the victorious United States wished to justify questionable wars in the postwar era, not to speak of the wars fought by their client state Israel. Fears of rising anti-Semitism, especially in European states with large Muslim populations, have not led to greater self-questioning by American and Israeli politicians but rather have supported and strengthened an ultimately destructive politics of fear.[96] In Germany, recent debates on anti-Semitism have increasingly equated critique of Israel's politics with anti-Semitism and all too easily accused the Germans of enduring anti-Semitism, suggesting that "das dumpfe Volk" would engage in anti-Semitic orgies the minute its moral-political guards looked away. Accusations of anti-Semitism have become more and more common, on ever more trivial provocation, often self-defeating and occasionally dangerous.[97] Members of the German political and intellectual elites who have invested their moral identity in battling perceived or alleged anti-Semitism have become a small but politically powerful party within or outside their respective parties (mostly SPD and Greens), but this narrow focus has diminished their understanding of the complexities of the present as well as the past—a dangerous shrinking of political imagination and memory.

In early 1945, at the end-stage of a total war, when death seemed to be everywhere, and a familiar rather than shocking phenomenon, the sinking of the *Wilhelm Gustloff* was not a memorable event. There was no public remembrance of it right after the war, at first because of the general chaos and wreckage. But for the next half century there was to be little or no remembrance of air raids, of expulsions, of the near total collapse of a civilization, the cities in ruins or burnt to ashes, the huge migrations of refugees and returning POWs, the many millions of dead and maimed soldiers, the hundreds of thousands of deaths during the first postwar years from crime, hunger, and cold, of so many people disappearing without traces, nobody counting. To the contemporaries, it must have been a present both totally ruptured and eerily enduring between the past and the future: the past now in an impassable distance and the future steadily retreating from the current devastation. It must have been incomprehensibly difficult for the women trying to keep their children alive in this world turned inexorably hostile to the living and for the fathers to return from a war that had, by means of total destruction, created this world.

The war had hit different regions and populations differently, but many millions of Germans had gone through terrible experiences. They were asked to forget them so that they could feel true remorse for the evil deeds of their criminal regime and remember forever its victims: as if there was and would be no space in memory to accommodate all the painful experiences of warfare; and on some level that was indeed true. Many Germans were profoundly shocked by what had become visible at the end of the war. To them, in the horrified moment of realizing the magnitude of the crimes committed in their name, it may have seemed natural to focus on the suffering of others, which in many cases seemed so much greater than their own. In ways not completely understood, mysteriously, making the past forbidden territory may have helped Germans to start rebuilding and cope with the catastrophic destruction of their country. The *Trümmerfrauen,* allegories of an obstinate determination that "life must go on," started to pick up and carry away pieces of rubble with their bare hands while the bombs were still falling. I remember that as a child, my mind filled with the images of ruins and the smell of burning, I once asked my mother how they could have done it, and she said there was no other way and we should leave past things in the past. We did; and I remember very little of what was for my family a traumatically destructive past. I do remember with great clarity that my mother did not want me to enter that forbidden territory, and that I minded her and feared it.

I remember thinking then, and often since then, but I don't remember whether I ever told her, that if I had been one of these women, I would have sat down, covered my face, and never got up again. But I also knew as a child that, being mothers, they could not have afforded to do so. It went together with my early understanding that we, the children, made it impossible for her and other mothers to even think about, let alone find, their own escape, and later her own small portion of happiness. I have remembered, but only as a fact, unable to watch it in my mind again, my mother returning to the basement where we were all sitting during air raids. It was a large old house with a solid cellar, and she would have run up to the attic to get rid of the small treacherous thirty-pound firebombs. It happened repeatedly, and I have sometimes tried to remember what it felt like, the ebbing of my fears, when I watched her jumping up, running, returning as if in one motion and silently, where the other women in the basement were shrieking with each shuddering thump. They offered their embraces to console us when she was gone, but my mother, who disliked their panicked praying and did not trust their judgment when things got tricky, had told us to stay put, close to the door, and not let anybody hold us till she was back, and that like always she would be back immediately.

I remembered as a child, and retained the memory without ever talking about it, how in a fearfully unfamiliar place where we had found ourselves unaccountably, my mother, who had left on a borrowed bicycle to get milk for us, had returned with blood on her face, arms, and legs, and without the milk. On the way back, the small group of women had been shot at from low-flying planes, the young soldiers laughing to see them topple into the ditch along the country road, the milk for which they had stood in line many hours trickling after them. The blood came from the bruises and cuts of the fall, not from a bullet, my mother said, wincing from the sting of the red disinfectant, probably the same stuff we feared all through our childhood. Many decades later I read accounts of such incidents and it was only then that I saw the soldiers as they laughed; they seemed impossibly young, both cruel and vulnerable.

At some ill-lit, menacing railroad station, waiting, with many other women and their children, for the train that did not come, my mother tore me away from a howling boy, one of a group of very young, very drunk Russian soldiers raping everything female in sight, they said from seven to seventy; and then she smeared my face with dirt. I only remember being violently torn away and something unpleasant being put on my face, only the fact; and, a later addition to that memory, the sadness that my competent mother must have been out of her mind with fear to hope that this would hide me where there was no place to hide. Curiously, I have always remembered the name of the station, Komotau (Northern Bohemia), and also the fact that for a while I would say the name to myself, sound-magic to protect me in other fearful situations, since what had threatened me in Komotau had not happened when even my mother would not have been able to save me.

In the early eighties, I taught for a semester at the University of Rostock, a then very unusual faculty exchange between an East German university and my home university, Brown. I occasionally saw very young Russian soldiers, very pale, with shorn heads, in their oversized stiff military coats and incongruously big boots that, I guessed, made them walk so awkwardly; their hands were never visible, hidden in the ill-fitting coat sleeves. Their barracks were on the shortest way from my apartment to the university, but I soon changed my route because there was something lost, unprotected, resigned, about them that made me uneasy. It was early spring on the Baltic coast; an everlasting grayness spread by the cold, watery winds that called for soft scarves to be pulled up and coats to huddle in. The young soldiers, scarfless, thin-necked above what looked like scratchy, unyielding collars, made me think of my young cousin who had visited us in Dresden on his way to the Eastern Front in early 1944. He was seventeen, small, very thin, with a scrawny neck, white-blond hair, gray-blue eyes, and big front teeth slightly protruding from a narrow, bony face. I must have been seven, excited by the visit of this new relative whom I had so far seen only on a photo. It had been taken a long time ago on a sunny day at the Baltic, showing a young, thin, but healthy, happily grinning boy next to a laughing, deeply tanned, handsome, incredibly young couple who would later be my parents and never look like that again.

I took the photo with me into the air-raid shelter because the people in the photo looked so reassuring, somehow inviolable in their physical ease. I still have it; it survived even our deportation from Czechoslovakia in my coat pocket. I remember that when I saw Wolfgang first smiling at us shyly in his oversized coat and boots, I immediately liked him and was afraid for him: he did not look like a soldier, who, I sort of assumed, would know how to take care of himself. He looked very young, more like me than a grown-up, and, as I would later remember it, uncertain and anxious. We would never see him again. A month later, he was missing in action. His father, a teacher, a gentle and kindly man, my mother said, had become *vermisst* the year before; just disappeared in some snowy, muddy wasteland. He had already fought as a draftee in WWI, and Wolfgang's mother, my mother's aunt, had worried about her fiancé. This time, neither father nor son, both draftees in an even more cruel war, came back: the fate of millions of soldiers, young, middle-aged, old; Germans and Russians alike.

I don't remember whether it was before or after Wofgang's visit that I overheard some women talking about what was worse, to be a soldier at the front or a woman with children in a basement waiting for the bombs to fall. As I remember it, they were undecided, but mostly fearing for their husbands to be killed or wounded, and I was undecided too, but perhaps only because they were adults and had to know more than I. Over the years I sometimes remembered them, their voices in the little corner shop where we all stood waiting for something, and I agreed with their anxiety about their men being shot at. They were not willing to weigh the men's ability to act, shoot, and run, against the women's sitting and waiting, their enforced passivity in the face of death by burning and suffocation. Both were humanly impossible situations. And I always remembered Wolfgang's uncertain, shadowy smile. I never learned how his mother had been able to bear the thought of her gentle, timid son conscripted into this terrible war and fearing it so much, having to go, never to return. I remember I asked my mother once and she did not answer; and I remember that I had thought she would not. The question was more for Wolfgang's sake than my aunt's; and I remember that I thought when my mother turned away from it that I had been unfair to her and Wolfgang's mother. They needed to leave things in the past; I was young enough to not be hurt so much, and it was much easier for me to ask questions and find the answers myself.

Half a century later, I would drive home late at night on I-5 in Southern California, floating directly, it seemed, uninhibited by the sparse traffic, toward the huge, smooth orange-yellow moon in the window shield. Losing my favorite music station, I turned the dial to an NPR talk-show, an interview with two women who had been army nurses during WWII. Those were the most wonderful years of their lives, about which they had finally written a book. When I got home, I had forgotten their names and the title of their book, but I think that I have remembered accurately what they said because I had found it so troubling, and so predictable. It was natural that all the soldiers they nursed had been heroes, every one of them, and that they had never forgotten them; natural that they also talked of parties, dancing at night, romance, the intensity of being alive and young in wartime. I remembered how over the years I had talked to many German women who had been young at that time and would mention this intensity too, in most cases apologetically, as if it was something sinful that had kept them from paying attention to the reality of their, of Germany's, guilt. I think I was smiling to myself during this part of the interview because I remembered my many attempts at reassuring them that we, born after them and growing up in already so incomprehensibly different, almost normal times, had no right to judge them. As if that could have quieted their unease in relation to me, the innocent one, the one who had more moral authority because she did not know. I remembered that, talking, we all knew that no matter how "natural" this intensity and other now forbidden emotions would have been then, after the war it seemed to be everybody's natural right to judge and condemn them.

But there was also that familiar and magic moonlit space of the spring night in which I was driving and the voices of the two elderly women, now softened in remembering. I tried to imagine them as young women and to recall a photo I had seen some years ago in an old issue of *Life*. I found it suddenly in the jumble of my stirred-up memories; it was in one of the famous issues published in May 1945 that brought the first documentation of the opening of the concentration camps into American living rooms. The photo I remembered shows three nurses in the foreground, close-ups of young pretty faces shot in profile, nicely made-up and coiffed under their helmets, facing the future with caring determination. And in the background, much smaller, three cheering GIs on the D-day beach, a hallowed, mythical place. There were two captions: "When those nurses stepped on the beach the men cheered!" and "The face of the woman who stands ready to help your man wounded in battle is a fresh, young American face . . . strong, eager, intelligent." The two nurses might even have seen that photo more than fifty years ago and thought it represented them too; and it could have; it was in fact meant to do so in its canny mixture of the individual and the type that could also be found in the often highly skilled Nazi war propaganda photography.[98]

The nurses shared with their listeners also darker memories of their, on the whole, wonderfully exciting war experience: they had had one profoundly disagreeable patient, a Nazi POW who because of his extreme youth, they thought no older than fifteen, and the severity of his wounds had ended up in an American field hospital. He might have been fifteen, since at the end of the war even younger teenagers were drafted for the "last effort." Listening to them, I thought of the Signal Corps photograph of a sixteen-year-old German *Luftwaffenhelfer,* conscripted to help with the at that stage hopelessly inadequate attempts to deter British and American bombers, a dangerous assignment that killed many teenage boys. The photo showed a youngster in a military coat much too big for him, tears streaming down his face, one in a series documenting teenage POWs I had found in the National Archives. If he had not been so severely wounded, their young patient could have been one of them.[99] The boy, the nurses said, as if still unpleasantly surprised, had no English; one could not talk to him; he would not listen because he was extremely suspicious of all Americans, must have been told nasty lies about "us." Small and bony, he tried to fight them off when they only wanted to help him and ease his pain, a typical, odious little Nazi, posturing and at the same time crying for his mother. This is what they remembered more than half a century later—"as if it was yesterday"— about a badly wounded child who could not communicate and, having been fed a lot of negative propaganda, could of course not trust "the enemy" and must have been frantic with pain and fear and longing for his mother. When they had become young again remembering these great times, talking about "our boys," their voices were girlishly high, soft and gushy. They became old again and their voices darker and sharper when they remembered the Nazi child-soldier who had justified all their enduring hatred of the enemy.

I was troubled by these two voices in which past and present mingled so strangely and familiarly because they seemed so impermeable. Nothing that did not fit their righteous arrangement of Good and Evil, their absolute belief in "our" good and clean war, would ever make sense to them. It did not make sense to the offended readers of the *New Yorker* who protested the "morality" of Sebald's descriptions of Germany's destruction by air raids. The fact that these two elderly women would soon be no more and their memories forgotten was no consolation. The issue is not the gradual disappearance of this still all-powerful Manichean scenario but remembering it as an important aspect of the history of that war and its aftermath. There is no sense in arguing that "the Germans also suffered": all people touched by that terrible war suffered, civilians and soldiers alike. But there is sense in including German wartime experiences into the historical memory of WWII—a complex of critically researched events, actions, and actors that might have led (and still might lead) to a larger, more general questioning of the meanings of war. Private memories cannot achieve that. My sparsely factual memories of *Luftangriffe* and *Vertreibung* are shared with many millions of Germans; and in their sparseness they are archetypical, redundant, formulaic. In another time and place, they are also unimaginable, even for those who share them and even though they are not imagined. The traces they left (if they left them) would have been hard to read. It was good that my mother, like many other mothers, discouraged us from trying to read them; what we could have seen then would have been too simple. Even now we would not be able to decipher it, because we still know much too little about the experience of extreme situations. Repeating them in memory may have its psychological and, in certain situations, political uses; but it will not help much to understand them.

As an adult, I have remembered my remembering as a child, and naturally questioned whether I had even remembered those bare facts or just been told them. But I am certain that, guided by my mother's reticence, I forgot what it had felt like sitting in the basement and listening for the bombs to fall; I could listen away from the women's sobbing prayers or look away from looking into that boy's face in Komotau, for a moment a huge inscrutable grimace above me. I know now that I must have been very much afraid then; but I was afraid of all kinds of things, particularly the passing of time. I remember quite clearly how as a small child I envied my sister because, being younger, she had more years left to live than I. I think I even remember what that irrational, real envy felt like: it was like something good to eat that I had already eaten; and also a general feeling of fear that pieces of the time that belonged to me might be just cut off. But I do not remember that I ever associated it with fear of bombs, or shots, or fire, even though I have always been easily panicked by sirens and have feared the sound of firecrackers and even the plopping of champagne corks, and above all the acid smell of ashes.

It was many decades later, when I researched my book on documentations of Germany's collapse in 1945, read the reports and saw the photos, that I started to come across some memories of my own and was grateful that there were so few of them. Had there been more, they might have distracted me from finding out more about the end of the war, the experiences of Germans as one group among others. Naively, working my way through the documentary materials, a part of me continued to believe that this should have been the war to end all wars; but I also knew by then that it is easier to bear the memories of others than one's own. Not wanting to talk much about the past was a gift of mothers to their children in dark times because it helped them to leave it behind in forgetting. In some sense it was a heroic gift because these women, so exclusively attentive to the survival of their children, might have been helped by remembering more, even if they did not think so at the time. In the second half of the sixties, when my generation first started to remember, building the moral high ground from which to attack our parents' guilty past, the memories were not ours but our parents', much less painful to us than to them, a weapon that was terrible because it was so easy to use and so effective. My generation's innocence was a fiction to punish our parents for their attempts at preserving it: "your lives, untainted, will be different from ours."

I never understood my generation's need to punish our parents with our self-righteousness; perhaps the impossible gift of innocence was too great an obligation. This, too, I have remembered only as a fact; I only watched from a great distance that these weapons were used, and how. By that time I already lived in America and could not forget that my mother had protected us from unimaginable dangers and that she said what she remembered were only her terrible fears for us—water under bridges. It was only then that I understood what that had meant for me; and I told her that I could guess what it had cost her to set me free from her past. It may be natural for mothers to do that for their children; but this particular past has meant for that generation of mothers the challenge to cope alone not only with bringing up their children but with their terrible, deeply feared memories of their own helplessness.

Until very recently I had never noticed that nobody in America ever asked about my German *Kriegskindheit;* none of my husband's relations, who had graciously accepted me into their family; none of our American friends and colleagues. It came up twice in the mid-seventies, both times in the context of my complaint of discrimination on the basis of sex against the University of California. One day a lawyer working for the Federal Equal Employment Commission called me from Washington to inform me that they had found in my favor—highly welcome news because at that time such complaints were rare and hard to win. And then he told me that he had been a pilot during the Second World War, dropping bombs on Dresden in the winter of 1945, and that he had often thought of the women and children who would listen anxiously to his plane overhead. Reading my file, he thought I might have been one of them, and the fact that he had worked on my case, and successfully, had given him much pleasure. Curiously, there was a parallel coincidence at almost the same time: the woman lawyer at the California Fair Employment Practices Commission who had worked on the complaint in its earlier stage and managed to move it on to the more powerful federal commission, was reserved, formal, and meticulous in giving shape to the case. I had been told that she had not been practicing law for long since she had attended law school only in middle age, as had many women at that time. I admired her professionalism and wanted to know what she thought of my case and, by extension, of me; but she would not say anything. When it was finally resolved and I thanked her again for all her hard and ingenious work, she said that she had always thought I had a very good case and that she enjoyed the challenge. She also told me—I can still see her smiling shyly—that she was Jewish and had been very unhappy when her daughter, who was studying international law in Germany, fell in love with a young German lawyer and wanted to marry him. Meeting him and his family, she liked them immediately and felt sad and embarrassed that, without knowing them, she had disliked and feared them. My file had arrived at the office around that time, and she had thought this an opportunity to make amends for her prejudice by giving my case as much attention as she could afford. I was glad and amazed that she would tell me about herself and that the issue of my German past had connected rather than divided us. I knew at the time that these were two particularly generous, spontaneous responses and that remembering them would always give me pleasure. I could not foresee then that over the next three decades such innocence of contact between different pasts would become much more rare: for these two American lawyers, I was simply a young woman academic who needed their professional help and who had a particu-

lar German history that was of personal interest to them when our paths
crossed for a while.

———

As for so many, and unimaginably different, immigrants, America
has meant promises, and, in the nature of promises, they have been
realized in surprising, puzzling ways. Not remembering much of my
Kriegskindheit, which stretched for quite a few difficult years into the
postwar period, I remember to this day how the CARE package came
from Benson, West Texas. It had to be picked up at the Red Cross distribution center in the small market town ten kilometers away. When we
first saw the large carton, it was tied to the bar of the bicycle, and our
mother was holding on to it as she swayed into the muddy slippery
yard. She seemed excited, as she was not even trying to avoid the most
treacherous chain of puddles. The family bicycle, squeaky with rust, its
tires made of patches, was our most glamorous possession; without it,
mother said, we would be even more hopelessly moored, lost in this tiny
village. It had traces of bright red paint and a thrilling shrill bell that
impressed the village geese I feared most, even more than the dogs. Wet
and shivering, mother patted the bike.

She was still holding on to the package, which was lumpy from the
rain, calling that we should close the window and let her carry the package in because she did not want us to get our feet dirty. That meant
pumping, carrying water in our two small cooking pots, warming it up
on the stove and finding rags to dry our feet. Everything seemed hard to
do and harder to find, and I was wondering how she had managed to
get the piece of rope to tie the package to the bike. She did not have it
when she left; and always suspecting that things would not work out
somehow as she always assured us, I had been almost sure that the
package would not make it to us. For days we had been talking about it,
speculating what it might contain. Mother maintained that it would be
lovely to get it in any case because it meant that people in faraway
places were thinking of us kindly. This, she said, was a promise of better
times to come. I thought it unlikely: how could they even know about
"us," much less think of us kindly? Who in the world, not even our
father, knew about us? Nor we about him; or the rest of the family. And
even if they did, how could that give us hope? As mother remembered, I
did not keep the objections to myself. I thought I had because she looked
so cold and exhausted. But she did not seem to have minded. In fact, she
sometimes reminded me of them as examples of my early suspicion that
things would most probably not work out. Sometimes I thought she

considered my shrinking away from promises with a degree of approval, certainly of amused fondness: the first word I ever said was "no"—an indication of future reactions and quite suitable for the times, she said. Trying to survive with the four of us, she would not have had the luxury of that "no."

I remember the fire we made in the stove, using up almost all the wood we had gathered the previous day to dry out mother and the package and celebrate their arrival. The festive sheath of warm air protected us for a little while against the familiar acrid smell rising from the skin of the long black stove pipe. The package sat on the table, inscrutable under its wet dark brown wrapping paper. First we looked up "Texas" on one of the maps that were leaning rolled up against the walls of the one-room schoolhouse to which we had been assigned for the time being. My mother believed in orientation—too much, as I remember thinking then: you have to know where you are or at least what questions to ask to find your way back. But what if you didn't, couldn't? If people didn't answer? If you are truly lost? Well, you must always try. Texas was easy to find; its emptiness occupied a large chunk of the huge United States. The name of the place where the people lived who had sent the package on its way, thinking of us, was not on the map. Probably too small, my mother said; or God knows how old these maps were. People were moving around more in that part of America; perhaps it was a newer town.

I remember asking, why would they move around if they did not have to? Where would they live, if they left their old place and all their things? They would build new houses and perhaps buy new things, my mother said. But who would build the houses and with what? There were men who had tools and they could buy wood—many houses in America were built of wood, and quickly, families and friends working together, she thought. It was all very different from where and how we had lived and especially from how we lived now. Families were together; there were fathers and older brothers, uncles, cousins.

It seems to me curious now, remembering, that we were so patient, letting the package sit there, all its promises still intact, as my mother warming up to them wanted it. But we were. We were amazingly "good," sober children, easily satisfied, adjusting without much hope to what we were told had to be our life for the time being. Children adapt more easily than grown-ups; their past has more room for losses. Not me, I would most likely have thought. I wanted my Steiff dachshund back and my book. When we left what was left of our house, the two older children were each allowed to carry two small favorite objects;

somehow they also vanished, like the house and everything in it. But she remembered that not even I complained much; even being the eldest and remembering more. Somehow I understood, she must have thought; I didn't, I thought then and think now.

There was a letter for us in the package: Mrs. Anderson wrote that she had three young daughters and thanked God that their family had a good home and did not have to be refugees. She had tried to imagine what it would be like for us and packed things that she hoped we could use. There was a photo of three little girls, impossibly pretty with their tidy curls and neat dresses and what seemed to be miraculously small, well-shaped shoes. We were three girls and a boy. There were no clothes for our brother, who would therefore get a larger part of the food that was surely there, underneath the pretty dresses, my mother hoped. I remember being doubtful that this decision was fair. The dress that might fit me next summer was light blue, with a lacy collar, much too pretty for me where we lived now, and I cried because I could not fit myself into the pleasure it promised. Mother always thought that the dress had pleased me. She reminded me that I did wear it often the following year, even though I had already outgrown it by then. I would not have cried over a dress; I was a sensible little girl who understood the situation. But I am sure I did cry; and later, still disagreeing about how "good" I had been, we both smiled, consoled in remembering.

There was lovely food in the package: hard yellow cheese, some cans of fruit, beans, and corn, and stony cookies that came to life when chewed for a while. There even was chocolate, the ultimate marvel, which I thought I had never tasted before. I remember that first taste—almost as violently distinct as the taste of pressure-packed peanuts. A smiling GI, gently pulling at my pigtail, had shaken them into my hand out of a can he had just opened. I had kept a portion for the others, telling them that I just happened to be there when the can was opened; I had not "hung around." You must never do that, never beg, mother would have repeated. I don't remember how we distributed the chocolate, perhaps because I was ashamed that I thought it was unfair or because I was angry that it could not but be so.

Much later I would be driving through West Texas several times, waving at the exit sign for Benson but stopping only for the picnic tables along the well-kept road shimmering in the hot light of the sun. I would gaze with pleasure at the harshly, beautifully exposed empty land: a splendid drive, purposeful, fast, unencumbered—air-conditioned. It would be light years after the child's distress that the place where the promised better future was to come from seemed so remote, so vast, so different. Mother would be proved right.

Later again, in yet another place, I would listen to an interview of a young woman soldier wounded in the American "war on terror" in Iraq, an unjustified war if ever there was one, but one frequently compared by its proponents with *the* just war in American History, WWII.[100] Private Conny Neal, a polite, soft-spoken, twenty-year-old gunner and MP about to return to Iraq, considered very seriously the questions asked by a sympathetic woman journalist. She spoke matter-of-factly and stoically about the scariness of patrolling, unprotected on top of a Humvee, mentioning briefly the aggressive enveloping heat that made carrying her heavy gear as MP an almost impossible challenge. Her neck had been injured by shrapnel, and she had been sent home to be stitched up. She was now going back with a rather prominent scar around her neck; it could of course have been much worse, and she was grateful that it was not, though she thought the scar unsightly. Asked how people had treated her when she came home, she said that they had talked to her as if she was much more grown-up than she felt and feels. She was nineteen years old when she was sent to Iraq and had just turned twenty: "I am really just a kid."

She spoke hesitantly about her feelings in going back to Iraq, and, asked whether she had a clear sense of what she was fighting for, she said shyly that she was not really sure of the reasons for her being there. I thought this a troubling question since the adult journalist was not about to be put in harm's way as was this girl-soldier and perhaps should not impose on her the reporter's wish to know and articulate what "we" are (or are not) fighting for in Iraq. But the young gunner considered this crucial and elusive question a serious matter and extended, even somewhat revised, her answer. It was very important to her, she said, not to have to think, or have others think, that the soldiers who died in Iraq had died in vain. The "parents and brothers and sisters" of the soldiers who died needed to know that they died for a reason. She herself needed to believe that "we went there because these people, they needed us to show them that you don't have to live like this because the world is a better place, if you open your eyes to what the world can give you." She was there to help them see what "the world can give you." She had to believe that "we were over there for a good reason, and I don't regret going over there."

So she went, uncomplaining, unhesitating, even though she really feared going: part of her temperament, part of her upbringing, part of the conditioning of military discipline. Still a teenager, she had volunteered to serve in the military "to get an education" when she could not possibly have foreseen what it meant "to be at war" for the ones who have to fight it. The context of this civilized conversation between the two women made the interview seem surreal: the younger one going to where she did not want to be but had to go; the older one staying behind, like the listeners, and wishing her "good luck" and to "take care of herself." But how could she take care of herself, save herself in the place where she went so reluctantly and fearfully, like my young cousin and the young Russian soldiers, and where we, the adults, know that the odds are against her. If she is killed, the coffin covered by the American flag that hides her torn-up remnants will be honored: this war, too, will end up as part of a moral history of destruction, fought for and won with a both obvious and incomprehensible technological superiority and for "a good reason" that remains obscure to those who fight it and those who endure it.

5 No End to "Auschwitz"

Historical or Redemptive Memory

When the news went around the (Western) world that California high-school students had laughed during a showing of *Schindler's List*, the recorded reaction was awe and outrage. At the school's graduation-cum-repentance exercises, the super cool mega-star director Spielberg joked with the adoring students, while the embattled Governor Wilson tried to refute their unauthorized attacks on his educational policies. It all went into a documentary film made for public television that included interviews with some of the students who had been involved in the incident. These spontaneous interviews were the best, because most revealing, part of the film. And it is indeed the beauty of documentary discourse that it can record the unexpected, accommodate the unpredictable. The students were unanimously cynical about the staging of the event, which included sprucing up their run-down inner-city high school for the benefit of the sensitive celebrities. They differed in their reactions to the ritual of repentance; the most interesting answer came from a feisty Latina who pointed out that the students had laughed at the infamous shooting of the young woman prisoner because the way she collapsed looked funny to them. After all, they were watching an actress pretending to die, not actually dying. Living in Oakland, they had seen a lot of people shot dead and falling down; they knew what it looks like; she didn't get it right. Their field trip had been disappointing anyway; they had expected a different movie, and then they laughed. How were they supposed to know that the "haulicost" was "so holy"?

Over the last six decades, the Holocaust *has* become "holy" in the West, and the resulting politics of memory and identity ever more pious and powerful. When *Schindler's List* was shown on American commercial TV, the sponsor, Ford, agreed to not having it interrupted by advertisements—an rare gesture of sensitivity. The astonished and presumably grateful viewers took note: a high point for the profitability of certain cultural pieties. German moviegoers were handed printed rules of conduct in a sacred space (no popcorn, no whispering) of allegedly American rabbinical origin. As to the young Latina: like the other students, she blamed Wilson for the shabby reality of the school and the skin-deep make-believe of its beautification. But Spielberg, himself a cultural icon, could do no wrong. Somehow he was above it all: responsible neither for the film they did not like nor for the extraordinary reaction to their ordinary laughter. In the current collective mind, including the elite media, *Schindler's List* had immediately become a documentary film, and the smart teenager had pierced that fiction—but only for the moment of purposeful self-defense. Because she had also demanded that a fiction film "get it right" when depicting details that were real in *her* world, in this case fatal shootings. For her, too, photographic images do not merely represent but *are* reality, especially where it is conflicted or troubled. The young woman dying on the screen had not been real enough—otherwise they might not have laughed. But they were also teenagers rebelling against a film that was imposed on them and, moreover, made unreasonable demands on their response.

There is an analogy in a series of photos taken by British army photographers in 1945 outside and inside a movie theater in Bergen-Belsen that recorded civilians forced to view a documentary movie about German "atrocities." One of them shows two teenage girls being marched back into the movie theater by five grim looking British soldiers for a repeat viewing: they had giggled the first time round. The caption condemns the girls' laughter as sinful denial of horrible crimes for which they, like all Germans, must bear responsibility and which they must never forget. But, teenagers, they might just have revolted against the blunt moral-political authority of the victors to make them show "real" contrition, imposing on them a deadly serious ritual of repentance.[1]

Half a century later, young German neo-Nazis would indeed deny that the atrocities had really happened. Like their Oakland counterparts severely "underprivileged," undereducated, and knowing next to nothing of the Nazis' resistible rise to power, they revolted in part against the last truly powerful taboo in post-unification German culture, the "holiness" of Holocaust remembrance. The morally outraged reaction to them on these grounds seems unwarranted given their obvious marginality (which does not exclude their potentially dangerous aggressiveness). But because of their elaborately anti-Semitic language and Nazi paraphernalia, they are seen as a political rather than social-psychological problem in Germany. In February 1998, with the ongoing heated debates of a Holocaust *Mahnmal* in Berlin—how monumental? how exclusively focused on the memory of Jewish suffering?—Green politicians defended their argument for monumentality and exclusiveness by claiming that Germany's position would otherwise be misunderstood by neo-Nazis. On February 13, 2005, the commemorative events on the sixtieth anniversary of the firebombing of Dresden were overshadowed by demonstrations of neo-Nazis against Allied air raids that caused Bundeskanzler Schröder to remind the citizens of Dresden emphatically that "they must never forget" their bad past. Much noted by the American and German media, this time-honored admonition was evidently more newsworthy than Germans remembering, on this one day, the pity of that city's near total destruction with its huge loss of lives.

Such preemptive defense strategies have always drawn on or led to taboos. If the Holocaust has become a "state religion" in Israel and its denial no longer a private stupidity but public heresy carrying a mandatory prison sentence of five years, public critique of Holocaust remembrance and publicly stated anti-Semitism can be prosecuted in Germany. In both cultures, this monumental national truth, drawing on the political mobilization of so much traumatic memory, might prove not only too isolating, but also too leveling. As Amos Elon points out, "remembrance is often a form of vengeance" but "also, paradoxically, the basis of reconciliation"[2]—in both cases a premature closure of critical inquiry. If the dead are to be honored in remembrance by recalling them for a time and making them speak once more to the living, ritualistic enactments of memory itself are not the answer.

It might indeed be necessary to practice partial forgetting in order to find a different, less exclusive way of remembering that admits questions posed by other voices. Multivocal, this kind of remembrance is arguably found more often in modern historiographical discourse, as critically shared and reflected documentation of past events, than in monological memory-stories. Memory is both chaotic and constructed, fluid and rigidifying; and memory-stories as a selective sequence of past events have often been vulnerable to the seductions of fiction. Not in the sense of deliberately evading the truth but of creating a narrative truthful to a preconceived, personally meaningful shape of the past that refutes all critical questions. If, in Augustine's words, memory is the presence of things past, it is so under the present conditions of the person

who remembers, and these conditions will be the more powerfully con-
ducive to fictionalizing, the more powerful and enduring the trauma of
the remembered events. Since the end of WWII there has been a tacit
cultural consensus in the West that because of its extreme nature, memory-stories concerning Nazi persecution of Jews need not be corroborated. Like fictional discourse, the discourse of the Holocaust as a construct of memory-stories has become a discourse of suspended disbelief.
But where fictional discourse is on principle nonassertive in relation to a
world shared with others, the supra-historical discourse of the Holocaust claims extraordinary authority regarding the truthful interpretation of life-worlds past and present, especially where it concerns the
memories of those who were not victims of that persecution.

Many decades after the end of the war, the equation of German and
Nazi that controlled and confounded U.S. occupational politics in the
immediate postwar period has reemerged as the equation of German
and perpetrator. Applying collectively the suspicion of guilt, this equation has taken the debate of German collective memory back to the
beginnings of German collective guilt after the collapse of the Nazi regime. Instead of clarifying the obscurities and fallacies of that debate
from the vantage point of historically informed hindsight it has left them
intact, partly because of the condensed, ritualized practice of remembrance where it concerns the enduringly sensitive cultural politics of
German-Jewish relations. Remembrance, public memory, draws on private memories that can be fit into a larger story of enduring cultural and
political significance and reliably affirm it. Selecting and then shaping
private memories so that they will neither change nor disappear, public
memory can stay the same over a long time. Left alone, the normally
fluid, unstable private memories retrieving fragments of a remembered
life emerge and retreat spontaneously. It is their very changeableness
and opacity that separates the past from the present by illuminating
differences and absences. Since they acknowledge the transformations
in time and with them the distances drawn by time passing, they are not
and cannot be the stuff of public memory.

What German civilians were told and shown of their regime's crimes
in 1945 seemed to them unbelievable, but they could not escape the
meanings of what they saw. The notorious German "inability to mourn"
collectively the victims of National-socialism had nothing to do with
Freudian repression and everything with individual Germans' difficulties in accepting as their memories events that they did not remember
having known of at the time when they occurred. Now they knew—
they had seen and heard it; then they had not known, not in the way in

which they knew now. Whether or not in the victors' hindsight perspective they "*must* (all) have known"—they knew now that in the eyes of the world they *were* guilty perpetrators because they had no authority to deny or qualify their past knowledge of acts of terrible victimization and thereby their complicity. Accused collectively, unable to appeal, they were collectively stripped of the authority of their memories—an authority that was granted collectively to the victims. The purity of victimhood revealed in *their* memory-stories underlined most effectively the enduring purity of Allied (American) victory.

References to this purity would be of great importance to postwar political uses of the justness of WWII and would support arguments for an enduring uniqueness of Nazi persecutions. They depended to a high degree on the photography of Nazi atrocities with which the civilian population was confronted at the end of the war to make them see what their regime had done in their name. Whether shot spontaneously by young, largely untrained U.S. Army Signal Corps photographers or carefully staged by famous *Life* photographers, these images were so powerful that they could only speak the truth of German guilt.[3]

In general, truth claims for documentary photography were little questioned at the time. Roy Stryker, head of the Farm Security Administration (FSA) photography section that established the cultural importance of documentary photography in the thirties, had sent out his photographers to some of the most remote places in America to "show it as it is"—extreme, exotic poverty in the richest country on earth. Almost a decade later, Stryker's picture files at the FSA headquarters in Washington were consulted as a model for war photography, and the young, inexperienced, often astonishingly talented Army Signal Corps photographers accepted the moral imperative of their documentation: their horrified disgust of what they saw went into their photographic images meant to "show it as it is" to the horrified German (and American) viewers. In certain ways, their pure documentation was more effective than the direct physical confrontations experienced by German civilians on their forced visits to the just-opened camps. Women with their children, often under ten, would be pushed close to rows and piles of dead, many of them typhoid victims, and their horror was not purely for the victims but mixed with fear for themselves.[4] In both cases, the rituals of "confronting the atrocities" defined their new collective identity as guilty Germans and thereby disrupted the normal temporal fluidity of identity and memory.

It is a truism that the person who remembers something having happened is no longer the person who made it happen or to whom it happened. At the time, when what she now believes happened was happening, she did not know, at least not in the same way, that it was happening as she now knows it to have happened. In 1945, this familiar experience of changing in time, being a different person at different points in time, was suspended. Frozen in their collective role as guilty Germans, they were stripped of their individual memories because these did not fit the public memory imposed by the victors and then internalized by them. These individual memories, elusive, fragmented, and contradictory, should have been elicited more patiently and then should have become part of the historical memory of the war they had just survived. But the victors did not want such historicization of the Nazi period for fear that the moral lessons to be drawn from the public remembrance of its crimes might be relativized.

This fear that has been strong and enduring.[5] Yet the perceived need for near absolute control over collective memory has obscured what is highly important to historical understanding: decisions made in the past are unambiguously right or wrong only under the conditions of hindsight, when competing contingencies have been resolved by (right or wrong) decisions. Attempts at reconstructing their meanings in the past require that the certainties of hindsight be temporarily suspended so that the temporal nature of experience can be accommodated and its historicity acknowledged. Looking back now, one understands that one saw, judged, things differently then; now one knows that one's judgment then was wrong. If one had suspected, known, even feared that wrongness then, it would still have been a different kind of wrongness. This difference is the crucial challenge to modern historical inquiry and documentation even, especially, where it concerns historically extreme situations such as the Nazi regime in its end-stage. It is a challenge that for the last sixty years seems to have been largely unacceptable.

———

In his study *The Holocaust in American Life,* Peter Novick lists some of the ways in which the identity politics of "Holocaust-centered Judaism" are played out, especially among the young, from "twinning" at bar and bat mitzvahs with a child that died in the Holocaust, to organized tours to Auschwitz and Treblinka for high school students who "were never so proud to be a Jew" as during their vicarious experience of the Holocaust, to college students "oversubscribing courses on the Holocaust" and proudly wearing yellow stars on Holocaust Remembrance Day. Adult Jews, Novick writes, "flock to Holocaust events as to no others and give millions unstintingly to build yet another Holocaust memorial";[6] it seems that almost every American town is proud to list such a memorial among its attractions. Every college, from the most distinguished to the most obscure, offers Holocaust courses that in most cases do not deal with the political history of the Nazi period, not even the history of the war, but focus on the extreme victimization at the end-stage of the war with a perspective of empathy that largely precludes intellectual engagement.

At the yearly meeting of German historians in 2004, Ute Frevert talked about the popularity and abundance of Holocaust courses in the Yale History Department, where she was currently teaching—striking in view of the wealth and variety of pressing global issues—and of her surprise at the students' pronounced lack of historical interest. She also mentioned the special professorships and special standards in Holocaust studies that contributed to its popularity. The emotionalizing of moral issues without historical information and the ensuing Good-versus-Evil scenarios supported by arguments of an essentially German Evil seem to her encouraged by a "very American, profoundly religious view of the U.S. as the bulwark of the Good. That position is intellectually unsatis-fying and politically fatal."[7] Her reaction may appear too colored by a critical European perspective on the growing influence of religion on American politics. But religious power has been feeding the still grow-ing power of Holocaust remembrance, which, in turn, feeds anxieties about growing anti-Semitism. Novick's shrewd, laconic account of the not always desirable influences of "Holocaust-centered Judaism" in American life was written before the events of September 11, 2001, that defined for George W. Bush his divinely approved mission to stamp out the evil of Saddam Hussein and, retroactively, Hitler and to spread the *Evangelium* of American democracy. Novick researched and wrote his book in more "innocent," certainly for the West less dangerous, times—a situation reflected in his tracing, patiently and sometimes amusedly, the not always pretty details of Holocaust-centered power politics.

In late February 2003, the American president determined to invade Iraq was reassured by Elie Wiesel that "Iraq was a terrorist state and that the moral imperative was for intervention. If the West had intervened in Europe in 1938, he said, World War II and the Holocaust could have been prevented. 'It's a moral issue. In the name of morality how can we not intervene?'" Complaining about European lack of cooperation that could only reassure "the killer" Saddam, Bush told Wiesel that he had read his "views on Auschwitz." In the days after the conversation, he repeatedly mentioned Wiesel's comments as a "confirming moment": "If Elie Wiesel feels that way, who knows the pain and suffering and

agony of tyranny, then others feel that way too, and so I am not alone."[8]
If the logic of this sentence is a bit uncertain, its political message is
clear. It was better to have Elie Wiesel, the Holocaust, and the just
WWII on your side supporting the parallel between Saddam's and Hitler's evil than to go it alone, as the older Bush had done ten years earlier,
when gathering support for the Persian Gulf War.[9] The older Bush, of
course, had better reasons and more substantial allies for the invasion
and did not need the authority of Wiesel's allegorical "pain and suffering." But he, too, had to call on the Nazis, standard American procedure when fixing to fight a particularly evil enemy; so, filled with righteous wrath, he proclaimed that Saddam Hussein was worse than Hitler
—a revisionist perspective that irritated some of the more pious political pundits.[10]

Unlike his father a believer by temperament, the son preferred to
invoke the "six million dead" to legitimize his "war on terror" during
his visit in Auschwitz. It was on the first day of his first trip abroad in
May 2003, after the premature "fall" of Baghdad, and Nazi gas cham-
bers were, as he said, a "sobering reminder of evil and the need for
people to resist evil." On the last day of this trip, he praised the then
still enthusiastic young soldiers in Qatar for having filled that need:
"Because of you a great evil has been ended."[11] Rejoicing in their victory, knowing nothing of the past, they believed their commander-in-
chief that good and evil could be separated so easily and that the war
they had won was just: they had invaded Iraq as liberators. This explicit
reference to the hallowed invasion/liberation mission of their grandfa-
thers fighting their way into Germany has become a staple in official
statements on the war, the more emphatic the more the situation has
worsened in Iraq. The young soldiers were now paying with their bodies and their lives for the explosive ideological division between the pure
Good of the American mission and the pure Evil of Saddam Hussein
alias Osama bin Laden alias Hitler; so was the Iraqi population.

Like all moral-political ideologies, this divide came with lack of
critical thought, foresight, and information. It is true, the curiously existential separation caused by the events of September 11 between a pre-
and post-lapsarian America increased the potential power of that ideology; but its Manichean seductions have played an important part in
the American political imagination ever since the victorious justness of
WWII; the younger Bush was just more disturbingly fundamentalist in
using it so literally. It was clearly reflected in the 2004 election rhetoric
of both parties, most strongly in the condemnations of all critique of the
Vietnam War. A generation later, the wounds of this most problematic
war in American history are not yet healed; but it is still an American

war in the tradition of the just and clean WWII and has to be exempt from all criticism, no matter how dirty its reality and how futile its huge human sacrifices, especially the civilian "enemy" population.

The aggressive literalness of the Bush administration's divine democratic mission may forestall any comparisons. But there are some similarities in Bill Clinton's war rhetoric during the Kosovo crisis. True to his uncannily diffuse political empathy, Clinton tapped into the cultural power of the victim status when trying to sell U.S. military intervention in Kosovo where Serbian "evil" was poised against "these innocent victims," the rest of the Balkans. Never mind that all the other ethnic and religious groups had created this mess together with the Serbs and that American and European governments had considerably contributed to it. But the morally all too clear, chaotic end of WWII had bestowed absolute Goodness and innocence on the declared victims, and absolute Badness and guilt on the declared victimizers.

The refugee problem, caused mainly by Clinton's and Blair's irrepressible humanitarian impulses to show off their fantastic toys by bombing a nasty upstart clan chief into unconditional surrender, was referred to as "Holocaust" from the very beginning. More specifically and importantly, it was presented in the established terms of Jewish persecution, namely absolute victimization, pure victimhood of the Albanians, and thus for NATO nothing less than the absolute purity of victory. All Serbs, even declared dissidents if they were against NATO bombing, naturally all Serbian conscript soldiers (like German conscripted "Nazi" soldiers) were heinous criminal perpetrators; all Albanians, regardless of previous conduct, were "innocent people," as Clinton never tired of repeating in his speeches about the plight of the refugees that had brought out the best in the American people and their leader.[12] The enforced passivity of "these innocent victims" called for the enlarged activity of the righteous interveners: they could rush to the rescue and, proactively, drop more bombs. If it was the familiar politics of innocence and victimization that lent so much needed moral support to NATO intervention in Kosovo, it was also Clinton's notorious responsiveness to the right moment in political culture. Invoking "these innocent victims" in Kosovo was for the duration of the conflict almost as "holy" and politically useful as invoking Holocaust victims, since referring to ethnic exclusion in Kosovo as "Holocaust" helped to shield NATO bombing from critical questions regarding the air raids' nature and justification.[13] The official victims' pure innocence justified and purified the destruction that fell from the sky on all the others, who were guilty because they were not purely innocent.

The power of Allied remembrance of WWII as the clean, good, just

war has drawn above all on the collective purity and innocent helplessness of the enemy's victims and the collective guilt of the enemy
population stripped of its civilian status.[14] In her letters to Karl Jaspers
immediately after the war, Hannah Arendt foresaw and pointed out
repeatedly that no matter what the victims of Nazi persecution had
done before or would do afterward, the nature and the scale of their
victimization had made them nothing but victims, forever innocent. This
was in her view a serious problem for German and U.S. postwar political culture because it erased all consideration of historical agency for
Jews and other groups who could lay claim to victimization. Sixty years
after Czechs and Poles committed atrocities against German civilians, it
seems still difficult for both groups to even consider, much less acknowledge, these acts of victimization because both have internalized the unquestionable authority of their own official victimhood. Mentioning the
historical fact of Czech and Polish agency is tantamount to questioning
their victim status and considered offensive—depending on the circumstances, almost as bad as anti-Semitism.

The amazing growth of the Holocaust in the German and American
imagination during the last decades has fed on the symbiosis of demon-
strable political power and unquestioned moral authority going back to
the Good War: the new spirituality combined with the old victimization
to create a heightened, often aggressive sensitivity to the concept of
suffering that in the United States has also supported the growing social
and political power of religion. The connections made by the Clinton
administration between ethnic cleansing in Kosovo and Nazi persecution of Jews were historically wrong since they disregarded important
differences concerning both the ideology of exclusion and the scale and
method of persecution.[15] Yet the Nazis' absolutely and enduringly innocent victims, as the victors presented them at the end of WWII for both
moral and political reasons, suggest a formal connection.

Clinton used unmistakable, if generalizing, references to Nazi persecution of Jews in his war rhetoric: "We don't want to make the same
mistake"; we made the mistake in WWII to "let it happen"; "we will
not stand back again." Jewish leaders took this rhetoric one step further
to speak authoritatively for the victims of the Holocaust in declaring
their full support for NATO (U.S.) bombing in Kosovo. In both cases,
presenting these events in the established terms of absolute victimization meant nothing less than a clean, just NATO victory that protected
the leaders from considering the connection between the dynamics of
their deadly state-of-the-art air show and Milosevic's increasingly brutal strategies on the ground. The debates for and against U.S. interven-

tion in Bosnia were also about the comparability and incomparability of these events with the Holocaust. Where for many Jews this analogy undermined the uniqueness of Nazi persecutions, others seized on the opening of the Washington Holocaust Museum in the spring of 1993 to argue strongly in support of intervention. Nonintervention, they claimed, would make the opening ceremonies "empty gestures," reduce the Museum to "empty symbolism," proof that "we have learned nothing from the Holocaust." Instructively, a few weeks after the opening the first Clinton administration gave a clear signal that it had "abandoned any Holocaust framework for the Bosnian events" since the issue was not genocide but, as Warren Christopher put it, "a morass of deep distrust and ancient hatreds; there were atrocities on all sides."[16] Yet six years later Bill Clinton would still point out emphatically an essential similarity between the events in Kosovo and the Holocaust in his speech to American veterans (May 13, 1999) after the American Legion had strongly recommended U.S. withdrawal from Kosovo.

Clearly political references to "the Holocaust," either directly or by analogy, and to the general justness of WWII as model for all U.S. interventions abroad seem to have become more frequent and powerful in the aftermath of the implosion of the Eastern Bloc. German reunification brought with it intensified soul-searching about the lessons of Germany's bad past now that it had been ratified as a unified nation and was again accountable as a major economic, if not yet political, power in Europe. For West German intellectuals who had been remarkably soft on the cultural politics of East Germany (where they would never have chosen to live) reunification meant a reorientation away from the ideologically correct pieties of (Hegelian) Marxism to those of Auschwitz. They needed to believe in themselves as upholding the correctness and therefore purity of a belief system. "Left" and "Right" would from now on be mainly distinguished by different degrees of concern for the purity of Jewish victims of National-socialism and of German belief in German collective guilt.

Though the 1985 Bitburg affair caused a great deal of media-driven consternation in both Germany and the United States, there was less explicit invocation of the Holocaust. "Bitburg" has remained active in German remembrance mainly as an offensive lack of *Betroffenheit* exhibited by Bundeskanzler Kohl when he asked the American President Reagan to pay a formal visit to a military cemetery, because this would obscure the crucial distinction between perpetrator and victim. In German public opinion, official visits to any German military cemetery would have been provocative because all the dead buried there, no matter how they got into this war and how they had lived through it, would have been "militarist Nazi" soldiers undeserving, to say the least, of such honor. The discovery of the few SS graves at Bitburg, so truly offensive to the American public, would for the German public be just the icing on the Evil cake. Had the visit happened a few years later, it might have provoked even more bitter debates, perhaps also in America. Part of the reason for the, in the end, relatively moderate American reactions was Reagan's vicarious and all the more powerfully accessible association with the "good war" in Hollywood remembrance. It enabled him (and his party) to disregard Elie Wiesel's and other Jewish leaders' intense lobbying against his visit to Bitburg.[17]

During the preparations for his official visit to the *Bundesrepublik* in early May 1985, Reagan had expressed the wish to visit the former KZ Dachau, but the *Bundesregierung* did not think it appropriate in view of the occasion. Reagan, in turn, declined a request to give a speech in the *Bundesrepublik* on May 8, the day of the fortieth anniversary of Germany's unconditional surrender, and spoke instead before the European Parliament in Strasbourg. Finally, the *Bundeskanzleramt* persuaded him to go to the cemetery with Bundeskanzler Kohl on May 5 and lay down a wreath.[18] The storm of American protests when the SS graves became an issue caused Reagan to fit in a visit to the former KZ Bergen-Belsen in the morning of May 5. There was much praise for his dignified conduct on this difficult mission and the equally dignified address to the *Bundestag* by President Richard von Weizsäcker on May 8. Known for his considerable diplomatic skills on all levels of mediation, he defined the German historical position forty years after the end of the war in ways acceptable to both the international and the German public. If May 8 was to be celebrated as a day of liberation from National-socialist terror, this should not obscure the fact that the date also meant for many Germans the beginning of even greater suffering. But this concession did not come without the familiar pedagogical admonition to the Germans to find the causes of *Vertreibung* and political oppression in the beginning of the war and not in its ending. May 8, 1945, should not be separated from January 30, 1933, the beginning of Nazi rule by terror. Still, Weizsäcker also emphasized on this occasion the importance of a historical remembrance that would enable political reconciliation.

Three years later, with the implosion of the Eastern Bloc imminent and the heated Historians' Dispute of the meanings of recent German history at a stalemate, Weizsäcker would instead emphasize the enduring supra-historical singularity and centrality of Auschwitz for all Germans—a singularity that would have far-reaching consequences for the future of German political culture.[19] Had his position changed significantly? Already in his 1985 speech, Weizsäcker had smoothly overridden all those Germans who might have had some relevant reservations about the ending of the war. Many of them might have thought that it was time to express some doubts about the wisdom of some of the victors' decisions forty years earlier. For the next twenty years, neither Weizsäcker nor his successors would be able to say anything even faintly critical about WWII to the victors; and this will not have changed by 2005, the sixtieth anniversary of Germany's unconditional surrender. Neither Weizsäcker's invoking the historical memory of Nazi oppression and American liberation in 1985 nor his postulating a redemptive memory of the uniqueness of Auschwitz in 1988 helped Bundeskanzler Kohl to be included in the memorial celebrations of the fiftieth anniversary of D-Day in 1994. It took another decade and the special invitation by Jacques Chirac for Chancellor Gerhard Schröder to be "allowed" to participate in the 2004 D-Day festivities.[20]

Twenty years earlier, the controversy over Reagan's visit to a military cemetery with a few graves of young SS men had divided American opinion. The media debated hotly whether he would or would not visit the cemetery and would or would not go to a concentration camp: well advised, he did both. God knows what he thought of the offended Jewish leaders or the easily spooked Germans. Burdened with fear of what the world might think of their bad past, the Germans have been curiously immune to the absurdities created by that fear. At the time of the visit, American approval and disapproval of Bitburg was almost even, and a small majority agreed with Reagan's remark that "German soldiers buried in the Bitburg cemetery were victims of the Nazis just as surely as the victims in the concentration camps."[21] Presumably he somehow excluded from this humanely realistic assessment the few young SS men—something he would also have to do now, another twenty years later.

The SS was declared a criminal organization at the end of the war, and its members were treated accordingly, which after the first chaotic years of rough justice meant meting out punishment more or less according to their conduct during the war, in addition to general professional restrictions. But in today's public imagination they are still collectively demonized as pure Nazi Evil. This may explain the public's lack of interest in historical information about this large and quite varied organization. The young SS men buried at the Bitburg cemetery might have been conscripts: at the end-stage of the war, the *Waffen-SS* re-

cruited sorely needed combatants by conscripting teenagers from the
school bench if they met certain physical specifications. Since their training would have been in any case better than that of other young conscripts, who would die in droves on the eastern front because they were
thrown into vicious battle with almost no preparation, even mothers
hating the Nazis' war might have preferred the elite fighting troop of the
Waffen-SS for their young sons because it gave them a slightly better
chance at survival. This was common sense in wartime, though it may
seem painfully, even criminally, skewed now. Was there nobody among
the highly offended protesters in Germany and the United States who
looked at the situation with some degree of historical realism? Novick
reports that later that summer a national survey commissioned by the
American Jewish Committee found that "the educated were much more
likely than the uneducated to approve of Reagan's visit—probably, a
Committee staffer wrote, because they saw it as a contribution to international goodwill and 'the healing of old wounds,' while the less educated were more nationalist."[22]

The upcoming fortieth anniversary of May 8 in 1985 had provoked
an unexpectedly lively discussion of the different meanings of this date
for different groups: while the Social-democrats (SPD) and the unions
saw in it the day of liberation from National-socialism, the conserva-
tives (Weizsäcker's party) saw in it more the beginning of the oppression of the eastern half of Europe, the end of Germany as a nation state,
and the division of Germany. There is truth in all these interpretations,
though an exclusive focus on liberation from National-socialism neglected the historical reality of Allied occupation, notably the problematic aspects of the victors' eagerness to instantly and forcefully prepare
all Germans for rebirth into democracy and freedom. Directive number
1 of the U.S. propaganda division (PWD), distributed two weeks after
capitulation, postulated that the first phase of reeducation had to be
"German confrontation with those irrefutable facts that will make them
accept German war-guilt and collective guilt for such crimes as concentration camps."[23] General Eisenhower's "Geleitworte" on the first page
of the first edition of the Munich *Neue Zeitung* (October 18, 1945), a
paper published in München by the American forces for the German
population, were a fire and brimstone sermon ordering the Germans to
change their evil ways or else, punctuated by a large number of "musts"
(*muss*): "the moral, spiritual, and material reconstruction of Germany
must come from the people themselves. . . . The German Volk must
recognize that it must distance itself from the *Herdengeist* (horde mentality) of the last twelve years. . . . Germany must become a country of

peace loving workers. . . . German militarism must be exterminated." In April 1945, Eisenhower had told the troops that they had come into Germany as victors, not as liberators, and should behave accordingly.[24] His tone would eventually mellow a bit, but he remained the victorious invader rather than liberator, deeply mistrustful of the Germans.

The term "liberation," however, had its uses for the victors if it was redefined. The now visible enormity of Nazi crimes, particularly the mass destruction of European Jewry, was so shocking that it defied understanding: crimes of such magnitude could not but be seen as singular, incomparable, outside and beyond human history. This literally "unspeakable" Nazi criminality was pure Evil, which had to have tainted the whole German population, which then could not but be collectively guilty. To be German meant to be guilty; the new definition of German identity was membership in a collectively guilty nation. And so the Allied invasion presented itself as liberation from both Nazi oppression and the old guilty German identity, as long as all Germans accepted collective guilt, showed remorse, and embraced rebirth into democracy. As soon as the occupation was in place, posters were put up in public places telling the German population "Diese Schandtaten: Eure Schuld!" (these shameful crimes: your guilt) and showing photographs of the camps with the (approximate) numbers of Jews killed by the Nazi regime.[25] In these public accusations no connection was made between German guilt and political organizations or institutions; all Germans were held responsible individually regardless of what they had done or not done. The question of guilt became a question of national self-perception: I am a German; therefore I am guilty.

This general German culpability would not be a legal issue but a powerfully intertwined moral-political instrument of control. The chief American prosecutor at the Nürnberg Trials, Justice Robert H. Jackson, made it clear in his opening speech on November 20, 1945, that the intent of the tribunal was not to incriminate all Germans, who had not in their majority voted for the Nazi party and who themselves had good reasons to want Nazi criminals brought to justice.[26] Claiming legitimacy for the Nürnberg tribunal to deal with a new kind of criminality, crimes against humanity, Jackson had to clarify that the court was not interested in a vast, fuzzy collective guilt of the Germans but in the criminality of individual National-socialists. However, defining individual guilt was limited to war crimes, and then pertained to military leaders, who could be held accountable since they were not immediately immersed in the confusions of combat and thus were better prepared to make distinctions between the morally permissible and impermissible.

In the case of crimes against humanity, German civilians were seen as subordinates of the criminal Nazi regime, and even though important distinctions were made between political leaders and followers in terms of punishment, the question of German guilt was indeed posed in general, comprehensive, collective terms.[27] The distinction between "war crimes" and "crimes against humanity" was not clearly drawn at the Nürnberg Trials because of the nature of that particular war (the eastern front) and of the regime in whose name it had been fought.

This would be true about subsequent American wars with their inhuman acts against civilian populations—the Vietnam War with its notorious free-fire zones, where no distinctions were made between combatants and civilians, being a prime example. It is also true about the bloody, chaotic situation, in the wake of the preemptive strike against Iraq, threatening to become "another Vietnam." The real issue here has been the nearly absolute power of the victor to interpret the law and assign guilt and innocence according to the maxim "might makes right." The unusually destructive air war and large-scale deportations of German civilians were (and are) not considered a crime against humanity because Germany had surrendered unconditionally. In his opening speech at Nürnberg, Justice Jackson had warned the victors not to forget that the standards by which they judged the accused would also be applied to them in the judgment of history. But the mills of history have been slow in the case of the victors and instantaneous in the case of the vanquished. German civilians were not combatants concerned with the connection between the line of command and group and individual survival. Yet they also did not have the protected status of civilian but were seen as "the enemy" in a total war. They all had been, and all in the same way, followers of a criminal regime who were now expected to have used their own judgment as to the kind of order they followed. They could and would be held co-responsible for not having resisted the criminal regime's rise to power and later its criminal acts.

Accusations of co-responsibility involve the question of knowledge, which is central to the definition of guilt. At the end of the war, the issue of knowledge turned into a collective accusation against the German civilian population, who when asked, "Why did you not do anything?" would respond, "We did not know anything." This made them all collectively guilty because in the eyes of the victors "they must all have known." Moreover, their denial could not but signify their lack of remorse, which intensified their guilt. It was precisely the combination of the Germans' pleading ignorance, and thereby innocence, and the victors' insistence on their full knowledge, and thereby collective culpability, that made criminals of all Germans. Since in the Allied view, their crime had been both active support for the criminal Nazi regime and passive lack of resistance to it, their identity was defined by their criminal regime; all of them were and would continue to be Nazis regardless of their former and present attitude toward National-socialism. Did they ever vote for Hitler? Did they welcome his war? Did they over time change their attitude to the regime? Did they embrace the total war? Their saying "no" was as expected as it was suspicious; by virtue of their victory, the Allies knew that the defeated were lying.

This dynamic of the victors' desire to get the full truth out of the Germans and, at the same time, to accuse them of not telling the truth was reflected in the Allied photography of the opening of the camps— "the German population" (nameless women and their children) "confronting the atrocities committed by their regime in their name"—and of the wholesale destruction of German cities that in these images were indistinguishable.[28] Where the strategists of the war in the air resulting in this destruction did not speak of punishment but simply of the reality of total war that no longer allowed the distinction between the civilian population and their regime, the victors looking at this reality spoke of the Germans' collective guilt and their lack of remorse. Whatever had happened to them, they had brought it on themselves—a sentence that by definition could never be appealed.

The victors' assertion that the Germans had brought it all on themselves, total air war as well as mass deportations, drew on the concept of collective guilt as a plurality of the same guilt for everyone regardless of what individuals had done and had remembered having done. The victors' judgment that in this huge collective of the guilty everyone was personally responsible for the deeds of their criminal regime confirmed their absolute moral, military, and political power. Many Germans, horrified by the revelations of Nazi atrocities, accepted the reality of that power, and the immediate postwar years saw much soul-searching and debating of the modalities of guilt and responsibility. But the concept of collective guilt remained something alien, an instrument of political control too blunt for understanding what had happened. The German nation had become a nation of criminals; the individual's membership in this nation meant his/her criminality, and for this reason Germans were excluded from the proceedings of the Nürnberg trials.[29]

During the postwar years critical contemporary voices across the whole spectrum of political associations drew attention to the fact that the Allies insisted on a kind of national collective responsibility and guilt that suggested Nazi *Sippenhaftung* (clan liability) and (a form of) racism. In his *Erinnerungen,* Willy Brandt used the phrase "umgekehrter [reversed] Rassismus" to describe what he thought about the Allies' mistaken collectivist suspicions of and accusations against all Germans for the sole reason that they were German.[30] There was an overwhelming majority of Bad Germans and a small number of "Good Germans" —a designation used by the Americans for all "official" victims of the Nazi regime and proven dissidents.[31] This small group constituted the "other Germany," to which Germans who had not been persecuted and had not spoken out publicly against persecutions were not admitted. Only the distinct public act of rejecting Nazi rule freed individual Germans from membership in collective German guilt.

As the poster had told the Germans, their guilt and shame was their collective silence, their individual failure to make their outrage heard. This accusation particularly was debated at great length in the immediate postwar era: the criminality of silence; of standing aside; of letting terrible things happen; the individual's moral duty to intervene no matter how high the cost to himself. But who in historical hindsight can make that judgment for another person about whose situation at that time she knows very little, not to speak of being able to share it imaginatively, as every responsible historian needs to do, at least to a degree and momentarily? Is it reasonable to expect such intervention if the act of speaking out literally meant leaving the relative security of collective silence and if the expectation is formed and articulated in a position of uncommonly protected hindsight: the victors' at the end of the war? the politicians' and public intellectuals' in the well-functioning *Bundesrepublik?*

Strangely, yet in a curious way logically, the most absolutist accusations of the collectively guilty Germans and demands for their enduring remembrance of this guilt and remorse have been made in the most politically secure and stable situations. The people who made them from a position of hindsight were the most removed from the dangerous chaotic conditions in which "the guilty Germans" had to make, or evade, the decision to break their guilty silence and speak out against the perpetrators. This seldom mentioned dramatic disconnect also excluded or repressed questions about the effectiveness of such interventions. Would it have meant a halfway realistic chance for rescuing a victim or just an a priori doomed attempt that would also doom the speaker? As one contemporary commentator put it: "Wer aus der Opposition des Schweigens [silence] heraustrat, wurde ein Märtyrer, aber nicht ein Retter [rescuer]."[32]

Should, could this realistic assessment be the solution of a painful moral dilemma, or should effectiveness not even be an issue in moral debates? How should or could the ethics of such humanly impossible situations be defined, and by whom? Taken together, the debates of the German *Schuldfrage* in the immediate postwar years touched on all these questions: the titles of the large number of essays published, responded to, commented on, criticized, praised, point to a remarkably varied, if inconclusive, discussion that demonstrated many Germans' desire to now speak about their nagging feelings of an uncertain but somehow real responsibility for what had happened. On the whole, they did not understand how it could have happened and what it really meant, other than destruction of human life on a scale so extreme that it did seem "incredible" and "unique," and certainly trumped the otherwise equally incredible destruction of their country by the Allies' air war.

The readers who half a century later protested Sebald's account of the air war in the *New Yorker* and sternly admonished the Germans to concentrate on their bad past instead of the Allies' conduct would do well to get some historical information about the Germans' enduringly intense and bewildered concentration on their responsibility for what they had let happen. The heady rush of soul- and mind-searching in the immediate postwar years, often highly articulate and nuanced, ebbed considerably after the 1948 currency reform (when the publishing and buying of journals became too expensive) and after the division of Germany (when other political and moral issues and problems moved into the foreground). But the seeds of later postwar intellectual analyses and sermonizing about the bad German past can all be found in these astonishing early debates, which in my view are very much to the credit of the Germans. There is an eagerness to understand the recent past by looking at it with a curious and often persuasive mixture of stoicism, social intelligence, and strong emotions—great sadness, shadowy hopes, and, thankfully, little spirituality. A strange in-between-time bridging the pervasive insanity of the last war years and the developing very different normalities of West and East Germany.

Outside of Germany, too little is known about those years, and Ian Buruma can claim in his detailed review of Jörg Friedrich's *Der Brand* that the "guilty German conscience about the Holocaust only emerged slowly and partially about twenty years after the war."[33] Had he been better informed and had his interest in Friedrich's book been less narrowly focused on an enduring German collective guilt, his review might have been the beginning of an American discussion of the issues raised in *Der Brand*. But reasserting the familiar hierarchy of suffering—the official victims of the Nazi regime at the top, the inherently guilty Germans below the bottom—Buruma is mainly suspicious of Friedrich's motivations for researching and writing the book. He asks "why a former leftist Holocaust researcher and neo-Nazi hunter would do this" and explains that "there are, of course, examples of people switching from one form of radicalism to another" (BU, 11). Buruma's pondering Friedrich's reactions to the destruction of Germany suggests that he finds them indicative of "one form of radicalism." He is not really interested in the wealth of the evidence of total air war gathered by Friedrich, who wanted to provide information for ordinary German readers about a largely forgotten part of *their* war and for that reason had excerpts of his book serialized in *Bild-Zeitung*. Buruma criticizes harshly Friedrich's choice of this "right-wing, mass-market tabloid": "It is as though he deliberately aimed his message at the crudest readership—not Neo-Nazi, to be sure, but relatively ill-informed, mostly illiberal, and prone to sensationalism" (BU, 11). Clearly, "they," *das dumpfe Volk,* are not worthy of information about their part of World War II, and their suspect conservatism fits what Buruma, without any explanation, repeatedly refers to as Friedrich's conservatism.

Most provocatively, Friedrich is more interested in detailed documentation of the specific German experience of air war than in lamentations of general Nazi Evil—the old parameters of German collective guilt to which Buruma still adheres sixty years after the end of the war. Buruma reprimands Friedrich for ending his voluminous study with a "long," "highly conservative" "lament" for the destruction of books and archival materials "as though, the loss of books, in the end, is even worse than the loss of people—which, from a particular long-term perspective may actually be true; but that does not make it morally attractive" (BU, 12). What does it take to be "morally attractive"? In Buruma's expectation, Friedrich "might have mentioned that by far the bigger blow to German *Kultur* was the murder and expulsion of the best and most intelligent people of an entire generation" (BU, 12). But Friedrich's concern here was a different blow, and one that has hardly been documented, in stark contrast to the Holocaust. In conciliatory conclusion, Buruma deems "perfectly respectable" Friedrich's "aim" to "wrest the history of German suffering from the clutch of the far right" and "to rescue the glories of German history from the twelve years of Hitler's thousand-year Reich" (BU, 12). Friedrich's "aim" is rather more radical: he is concerned not with German suffering but with the political and military ethics of the Allies' air war, and not with the "rescue" of those glorious cultural objects but with the mourning of their irredeemable loss—all the more so since their destruction was so senseless at that late stage of the war.

Over time, the Second World War seems to have become closer, of ever more contemporary moral-political importance, instead of retreating into historical memory. But this supra-temporal closeness has also meant greater interpretative difficulties that have proved a hindrance to critical rational discussion. Sixty years after the end of the war, Buruma is entirely comfortable in his role of judge castigating Friedrich for his "highly conservative" perspective on WWII without engaging with his arguments, not to mention his evidence. As far as the Germans are concerned, he has nothing to learn since they, in his view, have not learned anything from their bad past. Looking back at the immediate postwar years from what then seemed the considerable distance of two decades, Alfred Grosser could still point out sensibly that many Germans after a period of reflection did not hesitate to declare openly that their silence caused by their weakness and cowardice had indeed made them guilty in the sense that they shared some moral responsibility with those who had committed the atrocities. He also noted that this awareness of responsibility did not fit legal norms and could not be evaluated by a judge.[34]

The Allied occupation forces did not understand this situation when they initiated denazification. Wanting to impose collective guilt so that everyone was guilty by virtue of being German meant defining the question of nationality by the question of guilt; but the Allies also wanted to quantify individual degrees of guilt. Good Germans were easy since they had their own "Other Germany." At the time, many Germans accepted a general responsibility, if not the concept of collective guilt, nor the chaotic and eminently exploitable praxis of denazification. As far as one can tell from the wealth of debates carried out in the many public journals and reflected in private diaries and correspondences, they also accepted rather harsh interpretations of their silence as *schuldhaft*, guilty.[35] Eugen Kogon lamented the development of a guilty solidarity of silence instead of a responsible solidarity of protest, and located the source of German collective guilt in an "opportunism born of fear and ruled by fear."[36] Fear certainly was one of the important aspects of National-socialist rule, but it was itself a complex of differently motivated reactions: fear of whom? Fear for whom? In what situation? At what stage of the war? Was he talking about the elites? Ordinary people? Soldiers? Women with children?

In some of his essays, Kogon's argument was too generalizing in view of the multiple realities of the Nazi period, especially the end-stage

of the war. A communist and survivor of Buchenwald, he was profoundly disappointed by the Germans, and his condemning reaction
was understandable but not helpful. Speaking with the unquestioned
authority of the KZ survivor, he contributed to the overall abstracting,
de-historicizing tendencies in many of the debates of German collective
guilt that would eventually merge with the arguments for a supra-historical uniqueness of Auschwitz—a mythologizing process resulting in
politically exploitable moral certainties that would not have pleased
Kogon.[37] Where he argued from experience, as in his widely read *Der
SS-Staat* (1946), he was interested in detailed explanation rather than
general accusations. It is ironical and instructive that the title of this
sober analysis was mistranslated for an American readership as *The
Theory and Practice of Hell: The German Concentration Camps and
the System behind Them* (n.d.), a demonization that Kogon's factual
argument had clearly avoided but that was already present in the American preoccupation at war's end with German collective guilt and remorse. Since Germany had become to a high degree the mere object of
the victors' decisions and actions—in contrast to the end of WWI, when
it had been the recipient of a burdensome peace treaty but continued, if
with difficulties, as a nation—the *Schuldfrage* had indeed become the
nationale Frage, the question of historical national identity. Many contributors to the debates acknowledged a *Singularität* of National-socialist crimes and wrestled with the phenomenon of Hitler as "the dark
enigma of German history."[38]

Even though the question of "singularity" was not central to a majority of the discussions of *Schuldfrage,* they never related ("relativized") German crimes in WWII to other crimes in the history of European nations, not even of the Soviet Union. George F. Kennan would
later complain in his memoirs about a Soviet judge representing the
Soviet Union at the Nürnberg Trials—a regime that had committed so
many and so horrible crimes against its own populations and against
the (partly German) populations of the Baltic states. This seemed to him
to negate the only meaning the trials could have had.[39] Many decades
later, now a very old man, Kennan explained in a long letter of July 28,
1998, to Gordon Craig some of his disagreements with the Allies' han-
dling of the German Question at the end of the war. He had lived in
Berlin for several years, first as a graduate student in Russian studies at
the Friedrich Wilhelm University in the twenties and early thirties, and
then as an officer of the American embassy 1939–41. The city "meant a
great deal to me—was, in fact, largely formative for my own education
and thinking of the time." He was very disappointed by the "superficial

and, to my mind, frivolous actions of the victor powers in the immediate aftermath of the war. The cession of most of Germany east of the Elbe to the Poles appeared to me at the time, and still does, as a fateful and wholly unnecessary folly, the full and final effects of which we have still to taste. And the plans for the postwar occupation of Germany, and for the relations with the Russians over these problems, struck me as equally ill-advised." The basis for this realistically critical perspective on the Allies' precipitate actions, which had such disastrous consequences for many millions of German civilians, was Kennan's equally realistic view of the Germans. He has never shared, he writes,

> the tendency of so many in Europe and elsewhere to regard the modern Germany as by nature an aggressive and dangerous country. I have seen the Germans en masse as no better and no worse than other European peoples. The mantle of German unity [1871] was one that never sat well on them, to be sure. But from my own standpoint as a historian, I see their part in the origins of the First World War as certainly no greater, and perhaps even smaller, than that of the French and the Russians. And I see the entire terrible period of Nazi ascendancy as the product of the coming together of a whole series of quite abnormal factors. The reaction of the German people to Nazism . . . did indeed betray certain serious weaknesses, predominantly in the middle social classes, in coping with the heady influences of modern nationalism. But for those weaknesses they paid a terrible price; and I cannot believe that the weaknesses are going to be repeated in the years that lie ahead.[40]

More than half a century after the end of WWII, the rare fairness of this assessment is still reassuring.

There were critical remarks about the role played by the Soviet Union at the Nürnberg Trials, where all Germans, no matter how public their rejection of the Nazi regime during the war, were excluded from bringing the actual war criminals to justice. But these remarks were restricted to private diaries and letters, since all the journals were licensed by the occupation forces, who did not permit any critique of the occupation, at that time also including the Russians. Benno Reifenberg, during the Weimar period a well-known journalist at the respected *Frankfurter Zeitung*, stated in a 1946 essay, "Nürnberg," in *Gegenwart* that he "saw no reasons to doubt the integrity of the judges."[41] But many other observers, even though they might encourage their readers to accept the justice of the Nürnberg court, were not so sanguine. One of them was Erich Kästner, a well-known journalist and essayist of the Weimar period, and world-famous author of children's books. His books were burned and banned by the Nazi regime, but he stayed in Germany because, among other reasons, he wanted to be a witness. As feuilleton editor of *Die Neue Zeitung* (NZ) in the immediate postwar years, he tried to develop a more realistically differentiating view of the *Schuld-frage*. One of his strategies was to enlarge the "letters to the editor section," inviting his readers' openly expressed opinions, which he published and commented on, asking for further comments by other readers. It was an attempt to have a civilized, self-critical, sometimes even self-ironical conversation between equals who were all trying, in their different ways, to cope with the moral dilemmas of the aftermath of the Nazi regime as well as the many political absurdities of the occupation. The high-pedagogical American politics of German collective guilt proved intolerant of the substantive openness and grown-up tone of these conversations, and Kästner, frustrated by the constant petty, moralizing American interferences, resigned already in 1947. His decision disappointed and saddened many readers who had greatly benefited from his informal, dialogical encouragements to focus on what they could, and not on what they should, remember.[42]

From the perspective of almost two decades later, a critic of the American media control 1945–49 analyzed the presuppositions and consequences of the Allies' "austerity" politics based on their semi-religious belief in German *Kollektivschuld*. He pointed out their undifferentiated perspective on the Germans, who were then both accused of a "typically German" passive adaptability and suspected of hypocrisy because of their "atypical" public enthusiasm for the new political rules, such as the obligatory condemnations of the Nazi regime and acknowledgements of German guilt. In the view of the occupation forces, even the official opponents of the Nazi regime needed the victors' painstaking tutelage—an attitude that Kästner had thought not only irritating but profoundly counterproductive.[43] Kästner's description in *Die Neue Zeitung* (November 1946) of his first visit to the completely destroyed Dresden, the serenely beautiful, beloved city where he had grown up, is one of the most effective texts of the immediate postwar years because it interweaves mourning and hope, emotion and reason. There are the devastating images of irrevocable transformation, radical reduction, and yet, at the moment of the visitor's speechless despair, they are already retreating into the past. It will be a past that, though painful, will not resist a future gradual normalization, because the war left the Germans with "the two fires of guilt and of pain." Inconsolable, Kästner does not search for a "higher" meaning of this "unspeakable" absence of what was once Dresden. In order to accept the openness of the future, he looks for ways of coping realistically with the challenges of the past and the present. Half a year later, his essay "Reisebilder aus Deutschland," a detailed report on the exotic difficulties of the cruel winter of 1946–47—hunger, cold, lack of shelter, illness, death on a catastrophic scale—linked these horrendous problems to the questionable Allied power politics of separate *Zonen* (NZ, May 12, 1947). They responded to the individual victors' politics of self-interest but not to the desperate needs of the German population, in their great majority still women with their children and old people.

Allied moral truth-claims for German collective guilt as the substance of a new German collective memory were based on the victors' absolute military-political power. Kästner, who had survived the war in Germany and saw Nazi crimes as a part of WWII, questioned the Allies' claims to absolute moral authority and acknowledged the temporary reality and legitimacy of their power. The experience of the "two fires of guilt and pain" could be useful only if permitted to be remembered individually, namely calling on the partial, unreliable authority of fragmented, questionable private memories. Kästner's main concern at the end of the war was a better understanding of the possible connections between past and future experiences—the still obscure but crucially important potential of transition. But the American victors mistrusted precisely the potentiality of transition and insisted on an absolute separation between what they saw as the certainty of the evil Nazi past and the good democratic future. For a variety of reasons, still insufficiently understood, this separation today prevents a more sober, more inclusive historiography of the Nazi period that would permit questioning the politically powerful permanent identity of the status of the victim and of the perpetrator.

The "singularity" argument regarding German history never coalesced into a thesis, but it was considered in many debates and implicit in many German historians' reflections on the German past, especially in the dark times of the immediate postwar years. The influential conservative historian Gerhard Ritter wrote in 1946 that there "must always have been something deeply wrong or at least dangerous in our political life, since we have slid into so many abysses and catastrophes."[44] Ritter's statement reflects its historical moment rather than a determinist perspective on German history. But such perspective was attractive to many at the time because it promised much needed meaning, even if it took the rather extravagant form of assigning to the crimes of German National-socialism a special place in world history—as German high culture had had a special place in European history in the view of many German intellectuals, Jews and gentiles alike.[45] In this view, the German *Volk* appears as "unfathomable," capable of evil as well as of good, a *gens sacra* that by accepting the singularity of its collective guilt could move on from the "unique" crimes of National-socialism into a better future.[46]

Though quite rare in its pure form, this concept survived through the decades as a desire for a supra-historical memory of the Nazi period increasingly important to postwar (West) Germany's moral and political identity. Weizsäcker's ending the Historians' Dispute by prescribing an enduring supra-historical singularity and centrality of Auschwitz for all Germans is one important instant of redemptive rather than historical memory. His fiat that "Auschwitz remains unique," an "immutable" truth that "will not be forgotten," has been embraced as the enlightened acknowledgment of an enduring collective responsibility felt by all Germans for what they had let happen. However, Weizsäcker's argument does not concern historical events, the criminal acts of the Nazi regime, but rather their "holy" status at the center of German history, their remaining the same forever, like a saint's relic.[47] This supra-historical status will have to be accepted by all Germans not only now, but also into a future emptied of unpredictable human acts and thoughts. It is this assertion of moral authority over the future that silences historical memory by closing it prematurely.

The openness of historiography is based on the ethos of factual accuracy because it arises from sharing experiences and information with others and thereby subjecting it to others' critical inquiry and provisional judgment. Facts are not found "out there" but indeed "made" (*factum*) in the mind, and in that sense they are not unlike myths. But there is the fundamental difference that facts are subjected to a critical process of establishing their validity, and that process has to follow the modern standards of an informed trust in evidence. The processual nature of trusting evidence calls for the argument of plausibility rather than truth: at this particular time, in this particular place, among these particular observers certain facts seem more probable, certain kinds of evidence more trustworthy, than others. And since facts are made in the mind, and trustworthiness depends on the shared effort of constructing evidence, they can also be unmade. In the documentary discourse of historical inquiry, facts can be and often are revised, evidence reargued, the fluidity of memory and identity acknowledged and explored: historical memory will be valid only for a time; it will change in time. Not so in the mythopoetic memory of supra-historical persecution, where there is no articulation of historical time in a plurality of conflicting and shifting memories. Here the distinction between victims and perpetrators has been established as so enduringly absolute that the former are purged of all historical agency and the latter of all historical credibility, to the point that they are not asked any questions because their answers could only be lies.[48] The historical Auschwitz, with its 1.1 million dead, more than 900,000 of them Jews, will probably remain for a while an important part of the historical memory of twentieth-century mass destruction of human life. Yet, seen from the perspectives of other centuries and other continents, its place within that memory will change.

The general sense, in the immediate postwar years, of some degree of guilt in German passivity and silence under the Nazi regime was motivated by the desire of German intellectuals to speak out against this silence and educate the less enlightened *Volk* to deal with their guilt—the beginning of the postwar mantra of an *unbewältigte Vergangenheit,* the "unmastered," "unredeemed" past.[49] Their efforts increased after the Allies, discouraged by the chaotic implementation of denazification, had more or less given up on directly promoting Germany's collective guilt. In a curious way, the old authoritarian state, *Obrigkeitsstaat,* always said to have been the indispensable precondition for Nazi dictatorship, had made a comeback in a "democratized" form: instead of directives from above, Germans should be shaped in the image of their more enlightened teachers by means of public articles and lectures about their bad past.[50] Reeducation of the Germans had been an American concern for several years before the invasion/liberation and included the thesis, supported especially by the German exile community, of a collective German psychopathic guilt: collective German criminality was seen as psychological-political illness. This thesis was stated in the occupation newspaper *Münchner Zeitung* (June 30, 1945) as "Kollektivtatsache," which meant that it was "one of the most important tasks of therapy to make all Germans acknowledge this guilt," presumably as a step toward moral-political health.[51] In the current perspective of public intellectuals, ordinary Germans, with their allegedly inherent *dumpfer* anti-Semitism, are still as much in need of therapy now as they had been then. Their authority as educators derives from the dramatically uneven power relation between the analyst and the analysand: the physician who reads the patient's symptoms as signs that he, and only he, can interpret.

The Freudian echoes here are quite instructive. For Jung, German *Kollektivschuld* was "a psychic phenomenon" that he observed, not a moral indictment; and he argued against a moral interpretation of collective guilt. In contrast, Alexander Mitscherlich accepted the moral uses of the results of psychoanalysis already in his early essay "Ge-schichtsschreibung und Psychoanalyse."[52] More than two decades later, in their highly influential study *Die Unfähigkeit zu trauern* (1967; *The Inability to Mourn*, 1975), the psychoanalysts Alexander and Margarete Mitscherlich would diagnose the malaise of the collectively guilty Germans as a collective "inability to mourn" the victims of the Nazi regime and would prescribe the redemptive collective "labor" of remembering and mourning, *Erinnerungsarbeit* and *Trauerarbeit*. Moral imperatives rather than psychological concepts, these prescribed psychic activities were based on the Mitscherlichs' rigidly Freudian model of regressive repression. It was an unfortunate model in that it abstracted and re-duced the complex political-psychological reality at the end of the war, when Germans had to accept both the newly visible enormity of Nazi atrocities *and* the burden of their own collective responsibility for these acts. But since acceptance of the diagnosis came with the promise of political-spiritual healing, this model appealed greatly to the student generation of 1968, who would invoke it with religious fervor.

The terms *Erinnerungsarbeit* and *Trauerarbeit* quickly became buzz-words that proved to have great staying power in Germany and also in America. I remember with irritated fondness the many young earnest American students who in the 1980s and 1990s were sitting in my office explaining in great detail the fruits of their profound involvement with the labor of remembering and mourning, trying to protect it from my attempts at debunking this culturally potent illusion. To no or little avail: their master's theses and doctoral dissertations on postwar Ger-man literature and culture reflected a labor rich in empathy and trust in the illuminations of art, and poor in conceptual discipline and historical information. Having read the Mitscherlichs, they knew with certainty that they were right. Still, they were much more politely innocent than the earlier Mitscherlich-followers, the German students of the 1968 gen-eration, who, assuming the analyst's authority, used the diagnosis to lecture and blame their parents. As they saw it, the *Täter* generation's "inability to mourn" had cost them the loss of redemption. From hind-sight, the children's anachronistic threats seem silly, though perhaps politically expedient, like many other threats they would make later as public intellectuals and politicians browbeating "das dumpfe Volk" about their inability to comprehend the "uniqueness of Auschwitz." At the time and seen from the distance of another life in another country, they struck me as bizarre, unfathomable.

It is a familiar fact that the rejection of the parent generation that defined the identity of the generation of 1968 was above all the concern of the sons; daughters played a much less important role in this "move-ment," despite highly intelligent, ill-fated women radicals such as Ulrike Meinhof and Gudrun Ensslin. And I know "as a fact" (or, perhaps bet-ter, "psychic phenomenon") that the sons who had grown up fatherless "needed" to punish their mothers who had failed to protect them from this fate; but I never understood that need. It has always seemed to me tragically unfair to that generation of women who had risked and sacri-ficed more for their children than any other generation in recent West-ern history. On the whole, it may have been less difficult for daughters to grow up without fathers and with inevitably "strong" mothers; or perhaps the daughters' difficulties were more subtle, less urgent in ado-lescence. The result of this need may also have been a greater vulner-ability among the sons to the seductions of redemptive remembrance; and it would be interesting to speculate whether this played a role in the enormous attraction of the Mitscherlichs' diagnosis: their psychological and political simplifications should have been more obvious to the gen-eration of the children whose principled abstention from historical in-formation enabled them to simply condemn the *Täter* generation of their parents.[53]

Holocaust remembrance has been a highly visible phenomenon in both German and American postwar culture. There is a certain parallel-ism in the development of Jewish and German memory discourses over the last three decades, not the least because the official German manage-ment of Auschwitz has shown exquisite sensitivity to worldwide Jewish interest in an enduring uniqueness and cultural centrality of the Holo-caust. Many observations in Peter Novick's critical, remarkably un-guarded analysis of Holocaust memory in America also shed light on the more taboo protected German situation, beginning with his empha-sis on the circular dynamics of public memory. The most potent, collec-tive memories are those that claim to express "some permanent, en-during truth" that can become central to the definition of a group's identity in the present. "We embrace a memory because it speaks to our condition; to the extent that we embrace it, we establish a framework for interpreting that condition" (*HAL,* 170). This seems obvious (and harmless) in normal situations, but not in the case of Holocaust remem-brance. In a conversation about *The Holocaust in American Life* in the Internet journal *Slate* (July 21, 1999), Novick pointed out that his concern was not, as one participant had maintained, to argue against a reprehensible "instrumentalization" of the Holocaust, since "Jewish collective memory, religious and secular, has been selective, focusing on what were perceived to be useful lessons at any given time. Consequently, to say that a collective memory is 'instrumental' is to say nothing that isn't implicit in its being a collective memory." Drawing on Maurice Halbwachs's study of collective memory, Novick wanted to explore "the ways in which present concerns determine what of the past we remember and how we remember it," rather than search for influences of the past on the present (*HAL,* 3).

It is of course true that the concerns that shape collective remembrance are themselves shaped by past events, by experience. But in larger terms, Novick's focus on collective memory as morally or politically "instrumentalized"—determined by respective present concerns—freed him to write this useful *historical* study of the role played by the Holocaust in American life. Arguing from a wealth of evidence, he has located the growth of an ever more focused and exclusive Jewish Holocaust consciousness in a sequence of responses to certain political events and cultural trends beginning in the early sixties: The Eichmann trial first presented to the larger world a Jewish identity defined by a singularly fateful history of persecution and suffering. The Yom Kippur War reawakened anxieties about Israel's security, which resonated strongly with American Jews. The growing power of Jewish economic and political influence, together with the dwindling of any measurable anti-Semitism, and the increasing popularity of intermarriage created anxiety about maintaining Jewish distinctness. Larger Western cultural trends of basing group identity on memory discourses of previous (and somehow enduring) victimization both contributed to and were influenced by Jewish Holocaust consciousness.

Before the Eichmann trial, many American Jews had interpreted their suffering in more universal terms as that of one group among others mourning their losses in WWII.[54] But presenting on a worldwide stage the destruction of European Jewry as the core event of the twentieth century, the Eichmann trial also focused the audiences' attention on the memory-stories of individual witnesses, representing unspeakable, uniquely Jewish suffering. Here is the source of the sanctification of the Jewish Holocaust and of the Holocaust survivor as witness: it "has become standard practice to use the term 'sacred' to describe the Holocaust and everything connected with it. . . . Survivors' accounts are routinely described as sacred, as are the survivors themselves." Elie Wiesel, the most visible and influential proponent of this position, regards all attempts to "desanctify" or "demystify" the Holocaust as anti-Semitic, insisting that "any survivor has more to say than all historians com-

bined about what happened." This extraordinary much-cited claim provoked the complaint made "with some irritation" by the education director of Yad Vashem that "the survivor has become a priest; because of
his story, he is holy," and often not a reliable witness (*HAL*, 201).

A recent close analysis of the decision made by the chief prosecutor,
Gideon Hausner, to derive the dramatic structure of Eichmann's trial
exclusively from the stories of witnesses rather than the extensive collection of Nazi documents gathered by the Israeli police comes to intriguing conclusions. A large number of witnesses, chosen by Hausner
on the basis of their written testimonies and his subsequent interviews
with them, told their stories at the trial in the presence of hundreds of
journalists, "the world." In her still controversial *Eichmann in Jerusalem*, Arendt was very critical of this carefully choreographed staging of
Jewish collective identity in the experience of Nazi persecution as unique
Jewish victimization. Hausner had assumed that this experience could
become real for the millions of readers, listeners, and viewers only if a
large number of survivors testified in person and thereby individualized
the uniqueness of unspeakably cruel persecution. In the act of recitation, however, these stories would not draw on collective memories re-
freshed by the witnesses' recorded testimonies as Hausner had hoped.
Rather, the stories told by the witnesses at the trial *became* their memories.[55] These memory-stories and the modalities of "performing" them—
the fainting of a witness overcome by the horrors of his memory-story
in the act of telling it was shown repeatedly on TV and published in
thousands of newspapers—caused the presence of the witnesses to over-
whelm and obscure the presence of the defendant Eichmann. One observer noted that the witnesses were "the authorized delegates of the
Holocaust, they were the facts" (*EZ*, 150). There were very few critical
voices such as Arendt's that would question the claims made by the
organizers of the show trial regarding its authority and responsibility to
write the history of the persecutions, of WWII, of the twentieth century,
of modernity, of mankind.

And what would all of that mean for the judgment of Eichmann and
the historiography of the Nazi period? The Eichmann trial "set free the
language of the witnesses"; it helped them to "achieve their social identity as survivors," and the core of this identity was the fated calamitous
course of history (*EZ*, 151–53). Arguably, this situation changed the
long-term conditions of writing the history of the persecution of Jews:
the witness became an allegorical memory figure, signifying that the
past was nothing but that enduringly unspeakable experience closed to
all search for and checking of evidence. The memory-stories of wit-

nesses presented the Jewish genocide as a sequence of extreme, unspeakably painful experiences, asking the public to both identify with that suffering and accept its unique transhistorical, translinguistic status. The Nürnberg trials at the end of WWII had focused on the actual war criminals and the mechanisms that enabled mass destruction of human life. Their intention had been to arrive at reasonably fair judgments and sentences and thereby establish a new international legal system that could accommodate new kinds of crime and criminals. Two decades and many Israeli-Arab conflicts later, the Eichmann trial focused exclusively on memory-stories as building stones of an enduring (and enduringly binding) collective memory. It would be encouraged to grow in volume, but prohibited from changing in substance. Annette Wieviorka points out two different accounts of the Holocaust beginning at the end of the war, one concentrating on the machinery of the historical final solution and one on the victim, the *Hurbn,* who was immeasurably energized by the Eichmann trial. For her, as for many historians, the popular success of Goldhagen's *Hitler's Willing Executioners,* with its open disregard for historical evidence and preference for emotionalist, sensationalist over rational argumentation, was a disturbing event (EZ, 155–57).

Modern historiography, especially where it concerns events such as large-scale persecution and mass murder, has to create the mental and emotional distance needed to understand the *historical* events. This distance does not prevent horrified empathy with the victims; it does not lead to a frozen history that has to be thawed with the fire and blood of the victims' memories of extreme suffering. Arguably, it has been precisely the overreliance on such memories that has frozen historical accounting because of the often observed redundancies and rigidities of memory and the sensationalist interpretative liberties that a popular historian such as Goldhagen can take with witnesses' testimonies.[56] In Hausner's (and Goldhagen's) interweaving of memory-stories of unspeakable suffering, the focus is not so much on the terror of the victim but the terrifying, demonic criminality of the perpetrator, reflecting the prosecutor's goal to judge, accuse, and convict. In gathering the evidence and making it accessible, the historian's goal is understanding; and in that she depends on sharing information, critical questions, and reservations with other historians. Wieviorka ends her essay with the apprehensive question whether the historiography of these extreme events will be able to assert the normal standards of evidentiary documentation or whether there will be a more general replacement of historical research and analysis by personal story and opinion.

The control of the past by present concerns appeared literally in the choreography of the relations between the witness and the witnessed, one of the reasons why the Eichmann trial resisted and eluded historical representation—as "the Holocaust," a huge and opaque complex of memory discourses and politics, has done ever since. The useful provocation of Novick's study is his attempt to disentangle at least a part of this complex to give a clearer account of its historical growth. But his book's sharply divided reception seems based on a curious misunderstanding by quite a few critics who claim that this "obsessively" historical account of the remembrance of Jewish persecution reflects back on the historical status of the remembered events of persecution. They reject, on principle, a historical perspective on *everything* that has to do with the Holocaust and thus confuse the historical persecutions themselves with the memory discourses that have grown around and over them.

This confusion has also been central to most of the German memory debates: the uniqueness of Auschwitz does not concern the historical events connected with the historical concentration camp, but their unique, and then unchangeable, place in a German collective remembrance that is increasingly removed from, independent of, the past actuality of what happened in Auschwitz. Nobody in their right mind would deny the historical events underlying the Holocaust; many people in their right mind have been intrigued by the uses of these past events for present cultural politics. Tony Judt noted that Novick has "apparently trawled every archive and every publication of every American Jewish organization for the past half-century, and he has read what must be tens of thousands of pages of periodicals, pamphlets, and speeches by every American Jewish intellectual and spokesperson you can name, and many you could not name." He finds the result "ultimately inadequate to its theme." Novick should not have "abandoned" engaging with the Holocaust "on its own terrible and fundamental terms" "to criticize the troublingly instrumental uses to which the catastrophe is put."[57] But in contrast to Judt, who refers to himself as "a Jew and a historian," Novick is an American historian who happens to be Jewish and who is interested in the phenomenon of collective memory in the case of extreme events that in his view are not, as they are for Judt, supra-historical, unique, and exclusively Jewish.

Judt is existentially "irritated" by Novick's "disturbingly superficial treatment, in which the Holocaust itself is largely incidental to the narrative." But the historical events that we now refer to as "the Holocaust" are of course essential to Novick's historical narrative, since they

are the substance of the development of the American (Western) Holocaust piety that he documents. For a secular Jewish historian such as
Novick, the "Holocaust itself" does not exist, since it is a complex, still
partly obscure historical phenomenon reflected over time in collective
memory. It does exist for Judt as a profound and enduring moral message badly needed in contemporary culture: "Because the Holocaust,
for many people today, can speak to us mainly as a deracinated account
of absolute evil, it has a special value in a world adrift on a sea of ethical
and ideological uncertainty." Concerned about others' spiritual rou-
tines, Judt highly approves of the current "ubiquity of Holocaust awareness" and wants it "encouraged." "Is it good for the Jews?" he asks in
conclusion. He is not entirely sure; but he is "absolutely" sure that it is
"good for America." Evidently, the gentiles are more in need of redemption than the Jews.

Novick, too, asks that question, and his answer is unequivocally
negative. It is an old question that reflects the insecurities of minorities—most single-mindedly, perhaps, in the case of Jews because of their
composite historical experience of dispersion, persecution, and fear of
assimilation. It also ought to be a moot question in an immigration
country. A recent immigrant to the United States, Arendt noted with
relief that here one could be a Jew and an American; not for her the
currently fashionable, mutually exclusive hyphenated identities. When
Adam Bresnick praised Novick for having "produced an altogether ad-
mirable Jewish book"[58]—a (to me) somewhat puzzling conclusion to
an intelligent review—he may have had in mind the importance to Jews
of Novick's argument for a nonexclusive, universalist attitude in these
matters.

The moral certainties to be derived from the Holocaust are for Novick cultural symptoms to be studied with "curiosity and skepticism."[59]
There is also the historian's aversion to wringing lessons from the past,
since it is always qualitatively different from the present—most obviously where it concerns the chaotic end-stage of a total war of unheard-
of dimensions. Yet what he rejects as "the absurd maxim *In extremis
veritas*" (*HAL*, 181) has been at the core of the poetics and politics of
Holocaust remembrance from the beginning. His critique of simply repeating the irrationalism of extreme situations underlies his denial of
the uniqueness of the Holocaust—Jewish and German exceptionalism
—which is based on his commitment to the historicity of all human
experience, no matter how extreme.[60] Historicization of Jewish persecution has been routinely rejected by many professional historians of the
Holocaust because it does indeed mean relativization. Removed from

the protection of supra-historical uniqueness, the Holocaust can then be seen in the context of historical time, namely in relation to other events.[61] As a historical phenomenon of great but not of singular importance, the persecution of Jews by National-socialism is not the forever unfathomable, unspeakable Evil requiring mythopoetic representation. Temporal and relative, these persecutions can become at least partially accessible to rational argumentation and historical documentation. No moral certainties and guidelines can be found in the Holocaust—not in the historical events and even less in their memory discourses. As one perceptive reviewer sums it up, "Novick's harsh but unavoidable conclusion is that the Holocaust doesn't teach lessons at all."[62]

Like every historical event, the Holocaust in

> some ways resembles events to which it might be compared and differs from them in some ways. These resemblances and differences are a perfectly proper subject for discussion. But to single out those aspects of the Holocaust that were distinctive (there certainly were such), and to ignore those aspects that it shares with other atrocities, and on the basis of this gerrymandering to declare the Holocaust unique, is intellectual sleight of hand. The assertion that the Holocaust is unique—like the claim that it is singularly incomprehensible or unrepresentable—is, in practice, deeply offensive. What else can all of this possibly mean except "your catastrophe, unlike ours, is ordinary; unlike ours is comprehensible; unlike ours is representable." (*HAL*, 9)

Novick is dismayed by changes in social consciousness and conduct that accompany the growing power of a religious Holocaust consciousness to which concepts such as "sacred" and "evil" are central.

In the ever more rigorous hierarchy of suffering, the greatest achievement is "to wring an acknowledgement of superior Jewish victimization from an another contender. Officials of the U.S. Holocaust Memorial Museum tell, with great satisfaction, a story of black youngsters learning of the Holocaust and saying, 'God, we thought we had it bad.'"[63] This lesson underlines his point that little of use can be learned from the Holocaust as long as the guardians of its remembrance insist on the absolute uniqueness and therefore unquestioned superiority of Jewish suffering. If Novick shares with Hannah Arendt the insight that extreme situations do not necessarily reveal the truth about the human condition, he also shares with her a secular abstinence from the certainties of evil. Like Novick, Arendt did not believe in the usefulness of an existential "evil" but was curious about its cultural status and meanings.

Over the last four decades, mainstream Western culture has become more dependent on absolute certainties as they are amply provided in the Manichean scenarios of the Holocaust. At the same time, the debates of these issues have become much more guarded. Judt's self-protective rejection of Novick's arguments is mainstream, preaching to the converted: large general educated audiences to whom Novick's historical approach is simply heretical. It is a heresy that can best be dealt with by not making it a public issue in the way Arendt's arguments in *Eichmann in Jerusalem* became public. The fact that Novick's book has not been debated on the American Public Broadcasting System is quite instructive, because that system, with its increasing investment in quality talk shows, has become, in the last ten years, the arbiter of mainstream culturally "correct" opinion, including Holocaust remembrance. The virulence of the attacks on the Eichmann book were certainly painful for Arendt, but they also ensured that her argument would not go away. It was then, as it is now, an importantly secular argument—as is Novick's. But where she was confronted with the still raw emotion of her group's experience of precariousness after mass destruction, Novick has had to confront a by now monumental Holocaust discourse that has successfully ritualized that precariousness and, at least for the time being, may very well resist all attempts at historicization. The power of collective memory, it seems, has become much more important than the remembered events, a situation that Arendt did not yet have to deal with.

This shift in emphasis would have motivated Novick to document the circular dynamics of collective memory. It was not the aim of his inquiry to explore the relation between collective (public) and individual (private) memory. Yet this relation may in certain ways be relevant to the question underlying his argument: why does the qualitative difference of the past seem to hold so little interest for most people today, intellectuals very much included? This lack of interest has arguably made possible the currently dominant conjunction between largely unchecked collective memory discourses and definitions of group identity—a conjunction that in turn has weakened whatever is left of historical curiosity and imagination. The inevitable and inexorable separations created by time passing have never been more potent than now, when public memories of victimization have become ever more politicized and ever less tolerant of the remembered events' historical contextualization and differentiation.[64] The general tendency since the end of the war to embrace all "official" survivor memoirs, no matter what they actually say or how they say it, has had important, if perhaps unforeseeable, consequences. Among other things it has upheld an exclusive and inhibited cultural memory of the in many ways still obscure, incompletely understood political and generational catastrophe of WWII.

On a visit to Berlin in the summer of 1999, the American literary
historian Stephen Greenblatt was struck by the presence of ghosts all
around him, a strange and powerful sensation he described in a *New
York Times* article, "Ghosts in Berlin." He was sure that many visitors
to the city would share this feeling, "certainly all Jews." He might have
heard the eerily hushed recitation of the names of murdered Jews, un-
evenly punctuated sounds flowing continuously out of an installation
on the now again chic Friedrichstrasse. I heard them on a visit at about
the same time, was not sure what to think, and am less certain than
Greenblatt about "all Jews." But there is John Updike, visiting Berlin
and admiring its art museums, who also felt Nazi Germany right underneath the "deceptively smooth scab" of an "Americanized, prospering,
democratic" country. His verdict: "an American visitor to Germany
does not have to be Jewish to feel there a frisson, a shudder of fascination at the abyss beneath the carpet."[65] It is curious that both the literary critic and the creative writer did not distinguish between (historical)
reality and representation. Berlin is heavily populated by all manner of
signposts to the guilty memory of dead Jews who once lived here—
representations of ghosts to assuage the appropriately guilty conscience
of the living. Berlin is all about the living: their ingenuity, their greed,
their power—their treasure of the most important dead.

Greenblatt was negatively impressed by the dedication "Dem
Deutschen Volke" on the façade of the newly opened parliament building and the "triumphal" *Brandenburger Tor.* Looking at the desolate,
muddy field set aside for the Holocaust *Mahnmal*—the *Bundestag* had
finally decided on the American architect Peter Eisenman in June 1999
—Greenblatt thought it best to simply surrender to nature this space in
the heart of contemporary Berlin. A German acquaintance familiar with
the strategies of Holocaust topography suggested to Greenblatt a simple
sign to go with the emptiness of uncontrolled, undifferentiated natural
growth. It should read, "Despite all their efforts, the German people
have failed to create an appropriate memorial for their Jewish victims."
The exotic wilderness in the center of a thriving metropolis would be
the most appropriate *Mahnmal* of German collective failure to redeem
the promises of remorse and atonement.

The completed *Mahnmal* will be quite different from Greenblatt's
"anti-design," and, emphatically, it will not admit to the failure of redemption. In August 1988, the colorful, opinionated, self-invented
"Jewish" journalist Lea Rosh (she may or may not have had a Jewish
grandfather) had called for a "monument for the murdered Jews of

Europe": "I demand a *Mahnmal* from this land of the *Täter.*"[66] An energetic talk-show moderator and "moral entrepreneur," she immediately gathered the support of SPD politicians and public intellectuals, among them Willy Brandt, Günter Grass, Otto Schily, Walter Jens, and also several well-known and well-traveled East German intellectuals such as Heiner Müller and Christa Wolf. An open letter was sent on January 30, 1989, the anniversary of Hitler's *Machtergreifung,* to the Berlin senate, the *Bundesländer,* and the *Bundesregierung* complaining that the lack of a central *Mahnmal* was a "public scandal" and "shame." The group "Perspektive Berlin," headed by Rosh, used the familiar strategies of generalizing, moralizing, and emotionalizing in the attacks on German "repressed memories" of the Nazi past and insufficient mourning of Jewish victims. Most signatories of the open letter withdrew at the early stages of what was to become the longest, most erratic, most literally politicized and morally conflicted of German memory debates, spanning the last years of the *Bonner Republik* and the first five years of the *Berliner Republik* (*NM,* 85–88). But others joined, withdrew, rejoined at different stages in response to changing political constellations. In the end, Rosh's single-minded, sensationalist politics of *Täter* and *Opfer,* helped by the usual unforeseeable shifts in political power, paid off—for her. In an interview with *TAZ* of February 18, 2004, a triumphant Lea Rosh repeated the motto of her *Lebenswerk,* the victorious battle of the *Mahnmal:* "I claim the right to be involved." There were no questions as to the usefulness of her involvement since it has been exclusively speaking for the victims of the Holocaust. The *Mahnmal* in the heart of Berlin, south of the *Brandenburger Tor,* was close to completion, scheduled for inauguration on May 8, the sixtieth anniversary of the end of the war. The reporter's comment: "She has made the monument for the Jews her own. . . . The steles of the *Potsdamer Platz* seem to belong to Lea Rosh and she has the say in what other people can say about it."

It was of course not only Rosh who pushed the project through; but she has had an astonishing influence on a debate always close to exploding under the combined stress of lofty moral certainties regarding Jewish victimization and the divisive self-interest politics of Jewish Germans, non-Jewish Germans, and international (American) Jewish groups. Remarkably media-savvy, Rosh has always managed to stay in the limelight, whether she was praised or, more often, ridiculed in the press. In her fierce competition for control of the project she was helped by the fact that most of the active participants over the long duration of the *Mahnmal* debate were public intellectuals, writers, literary scholars and critics rather than professional historians of the Nazi period.[67] Her

melodramatic identification with the victims and the authoritarian absolutism of the demands she made in their name were favorite fodder
not only for the notoriously irreverent *Spiegel*.[68] It is her curiously literal self-inflation—a vessel holding the voices of (almost) all dead Jews,
right out of Grass's *Tin Drum*—that makes her appear excessively *betroffen*. Her strength is precisely her moral contempt for rationality where
it concerns the indeed difficult questions raised by the whole *Mahnmal*
idea; and in this she is a strangely fitting allegory for much of German
Holocaust remembrance. In her concluding remarks to the ambivalently
admiring *TAZ* reporter she acknowledged that "I am not as talented as
Schubert, and I am also not Goethe. But with this monument we will
bestow something on this land that will stay for a long, long time."

Disarmingly ridiculous; and she cannot even be told to "get real"
because she *is* very real: somehow she has held on to the power of being
the Conscience of this *Land der Täter*. The monument itself, not its
moral-political message, is another matter. The Jewish-American architect Peter Eisenman, with the support of Bundeskanzler Kohl eventually
the winner of the second competition (1997), wanted his arrangement
of 2,751 differently sized steles (there are 2,750 Holocaust memorials in
Germany) to create a sensation of "strangeness" (his word). According
to many viewers, he has achieved this sensation: the steles made of concrete seem to move in a strangely serene rhythm, as if stirred gently by
the wind. This, under the circumstances, "strangely" pleasant sensation
is created by the steles' considerable variations in height, though they all
have the same width and depth. Experts project a million visitors yearly
who will be impressed by, and talk about, the intriguing visual pleasures
of the architecture of Daniel Libeskind's Jewish Museum and Peter
Eisenman's Holocaust *Mahnmal*—high-art like Schubert and Goethe. It
is these visitors that will come "for a long, long time" and justify Rosh's
absolute belief in her *Lebenswerk*.

The Sinti and Roma and the homosexuals who had demanded to be
included in the *Mahnmal* will eventually get their own monuments:
there are already signs posted at the prospective sites announcing the
future structures. There are also the Poles murdered by the Nazis, the
Russian POWs who died in German camps, the many German political
enemies of the Nazi regime, large numbers of Russian civilians and,
finally, of German civilians killed in the air war and on the trek from the
East. But all these groups will have to go on waiting indefinitely; the
Germans probably "forever." In the meantime, there is an *Ort der Information* underneath the *Mahnmal* where, among other things, a voice
reads continuously the names and short biographies of the known 3.5

million Jews killed by the Nazis, and representations of mass shootings are shown. I wish there could have been one simple, silent monument in memory of *all* the dead of WWII in the center of the European city of Berlin. As far as we know, in reality, all the dead are equally gone: the only "incomprehensible," "unrepresentable" "truth" of the human condition.

The most difficult time for the *Mahnmal* project was in early 1998, when a group of historians, writers, and public intellectuals signed a statement against going on with a project they thought too monumental and morally obscure (*NM*, 99–104). Among the signatories were Günter Grass, Walter Jens, Klaus von Dohnanyi, and several Social-democratic politicians. For years, Rosh and Ignatz Bubis had urged to speed up the *Mahnmal* debate whenever it threatened to get bogged down in the many unresolved issues of memory and identity: they wanted the *Mahnmal* completed as soon as possible, to seal in stone the enduring memory of Jewish victimization. When the design chosen in the first competition was rejected by both Bubis and Bundeskanzler Kohl in 1995, Rosh immediately lamented the notorious German "inability to mourn." The American-Jewish literary scholar and monument expert James E. Young, a participant in the debate, had at that point made the presumably Derridian suggestion that the German Holocaust *Mahnmal* "should be unfinished, unbuilt, a forever incomplete thought process" (*NM*, 93)—certainly not what Rosh wanted to hear. There was a general sense of embarrassment, also regarding possible international reactions, but Rosh and Bubis pushed on, and the discussions in smaller groups picked up again, though they became less and less transparent.

The 1998 disruption was much more serious and could easily have led to abandoning the whole project. In July 1998 Schröder, then candidate for the office of *Bundeskanzler,* let it be known that the SPD was not interested in going on with the project in the case of a regime change. This caused Rosh to speak of a German declaration of bankruptcy and to appeal to the SPD to become the *Judenschutzpartei,* the party that would protect the Jews—a curious request in view of the realities of contemporary Jewish life in Germany. Surprisingly, Kohl came to her aid shortly before the election on September 27 by stating his support for the *Mahnmal:* "We would be cursed by the whole world if we now said, it's too difficult, we better leave it alone" (*NM*, 103–104). In August and September 1998 the designs of the four finalists in the second competition were again exhibited, Eisenman's with the alterations Kohl had wanted, and there were lively discussions of their esthetic-moral merit in the media. Kohl's intervention in favor of Rosh and her group was commented on ironically in a *Spiegel* essay as the folly of the "Skandal-Kanzler von Bitburg."[69] But public opinion had turned against the project, which seemed too focused on the esthetics and too fuzzy where it concerned the large issues of German guilt and remorse—the unique *Mahnmal* holding the Germans to their unique moral obligation instead of just another museum or information center.

Ironically, it took Walser's peace prize speech and Bubis's reaction to it to get the SPD back to the table. Walser, who had argued against the all-pervasive pedagogical moralizing of the self-declared guardians of the nation's conscience (Lea Rosh), was largely responsible for the survival of the *Mahnmal* project because he had inadvertently threatened Bubis, already nervous about the survival of his pet project. It was a threat that stirred him to action—accusing Walser of Holocaust denial, anti-Semitism, and closeness to right radicalism—which in Germany could not be, as it could have been elsewhere, shrugged off as rather absurd momentary overreaction. Schröder joined Rosh in attacking Walser: Rosh declared that the Walser-Bubis controversy had made building the *Mahnmal* a historical-moral imperative; Schröder declared that Walser had made it impossible to be against the *Mahnmal*. All critical questions concerning the moral, political, and historical meanings of the project had now been laid *ad acta*. The *Mahnmal* was certain to be built, and for the intervening years before its completion the building site became the place of demonstrations against anti-Semitism, regardless of political and social realities.[70]

The area of the Holocaust *Mahnmal* is open to everyone; its sensitive, light gray steles will have to be guarded around the clock. Berlin has infinitely more dogs than neo-Nazis, and lots of birds who like to fly above and through that mysterious field of concrete structures and cannot be prevented from leaving traces. There will be people picnicking on some of the steles. Perhaps there will be wineglasses raised to their beauty. Art, where it works, is not about truth but resistance to its interference. The exclusive certainties of redemptive memory are not represented by the monument but enacted at the *Ort der Information* beneath it. It says that the judgment of the *Generation der Täter* in the *Land der Täter* has always been certain for postwar Germans.

But it seems that it can never be certain enough, despite—and then also because of—the many promises made at the many commemorative ceremonies during 2005, the sixtieth anniversary of the end of WWII: solemn oaths ringing out like church bells that Germans in their collectivity will always be aware of that judgment and always remember what they let happen so that "it will never happen again." Inevitably, since the exact combination of the historical facts underlying "Auschwitz" is indeed unique in the sense of not likely to occur again, these promises are part of the rituals of remembrance. No matter how good and grave their sound, they are easily suspected of not being for real, not deeply felt, not intended to be kept. And the allegedly best argument against their sincerity has been the recent thawing of prohibitions controlling German wartime memories that allows Germans in their collectivity some, albeit cautious, revisiting of their pasts on their own terms.

The suspicions have increased with the approach of 2005. Non-Jewish German observers have warned that the mass of non-Jewish Germans would be motivated by the anniversary year to insist on presenting themselves as "victims of bombs, of rape, of captivity, and, of course, victims of flight and expulsion [*Flucht und Vertreibung*]. The general German feeling [*das deutsche Volksempfinden*] has regressed to a state characteristic of the Fifties that one would have thought left behind long ago [*überwunden*]." The obviously progressive author of this lament writes of the failure of the "historians and the other *Volkspädagogen* trying, over many decades, to teach the Germans to acknowledge that they were also, and above all, *Täter*."[71] Speaking in the name of German guilt, it is uncannily easy to pass summary judgment on "the Germans" without knowing anything, not to speak of thinking.

Then there is the pessimistic assessment voiced by Richard Chaim Schneider that during the "*Gedenkjahr* 2005," with its flood of publications, TV programs, commemorative ceremonies and speeches, Jews will be nothing but *Statisten,* extras, pushed to the edge of what should be *their* stage for presenting once more and more fully than ever before their suffering during the Holocaust.[72] He is not concerned with a receding memory of the Holocaust (hoped for, he claims, by many Germans) but with the rapidly aging witnesses to the Holocaust who will be gone by 2015, which for him makes 2005 an especially important anniversary year. Even though Jews have been invited to speak at all the commemorative events, their speaking out about their suffering will be ritualized, as will be the "politically correct" speeches of non-Jewish Germans and the larger world, with their empty promises of remorse and never forgetting.

When Schneider stated his complaint, he did not know yet that the commemoration of the sixtieth anniversary of the liberation of Auschwitz on January 27, 2005, was "the largest ever," bringing together "the presidents of Russia, Poland, Israel and Ukraine, as well as Vice President Dick Cheney and other world leaders"—such as Bundeskanzler Schröder, who also presided over a week-long commemoration of

Auschwitz in Germany in late January. The UN had already commemorated the liberation on January 24 with pledges of "never again" in a day-long session, the first such commemoration at the General Assembly. It had been requested by the U.S., who had also asked for that date to avoid conflict with the Auschwitz ceremonies—a successful worldwide coordination in memory of the centrality of Auschwitz.[73]

Yet all these commemorative activities, and the many, many more to come during the anniversary year 2005, would never reassure Richard Chaim Schneider, because they would not counteract the, in his words, "recently opened debate of Germans as victims of W.W.II." He finds it deeply troubling that "the literature about air raids on Dresden, Hamburg and other German cities has reached the bestseller status," and that 1945 will be remembered by a Munich exhibition of personal *Erinnerungsstücke* (commemorative objects) of Munich air raid victims, among them Jews. Moreover, he is certain that if this kind of memory of WWII becomes more predominant, "there will be no place for the Jews, not even as *Statisten,* because their very presence will remind the Germans who see themselves as victims what they do not want to be reminded of: their guilty past." At the very beginning of 2005, he concludes bitterly that "Germany is much too self-involved to find time during this commemorative year to finally engage more deeply with Jews and their experiences"—an observation that, given Germany's serious attempts over many decades to do just that and thereby make amends for its bad past, seems unfair but, above all, unrealistic.

Schneider's innocently high expectations where they concern a both spontaneously expressed and enduringly well managed German guilt are of course not shared by all Jews, German or non-German. But they are shared by too many Germans, and they have been at the core of the enduringly difficult relations between Jews and Germans. It may be precisely a changing German perspective on WWII, one no longer so exclusively dominated by the centrality of Auschwitz and therefore more able to quietly accommodate a greater plurality of memories, that could be helpful to both Jews and Germans in finding some degree of commonality in the human experience of this inhumanly horrible war. And to take it from there.

6 This Side of Good and Evil
A German Story

The SS officer Hans Ernst Schneider changed his name to Hans Schwerte in May 1945, that chaotic month when the past seemed to be as unimaginable as the future, and everything seemed possible and impossible. He was thirty-five years old, and as far as we can know, he would never turn back. As he said half a century later, he wanted to avoid punishment for his past activities and associations, which he feared would imprison him forever—a very long time—in this now criminal past and make it impossible for him to have a voice, a share, in the future.[1] His new identity, like postwar (West) Germany's, would turn out not the result of that significant moment of conversion in May 1945, as the victors had demanded it then and as Schwerte would remember it, if ambiguously, fifty years later. It would be a process of learning in time, a gradual development toward a democratic attitude and later, in Schwerte's case, an explicitly liberal position. He would become a successful professor of German studies involved in many research projects in literary and cultural history, and a high-ranking, much honored university administrator and reformer admired for his good judgment and remarkable organizational talents.

Notwithstanding his magisterial, well-received study of Faust and the Faustian idea in German culture,[2] it was his social and political intelligence rather than his academic performance that made him the friend and ally of many influential academics and Social-democratic politicians, including Bundespräsident Johannes Rau. Schwerte's undeniably useful life over the first fifty years of the *Bundesrepublik* would not have been possible without the reestablishment of that country's political and cultural institutions; in turn, their stability and growth depended on people like him who were willing and able to undergo significant transformation, even at the price of self-invention. In 1995, when Schwerte informed the authorities of his true identity extinguished by his act of deception half a century ago, the general condemnation was extraordinary, especially coming from his friends in high political places and his fellow-academics, concerned above all that they might be tainted by the dark ghosts rising from the past.

There was a powerful, panicked impulse to extinguish the Schwerte part of that troubling equation as quickly and completely as possible, to leave nothing but that shadowy heinous SS officer from fifty years ago. By now a very old and sick man, Schwerte was excommunicated from civil society, stripped of his social associations, his decorations, his pension and medical insurance. He was left to fend for himself in the old sense of *vogelfrei*—like a bird free of, outside, human community. Once the expulsion was complete, the media had had their feast, articles and books had put together hasty speculations, this "incredible" story was quickly forgotten, locked away with all the other bitter memory debates that had come and gone over the years. I am telling it here once more, and to a different audience, to demonstrate the difficulties of understanding fully what happened to the Third Reich and to its memory, but also the importance of trying anyway, with more realistic expectations and less pieties. In this perspective, Schneider-Schwerte's story will have to remain inconclusive, especially where it concerns the arch-German— and, to a degree American—issues of guilt, memory, and remorse. But it may also turn out to be less exclusively German, less provincial, more contemporary than his accusers might have thought—certainly less redemptive than they, if not he, had bargained for.

———

The concept of "the political" that Arendt developed in *The Human Condition* as a counterprojection to totalitarian rule is in many ways too pure and restrictive.[3] But her core argument for an essential interdependency of democratic political freedom and lawful authority, good citizens and good people, emphasizes usefully the importance of good cultural and political institutions for independent, responsible thought and action. Such institutions had been damaged by radical politics on the Right and the Left in the aftermath of WWI and would be all but destroyed during Soviet and Nazi totalitarian rule. Institutions are established and develop within a complex web of connections between individuals' temperaments and activities, institutional structures and

political agenda—all the more so where they concern high cultural issues such as German studies as part of the humanities, *Geisteswissenschaften*. Currently, the survival of *Germanistik* as a theory-heavy academic discipline, *Literaturwissenschaft*, is widely debated in Germany
across the political spectrum. In view of the SPD's need to reign in the
high costs of academic education and to acknowledge the changing cultural priorities of the new *Berliner Republik* in the age of technology-
driven globalization, contemporary *Germanistik* appears anachronistic.
The issue is not for or against education but the kind of education
deemed appropriate at this time, and we can only judge the respective
decision if we know enough about its context. It has not been useful to
simply dismiss as odious propaganda all cultural and educational activities during the Nazi period: we have to ask how these activities played
out both within inherited (if modified) and newly established institutions, notably by the SS. The Third Reich claimed the old-new utopianist energies of the *Reichsidee*, which in various ways had been an
important part of Weimar political culture, including left-intellectual
Messianism with its eschatological concept of history.[4] Promises of a
new order drawing on the cultural and political glories of a distant past
to create, nurture, and educate the *New Man* and *New Woman* in new
or (radically) reorganized institutions emphasized the importance of
utopian men and women and of utopian institutions in the service of a
new sturdy and vibrant national and socialist community. These promises were attractive to large population groups who had lived through
WWI and its aftermath and felt besieged by the profound political, cultural, and economic difficulties of Weimar modernity.
The cultural politics and political processes of national and social
self-invention seemed particularly persuasive to the large group of severely underemployed young (male) academics. The fact that the new
regime was the outcome of a revolution from the Right and had a history of political violence did not deter them as automatically as we,
looking back from a distance of more than seventy years, would have
wished. Arguably, our perspective on Weimar political culture has been
shaped too much by the assumption *Der Geist steht links,* that is, all
meaningful change can come only from that position, regardless of the
many historical correspondences between the revolutions—their promises and violence—from the Left and the Right, and similarities between
the resulting totalitarian dystopias and their institutions. It is true, the
Nazi version would lead to a more focused, consistently violent exclusion, but we cannot therefore simply disregard the power of its initial
promises in their contemporary context that favored utopianist hopes

and desires—on the Right as well as the Left. And by far the most important difference at that stage was the role played by political and cultural nationalism, the politics of authentic identity.

There is an instructive exchange of letters between Karl Jaspers and Hannah Arendt in early 1933 about Jaspers's *Max Weber: Deutsches Wesen im politischen Denken, im Forschen und Philosophieren* (1932). On January 1, 1933, Arendt writes her admired and supportive teacher from Paris to thank him for sending her his book; but she also tells him about her difficulties with it. She can accept Jaspers's view of Weber as "the Great German" but not as the incarnation of "German *Wesen*" (essence), which Jaspers defines as "reasonableness and humanity with their source in passion." Since she is Jewish, her agreement with this view, as with Weber's "impressive" patriotism, would be as inappropriate as her disagreement. Germany is existentially important to her since it signifies native language, poetry, and philosophy, but she cannot but distance herself from Weber's "magnificent" statement that he would enter into an alliance with the devil to help restore Germany.[5]

Jaspers's immediate answer is concerned about Arendt's rejection of German *Wesen* and her distancing herself, as a Jewish woman, from "Germanness." His decision to use that term had been, he explains, a historical "Totalitätsintention" to emphasize for his intended audience, Germany's nationalist youth, the future-oriented "ought" in the equation German = reason. He has found much good will and much confusion among the young, and precisely for this reason, he chose a nationalist publisher's series, *Schriften an die Nation,* and compromised on the subtitle to make it more suggestive for his young readers. In his opinion, Arendt only needed to add Germany's "historical-political fate" to her concerns about native language, poetry, and philosophy to erase the difference in their views. For the present and in political terms, Jaspers wrote, Germany's fate had to be linked with a unified Europe. But, distinguishing between a self-restrained "Reich *der* Deutschen" (empire of the Germans) and a "Reich *des* Deutschen" (realm of German culture), he also projected the role of the latter as essential for the establishing of connections within Europe—between Holland and Austria, Scandinavia and Switzerland.

For Jaspers, this "Reich *des* Deutschen" signified the idea of a viable cultural expansion through German (high) culture, which he shared with many Weimar intellectuals, young and old, Jewish and Gentile, across a broad spectrum of political sympathies and affiliations that would soon include the SS institution *Ahnenerbe*[6] with its staff of young Ph.D.s in German literature. Given current sensitivities, it may not be needless to say that I am not claiming here even the slightest connection between Jaspers's views and Nazism. Rather, the issue is his and many other highly educated and well-intentioned Germans' intense preoccupation with cultural Germanness—a preoccupation that Arendt would share to the end of her life and that goes a long way to explain her enduring fascination with Heidegger's philosophizing. In early 1933, however, she clearly distanced herself from Jaspers's belief in the redemptive expansion of German culture because, in contrast to many of her German Jewish intellectual contemporaries, she shrewdly saw the dangerous implications of Nazi political and cultural nationalism.[7]

These implications would surface gradually; and it is precisely the historicity of the Nazi regime moving in time through different stages that needs to be explored with an awareness of the fallacies of hindsight. Looking at National-socialist concepts and uses of German culture, we have to look at individuals involved in redirecting, rebuilding, or establishing the institutions within which and through which the humanities would operate, among them importantly the complex of new institutions under the control of the SS. Curiously, the taboo on talking about these individuals and their institutions soberly as historical phenomena, without invoking at every step of the argument the self-protective warnings of "monstrous," "heinous," "atrocious," has increased rather than diminished over the years. Since the end of WWII, any person involved in any way with an SS institution, regardless of that person's actual activities during that period, has been automatically criminalized and, with the growth of Holocaust memory discourses, also demonized. This existential-moral rather than political-institutional excommunication is not found where it concerns individuals in at least partially comparable Communist (Stalinist) institutions. But it takes this sober perspective to yield any useful information: What exactly were their tasks? What were their institutions meant to achieve?

Charged with the articulation and communication of Nazi cultural politics, these institutions were outside but in many ways parallel or linked to the established academic institutions for research and teaching in the humanities. Such connections became increasingly important once the *Wissenschaftsministerium* (ministry of science) had initiated the project of a special contribution of the humanities to the war effort (*Kriegseinsatz der Geisteswissenschaften*) headed by the rector of Kiel University and professor of international law, Paul Ritterbusch, who joined the *Wissenschaftsministerium* in 1940. One of the first sub-institutions was *Kriegseinsatz der Germanisten*, headed by Franz Koch and Gerhard Fricke, which promptly produced a five-volume study, *Von deutscher Art in Sprache und Dichtung* (German identity in language and poetry)—a project that had the support of a large majority of senior professors heading the institutes for the study of German literature at various universities (*MW*, 97, 171). At the time, that support was clearly politically expedient. It was important to the regime, for reasons of cultural legitimation, that its cultural institutions share academic projects with university institutes, which were then rewarded for their cooperation. But the project itself, the collective of contributors and contributions, was also symptomatic for the many different ways in which the appeal of cultural-political nationalism could express itself, even under the conditions of an increasingly totalitarian regime and total war.

One of the contributors was Hans Rössner, who is also a good example for the connection of careers and research projects at the universities and at Nazi institutions. Temporary membership in the SA, with its informal net of local cultural-political programs and organizations, was a common career pattern among young, otherwise unemployable academics in the humanities. Rössner left the SA in 1934 to work for the SS-supported "Academic Self-Help Saxony" and, part-time, for the *Sicherheitsdienst* (office of national security). He was appointed to the position of assistant professor at the German department at Bonn University in 1936 and finished his dissertation on "Georgekreis und Literaturwissenschaft" in 1937. Stefan George was at that time wooed by the Nazi regime, partly as an inspirational figure to *Jugendbewegung,* the both conservative and progressivist, loosely organized, influential movement of young people that had become emblematic for the general cultural mood of new beginnings around 1900. It shared with Nationalsocialism the neo-Romantic celebration of nature, the organic, the local, rootedness, significant community, and, up to a point, cultural nationalism (especially German music) but differed dramatically from its political goals, strategies, and methods of organization. George's highly mannered poetry was much admired for its priestly *gravitas* and elitist style (some of his poems *are* beautiful in the mysterious manner of "good" poems); his homoerotic circle, as high-serious as the master himself, had a number of Jewish members.

Rössner's dissertation topic could have been interesting to a variety of readers and students for a variety of reasons. A talented young scholar, he went on to organize and then head (since 1940) the section *Kunst und Volkskultur* (art and folk culture) within the large and increasingly powerful institution of the *Sicherheitsdienst.* He would have been the only non-*habilitiert*[8] contributor to *Von deutscher Art in Sprache und Dichtung* if the project's rigorous deadline had not forced him to withdraw. Despite his heavy workload in the *Reichssicherheitshauptamt*, Rössner kept his teaching position at Bonn University from 1940 to 1944, planning for a proper *Habilitation* and a professorship, as did other young cultural-nationalist academics who had found work in the newly established Nazi institutions (*MW*, 98f). Their rehabilitation after the war differed greatly, depending on the time and place of their denazification. After the beginning of the Cold War, their membership in an organization retroactively declared criminal tended to be judged relatively mildly in the courts, but not so in the immediate postwar period. Rössner, who had testified against the major war criminals at the Nuremberg trials and was imprisoned till April 1948, was lucky in that respect. But his postwar career was less spectacular than that of another young Ph.D. in German literature, Hans Ernst Schneider, whose professional experiences during the Third Reich were in important ways similar to Rössner's, with the exception that Schneider's superior in *Ahnenerbe* did not support his plans for *Habilitation* and that Schneider liked organizational challenges and teamwork better than scholarly research.

Schneider's membership in the SS began in the fall of 1937.[9] He had a short stint at the *Rasse-und Siedlungshauptamt* (office for issues of race and population) in 1938 and then joined the SS project *Ahnenerbe*, with which he would be associated to the end of the war. Schneider organized and then headed the loosely connected subsection *Germanischer Wissenschaftseinsatz* (mission of Germanic studies), originally an *Ahnenerbe* project charged with promoting the idea of a culturally (and then politically) Germano-centric Europe, an extension of *Reichsidee*. In 1945, avoiding imprisonment, he changed his identity and became Hans Schwerte—and half a century later the "Schwerte case." The extraordinary hostility of the reactions to the uncovering of Schwerte's former self, Schneider, and his activities for a variety of Nazi institutions, illuminates the imperfections and lacunae of hindsight perspective that have created many difficulties for the historiography of the Third Reich. The Nazi regime had become so criminal, the political and military collapse was so extreme, the cultural rupture was so total that it profoundly disrupted the modern historian's habit of time travel: going back to the historical actors and events as they had been in the context of their temporal contingencies became near-impossible. Where "the Nazis" are concerned, historians have found it very difficult to establish the usual observational position of flexible distance that allows for an essential human commonality spanning extensive separations by time and helps to recognize both differences and similarities.[10]

There could be no such commonality with anybody who had actively participated in the Nazi regime. The historian encountering such a person on the reservation, as it were, of his Nazi past, could never imagine that he himself might have been like that person, sharing the ambitions, confusions, desires, anxieties, ambiguities, and deceptions of another life in another time. Yet the ability to imagine what it would have *felt like* to be that other person, to develop historical *sym-pathy* in a literal sense, has been central to the success of historical research. The issue here is not learning to feel with or for that other person; it is, rather, learning how to make sense of that person's life by allowing it to make sense on its own terms—even if in certain cases that can be done only with grave reservations. It stands to reason that such historiographical sympathy cannot develop where it concerns the great historical villains, a prime example being Kershaw's portrait of Hitler as the non-person of huge dimensions, an evil absence in the center that allowed the Germans to project their most heinous fantasies and fears on him.[11] But the phenomenon of National-socialism seems to have demanded a degree of historiographical distancing that would make all Nazis appear as monstrous aliens and all Germans as Nazis.[12]

In the American popular culture (films and literature) of the forties and fifties, all Germans were presented as grotesque, unredeemable fascists, whereas Russians were shown as ordinary people oppressed by Communist rule, the suffering victims of an alien ideology.[13] Germans, in contrast, were existentially infected with Fascism, and it stayed with them—once a Nazi, always a Nazi—a view that has endured in the American collective psyche to this day. As in Germany, in the United States too, this myth of an enduring infection has become more morally certain and politically exploitable over the years, whether it means selling a war or a movie: the young Nazi soldier in Spielberg's *Saving Private Ryan* repeating successfully a then fifty-year-old U.S. war propaganda cliché.[14] However, during the first decades of the Cold War, when the phenomenon of totalitarianism was much debated, the American official view was to morally equate Soviet Communism and German Fascism. This equation disappeared with the implosion of the Eastern Bloc, leaving Nazi Evil as an all-powerful, semi-religious, absolute negativity in Western culture that, like a black hole, has sucked up all attempts at historical differentiation.

From educated hindsight, the ideological context for Schneider's work in *Ahnenerbe,* National-socialist philo-Germanicism, with its new visual and linguistic archaisms and its combined utopianist exclusiveness and desire for expanded territorial domination, appears both ridiculous and dangerous. Curiously, it seems to have been the grotesqueness rather than the sinister awfulness of Nazi "Newspeak" that has led to simply rejecting the whole Nazi phenomenon with high moral contempt for its deadly silliness instead of studying the reasons behind this new "primitivism." The linguistic control through (Orwellian) "Newspeak" is as effective as it is common in utopian organizations. Moreover, in contrast to Communist Newspeak, Nazi philo-Germanic rhetoric fit certain important aspects of the utopian tradition since Tacitus's *Germania*, within which Thomas More situated his *Utopia*. It concerns the topos of "relearning barbaric virtues," an important issue in eighteenth-century intellectual discourse (Rousseau, Diderot, Herder, Kant, Georg Forster). It reemerged in the nineteenth century after the Industrial Revolution, this time not as a topic for intellectual debate but as a cultural desire to go back to a mythical shared Germanic past of pre(anti)-capitalist natural wholeness and simplicity. The paradisiacal equality and community promised by such "going back to the roots" would, so the expectation, somehow heal the political, social, and economic division associated with the experience of technological modernity.

William Morris's utopian classic *News from Nowhere* (1890) was written as an explicit counterprojection to the American writer Edward Bellamy's celebration of liberalizing technological progress in *Looking Backward* (1888). Both authors had been working actively with labor organizations, but in very different cultural-political situations. Where Bellamy's text is an early example of affirmative science fiction in its projection of liberating technological complexity, Morris's utopian fiction is influenced by Rousseau's argument for a cultural simplicity that goes back to an early developmental state, before the notion of property and therefore identity. Following Thomas More's *Utopia*, Morris also embraces Tacitus's praise for Germanic peoples as exemplifying healthy and nurturing communal closeness to nature, in contrast to Roman (European) hyper-sophistication and individualistic, decadent, self-destructive reliance on technology. The German post-WWI experience of accelerated, for many frightening, technological changes in the workplace, increasing pressures of overcrowded urban living, political polarization and violence, and extreme economic uncertainties made particularly attractive promises of mental and physical health through national community and unity. The "new order" of the new-old Third Reich exploited old anxieties and desires in propagating "the roots," the "organic" ties of blood and soil, of family and cultural traditions, and it did so with the efficiency of the new communications technology of radio and film.

No matter how well they may communicate on the inside, looked at from the outside, utopias tend to be islands, separate, remote, uniform, and secretive, in order to protect utopian self-invention. A common feature of utopian organization, this exclusiveness would assert itself with full force at a later stage of the Third Reich, when, partly due to the moral inversion of a total war—killing as a positive cultural value—it became surreally violent and finally self-destructed. Thomas More, whose foundation fiction *Utopia* would become a "holy" text of nineteenth- and twentieth-century political Communism, had already anticipated that danger in the early sixteenth century, when he stated his fear of the "corruptio pessima optimi," the change from utopia into dystopia when the ideology of the new order would become all powerful: an end, and then the total and explosive end, in itself.

This is not to suggest that National-socialism at any stage of its rule represented the optimum, that is, the projection of a better life through better organized community in the sense of writers such as More, Marx, or Morris. There had been too much exclusion, too many enemy groups, from the very beginning. Like all (dys)utopian constructions, the Third Reich created its own cultural-political institutions in its efforts to dismantle the preceding political order, and its specific exclusiveness was partly due to the undermining or removal of the old liberal democratic institutions of the Weimar Republic. This process was not essentially different in a left utopia such as the Soviet Union—*vid.* its sophisticated, shrewd analysis in Zamyatin's dystopian satire *We,* written in the early twenties. It is true, there has been a general utopianist exclusiveness and paranoia through the centuries: since More's *Utopia,* utopian communities have been predicated on walls and silence to protect "us" against the world outside. But paranoid exclusion was intensified in the Third Reich by the importance of race for the selection of undesirable (outside) and desirable (inside) groups, an importance that in the end became disastrously all-consuming.

Controlled breeding, a related issue, has also contributed to utopian exclusiveness. The "natural" ranking system of Plato's *Republic,* in some critics' view "protofascist," relied on it to deal with the chicken-and-egg question of utopian people and utopian organization. Aldous Huxley's satirical *Brave New World* (1932) took it literally, that is, to the absurd. It was at first meant to be an ironical argument directed against H. G. Wells's overweening cultural optimism regarding scientific and technological developments; but, as Huxley said in a foreword written after WWII, it should be read as a warning against their dangerous potential. Seven decades later, his vision of a future biotechnology has become entirely contemporary to our current debates of the powerful and troubling realties of human fertility technology and cloning. In the early thirties, when such technology and, more important, its social impact were still in an exotic utopian future, the interest of Huxley's text lay in its consequences for utopian politics: from now on, dissent in utopia would be impossible, and yet only dissent could reveal the essential badness of the presumably good place, the dystopian reality of utopian promises. From now on the dissenters' arguments will be a priori inaccessible to their fellow-utopians, who are equal by virtue of their biologically controlled inequality, and therefore all of them equally unable to entertain ideas that have not been part of their respective bio-social group programming.

In that, the destructive potential of Huxley's colorful, hedonistic, rigidly stratified *no-place* is much more frightening than that of Orwell's grim, drab, oppressive communist society. In a world largely changed by the catastrophe of the Great War, the first modern technological war, whose consequences have dominated the twentieth century and are still with us in the new millennium, it has been the possibility of realizing utopia that made it impossibly dangerous—as Huxley foresaw before the Second World War and Orwell realized at the end of it. In the beginning of the century, H. G. Wells's *A Modern Utopia* (1905), with its mix of modern technological progress and a culturally conservative hierarchy of values, propagated breeding for mental and physical health in the interest of achieving a less chancy combination of nature and nurture— an optimistic desire for control that Huxley thought at best outdated. And yet, despite its Platonic features and indeed overly optimistic belief in the liberalizing energies of technological advances, Wells's utopian projection (rather than construction) was meant to develop workable ideas for a better life for more people. Many of the inventive suggestions throughout *A Modern Utopia* are appealing today, worth being revisited, precisely because he sees his project as open-ended, for once not closed in by walls and silence.

Yet, like all utopias, this one too is a creation of its time and significantly separated from the future into which it has been projected. Conceived after WWI and two revolutions, Huxley's and Zamyatin's dystopias, in contrast to Plato's, More's, Marx's, or Morris's utopian constructions, were not meant for human habitation, pointing to the inherently inhuman aspects of social-political and technological revolutions. H. G. Wells's projection of a better world in progress still seems habitable today. His ideas would be more attractive to the elites and to men than to the undereducated and women, though even his suggestions for women make sense, if only by illuminating our very real contemporary problems of raising children into a reasonably livable future. His "remodeled" rather than new world dealt intelligently with the issue of biological and cultural heterogeneity and inequality, of racial and cultural prejudice, with the promises and problems of globalization, the mixing and separation of peoples. It tackled what we seem unable to do, the difficult balancing of diversity and homogeneity. A modern utopia, this remodeled world was presented as one among other projections; above all, it was agnostic and did not promise redemption, in contrast to, among many others, the utopian constructions of Marx and his admirer Morris, and the Third Reich.

Considering, much less building, a modern utopia along the lines of Wells's projection was not an option for the group of well-educated but culturally uncertain and politically bewildered young men from which the elite SS institutions recruited the "new men" to build the new Germanic-German order of the Third Reich. What these young men sought was a new social and economic order, political direction, and above all a place in the world for themselves. The gainful employment offered by these SS institutions was the first, immeasurably important step toward finding that place. In East Prussia, where Schneider was trying to support himself with freelance journalism while studying German literature at Königsberg University, the unemployment rate in the early thirties was about a third of the population, and worse in fields such as literary and cultural studies. Like many other German students, Schneider believed that the old bourgeois capitalist order had been vastly corrupt, a spectacular failure, and that the new socialist future lay with national rather than international socialism, even if he and many others were occasionally troubled by the enduring violence used as a political tool by the National-socialist party.

There had been political violence on the Left too, but it seemed on the whole less intrinsic to its ideological position. In his conversations with Claus Leggewie after the dicovery of his "true" identity, Schwerte remembered that Schneider was repulsed by the brutal behavior of "grossdeutsche" National-socialist students against Jewish students and professors in Vienna in the summer of 1932 and that he was on the whole not impressed by National-socialist student organizations.[15] In 1933, he knew very little about Hitler's program and the goals of his national revolution, but he did share the anti-bourgeois and anti-church sentiments of many young Germans, and the Nazi movement seemed to represent this position—more so, or more familiarly, than the Soviet-influenced Communism of the late Weimar period. After Hitler's *Machtergreifung*, Schneider, like many middle-class Germans across the age and political spectrum, believed that once established, the new regime would change its aggressive style. Up to a point they were proved right; but only for a while and only if they were the intended inhabitants of the Third Reich, the people inside the walls of utopia.

What did the twenty-three-year-old Schneider really feel and think at that time? The questions and probings in Leggewie's attempts to trace the developments of Schneider, of Schwerte, and of Schneider as Schwerte arguably helped the old Schwerte to try to find his way back to Schneider. Yet it is hard to say how far his memories are reliable, given the unusual circumstances of two radical changes of identity and great temporal distance. What Leggewie recorded sounds on the whole plausible, keeping in mind the biographer-historian's inevitable difficulties in "really" getting back into the past by getting full access to his subject's past states of mind. Critics have pointed out rightly that Leggewie's account shows signs of having been written in haste because of the great interest, the newsworthiness, of the topic in the late nineties. But in contrast to most commentators on the Schneider-Schwerte case, Leggewie has also been more interested in understanding than condemning Schwerte. Instructively, he mentions in his acknowledgements that he wrote the book during a stay at New York University. If the spatial distance from Germany made research more cumbersome, it also contributed to a useful intellectual distance in that it gave him access to other perspectives. He learned from discussing the case with American students and colleagues, who "can look at the two German pasts more soberly and with more curiosity than the German public too easily caught up in retrospective competition for moral correctness and righteousness."[16] Not unexpectedly, Leggewie's account was found wanting in *Betroffenheit*, especially when reviewed in papers that have redefined their role as watchful guardians of German *Vergangenheitsbewältigung* after reunification, when they lost the built-in moral authority of their position on the Left.[17]

Schneider, as Schwerte remembered, was intrigued by communist intellectual debates at some point during the early thirties; but politically innocent and looking for guidance and direction, he became more interested in the idea of a "conservative revolution" proposed by the *Tat-Kreis,* an at the time well-known group of conservative intellectuals. It is useful to keep in mind that this group's defense of authentic

German culture against the abstracting and alienating systematism and inauthentic collectivity of Western technocratic civilization had distinct echoes in the intellectual Left, especially the subgroup of (what later became) the Frankfurt School.[18] The convergence in important aspects of left and right intellectual positions, particularly the revolutionary, utopianist energies directed against all status quo institutions in the search for meaningful community, has often been mentioned; indeed, it has become a cliché. But its implications have never been taken really seriously because the nationalist version of community has been so completely discredited by the Nazi regime. In some ways even more important: for intellectuals, meaningful revolutions could come only from the Left, since their arch-model has always been the French Revolution, never mind the bloodiness, the *terreur,* of its last stage and the resulting war and restoration. But the search for redemptive community, *Gemein-schaft,* was indeed shared by young people on the Left and Right, whether it concerned a national *Volksgemeinschaft* or the international *Proletariat.* It was exploited by both Nazism and Communism, among other things through youth organizations and athletics, causing young people (mostly men) to go back and forth between the two political movements till the Nazis won the game. The identity politics of nationalism seemed more promising and more reassuring to more young Germans than internationalist Communism, especially its association with Stalin's Russia.

The fact that the majority of politically interested and active German university students were on the Right has been a notoriously negative aspect of Weimar political culture, since in the aftermath of the Nazi regime, "right" and "radical" have seemed almost synonymous, and both have been summarily judged as Evil. By no means all conservative students showed aggressive and exclusive behavior against fellow students and professors who did not share their position; and that was also true for students in the sixties and seventies, who were then in their majority on the Left. In both situations—in the aftermath of a disastrously lost war and during a disastrously unmotivated war that could not be won—one political direction was dominant and could become radicalized to the point of political violence. Whether on the Right or the Left, radicalized students became, at least temporarily, part of a collective irrationalism in their overriding desire for instantaneous, redemptive community: whatever their position, it was eo ipso the only correct one.[19] Student radicalism on the Right during the Weimar period was potentially more dangerous than student radicalism on the Left four decades later; but there are some aspects that are comparable.

There are also possible comparisons with other radicalized ideologies. If the nationalist and anti-Semitic components of right radicalism have been responsible for its demonization, a more sober and circumspect historical perspective might tell us something about its re-activist grievances and hopes, not unlike Islamic re-activist fundamentalism. This re-activism needs to be analyzed rather than simply condemned as "unspeakable" Nazi Evil or the demoniacally Evil Axis of Islamic terrorism.

The young academics who joined SS institutions did so for a variety of reasons, one of them their willingness to see in this nationalist and socialist organization promises of greater political stability and more equitable social security—arguably *the* single most important desire of most Germans after the chaos of the Weimar Republic in its end stage. Being young, they also appreciated the ingenious Nazi mix of youthful energy and order, the dynamic and the static, the future and the past; most of all a new hopeful belief that it would mean a better life for themselves but also for others. In hindsight perspective, such belief has seemed impossible to many people living in a world changed beyond belief since the end of WWII. Though this lack of historical imagination is regrettable, it is also very common and understandable. In the aftermath of traumatic dystopian experiments, no matter how different the scale of their destructive power, such disbelief has been quite familiar among former believers, who would be asking themselves how they could possibly have once believed in the promises of political ideologies that produced the terror of the French and Russian revolutions, the mass destruction of human life in the utopias of Nazi Germany and the Soviet Union, the intricate, ideological pressures and petty but not therefore less hurtful restrictions and injustices in the German Democratic Republic. Who had they been? How could they even begin to perceive, much less reconstruct, that now largely submerged former self that seemed stripped off, left behind with the chaos of cultural and political collapse?

Hans Schwerte revealed his true identity to the authorities on April 26, 1995, anticipating by a few hours such revelation by a Dutch television station that he knew planned to expose him on his eighty-fifth birthday, normally the occasion for yet more honors and decorations. While only his family and very few trusted friends knew about his change of name and identity, rumors had been intensifying among the academic community in Aachen for several months, and Schwerte had been receiving anonymous letters and phone calls. Suddenly returned, reduced to Hans Ernst Schneider, Schwerte was ordered to "explain himself." He must have thought it possible to do so, since he made himself available for interviews in the print and television media during the days immediately following the excitingly scandalous breaking news of his SS past. In his statement to the authorities he had admitted his membership in the SS and co-responsibility for the extraordinary crimes committed by this organization; he had expressed his enduring "profound shame and sadness about National-socialism and particularly the SS whose uniform I wore." This statement was quoted in many newspapers. When the *Aachener Volkszeitung* asked him whether he felt co-responsible for the death of so many people, he answered, "Of course. I wore a uniform that is responsible for the unspeakable things that happened in Europe. But I myself have not killed anybody."[20]

Had Schwerte really imagined that his explanations would be heard? that the issue was listening to what he was saying? Should he not have anticipated that everybody, especially his fellow-academics, would want to excommunicate him from civilized society, to parade him in his fallen state as utterly contemptible sinner? In his public persona as academic administrator he had skillfully navigated the German minefield of politicized sensibilities regarding the bad German past of which he had now become an allegory. He should have foreseen the ecstatic reactions of German intellectuals and journalists to the existentially thrilling "impossible" combination of SS officer, *Ahnenerbe,* deceptive identity change, and evasion of just payment for his criminal past: no prison, no shame, no guilt, no remorse. Yet, Schwerte had evidently not anticipated the intensity of that religio-political, moral wrath and self-righteousness. The most striking aspect of the elite media hunt was the extraordinary verbal aggressiveness of the accusers' protestations that they were not, would not, could never have been in any way like that monstrous sinner. After fifty years of living as a good citizen and good man, having left behind a dangerously confused and misguided but not personally criminal past,[21] Schwerte could not accept that verdict, at least not in this form. When he revealed his SS past, he may or may not have been aware of the painful paradox waiting for him to be sorted out: the more his support for the Nazi *Reichsidee* must have seemed plausible to him then, the more difficult—but also the more important—it would be now to explain to himself and others, why.

That turned out to be impossible because his useful and decent life as Schwerte was not a mitigating (or at least neutral) but rather an aggravating argument. Suddenly reduced to the ghost of a wicked young SS man, this life was not only extinguished but also turned against him. Accused of having deceived and betrayed all his associates and friends, of never "facing" his Nazi past, he could have no acceptable response:

whatever he said could only be more lies. His original sin had been to deny and to conceal his past. This has been the worst crime in Germany, since such concealment always suggested the worst: the past reality of participation in mass murder. Prosecutorial questions were literally fired at him from all sides, across the political spectrum, to make him confess his guilt in the terms of the questioners. His deception was monstrous precisely because his life had been a success. As one of his more intelligent critics argued, Schwerte could only have "appeared to be such a convinced and convincing liberal, because his new life was built on deception. He took a more radical turn than Schneider could ever have done. The deception was so genuine that he himself became its victim. This also explains his being shocked at first by the shocked and furious public reaction."[22] But if the radical turn was indeed a turn for the much better than anybody could have expected, why—or in whose eyes —would he have to be a "victim" of self-deception? Why could he not be seen as somebody who had used it for good purpose: the liberal Hans Schwerte who in the spring of 1995 confessed to having left Schneider behind for good in the spring of 1945. It was his sense of the person he had become over the last fifty years, a temporally composite, layered, complexly unstable but familiar identity, that made it so difficult for him to accept, much less understand, others' furious denials of transformations that he had experienced.

What had Hans Ernst Schneider actually done during the Nazi regime, and who had he become in 1945? Nineteen thirty-three was not the best year to be writing a dissertation in German literature at Königsberg or any other university, since the new regime's promised or threatened radical change had created a great deal of uncertainty. In 1931 Schneider's original thesis advisor, Josef Nadler, author of a then muchused literary history that interpreted literary creativity in the terms of the author's regional origin, had suggested he write on Turgenev and German literature. But Nadler, whom Schneider admired, had since gone to the University of Vienna and left him stranded. His new advisor was a Baroque specialist and engaged Catholic who helped the young student out but did not show much interest in him or his topic.[23] Apprehensive about the regime change, Schneider spent the summer of 1933 with the *Freiwillige Arbeitsdienst*[24] of the WWI veterans' organization *Stahlhelm* (steel helmet). This conservative organization would soon be taken over by the SA, for which Schwerte then worked as "Referent für Volkstumsarbeit" in the "NS Gemeinschaft *Kraft durch Freude*,"[25] a part of the organization *Deutsche Arbeitsfront.* In 1936 he assumed an administrative position in the East Prussian branch of the organization *Volkstum und Heimat,* which had been taken over in 1934 by Alfred Rosenberg's *Nationalsozialistische Kulturgemeinde,* itself a result of a reorganization of *Kampfbund für deutsche Kultur.*

Terms such as "Kraft" (force), "Front," "Gemeinde" (community), "Bund" (congregation, community, association), and "Kampf" (battle) abound in the names of a plenitude of Nazi cultural organizations to emphasize their energetic, activist, communal nature. The organization and reorganization of institutions charged with propagating the cultural politics of the Third Reich's New Order was very lively in the thirties, reflecting personal as well as ideological conflicts and struggles for power. The foundation of *Kampfbund,* for instance, went back to the decision made at the NSDAP Parteitag in Nürnberg (August 1927) to found a "nationalsozialistische Gesellschaft für Kultur und Wissenschaft" under the leadership of Rosenberg, who would then also be responsible for the development of the new society's program and organization. Rosenberg's (undated) mission statement in the fall of 1927 concerns the "fight" for a hierarchy of values in the "battle" of internationalism with the concept of a racially grounded *Volkstum.* Internationalism signifies "Weltrepublik," "Materialismus," "Trusts," "Grossbanken"—unrestricted, limitless individualism and pacifism—on the one hand, and Marxism in the form of "liberale Sozialdemokratie" and/ or "terroristischer Bolschewismus" on the other (*MW,* 35 n. 3). There was, however, no reference to "Judentum" even though Rosenberg saw this group as representative of the purest and therefore most dangerous form of capitalism and globalism (ibid.). Instructively, this statement was much more explicit about the old negative than the new positive values. "Rasse, Staat, Sprache und Geschichte," Rosenberg declared, have to be cleansed of all the negative influences, but there was little advice how that should be done.

The statement of intention in the statues of *Kampfbund für deutsche Kultur* founded in 1929 was again quite general in declaring its goal to "explain to the German people the connection between race, art, science, moral and soldierly values" (*MW,* 39). The first issue of "Mitteilungen des *Kampfbundes für deutsche Kultur*" (January 1929) had a programmatic article, "Die Geisteswende" (change of mind and spirit), which equated Germany's political and economic collapse with an "innere Glaubenslosigkeit" (lack of faith) regarding the value of "Deutschtum." In this view, the aimlessness of German politics signaled a general lack of *völkisch* political and cultural ideals. Ordinary Germans suffered from loneliness, abandonment, and hopelessness because they worried about the spiritual and mental welfare of their *Volk*.

With their exclusive focus on "Weltrepublik" and "Menschheits-kultur" (mankind), (left) intellectuals have consistently failed to understand that the most important contemporary task is to save *Volkstum* grounded in blood and soil as the "eternal source of all creativity" (*MW*, 41–42). They have been distracted by their goal of "theoretically" joining individuals dissociated from race, nation, language, and history with millions of other disconnected individuals from other *Völker*, nations, and continents (ibid.) At issue was the modern danger of international-ist globalization that could be halted only by powerful physical and mental rootedness, utopianist fundamentalism. Germany's accelerated political and industrial modernization following the disastrous First World War had created many difficulties for large populations, similar to what we are experiencing now in the hypermodern new millennium, to which the attacks on the New York Trade Center and the Washing-ton Pentagon were the most strikingly allegorical reactions. At issue was also Germany's profound military and political humiliation, bril-liantly exploited by the Nazi credo of an irresistible will to power.

Kampfbund quickly built up a network of local and provincial as-sociations and by August 1933 had organized special groups for film, theater, music, fine arts, architecture, technical design, literature, adult education (*Volksbildung*), studies in folk culture (*Volkstumsarbeit*), phys-ical education and dance, and ancient Germanic history. There were also mergers with new cultural organizations and alliances with older established organizations pertaining to theater, literature, continuing education for low-level white-collar workers—an endless array of asso-ciations supporting various cultural activities (*MW*, 43). The result was a formidable complex of firmly coordinated cultural and educational projects and institutions that was to go on growing after *Kampfbund* had turned into *Nationalsozialistische Kulturgemeinde* and had incor-porated *Volkstum und Heimat*.

Schneider's immediate superior here was a staff member of the *NS-Kulturgemeinde* and the "Gaupropagandaleitung Hauptstelle Kultur" East Prussia, the clunkily titled "Gauvolkstumswart," Alfred Zastrau, like Schneider a 1935 Ph.D. in German literature and culture from Königsberg University.[26] He had distinguished himself at the university with the argument for replacing outdated nineteenth-century philology with a new linguistics: a concept of German language as the historical form of German life and reality-perception. This approach yielded silly but politically correct etymological "evidence" for links between the roots of *sprechen* (speak) and *sprühen* (spray), emphasizing the activist, performative dimension of (German) speech; or between *Wahrhaftigkeit* (veracity) and *Wehrhaftigkeit* (valor). But such speculative self-enhancing arguments can be found in the politicized identity studies of all shapes and colors offered currently at Western universities; and at that stage the Nazi experiment of philo-Germanicism was—or seemed to be—all about the cultural politics of identity.[27] There *was* National-socialism's tradition of political violence and of political anti-Semitism, but the former had been shared to a degree by the Left, and the latter appeared to be toned down as the party became more respectable, gaining in real political power.

As Zastrau argued in a lengthy memorandum of July 31, 1936, the cultural-political importance of *Volkstum und Heimat,* an organization with a small power base, was located primarily in its networking activities, notably through informal *kameradschaftliche* contacts that would be *gleichgeschaltet,* that is, subsumed into "prompt, reliable cooperation with all appropriate State and Party organizations." The most desirable components of this organization were the "correctness of its ideological and cultural-political principles" and its "growing expertise in taking initiative and its effectiveness as role model" (*MW,* 52). The weird mix of pseudo-Germanic archaic neologisms, ideological buzzwords, and pep talk about the organization's super-achieving, combative, energetic motivations and strategies was typical for the utopianist activist constructivism of the earlier stages of the Third Reich in its efforts to distinguish itself from the old, tired, compromised politics of the Weimar *System.*[28]

Following Rosenberg's directives, *Volkstum und Heimat* has to account for all the various local expressions of "earth and homeland" grounded in *Volkstum: Volkskunde, Volkskunst, Volkssprache, Volksmusik, Volksspiel, Volkstanz, Volkserziehung, Volksfest*—all of them important cultural activities in that they communicate the energies and creativity of a "genuine and original cultural life of the *Volk.*" *Volk* is the justification for and incarnation of the all-important *Gleichschaltung,* the arch-utopian principle of obligatory coordination of all utopian subsystems. Its goal is the elimination of all existing democratic institutions with their rational checks and balances, to the point where independent political thought and action could be "switched off" (*ausgeschaltet*) like all the lights. And they were "switched off" as the regime became more totalitarian and the war more and more total.

The cultural values of blood, soil, the homeland, the local, authenticity, native origins, the inherently spontaneous creativity of the *Volk* itself, are all parts of the familiar Nazi ideology. They were derived from early-nineteenth-century concepts of Romantic cultural-political nationalism and its neo-Romantic versions of cultural-political conservatism through the nineteenth century that are still active in many previously underprivileged or oppressed groups' contemporary celebrations of their rooted identities, their "cultures." Previous oppression and alienation are central to both Nazism and Communism; and so is the all-important, irrational, and exploitable fiction of an inherent existential power, wisdom, and total solidarity of the collective—notions that can also be found in the identity politics of minorities in the United States and the former Soviet Union, and in fundamentalist Islam. In Nazism and Communism this translates into a significant community of the masses, *Volk* and proletariat, though they are divided by the different shapes and functions of the collectives: differentiating organic nationalism versus homogenizing technological internationalism; solidarity based on supra-historical blood ties versus historical class consciousness. Accordingly, Zastrau's memorandum emphasized the wealth and variety of *specific* cultural articulations of the central Nazi values of blood, soil, and homeland. He had drawn extensively on an article, "Heimatmuseum und Volkstumsarbeit," just published by Hans Ernst Schneider in the June issue of *Der junge Osten,* the house journal of *Volkstum und Heimat.*

At that time still relatively informal, the administrative structure of *Volkstum und Heimat* would have reflected some indirect methods of influence and persuasion the Nazis had learned from the youth movement and reform pedagogy. They would have been important for the success of National-socialist *Basisarbeit,* also in the context of Schneider's later propagandistic activities for the cause of Germano-centrism in Holland. But the democratic impulses at work in these movements were too marginal and therefore too vulnerable to survive in the politically charged NS educational projects for German youth. Zastrau's and Schneider's level of activity at that time in the area of *Volk*-related artistic education, events, and production was noted as impressive—arranging thirteen week-long performances of folksongs, ten two-week courses in playing the recorder, thirty-four folksong and folkdance evenings, five hundred afternoon performances of puppet shows, six folk art exhibitions, lectures on these subjects, and also folksong awareness courses for political leaders.[29] This program may look oddly idyllic, but *Volkstum,* the core of Nazi ideology, was celebrated like Mass: a high-serious religious ceremony to honor collective German identity. Teaching "political leaders"—young men and women working with youth groups—

to sing folksongs in harmony was serious business, like teaching young American Indians ritual war songs and dances.

Teaching was part of Schneider's *Schulung* activities, namely direct or indirect propaganda for Nazi ideology through courses in folk art and customs, rehearsing *Volksspiele* performed by nonprofessional actors, or arranging for folkdance events, one of his favorite activities. Communist *Basisarbeit* used similar propaganda methods, especially in the youth organizations, and it also emphasized the importance of spontaneous and creative community activities such as singing, dancing, and lay theatre, in celebration of the identity of the larger collective. These were methods that both movements had learned or copied or transferred from the youth movement, together with its anti-bourgeois, utopianist communal energies, and they would resonate in certain ways in the great American interest in folk music in the seventies. The various realizations of radical communalism had great appeal for young people after the radical individualism of the Weimar period, and Schneider was no exception during these years.[30]

Schneider would soon leave the SA to join up with the SS in the fall of 1937. He was sent to Austria to teach *Volkskultur* in an Austrian *Landesdienstlager* for teenage girls and boys, to work with NS student organizations, and to report on "political Catholicism." After this probationary period, in February 1938, he was called to the Berlin headquarters of the SS *Rasse- und Siedlungshauptamt*[31] and that was the end of what Schwerte would sixty years later remember as the good time in Schneider's life. He qualified for him mostly positive memories of the years 1934–38 with a reference to the dark years still unknown in the future. Had Schneider looked more closely, he might have seen danger signs; but he saw during these years a rigid bourgeois status quo breaking up after the Nazi revolution: there was new social openness and community, a new sense of purpose; his writing was published, there seemed to be a future for him and young people like him; they were employed, they had become upwardly mobile.[32] These were relatively good years for many working- and lower-middle-class Germans who at first benefited from the utopia created by that revolution from the Right and hoped that this time things would turn out all right. But with his new position in the *Rasse- und Siedlungshauptamt,* Schwerte had moved closer to the increasingly destructive—in the end self-destructing—center of power, even though he would stay on its margins, and, with luck and relatively protected, he would emerge relatively innocent.

In 1937, the Berlin headquarters of *Rasse- und Siedlungshauptamt* had a staff of about one hundred working on the development and application of the criteria for racial categories; there were numerous subsections, and new offices and positions were constantly established, dissolved, changed.[33] Some of the higher-ranking officials were also involved in the establishment of *Ahnenerbe*, though by the time Schneider arrived, the influence of *Rasse- und Siedlungshauptamt* had already been reduced, and in the late summer of 1938 *Ahnenerbe* took over its *Wissenschaftler,* academics trained in the sciences (*Naturwissenschaften*) and humanities (*Geisteswissenschaften*). The latter were important to the Third Reich as the "theological" guardians of National-socialist orthodoxy in the service of an alternate modernization process fusing past-oriented ancient values such as blood, soil, and clan and the future-oriented, brand-new achievements of technology.

This fusion bestowed premodern magical properties on modern technology and thereby contributed to the curiously open irrationalist aspects of German Fascism. Charged with protecting the New Order from its "enemies" and working out the selection of the National-socialist New Man, Woman, and Child, the SS did not model itself on the old European elites but saw itself as a New Elite, a populist neo-aristocracy of the racially best that would gradually replace the old elites.[34] With all this, the SS was a surprisingly loose structure in which organizations, offices, bureaucracies, associations of all kinds were connected by personal contacts and ties—in stark contrast to the rigorous general political *Gleichschaltung* of all existing cultural and political institutions with National-socialist organizational power interests. Though the different SS units' competencies and duties often intersected, their politics were remarkably independent, and they were resentful of the superior authority of the Reichsführer-SS Heinrich Himmler. This structural informality, reflecting partly the instability of Nazi organizations before 1933 during the movement's *Kampfzeit* and partly an imitation of traditional German ministerial bureaucracy, enabled the SS to maintain its own ideological and political power base in the Third Reich, a state within Hitler's state.

Schneider moved over to *Ahnenerbe* in late 1938 and assumed his position in research and *Schulung* on January 1, 1939, one of his activities being to edit the journal *Weltliteratur.* Since *Literaturwissenschaft* had been excluded from the program of *Ahnenerbe*, its director, Wolfram Sievers, Schneider's supportive superior, had to argue for the journal's importance to *Ahnenerbe* as a significant part of the special mission of the humanities in the *Kriegseinsatz der Geisteswissenschaften.*[35] They were intended as "scientific" support for National-socialist goals such as the cultural and political commonality and recognition of blood ties between all Germanic peoples, and a rejuvenated concept of *Reich*.[36] Schneider's specific *Kriegseinsatz* in Den Haag, where he was sent in July 1940, was to influence *Wissenschaftspolitik* in Holland, later also in Flanders and Norway, in the philo(pan)-Germanicist terms of *Ahnenerbe*. Schneider was—or was perceived to be—so successful that the project was given an official administrative status as *Germanischer Wissenschaftseinsatz* under his leadership in 1943. In his strategies he was partly following ideas proposed by Joseph Otto Plassmann in a mission statement of October 1939.[37] A colleague in *Ahnenerbe* and a Holland specialist, Plassmann had advised continuous examination of the Dutch press regarding Dutch attitudes toward Germany and attempts at influencing certain Dutch newspapers and journals and certain population groups in Holland to be more sympathetic to Germany's goals.[38] This should be done by organizations that already had cultural connections with Holland, for example, *Ahnenerbe* with the Germanic-*völkisch* Dutch "Parallelorganisation," *Der Vaderen Erfdeel*. Their task would be to emphasize the commonality of Dutch-Germanic and German culture, avoiding, as much as possible, obvious political implications (*MW*, 78).

Schneider seems to have taken to heart the latter suggestion, a strategic decision that also suited his temperament and would have contributed to his success. He was liked by his superiors and others who had contact with him for his initiative, his administrative and organizational talents, and—most elusive and perhaps most important—"people skills." The introduction to the first issue of *Weltliteratur* (November 1940) on which the *Volksche Werkgemeenschap* had collaborated with Schneider, was a mission statement praising the contributors as the young combative part of the *völkisch* vanguard in Holland and Belgium spreading the idea of "pan-Germanic commonality" in preparation for a New Order of Europe.

Schneider claimed that the best and brightest in these countries, though at that point only a small group, had already accepted the "might and force" of this idea "emanating from the Führer" and become "passionately and forcefully devoted" to it. He also maintained that it was the powerful idea of a New European Order that had affected them and not German political power supported by military might, though the language he used clearly connoted the aggressively activist nature of that New Order.[39] In addition, Schneider cooperated in establishing offices for the administration of faculty exchange in occupied countries and participated in meetings in Berlin in late 1942 in preparation for a conference for foreign scholars. Again, the stated intention of this conference was to make more accessible to the visitors a "common Germanic world view" by emphasizing Germany's *geistig-kulturelle* rather than political and military claims to leadership and disguising the actual cultural-political purpose of the whole meeting by proposing lecture topics as innocuously academic as possible.[40]

Whether or not Schneider at that point still believed in the legitimacy of Germany's leadership or, if he did so, in his own ability to mislead the foreign scholars as to the real goals of the conference has to remain in the realm of speculation. The discovery of Schwerte's true identity did not lead to the recovery of Schneider: the suspicious, accusatory questions thrown at him by large crowds of hostile, self-righteous journalists did not allow any answers that might have helped with the reconstruction of Schneider's activities and motivations to get a sense of that person in that situation. We know from archival materials that he gave a lecture in Salzburg in early 1943 on the political tasks of German *Wissenschaft*, where he emphasized the importance of studies in the folk cultures of western and northern Germanic border areas, pointing out to listeners "the extent to which these Germanic peoples have forgotten their historical roots." One of his examples here was the German *Mischlingsgesetz*, the law forbidding mixed-race relationships, which caused the leader of the *Nationaal-Socialistische Beweging der Nederlande* (NSB) to complain that "Jews were excluded from the Dutch National-socialist movement."[41] Schwerte's reaction to this, under the circumstances curiously innocent, complaint was the professional conclusion that German propagandistic activities had failed to persuade the members of that small but important Dutch movement that racial homogeneity and purity was inherent in the pan-Germanic *Reich* led by National-socialist Germany.

The foundation myth of the Third Reich was the significance of race as a political and cultural basis on which to build a unified northwestern Europe. How did Schneider regard this foundation myth? Did he have privately held reservations? If yes, to what extent? How much did he know of and what were his private reactions to the exclusion of Jews—in the mid-thirties? in the late thirties? in the early forties? Half a century later, Schwerte would express feelings of sadness and shame when speaking of Schneider's wartime visits to Holland, yet also of enduring and nostalgic memories of pleasant encounters then with Dutch people and seascapes. He liked Holland and thought it important to win it over to the expansive Germanic *Reichsidee*; his overriding desire to carry out his mission successfully blinded him to the meanings of the signals of danger that would have been visible at that time.

In a long, tortuous essay in *Weltliteratur* (October 1943), Hans Rössner emphasized the important role of "deutsche Geisteswissenschaft" in supporting and strengthening the *geistig* and spiritual resistance of the German people in both its defensive and offensive aspects. There would have to be *geistige* defensive confrontation with the ideas and the worldview of Germany's enemies, but also the conservation, new organization, and creation of Europe according to the rules of its organic substance and basis, militarily but at the same time as the beginning of a future peaceful order. These tasks would lead to a "Neuordnung der Wissenschaft" (*MW*, 172–73). One year later Schneider would draw on this essay for his concept of a "Totaler Kriegseinsatz der Wissenschaft" within the section *Germanischer Wissenschaftseinsatz*. In September 1944, with the Allies approaching from all sides, he proposed an *SS-Arbeitsgemeinschaft Wissenschaft*, gathering together all the *Wissenschaftler* still active (read: alive) in the various SS-*Hauptämter* to counter the existing *Zersplitterung* (fragmentation) of responsibilities and personnel (*MW*, 231–33). *Germanischer Wissenschaftseinsatz* can no longer be expressed through scholarly debates but has to "be decisive in its support for the most important tasks of political warfare as demanded in the hour of our people's utmost effort and need."

Going beyond rhetorical admonitions, Schneider proposed the foundation of a *Germanisches Reichsinstitut*, which, in addition to its essential Germanic goals, would deal with pan-European issues in relation to their importance for a "germanische Gemeinschaftsleistung" (community effort) and thus make it possible for Flemish and Dutch *Geisteswissenschaftler* to join with their German colleagues in fighting the "scientific" battle against all ideologically opposing powers.[42] Schneider's suggestion to involve in this battle all still "available," politically suitable German scholars was supported by, among others, Hans Rössner; and his activist Germano-centric *Europagedanke* was echoed by Sievers (*MW*, 239–46). He was most interested, it seems, in the challenge of a more effective organization of the sciences in general and *Geisteswissenschaften* in particular, insisting that every great scientific achievement was built on *Wissenschaftsorganisation* and that so far the effectiveness of *Kriegseinsatz* had left much to be desired.

Schneider's memoranda on *Kriegseinsatz der Wissenschaften* reflect his National-socialist convictions as much as his frustrations regarding the lack of efficiency on this front.[43] There are resonances in these texts of Schneider's earlier, youthful fantasy of a dialogue, during the Seven Years' War, between Frederick the Great and the poet and literary scholar Johann Christoph Gottsched: a *Königliches Gespräch* (1936) between a great ruler and an important *Geisteswissenschaftler*. Energized by the cultural-political importance of his project, a theater not derivative of French language and culture but drawing on a German language and cultural identity not yet consolidated in the second half of the eighteenth century, Gottsched tries to motivate the aging, tired warrior king to help him. He explains that in the absence of a German *Volk* in which the centrifugal cultural interests and energies of German-speaking people could be culturally united, his lifelong fight for a German theater had been doomed from the beginning. Only the king, the political actor, was in a position to create what the poet needed, a *Volk:* "That is your contribution to the poetry of the *Volk* still in the future. . . . Nobody could carry out this task for you. Others may curse your wars, I bless them for I see them as the advent of a more genuine way of being. This is why I say we can only be silent now; because the deed is yours. . . . Today your soldiers are marching with the poet of times to come."[44]

From hindsight, these are badly written, dangerous sentiments of a politically confused twenty-six-year-old who could have been one of the nationalist young people for whom Jaspers had written his book on Max Weber, had it not already been too late. In the meantime, Hitler had seized the power, and the promises of the Third Reich had been too great a temptation. Obviously, the young Schneider identified emotionally with the poet's desire for significant cultural-political participation in the proverbially better future. Did this desire move him toward a Faustian pact with the devil famously played by Gustav Gründgens, the darling of Göring? But was not this Mephisto much too sophisticated, ambiguous, treacherous for the naïve young man who joined the SS in 1937? Eight years later, his world had changed unimaginably.

As late as March 1945, Schneider submitted a list of six topics, surreally irrelevant under the circumstances, for an all-out propaganda effort involving the press and radio as planned by the *Sicherheitsdienst:* 1. the idea of race in a newly organized Europe; 2. the political concept and reality of European *Lebenraum* (one of the central concepts of Nazi ideological-territorial expansion); 3. the *geistig* situation in the European countries; 4. the meanings of Germanic influence in the community of European peoples; 5. achievements and leadership failures in areas under German occupation during the war; 6. special European achievements in Asia and the Americas.[45] In certain ways, Schneider's and his colleagues' reactions to the imminent collapse of the Third Reich reflect the panicked hyperactivity of all the other "letzte Einsätze": the insanely detailed and enforced orders going out to everybody still alive,

old men, women, teenage boys and girls, to defend the besieged fatherland to the inevitable, unimaginably bitter end, which would also be
theirs.[46]

But there is also the enduring self-deception of these *Geisteswissenschaftler* that anybody would be interested now in what they had to
say about Germany's cultural hegemony in Europe. With the war obviously lost, their attempts at creating "a new European order for a developing community of peoples under German leadership" had failed
spectacularly, but one would not have guessed it from that document,
despite some faint indications of self-doubt, perhaps even self-criticism.
Referring in the fourth theme to basic Germanic values, such as loyalty,
honor, and freedom, that have defined the self-perception and acts of
Germans and other Europeans since Tacitus, Schneider asks, "to what
degree can one activate these basic values today?" and the fifth theme
even admits to failures of German leadership. But this makes the document even more terrifying because, in its helpless pretense of carrying
on into a future, it reflects (whether or not Schneider and his colleagues
ever sincerely believed in it), the utopianist irrationalism of Nazi ideology that in the end caused the death of so many people.

In their detailed study of SS institutions on the occasion of the
Schneider-Schwerte case, Joachim Lerchenmüller and Gerd Simon com-
mendably do not demonize Schneider's activities but focus on reconstructing the institutional settings on which he depended and which he
helped to develop. Equally important, they trace the cross-fertilizing
connections between him and members of his generational cohort in
Ahnenerbe. The resulting mosaic-like portrait is of a young enterprising
CEO of *Germanischer Wissenschaftseinsatz* exploring the cultural-political intervention strategies of Germano-centrism rather than a rigidly
aggressive *Ahnenerbe* ideologue. Their portrait is certainly more helpful
than that of the proverbially, allegorically evil SS man, yet it does not
address the issue of Schneider's and his cohort's cultural and political
nationalism, the *Volk*-based *Reichsidee* that later metamorphosed into
a Germano-centric *Europagedanke* and that had led to their interest
in the Nazi ideology of a Third Reich. Looking at Schneider's development between 1937, when he joined the SS, and 1945, when he became
Schwerte, the continuities are as striking as are the changes, and, from a
reasonably unspooked hindsight, both are understandable—in the terms
of their own dangerous dynamics. The circumstances of this choice suggest that, like his other career moves in the thirties, it had more or less
"happened": the conservative but not radically right *Stahlhelm* was tak-
en over by the SA, and Schneider was just swept up with it; *Königliches*

Gespräch (published by the respected Westerman Verlag), caught the attention of Rudolf Jacobsen, a high-ranking official in *Rasse- und Sied-lungshauptamt,* who then became Schneider's mentor and among other things helped him out of a difficult situation by moving him from the SA into the SS.[47]

Yet, the issue is not so much Schneider's relative naiveté, his letting himself get involved in these organizations—did he really want to move over to the SS, with its decidedly better employment prospects, or did he mainly want to escape the SA?[48] It is, rather, that *Ahnenerbe,* like other SS institutions, changed once the war had started, and dramatically so in its end-stage. Schneider got caught up in these changes, as his writings and lectures during the last war years show quite clearly, but not, as far as we know, to the point of involvement in individual criminal activities. In this respect, he seems to have been lucky throughout. His greatest luck in the end was not to be sent to the eastern front and forced to participate in mass murder like his colleague Otto Ohlendorf, an economist disliked by Himmler, who saw him as a rival and a "Non-konformist" drawing attention to the German population's growing discontent with the Nazi regime.

Ohlendorf was transferred to the eastern front as "Leiter der Ein-satzgruppe D" and became involved in the murder of nine thousand Jews, Roma, and Communists, for which he was sentenced to death in 1948 and executed in 1951—a decision that was questioned by many observers across the political spectrum at the time. The fact that Ohlendorf had taken considerable risks as editor of the often openly critical security (SD) reports on domestic issues, one of the reasons why he had been given that "dirty" assignment, did not help him. Schneider did not have such personality problems, if only because he was younger, had less political insight and influence, and was out of view for much of the time. It may have been his immediate superior Sievers, later executed for his involvement with Himmler's notorious *Unterkühlungs-experimente* (cold experiments), or even Himmler himself who protected him from this fate. The psychopath Himmler thought mass killings of Jews and other "enemies" of the Third Reich the most honorably dreadful task in the service of Germany's historical mission and, with terrible logic, he might have sought to spare from this hellish assignment the people he liked.

In a broader moral sense, Schneider was co-responsible for the murderous deeds of the SS even though he was lucky not to have been involved personally. Fifty years later Schwerte would acknowledge that co-responsibility explicitly and repeatedly: he had worn "die Uniform von Auschwitz." He was aware of the crucial importance of several fortunate accidents that spared him having to make certain impossible decisions that others had to make with terrible results. But, then, the principle of accident is more obviously powerful in extreme situations; fortune, good luck or bad luck, is the goddess of war. In his interviews, Leggewie was particularly concerned about Schneider's participation in a *Sonderaktion* in Krakow in late October 1939 in connection with the *Ahnenerbe* assignment to confiscate politically important art—an assignment that might have been protected by one of the notorious special *Einsatzkommandos*. Schwerte, Leggewie writes, was adamant that he had never been in Poland during the time when he worked for *Ahnenerbe* (this time the, in hindsight, lucky coincidence had been a verifiable illness). He was also profoundly disturbed by the insinuation of such connections made by many of his accusers, who could not provide evidence but nevertheless claimed moral authority for their speculative suspicions of an evil SS man: a semi-religious authority that since the end of the war has sought to silence attempts at sorting out facts from fictions, and irrational from rational arguments.[49]

Luck seems to have stayed with Schwerte during his second, his "real," life in postwar Germany. Was he still protected by his "pact with the devil," an overreaching desire for more than the common lot, when he "sold his soul" to the SS for the promises of the Third Reich that would last a thousand years? The Faustian parallels are of course suggestive, if only in adding to the "Germanness" of Schwerte's story; and also in view of the fact that in his most important book, *Faust und das Faustische. Ein Kapitel deutscher Ideologie* (1962), he would later sort out critically the Faustian impulses in German culture. If there was a conscious decision in 1937 to bet on the SS rather than drifting into another job, Schneider's momentous self-invention in 1945, which marked the beginning of his gradual significant transformation over the next fifty years, would have meant a break with the devil: the earth opening underneath him, hellish shrieks and then deafening silence. But this was a modern break, more modern even than the transformation of Goethe's Faust, who in the end would be forgiven because his useful life was *his* achievement, not the devil's.

As in the case of Goethe's Faust, Schneider/Schwerte's break with the devil could be survived without eternal condemnation. For Schwerte this did not mean hope for forgiveness as much as a notion, probably almost an expectation, that in looking at his life over the last half century people would make attempts at understanding its relative value in its continuities and discontinuities. Understanding is less complete and

more ambiguous than forgiving because it does not compress past decisions and acts into a significant moment of judging them "worthy" of
forgiveness. Understanding is a process that extends into the future: its
cumulative, composite perspective on the past and present is open to
other not yet existing or imaginable views that themselves will be con-
tingent on future developments. Contemporary attempts at understanding the issues raised by the Schneider-Schwerte case may differ, even
dramatically, from those in the future. But there would always have to
be the historicity of their own and Schneider-Schwerte's respective situations and thereby their taking into consideration the role of accident
and contingency.

Forgiving assumes, if momentarily, an unquestionable, a priori authority that, beyond all contingencies, redeems the transgressor fully.
The moment of forgiveness may have been unpredictable, unexpected
(if hoped and prayed for); but the status of having been forgiven is
enduring. Understanding does not work on this semi-religious level because it is temporal and provisional. Yet only attempts at understanding
will clarify how in the Schneider-Schwerte case the role of accident in
human affairs would indeed result in a greater, more self-conscious responsibility where it concerned social and political decision making.
Schneider may or may not yet have known that when he turned himself
into Schwerte; but Schwerte evidently did. He could have been successful in postwar Germany in many different ways, but the way he chose
emphasized the crucial importance to social well-being of rational,
stable cultural and political institutions. And in his role of teacher, according to the statements of many of his former students, he would
educate young people to use well the intellectual independence supported by these institutions, and thereby ensure their future.[50]

After the discovery of his true identity, Schwerte was asked in an
interview with *Westdeutscher Rundfunk* (WDR) why he had changed
his name since, according to his own statements, he had not been a
high-ranking member of the SS. His answer was that he had shed his
identity fearing for his life, his freedom and, equally important, his professional future in the field of *Geisteswissenschaften*. He knew that it
would probably take at least ten years "till people would listen to me
again. That much is clear. Perhaps I would never have been listened to
again. Because people would have said what you said, that I was a high-
ranking official and had done bad things. Who, do you think, would
have listened to a man wearing the uniform of the SS? It would have
been a very rare case. We knew what they thought of us, and they were
right, they were right" (*MW,* 282). It was a remarkably unguarded re-

sponse, as were most of his statements in these early interviews. His innocence in dealing with the media points to his initial assumption that the issue would be (however critical and tough) questioning for the sake of better understanding, not sentencing for the sake of excommunication. They would ask him "how did you come to do it?" rather than "how could you possibly have done it?"

The more level-headed of Schwerte's critics argued that his decisions and acts had been centrally motivated by *Geltungsdrang*, the desire to do something noteworthy, be somebody (*MW*, 282). The German word used here, though somewhat derogatory, refers to what American elite universities, the business world, and the army call "leadership qualities." It is an elusive but important talent that served Schwerte well in the postwar era, but it also benefited the institutions for which he worked. He had always been an ambitious doer with a distinct talent for organization and self-presentation. Open to new ideas, flexible, and adaptable, but also self-assured, disciplined, and purposeful, he fit the profile of the ideal manager outlined in the glossy employment sections of *Frankfurter Allgemeine Zeitung* or the *Wall Street Journal*. In the midst of unbelievable chaos and confusion—arguably the worst in European history since the Thirty Years' War—Schneider wanted to have the chance to eventually regain a position in which he could contribute to and exert some influence over future cultural developments. He wanted visibility, to be heard and seen in the world—as it turned out the best way to deal with the problematic past in practical terms. His success in this respect, his having taken the chance and done so well, may have been the most provoking aspect of the Schneider-Schwerte case. Settled comfortably in the authority of their moral arguments for decades, Schwerte's accusers were more than ready to judge and sentence him. Was the old Schwerte simply spontaneous when he gave this answer, expecting his interviewer to understand his situation? Or was he deliberately taking a risk in being honest about his motivations?

Up to a point, some of his critics understood and accepted that Schneider wanted to play a role in postwar Germany, especially since it had turned out to be a very useful one. Not everyone argued that his treacherous change of name and identity, his *Namensbetrug*, made his whole life in postwar Germany a lie. But the terms "lie," "betrayal," "deception," "trickery," "sham," "façade," "charade," "fraud," "mask," and "impostor" appear in the titles of almost all the articles written on the occasion of the scandal. Schwerte's successor at Aachen University and one of his most relentless accusers used as a motto for a gratuitously spiteful attack Adorno's apodictic aphorism "Es gibt kein richtiges Leben im falschen."⁵¹ In this as in much of the troubled German past, Right and Wrong are not that easily separable; it is too simplistic to argue that under the conditions of *Namensbetrug* a convinced Nazi could never have become a convinced democrat. There were the few voices of reason in the stunningly heated, venomous debate that pointed to the significance of Schwerte's eventual transformation into a "convinced democrat." Yet even they did not want to engage with the historical meanings of the young Schneider's idealistic if, from hindsight, dangerously irrational cultural nationalism. For what kind of *Evil* was this nationalism responsible? And did the convinced democrat Schwerte accept that responsibility?

In the radio interview with WDR, Schwerte had said that one of the reasons for changing his name had been the insight in April or early May of 1945, when "the end of this megalomania" had become obvious, that he and others like him felt they needed to contribute to the rebuilding of a Germany that had to find its way "back to the humanity of the world": "we, particularly we who came from the seemingly most radical corners of the world, we had the obligation to acknowledge our responsibility for what we had envisioned, that it simply had to go wrong, and this way we slowly moved toward democracy" (*MW*, 284). It was difficult, even for relatively fair critics, to take seriously Schwerte's invoking *Humanität* and *Demokratie* at this turning point. Schwerte said himself in the interview that claiming for his experience of conversion values so conspicuously denied by the Nazi regime might seem "pathetisch." It had indeed taken a gradual learning process to find his way toward meaningful participation in democracy.

Schwerte attempted to refute some of the core accusations in a letter to the editor of *FAZ* (November 13, 1996), "In 50 Lebens- und Arbeitsjahren gewandelt [transformed]," in answer to Hermann Kurzke's "Germanisten unter Hitler–Wie aus Hans Ernst Schneider Professor Schwerte wurde" (*FAZ*, October 28, 1996). He focused on the central argument that since he had lied in 1945, he had to go on lying, would always lie: and insisted that he was not denying or hiding his activities till 1945. He acknowledged his guilt and shame and had spoken openly about his past, as much as he could remember of it after so many years.

Schwerte linked the suspicion that he would never speak the truth to the explicit denial of a possible transformation over a period of fifty years. This denial would then also concern his "'Konversion' (Mai/Juni in Lübeck)" and acceptance of "a new responsibility after the catastrophe of a life gone radically wrong." Instead, his life after 1945 appeared to have been nothing but "a lie and a cheat," following the maxim "once a Nazi, always a Nazi," no matter how much he had tried to turn his life around and this time work for the good. He agreed with Kurzke that it was not indignation and rage (*Empörung*) that would contribute to a better historical understanding but reasoned, critical elucidation (*Aufklärung*)—a task he had set himself for the last decades. As he said repeatedly to interviewers in 1995: "I wanted to become a teacher; any kind of teacher." In this desire to teach, Schwerte seems to have been remarkably consistent (even though the contents of his teaching would be dramatically different); some of his interviewers would discover in the archival materials that he had expressed this goal several times in job applications during the Third Reich.[52]

When confronting Schwerte with his evil past, even partly sympathetic critics would see all of his statements since 1995 as "the largely unreliable result of retrospective wishful thinking and actual difficulties to remember" (*MW*, 285). Yes and no; the reliability of these statements may be fragile, but they do deserve our attention, since they tell us something about Schwerte's former self, Schneider, a man in circumstances already unimaginably different from, distant to, ours. Schwerte's ongoing processes of transformation have confirmed his becoming an active participant in postwar democratic culture and politics; yet it was the difference and the distance that made it so easy for his critics to construct Schneider as an uncommonly wicked defendant, whose crimes against humanity and transgression against all Western values would have made such transformation simply impossible. Arrested in this role, Schwerte was in no position to question and perhaps modify the accusations and the demands to profess, again and again, his shame and guilt. When he wrote in his letter to *FAZ* that he had already acknowledged his shame and his guilt, he did not realize that his critics' and their audiences' appetite for such declarations was insatiable. He was not encouraged to engage in patiently searching his memory for details of the events and acts of Schneider's past because his questioners were a priori certain that what he would find had to be monstrous. Where the bad German past is concerned, demonstrations of indignation and rage still win out easily over sober attempts at *Aufklärung*.

On May 17, 1995, Schwerte wrote to Marita Keilson, a former dissertation student who had contacted him on April 30, immediately after the news broke: "Still in the middle of the 'hell of the media,' day and night, it is almost impossible for me to write, to answer, to express my gratitude for the many letters." Her letter particularly had given him back momentarily the "composure" of a lived continuity—something that would elude and haunt him for the last years of his life—and so had her article "Hans Schwerte und das NS-Erbe" in *Berliner Tagesspiegel* (May 5): "your article was almost the only one in the media chaos that managed to communicate what I had done during those 'ominous' fifty years, apart from 'falsifying documents.'"[53] Both Marita Keilson's first letter and her article had focused on Schwerte's importance as a teacher, particularly for students in the sixties who needed, as she did, to be introduced to the study of literature in a cultural-political-historical context that very much included the troubled German past. Her article and a later lecture did not attempt to find excuses for the Schneider-part of his life but to argue the value for others of the Schwerte-part and make that the issue of the debate.[54] For this reason, too, Marita Keilson and her husband, the German-Jewish psychoanalyst Hans Keilson, who had emigrated to Holland and for many decades worked with traumatized Jewish orphans, argued against the government's withdrawal of Schwerte's pension and medical insurance.

Hans Keilson called this act "shameful," asserting that the man who wrote the *Faust* book was no longer an SS man and should not be treated as such.[55] In a letter of November 17, 1996, both Keilsons agreed with Schwerte's arguments in his letter to *FAZ*. It was not so much the punitive, constrained conditions in which he had to live out his last years but the denial by postwar German society, and in this petty way, that he had existed at all over the last half century. In his first letter to Schwerte, Hans Keilson expressed the wish to meet him personally so that they could learn about and from each other because

> After all, you and I are almost the same age, and we are the surviving witnesses to a time whose inner topography still holds many secrets and mysteries waiting to be answered and clarified. I have often asked myself, what would have become of me, if I had not been born a German Jew. I am convinced that in a conversation between us which perhaps should be recorded, a part of contemporary history would become transparent that has so far been obscured by half-true and false moral stigmata but could elucidate the real decisions in both of our pasts, conflicts and misfortunes.[56]

There would be more letters that touched on this issue, and they would meet and talk. But the conversation seems to have been more private and not appropriate for the public space of a radio broadcast, as Hans Keilson seems to have envisioned originally and Schwerte seems to have thought desireable.[57]

Marita Keilson's spontaneity made it possible for Schwerte to talk about his past more openly than to anybody else outside the circle of his family and a few old friends. But the limits of his opening up in remembering are as instructive as are the memories themselves. In her first letter, Marita Keilson had immediately reassured Schwerte that he should not feel obliged to "explain the situation" though she "also understood that it would be difficult for you in the immediate situation to write to anyone without explaining yourself." This was the core of Schwerte's difficulty, especially in 1995: he was bombarded with requests to "explain himself," but nobody listened to his attempts at explanation because they knew them to be nothing but pure apologeticism, above all profoundly lacking in remorse. Given the German cultural and political preoccupation with confronting their troubled past "honestly" and the media's hyper-thorough prosecution of any failure in this regard, particularly in this dramatic, allegorical case, their feeding frenzy was not surprising. Nor was the general summary condemnation, even if the number and fervor of the politicians, journalists, public intellectuals, and fellow-academics rushing to judgment was astonishing.[58]

Where Schwerte was not pressed in this way, in situations where friends wanted to understand better the interdependencies of rupture and continuity in his life—the most familiar and most puzzling phenomenon in postwar (West) Germany for his generation—he did try to get back to his former self and to explain at least some aspects of his former life. Yet half a century after what had been deeply traumatic events, the past had become and remained too remote, too separate, and memory too uncertain. Trying to clarify who he had been in that now so strange place and time of the Third Reich, but also, inevitably, concerned not to appear too tainted to keep their friendship, he could not ultimately remember much more about this past than they had generally known. This is not to say that there was anything in his past that would have tainted him in legal terms and that he was therefore deliberately holding back. But Schwerte knew that the Nazi period has been a peculiarly exotic past, both more distant and more present in the collective imagination than other pasts and thus more vulnerable to misunderstandings and misinterpretations. Fears in this respect might have diminished his ability to recall it, beyond the difficulties of unstable memory in old age and, perhaps even more important, his active rather than contemplative temperament and conduct over many years.

Were these fears even conscious? Would they have been justified in the case of his friends who had known him as Hans Schwerte and accepted the opacity and obscurity of the part of his life that was in the past? Since he was not on trial with them, they respected the privacy of his feelings about the past and did not probe their sincerity. And yet, as his correspondence with Marita Keilson suggests, it was not quite that simple, neither for him nor for her. In a letter of June 20, 1996, he asks her anxiously to keep to herself the nostalgic memories of wartime Holland he had just shared with her in a long telephone conversation:

> it was a momentary memory image of the landscape and the sea. I was of course aware every day that I was part of the German occupation; I knew of course about the raging war 'out there,' and the air raid nights at home. And many other things. And yet the other image has stayed in my conscious-unconscious memory like, as you reminded me, the images of my native East Prussia and the seacoast there. These images are in some way interconnected. Please understand me. I could never have mentioned this in front of your husband; that would have been cynical.

Marita Keilson answered promptly (June 24, 1996) to reassure Schwerte: it had seemed to her that these "sunlit" Dutch memories emerged as if he was talking to himself. Her husband, she knew, would understand very well Schwerte's layered memories as well as his scruples about them. Moreover, on the basis of what he had read of Schwerte's work, he would know how to appreciate the ambivalences. Comparing Schwerte's and her husband's experiences with their memories, she points out the difficulties, in both cases, of finding a balance between the sunlit and the dark ones: "but why should that be easy, especially for his and your generation. Perhaps it is a part of what you call the 'homelessness of this century.'"

Inevitably, this homelessness appears different in different perspectives. Neither Marita Keilson, secure in her Dutch identity and the moral authority of her German-Jewish husband, nor Schwerte, more lost and uncertain of "himself" than he could ever have imagined, would have wanted to explore honestly the suddenly inverted power relations. In her lecture at Erlangen University before an overwhelmingly hostile audience of Schwerte's academic peers and young students, the grandchildren's generation, Marita Keilson referred to Schwerte's short fiction "Begegnung auf der Strasse" (1954; encounter in the street), which, she thought, dealt with the issue of remorse. Witness to a fatal motorcycle accident, the protagonist is stained with the blood of the victim. Having washed it off and continuing on his walk home, he realizes that despite the coincidental nature of his involvement and the accidental nature of the victim's death, there was still the question whether it was possible "to wash off the blood, to really wash off the blood of the victim? This encounter could not be extinguished. He would have to try to live with it."

While Marita Keilson emphasized the protagonist's insight that the victim's blood cannot just be washed off,[59] the sociologist Karl-Siegbert Rehberg read the text quite differently. Himself a successful academic administrator and former colleague of Schwerte at Aachen University, Rehberg remembers Schwerte's political and organizational intelligence, gift for mediating between opposing positions, and, by implication, pleasure in power. Schneider is for him a "technocrat" in a future Nazi-ruled Europe with an "opportunistic talent for adaptability to any kind of rule, ambition, vanity, and striving for the respective center of influence. Every system needs agile and talented actors." In the status quo climate of Aachen University, Rehberg argues, Schwerte would appear "progressive" and "supportive of reforms"; but he did not manage to atone, achieve *Wiedergutmachung* (reparation), because he "did not take the risk of choosing the shame of exposing himself to the judgement of others." This way, he "just kept muddling through, like most people," if with more dramatic consequences.[60]

Would Rehberg, roughly a generation younger than Schwerte but otherwise quite like him, have taken that risk and exposed himself to this kind of judgment? Reflecting on the mistakes his generation has made in their preoccupation with the Nazi past, Bernhard Schlink writes: "The lesson we learned from the past concerns morality rather than institutions. We reproached our parents, teachers, professors or politicians with having been blind, cowardly, opportunistic, recklessly irresponsible careerists. We accused them of their individual moral failure: their moral conduct should and could have been different." His generation's issue in this agonistic debate with their parents was for Schlink, in the self-ironical perspective of middle age, that generation's profound lack of moral and civil courage and the children's courage in confronting the parents with these reproaches; they were training for courage in the future.[61]

In some sense, Rehberg and most of Schwerte's high-serious critics are still training for this courage, avoiding it as much as possible in the meantime. Rehberg denies Schwerte's "conversion" and accuses him of having refused, to the end, to deal with what he had done as Schneider during the Third Reich and of having simply repressed, extinguished, that part of his past. For evidence he quotes the two concluding sentences right after the passage selected by Marita Keilson: Walking on, the protagonist has soon disappeared in the stream of people: "The bloodstain was no longer visible. It was quickly extinguished by people stepping on it." Rehberg does not consider the change in perspective here: who notices that the bloodstain was no longer visible and what, then, is the meaning of this last comment? In Rehberg's view, the "Megamaschine" of German postwar society had smoothed out the roughness of the past by the mid-fifties, "making it possible to believe that, on the whole, the traces of blood would be covered over and forgotten."[62] Rehberg's perspective on the Schwerte-Schneider case, though ostensibly more realistic and not as simplistically moralistic, still shares his generation's self-righteousness.

The protagonist of the story thinks and fears that the traces, the memories, will stay with him. Compared to others' comments on the subject, Rehberg's is relatively fair in its evaluation of Schwerte's considerable achievements aided by stable political and cultural institutions. However, the question whether Schneider should, would, or must have known about the cold experiments in particular and the mass deportations and killings in general remains an important issue for Rehberg, from which he cannot separate Schwerte's life. Not as aggressively as others, but still prescriptively, he charges Schwerte with not having met the challenge to create "something worthy of teaching and learning out of the most profound crisis of his life, its complete retroactive devaluation." He does not seem to question this general, complete devaluation, nor does he seem to completely share it. But the current cultural power of the memory-discourses of Nazi victimization must have seemed too great not too seek protection in ambiguity.

Rehberg did not think that he could say what Marita Keilson said, namely that as far as we know, Schneider was not personally involved in criminal activities; that it does not help to speculate what he might have done and should have known; that Schneider, as he was forced to realize himself, made bad choices and sought to overcome their consequences by seizing the opportunity to become Schwerte and lead a useful life. It is this life that she knows and that interests her now. The implication of a position such as hers—though she did not say so explicitly—is that questions of atonement and remorse are on a different level, both more immediate and more remote, and have to be treated accordingly. Sixty years after the historical events, it might be useful to pose them more tentatively, bringing to them more historical information and imagination and less judgmental emotion. Rehberg ends his essay with the question whether Hans Schwerte should not be granted a "second chance," have "a right to a new life." But then he cannot resist framing the question approvingly with the comment made by a former student of Schwerte that such second chance "would have to go together with never forgetting that it was not granted to the victims." As Schwerte's writings, lectures, and cultural-political activities since the early sixties suggest, he had not forgotten.

Marita Keilson's correspondence with Schwerte deals with many of the most difficult conundrums of his case, notably his double, or split, or continuous/discontinuous, composite identity reflecting the entwined German past and present—an issue that could not be resolved but perhaps could be better clarified. On September 17, 1995, she quoted from the letter of a fellow former student: "Schwerte will remain Schwerte for me and not Schneider," adding shrewdly that it won't do to "just want Hans Schwerte without Hans Schneider. It is not that simple, at least not in the German tradition. We got Hans Schwerte, and everything we owe him, that is, all he has done since 1945, because in so many ways it is built intellectually on the experiences of Hans Schneider." Schwerte's answer of September 26, 1995, might have pleased Rehberg as an attempt to fit his existential crisis into a pedagogically worthwhile example, but the fit is almost too perfect, and in that too much of a justification rather than an attempt at explanation. He writes that "the *geistig*-political experiences and thinking of Hans Schwerte are certainly based on the experiences and entanglements of Hans Schneider. . . . It was only because I was at the center of the insanity and criminality of that regime and could observe them from up close . . . that I could, after the war and a period of searching, begin my 'work' and finally write my hidden autobiography in the book on 'Faust and the Faustian.'" His "bitter experiences and errors" should not be overlooked; but neither should his "efforts in support of opening the eyes of the developing new Germany to the disastrous German past." He desperately wants these efforts to be recognized in a more generous view of his postwar life, his half a century of working and living in postwar Germany.

Marita Keilson's view of an underlying continuity was more realistic. In a letter of February 2, 1997, Schwerte described the difficulties of having to deal with a multitude of former selves as they appeared in the many accusatory analyses of Schneider/Schwerte—"how could I not mislay myself"—and the feeling that he no longer was "a contemporary to anyone, at best a *Paradigma*." Her comment was that the inner integration of Schneider-Schwerte had probably worked quite well and the problem was the practical question of how to make it public. The *Paradigma* seems to her a somewhat dangerous distance to himself, Schwerte (March 23, 1997). She was right about the temporal process of integration; but from her secure position—she had been attacked for her support of Schwerte, but nobody questioned her and especially her husband's general moral authority—she could not really understand the near impossible difficulties of that "practical question."

During his last years, Schwerte was in no position to deal with them, nor was he able to cope with the *Paradigma:* he could not disassociate himself from the many, mostly hostile, constructs of his then multiple selves. In early October 1998, Schwerte wrote to Marita and Hans Keilson about the impact on him of Leggewie's book, eager to get their reactions: he finds the first (longer) part about his life as Schneider harshly judgmental; but in the second part he sees attempts to come closer to his current existence: "Taking the book as a whole, I finally feel that I am taken seriously as a whole person and presented as such and not dissected into arbitrary pieces or layers." Leggewie's book has made him "whole" again, and at the same time has rendered "understandable" his own "confusion" at the end of his life.

Marita Keilson reacted less positively to what from her very different position looked like a rather summary "Aussensicht" of Schwerte's life and work. She was also noticeably unenthusiastic about more interviews and discussions of the identity-issue planned by the energetic Leggewie. No longer sure that the "moving" conversation between Hans Keilson and Hans Schwerte, tentatively scheduled for broadcast by *Bayerischer Rundfunk*, would be effective in the public sphere, she suggested that it would better be left in the private sphere (October 28, 1998). She was right; public discussions of the Schwerte case should have dealt with the question to what extent Schwerte's intelligent and well-informed attempts to open the eyes of his students and other readers to the powerful and dangerous irrationalisms of the Third Reich had depended on his own uncommonly immediate experience of them. But given the demonization of this experience, which inexorably collapsed Schwerte into Schneider, there seemed to be no public space for a rational exploration of the entangled, potentially so instructive issues raised by this case.

A small minority of German intellectuals thought Schwerte's professional life an example of successful transformation in time; a tiny minority said so openly. The single most intriguing and troubling aspect of the Schneider-Schwerte case has been the refusal of a great majority of intellectuals and other members of the German elite to consider the meanings of temporality where the bad German past is concerned, because the nature of Schwerte's past encouraged precisely that refusal. Judging from his unanimously harsh condemnation and rejection by the German government, most academics, and practically all the elite mass media, Schwerte's useful, "good" life over a period of more than fifty years was not only denied but turned against him as nothing but lies, "Lebenslüge." It was seen as personal, professional, and political betrayal and thereby deliberate "victimization" of all those who had "believed in him," namely had accepted his new identity as a matter of course and had enjoyed their contacts with him. Johannes Rau was among those who felt existentially violated by Schneider's "treachery," and, as always, he asked the media to share his profound pain. He had benefited considerably from Schwerte's administrative experience and expertise—as had Schwerte from Rau's making use of what he had to offer.

Rau had been an admirer of Schwerte's ability during the "wild" years in Aachen, students' discontent in the late sixties and early seventies, to "reconcile instead of divide" ("versöhnen statt spalten"). It was Schwerte's motto, adopted by Rau while running for the office of *Bundeskanzler;* but he sought to forget this now grotesquely embarrassing friendship as quickly as possible. Marita Keilson wrote several letters pleading to redress the issue of Schwerte's suspended pension and decorations by arguing the cultural value of his postwar activities. Rau's successor as *Wissenschaftsminister* in Nordrhein-Westfalen expressed her intense *Betroffenheit* that such a well-known academic could have kept secret for all these decades his criminal past. Her most important concern, she wrote, was the question whether "all of this"—his service to the university and the country—"had been but a mask and cover-up" for the sake of his career or had there "also been purification and expiation? Has Dr. Schneider become a better person? However, these issues do not touch on collective but individual responsibility and its acknowledgement." Notwithstanding the *Wissenschaftsminister's* intense concern for his spiritual health, "Dr. Schwerte was a civil servant, and in Germany this relationship demands special loyalties." Schneider-Schwerte had gotten his position by means of "cunning deception" and was therefore not eligible for a pension, and no redress was legally possible, since he had hidden his true identity and not taken individual responsibility for his past.[63] This letter, in its hypocrisy and "Goodness," sums up mercilessly the damages done by the German elite's internalization of German collective guilt.

The German *Bundespräsident,* Roman Herzog (Rau's predecessor in this office), whom Marita Keilson had asked to consider restoring to Schwerte the *Verdientstorden der Bundesrepublik Deutschland* awarded for his outstanding service (October 18, 1995), informed her that Schwerte would never have been awarded the order if the reproaches made against him had been known earlier (December 21, 1995). But the issue was, as Marita Keilson had pointed out in both cases, the reality of Schwerte's service, notwithstanding the accusations; the fact that they had not surfaced earlier to prevent the award was not an argument. Like the critics, the officials avoided an open discussion of the meanings and the value of postwar transformations. Training, as Schlink put it shrewdly, to have the courage to resist an evil regime in the future, they accused Schwerte of not having had that courage in the past (like their lamentable parents), and therefore denied him the experience of transformation in a future that he had wrongfully shared with them, the children.

The argument underlying all these complaints and lamentations was that being a good citizen and good man in a situation where one could draw on the lawful authority of political and cultural institutions did not count. No matter how honorable and useful, Schwerte's conduct could have only negative value because he had cheated his way into postwar West German society and then lived his life under the much too easy circumstances of a reasonably well functioning Western democracy. Most of his critics had never known anything but these conditions, at least in adulthood. But it seems that the generational difference served them well as an excuse for not even trying to imagine Schwerte in the time and place of Schneider, once Schwerte's changed identity had become an issue. The "real" part of Schneider/Schwerte could only be Schneider because it was *his* life, even though it was much shorter than Schwerte's, that carried the heavy weight of the German past. Where Schwerte had sinfully denied that evil past its due by not accepting punishment and not showing remorse, his critics confronted the German past "honestly" by condemning him. In this scenario, it made perfect sense that the German government withdrew not only his decorations for outstanding service, but also the pension Schwerte had earned with his good work over many decades, because he really *was* nothing but Schneider.

But why, if the indeed profound qualitative difference between Schneider's and Schwerte's worlds seemed so clear to the critics, were they unable to appreciate the difference between the two men? Was it not precisely the reality of an extraordinary collective change, enabled and supported by functioning political and cultural institutions, that over the last half century has made possible the development of a new democratic Germany? An overwhelming majority of Germans across the generational and political spectrum has rightly identified with this new Germany because it has offered them the choice to be good citizens. Yet that choice still had to be made; and Schneider-turned-Schwerte did indeed make it, arguably more consciously and consistently than many of his critics.

Schwerte's critics were adamant that he could not be allowed to survive Schneider's identity as *Täter*. Ironically, it might have been easier for him to reveal his past as Schneider twenty years ago, when the presence of the past was less politicized. The concept of "Täter" has become more generalized, collectivized, and virulent during the last two decades, leading up to and in the aftermath of the collapse of the Eastern Bloc.[64] The ease with which references are currently made to the "Tätergeneration"—as if all Germans living at that period had been guilty of mass murder—made it easier to condemn Schwerte immediately and absolutely. If all Germans of his generation were *Täter,* how could an SS officer not be super-guilty? Simon and Lerchenmüller based their "ranking" of Schneider as "Normaltäter" (as compared to those members of the SS who were personally involved in criminal activities) on the available archival evidence: despite his connection with *Ahnenerbe,* Schneider was, as far as we know, most probably not informed about and almost certainly not involved in the infamous cold experiments.[65]

Schneider was not the monster of unspeakable secrets but an ordinary, if intelligent and ambitious, man living under the conditions of a criminal regime whose ideological assumptions (if not its outright criminal acts) he had shared but would learn to reject. It is true, Schneider's approach to promoting ideological pan-Germanism, his favoring, on the whole, persuasive cultural over forceful political indoctrination, may have helped him to conceal from his audience and also himself the increasingly violent politics of total domination at the core of Nazi *Weltanschauung.* Yet it was also the irrefutable evidence of the catastrophic consequences of this domination that shocked Schneider to "convert" to a different future in 1945, and, judging by their conduct, it seemed to have motivated Schwerte and other former SS officers to rethink the concept of Europe. In the mid-fifties, Schwerte edited four volumes of a series on the concept of Europe, *Gestalter unserer Zeit,* together with Wilhelm Spengler and Hans Rössner. The three men had worked together on the *Europagedanke* during the last years of the war, when SS research was focused on questions concerning Germany's political leadership in a Germanic-German-centric Europe. After the complete discrediting of German nationalism, "Europe" had considerable cultural appeal for German readers in the fifties, but even though Schwerte was as attentive to audience reactions as Schneider had been, his understanding of the issues was significantly different. When he and Spengler now raised questions of political strategies, it was to argue the necessity of European peoples coming together after a war of unheard dimensions that had been started by Germany and cost Europe its "old central position." The historical Europe could survive only as a union subsuming the old nationalisms.

Yet if German-centrism and militarism were now safely in the past,[66] there was still some way to go to arrive at Schwerte's intellectual position in his *Faust* book (1962) and his political activities as a left-liberal academic administrator. Schwerte's, Germany's, transformation did not happen overnight, and his "conversion" in 1945 could have meant only its as yet unrealized potential. In the *Faust* book Schwerte would critically analyze "Germanic-German" celebration of significant national fatedness and tragedy and of the "great individual" that does not recognize limitations—at the cost of others.[67] But his most public statements about the dangers of political neo-Romanticism and irrationalism were made on the occasion of the 1965 *Nürnberger Gespräche,* a series of five conversations before large audiences in the Nürnberg *Meistersingerhalle* on the two questions of "How Was it Possible?" and "What Is the Connection between Auschwitz and the German People?" Invited guests included the historian Fritz Stern, the KZ chronicler H. G. Adler, and the *Generalstaatsanwalt* Fritz Bauer, chief prosecutor at the Frankfurt Auschwitz trial in 1965.

Schwerte, who had organized the event together with Hermann Glaser, made several important interventions that echoed his critique of irrational ideological nationalism in the *Faust* book. He also argued against the destructive right to dominance of "Germanic-German *Herrenmenschen*" since the early nineteenth century, which he connected with the mission of genocide, not only of Jews but of East European peoples—the East as fulfillment of this mission—and he quoted Himmler: "This will be our historic achievement, that we have killed thousands and millions and remained decent *(anständig).*" Schwerte thought this sentence a key to the understanding of National-socialism at the end-stage, when Himmler's influence was greatest:

> Killing was not just a robotic duty but was executed with *religious* conviction. . . . Himmler and his people thought in "Germanic" terms . . . the inhuman friend-enemy scenario. There are only the chosen ones and total aliens, the enemy who has to be destroyed to uphold the order of the world. Auschwitz, then, is the most shocking and radical example of the possible consequences of ideologies that have their source in early 19th century German political Romanticism, once they were no longer controlled by rational thought.[68]

Again and again during these conversations, Schwerte insisted on the cultural and political importance, particularly for Germans, of the intellectual achievements of the European Enlightenment. In this context he also spoke of shame for Germany's intellectual history in the nineteenth and early twentieth centuries. Less than two decades after his "conversion," Schneider's transformation was complete; Schwerte had "arrived in the West and he was to stay there."[69]

Another three decades later, the great majority of Schwerte's critics refused to believe this transformation, though there was now much more evidence of it. Ulrich Greiner expressed his utter, scandalized amazement that "this former SS-*Hauptsturmführer* was sitting on the podium of the *Nürnberger Gespräche* which he had co-founded, one of the first public attempts of *Vergangenheitsbewältigung,* sitting next to the *Generalstaatsanwalt* Fritz Bauer who had instigated the Auschwitz trial, and said: 'Killing was not just a robotic duty but was executed with *religious* conviction.' . . . This from the man who not only shared this 'religious' conviction but enforced it by draconic means." Quite apart from these undocumented allegations, Greiner also characterizes Schwerte's motivations as a combination of "blind denial and the desire to make amends,"[70] refusing to consider Schneider-Schwerte's learning process. He simply denied the significance of Schwerte's contribution to the *Nürnberger Gespräche,* namely his analysis of National-socialism, especially in its end-stage, as a premodern fundamentalist symbiosis of religion and politics.

This symbiosis is an enormous challenge to the West today and, like National-socialism, needs to be analyzed rather than demonized. But Schwerte's critics seemed interested only in accusations built on suspicious speculations that Schwerte must have been more criminally involved, must have known more than he said he had, and that such a person could never be forgiven. Arguably, the issue was understanding, not forgiving; but the heady authority to grant or withhold forgiveness, derived from the purity of their belief in Nazi Evil, made understanding a much less interesting proposition. Perhaps the most instructive aspect of the Schneider/Schwerte affair was the critics' lack of interest in National-socialism as a complex historical ideology propagated by Schneider and left behind by Schwerte—a transformation quite common among intellectuals who formerly propagated now historical Communist ideologies. But it is also true that the extreme acts of destruction at the end-stage of WWII seem to have sucked up, like a black hole, all attempts at understanding "how it was possible."

If Schwerte cannot be reduced to Schneider, it is also too easy to just erase him. In acknowledging the, in some ways, still obscure German past that, for the time being, still seems to resist or evade its place in history, we should not defer more open and critical discussions of these

issues into an indefinite future. In that respect, the *Nürnberger Gespräche* four decades ago were more productive than were most of the
recent German memory debates. No group, Jewish or non-Jewish, has
the semi-religious authority to forgive or withhold forgiving; they all
share in the responsibility to make Germany's troubled past more accessible in the (ideally) secular, rational, differentiating terms of modern
historiography—the terms of our contemporary scientific and technocratic culture.

———

Schwerte's critics denied him the temporal, processual nature of
transformation and of memory because they needed to insist on the
enduringly criminal identity of the man who had lied about his past and
cheated them of contrition and expiation. Not even Schneider's knowledge of, let alone his involvement with, the cold experiments could be
proved, yet the relentless attacks fed on the enduring suspicion that
Schneider must have known and was therefore involved. Keeping this
suspicion alive, his critics could argue that the discovery of Schneider
automatically identified Schwerte with "radical Evil," a monster that
had to be exorcized from civilized community. Rushing to judge and
condemn him, they presented him as an opportunist of such (super- or
sub-human) dimensions that it was precisely his apprenticeship in the
criminal *Ahnenerbe* that prepared Schneider for Schwerte's stellar rise
in postwar Germany. It had been all the same for Schneider-Schwerte
which political system he served; "der Opportunist Schneider" had not
undergone any transformation, but simply adjusted his career to the
changing times. In the words of his successor at Aachen, Theo Buck:
"Slowly but surely he made the expedient mental turn of 180. He was
intelligent enough to state, under a false name, exactly the opposite of
what he had written as Hans Schneider. Thus in a simplified procedure
of self-denazification and self-amnesty, the card-carrying SS man became an allegedly convinced model democrat who found that he had it
in him to help build a democratic Germany. 'Life with a Mask' could
begin."[71]
Buck's perspective may appear unpleasantly bigoted because of his
verbal aggressiveness; but it was essentially the perspective of most of
Schwerte's critics: they simply would not allow Schwerte to have "really" changed. The sincere contrition and absolute rejection of Nazi
ideology as precondition for a sincere conversion to the ideology of
democracy has been an all-important issue in the enduring old-new debate of an *unbewältigte Vergangenheit*. If Schwerte seems to present

an allegorically clear case, it is in the terms not of his own beliefs or non-beliefs but of the expectations underlying his condemnation. He is the incarnation of the sinful past-denier much lamented by intellectuals and politicians since the end of the war: lamentations that have always pointed to the regrettable shortcomings in that respect of other people. *Spiegel,* in an early interview with Schwerte in May 1995, was properly horrified that he had established a chair for Jewish studies: "he who was praised for the hate-speech journal *Storm* by Standartenführer Wolfram Sievers who was later hanged in Nürnberg."

Like other academic programs supported by the cultural politics of identity, Jewish studies has become desirable for humanities curricula at Western universities. Schwerte, a successful academic administrator, was no exception in taking the initiative to establish it at his university. He may have thought it a truly good project in the current situation, beyond its obvious political correctness value and beyond the issue of expiation for his past as Schneider.[72] Schwerte was always a man of his time, as Schneider had been in very different circumstances. He changed in time and with the times; he transformed himself and in this process was helped rather than hindered by his memories and regrets. When he put the past behind him, he did and did not look back. He repeatedly said that he had always been energized and exhilarated by the new and surprising impulses of cultural and political change. In the first part of the sixties it was his working with the politically progressive student theater in Erlangen and his establishing the new program in theater history. When he was considered for the position in Aachen in the mid-sixties, he was seen as a left-liberal interested in university reform.[73]

It is particularly this aspect of Schwerte's personality—his temperamental and intellectual willingness to change by making use of the potentialities of change—that makes Schwerte's case so instructive. If Jewish studies had become an important issue for a variety of culturally-politically entangled reasons, Schwerte would act in response to this new reality, as he had in the case of political liberalism, an important issue since the mid-sixties in the academic world. Pointing to a photo of Böll, Grass, and Brandt, Schwerte told the *Spiegel* interviewer that he felt "politically at home" with these men. For many years he had conducted himself as if he did, and there is no reason to assume that his democratic *Weltanschauung* was anything but sincere, judging, as we normally do, by the evidence of a person's conduct. But his situation was abnormal to the point that it skewed his critics' perspective and thereby the evidence: in the eyes of this interviewer as many others, Schwerte's sincerity was out of the question: he could never have been, never be, a sincere democrat since he had not always been one.[74] This refusal to engage with Schwerte's (and their own) temporality obscured the plausible assumption that Schneider, magically transported from *Ahnenerbe* to a postwar Western institution of higher learning, would most probably have soon turned into Schwerte. One of the few perceptive commentators on Schwerte's—and his critics'—difficulties pointed out that Schwerte/Schneider's "diachrone Schizophrenie" is a symptom that could also be observed in German postwar society as a whole, very much including the universities: "The Germans can probably recover and heal, because they have the use of several lives (generations); an individual, for the same reasons, cannot."[75]

One of the greatest problems caused by this *diachrone Schizophrenie* is the role of memory, which also has consequences for the modalities of remorse. When Professor Hans Schwerte went to Holland and Belgium in the early eighties as a highly welcome cultural ambassador sent by his friend Johannes Rau, then *Wissenschaftsminister* of Nordrhein-Westfalen, did he remember the darker aspects of the past? or more those "sunlit" images that might be a bridge to his good life in the present? Even if he had been able to remember the feelings of his former selves sequentially, not just immediately before and after the traumatic moment of radical change, would it not have been a near-impossibility to retrieve this former self as a process of transformations in time? Would it not always just be fragments, refractions of something that was elusive by virtue of its temporality? How can we know with certainty who we were in the past other than that we were different then from what we are now? How could Schwerte have answered questions who Schneider was; what exactly his activities had been; what kind of essays he had written, lectures he had given? Most difficult and important: what he had felt writing them? Even if he had not yet been so old, or if he had been questioned differently, could he have recalled more than the general drift of the official arguments he made then as Schneider, which appear so troubling now? Some of these documents are preserved; they can be read word for word today—but how do *we* read these words? What do they really tell us now about him then?

Questions like these may seem to detract from the magnitude of what happened then and what Schneider contributed to letting happen; in that sense they may seem "apologeticist." But they are also obvious when we are dealing with temporality and the vicissitudes of memory. It was impossible to learn from Schwerte what everybody wanted to know: who were you then? What did you really think and feel writing what you were writing? He could not have gone back to the person of the writer, not even under normal circumstances. Even if there had been diaries and if they had been preserved, we would have only partial access to Schneider's thoughts and feelings about himself and his work, because the persona of the professional writer would have differed from that of the private diarist who in recording his professional experiences would also have given them a different shape. We know in principle how difficult it is to assess the truth of any documentation of past states of mind. If it concerns certain interestingly dark periods, we may want to believe what we largely cannot know. Schwerte's questioners believed that his past as Schneider was criminal, that he should show remorse for having been Schneider, for concealing this fact, and for denying that he continued to be, indeed *was*, Schneider now.

As a modern, history-based, morally questioning collectivity, we need to be clearer about the uses of collective remorse: In the German case, what is it that we want from the war generation? That they feel what we think they ought to feel? Is what we think in this case reasonable? Does it help us to understand or does it hinder attempts at understanding? Why do we call it *Tätergeneration* or *Volk der Täter*? Remorse is a core of emotional, moral energy derived from the culprit's knowledge that what he did was wrong. But in whose terms can he know that? If it is in his own terms, he is in most cases a different person now. If it is in the terms of the people who judge him, he has to acknowledge rather than know that he did wrong, and he does so by *showing* remorse—the sign of German guilt and shame desired by the victors. When Schwerte refused to show remorse in the early interviews, insisting that he had led an honorable life and *was*, not just called himself, Schwerte, while his questioners wanted to reduce him to *their* version of Schneider, he refused to know his life in their terms. He was punished with increasingly hostile questioning, since denial of requests for remorse violates the authority of the inquisitors. Demonstration of remorse means symbolic restitution of the wholeness of the group or individual harmed by the culprit. Contrition, the religious version of remorse, is a symbolic reassurance of the inviolability of the divine being. In the context of the bad German past, requests for and demonstrations of remorse have tended to assume a supra-rational, quasi-religious dimension.

At the end of the war, the all-important demand of collective remorse and conversion to democracy was predicated on the assumption that gradual transformation in real time, with its contradictions, conflicts, and lacunae, would not do and that no proof of change of heart and mind would ever be sufficient: There had to be a radical, instantaneous German rebirth and then its continuous collective confirmation by the *Tätergeneration*. But in the case of a real *Täter*, if only in the "Normaltäter" version of an SS man guilty by association, such confirmation becomes blasphemy. Instructively, the Schwerte case did not produce another memory debate; it was too radical and therefore too rare a transformation. On the other hand, it was precisely the high degree of continuity—from one set of cultural politics to another—combined with the extreme disparity of value—from absolute disapproval (Evil Nazi) to a high degree of approval (respected liberal academic and administrator)—that made the case so scandalous.

In the *Spiegel* interview, Schwerte pointed out that his experiences after 1945, his life in a functioning democracy with stable, supportive institutions, had over the years made him immune against the ideology of racial community and solidarity that, in a very different situation, had tempted his younger self, Schneider. The reporter who conducted the interview knew better; Schneider's criminality was enduringly Schwerte's: "The old gentleman is bitter that he has been denied the image of a true democrat. He says 'I carried the virus, but I have become immune.' Anyone who had been in the eye of the tornado, in the middle of the SS, would not forget that. In the eye of the tornado, where in hindsight he would like to be, there is no wind." That last sentence is not Schwerte's and is a deliberate, serious misinterpretation of Schwerte's meaning. What he had said, partly quoted directly and partly in indirect discourse, concerned the phenomenon of transformation as a complex process in which changes and continuities mix in often contradictory, not fully comprehensible ways. This is especially true where the changes were so dramatic. Schwerte left behind his SS past, which he could not undo but also could not forget; its memory stayed with him, producing the "antibodies" that helped him in the process of *becoming* immune, but this process also depended to a very high degree on his experiences, activities, and conduct as Schwerte. Denying that *process,* the *Spiegel* interview, instructively titled "Ich bin doch immun" (I am immune), denied the possibility, the meaning of transformation.

Schwerte's concern in all these interviews was to explain himself, that is, his transformation into a new, better identity, and almost every interview, every article accused him of deceitfully wrapping the old self so that it would seem to be new. The Dutch TV reporters who forced Schwerte to give himself up called his case "a German career." *Spiegel* presents it as "*the* German career." Moreover, Schwerte-Schneider has lived "with the lie longer and more brazenly than most. Now he is held accountable by a society whose striving for uprightness he himself had supported." So it is not *the* German career but its distorting mirror image? But are these German political and cultural aspirations a priori suspect? The clichés, distortions, opacities, outright falsifications, the numbing hypocrisy in this as in almost all other reports on the Schwerte case, speak volumes about the enduring German *Vergangenheitsmisere* more than half a century after the events. The more his critics condemned him, the more irritated they were by the incongruously mundane nature of his case: a young handsome SS officer looking the part of Nazi Evil turned into an old, distinguished dignitary of a soberly, boringly democratic state.

Schwerte's in many ways troubling but not demoniacally evil past was not the stuff of a pact with the devil. Schneider had not made that pact when he went to work for the SS; his motivations were a mixture of ambition, a sense of adventure, and, from hindsight, dramatically misguided idealist nationalism. Goethe's modern Faust had very different motivations—dangerous idealism was not one of them; and if Schneider had sold his soul, he would have done so unwittingly, a deal that would not have satisfied the devil's requirements for successful temptation. Still, it was for fortune, not for grace, that he was able to retrieve whatever it took to become Schwerte. The sudden change, condemned fifty years later as sinful lie and betrayal, required the blind accidentality of luck. Schneider needed it badly because he was indeed closer to Nazi criminality and more vulnerable to becoming involved by virtue of his associations than most *Geisteswissenschaftler* working in academic institutions during the Third Reich. Was his career, then, *the* German career? He turned from the fantastic dystopia of the Third Reich to the sensible sobriety of postwar German democracy; over a period of five decades, integrating the Schneider and Schwerte identities, he gradually, naturally forgot much about his former self. For its larger part, his life was good, not just for himself but for others. But in the end, the cultural and political energies of a powerfully ritualized German collective guilt that has long since transcended modern secularity and temporality caught up with him; and it literally tore him apart again. Not *the* German story, but *a* German story, if a peculiarly instructive one.

NOTES

1. Historical Memory and the Uses of Remorse

1. See Dagmar Barnouw, *Germany 1945: Views of War and Violence* (Bloomington: Indiana University Press, 1997), ch. 1, "To Make Them See"; Manfred Henningsen, "Der Ort des Holocaust in der amerikanischen Ökonomie des Bösen," in *Deutsch-amerikanische Begegnungen,* ed. Frank Tromler and Elliott Shore (Stuttgart: Deutsche Verlagsanstalt, 2001), 251–67. "Myth" is used throughout this study in its meaning of culturally significant story.

2. The *New York Times,* October 31, 2002, quotes administration officials that Mr. Bush "has smoldered with resentment" and that the administration's policies regarding Germany were guided "by the personal anger of Mr. Bush over Mr. Schröder's campaign, and over one of the ministers in his cabinet, who compared Mr. Bush's tactics to those of Hitler. It was that remark that prompted Defense Secretary Donald H. Rumsfeld to say the German-American relationship had been poisoned."

3. Rumsfeld's accusations of German disobedience and bad soldiering, drawing comparisons between a well-functioning democracy and Syria and Cuba, did not go over well with the war-weary German population (*New York Times,* Feb. 6, 2003).

4. See the images reproduced in Barnouw, *Germany 1945,* ch. 1.

5. For a good example, see Tony Judt's sharply critical review of Peter Novick's *The Holocaust in American Life,* "The Morbid Truth: In Defense of Holocaust Obsession," *New Republic,* July 19/26, 1999: "Because the Holocaust, for many people today, can speak to us mainly as a deracinated account of absolute evil, it has a special value in a world adrift on a sea of ethical and ideological uncertainty."

6. The U.S. elite press misreported repeatedly what the undiplomatic minister of justice had actually said, missing the fact that both Hitler and Bush were caricatured in private conversation—a joke that should never have been misconstrued as an indication of reemerging German anti-Semitism. For many Americans across the political spectrum, twenty-first-century Germany is still outside the parameters of a political normalcy that Jane Kramer now seems to think desirable. ("Resentments," *New Yorker,* Oct. 7, 2002, pp. 39–40); see however her more opaque if no less

judgmental position in *The Politics of Memory: Looking for Germany in the New Germany* (New York: Random House, 1996).

7. Quoted on NPR, *Morning Edition,* Jan. 31, 2003.

8. Peace Prize of the Association of German Booksellers, Oct. 1998; see the documentation of Walser's speech and the reactions to it in *Die Walser-Bubis Debatte,* ed. Frank Schirrmacher (Frankfurt: Suhrkamp, 1999).

9. Elie Wiesel (*Der Tagesspiegel,* Dec. 1, 1998) and Israel's ambassador Avi Primor (*FR,* Dec. 7, 1998) also stated their being offended.

10. This fact explains why *Die Welt,* which had at first published the comments of Walser's defenders, by no means all of them conservative, soon made it known that it was no longer supporting the debate. For the media boycott by American Jews and fundamentalist Christians because of their "kindness" to the Palestinians in reporting on the Israel-Palestine conflict, especially the devastation of Jenin, involving the *New York Times,* the *LA Times,* the *Washington Post,* National Public Radio, and CNN, see Felicity Barringer, "Some U.S. Backers of Israel Boycott Dailies over Mideast," *New York Times,* May 24, 2002.

11. Martin Walser, "Auschwitz und kein Ende" (1979), in Walser, *Über Deutschland reden* (Frankfurt/M: Suhrkamp, 1989), 24–31.

12. *New Yorker,* June 16 and 23, 2003, pp. 69–70.

13. Bill Clinton used it a great deal when trying to sell U.S. military intervention in Kosovo, where for the duration all Serbs were evil perpetrators and everybody else "these innocent victims"; see ch. 5 of this study.

14. This includes the "elite" media; see the much discussed *New York Times Magazine* article "Reagan's Son" by Bill Keller (Jan. 26, 2003).

15. At their annual convention in Atlantic City in October 1944, American Zionists across the political spectrum demanded unanimously a "free and democratic Jewish commonwealth . . . [that] shall embrace the whole of Palestine, undivided and undiminished." See here Arendt's critical comments in her article "Zionism Reconsidered" (rejected by *Commentary* in 1944 as too disturbing): *Menorah Journal* 33 (Aug. 1945): 162–96; reprinted in Ron H. Feldman, ed., *The Jew as Pariah: Jewish Identity and Politics in the Modern Age* (New York: Grove, 1978), 131–77, 131. In her little known series of essays on the "Palestine question" 1945–48 (collected in *The Jew as Pariah*) Arendt predicted with uncanny precision almost all the problems met and created by a future state of Israel: see below this chapter and my *Visible Spaces: Hannah Arendt and the German-Jewish Experience* (Baltimore, Md.: Johns Hopkins University Press, 1990), 72–134.

16. On the personally important but historically often irrelevant stories of Holocaust survivors, see Peter Novick, *The Holocaust in American Life* (Boston: Houghton Mifflin, 1999), esp. 273–77. Novick quotes the director of the *Yad Vashem* archive about the unreliability of most of the twenty thousand testimonies collected: "Many were never in the places where they claim to have witnessed atrocities, while others relied on secondhand information given them by friends or passing strangers" (275).

17. See *Probing the Limits of Representation: Nazism and the "Final Solution,"* ed. Saul Friedlander (Cambridge, Mass.: Harvard University Press, 1992), and, in contrast, the interview with Volkhard Knigge, director of *Gedenkstätte Buchenwald,* "Punkt, Ende, aus," *Tageszeitung,* March 23, 2000: Knigge argues that the powerful buildup of Holocaust discourses, also in the United States, calls for a more rigorously checked historical recording. The important Stockholm con-

ference for "Holocaust Education, Documentation and Research" (2000) showed a lack of interest in "rational discourse" and documentary evidence, embracing instead a "*Zivilreligion* centered in radical Evil, the Holocaust" and favoring "empathy" and quasi-religious witnessing over the sober gathering of evidence. In this context, Knigge also criticizes Spielberg's Shoa Foundation as too undiscerning and dilettantish. The term *Zivilreligion* is used negatively by critics who share Knigge's rational position. Ironically, it goes back to the Romans and was used in eighteenth-century Enlightenment arguments to emphasize the importance of secular, rational discourse. For more discussion of these issues see ch. 5 of this study.

18. On the context for this problematic "renaming," see ch. 3 of this study.

19. Among them *Die Zeit, BerlinerZeitung, Tageszeitung (TAZ), Süddeutsche Zeitung (SZ), Frankfurter Rundschau (FR)*, and since the summer of 2002, after another anti-Semitism controversy, also *Frankfurter Allgemeine Zeitung (FAZ)*. With the exception of the latter, these papers had supported left positions before the collapse of the East Block, claiming the higher moral authority of *speaking for* the exploited victims of capitalism. I support intelligent left politics that *work for* the "masses" who are indeed exploited by rampant capitalism; I take issue with certain groups of (formerly left) intellectuals who have constructed and then exploited the moral authority of the (Jewish) victim status for their own reasons.

20. "Ihr! Ihr macht mich zum Juden. Zu eurem Musterjuden!": the last sentence of Rafael Seligmann, *Der Musterjude* (Hildesheim: Claassen, 1997), 353. The word *Musterjude* is based on *Musterkind*, a model child, with its ambiguous, contradictory connotations.

21. See his essay in *FR* (Nov. 16, 2002), "Wir sind alle Kinder Hitlers: Rafael Seligmann erinnert sich an seine Jugendzeit unter latentem Antisemitismus. Über die anhaltende Schockstarre der Angst in Deutschland." In Seligmann's scenario, non-Jewish Germans are either anti-Semites or slimy hypocrites in their relations to Jewish Germans.

22. See *Frankfurter Rundschau*, Dossier: Michel Friedman unter Verdacht, July 3, 2003.

23. "Die Provokation," *Der Tagesspiegel*, June 21, 2003.

24. The persecution of Jews, now officially a supra-historical phenomenon, has since 1981 been a "doctrine of national truth anchored in law," a "state religion" in Israel. Public denial of the Holocaust is then a heresy carrying a mandatory prison sentence of five years: see Amos Elon, "The Politics of Memory," *New York Review of Books* (hereafter *NYRB*), Oct. 7, 1993, pp. 3–5.

25. See Annette Wieviorka, "Die Entstehung des Zeugen," in *Hannah Arendt Revisited: "Eichmann in Jerusalem" und die Folgen,* ed. Gary Smith (Frankfurt/M: Suhrkamp, 2000), 136–59.

26. For a particularly transparent example of the dynamics of this power-relation, see the *Holocaust-Mahnmal-Debatte* discussed in ch. 5 of this study. Novick, *Holocaust,* 201, points to standard practice of using the term "sacred" in connection with Holocaust survivors and their stories, quoting here the remark made "with some irritation" by the education director of Yad Vashem: "the survivor has become a priest; because of his story, he is holy."

27. Hence in the United States the great popularity of old war documentaries and of computer games restaging WWII and in Germany the control of representations of WWII in the media and the availability of indexed books, WWII materials, and memorabilia, especially sales on the Internet.

28. Despite Sebald's explicit statements about German "shame" and "guilt," an excerpt from the English translation of his text, "A Natural History of Destruction" (*New Yorker,* Nov. 4, 2002, pp. 66–77) met with severe criticism from American readers who were "shocked and offended" by "implicit suggestions" of overly destructive Allied bombing and of "Nazi rhetoric" in Sebald's description of air raids. They argued that "the Germans were themselves responsible for this suffering," and that the fire bombing of Germans cities "will be forever trumped" by the KZs. (Letters, *New Yorker,* Dec. 2, 2002.) For more on this issue see ch. 4 of this study; see also the balanced account of German war experiences in Max Hastings, *Armageddon: The Battle for Germany* (New York: Knopf, 2005).

29. See the balanced collection of responses to *Der Brand* in Lothar Kettenacker, ed., *Ein Volk von Opfern? Die neue Debatte um den Bombenkrieg 1940–45* (Berlin: Rowohlt, 2003), and my detailed discussion of the book and its reception in ch. 4 of this study.

30. See *Germany 1945,* ch. 4, "Words and Images."

31. To balance the huge commercial success of his *Crab Walk* and preserve his image as guardian of German collective guilt, Grass signed a public protest against a planned *Zentrum gegen Vertreibung* (expulsion) in Berlin with a *Requiem-Rotunde* in memory of the victims of expulsion and a documentation center pertaining to the expulsion and deportation of more than 16 million Germans. Grass and other intellectuals' and politicians' concern in both Germany and Poland is that such a center might be too much of a "national project" and provoke the mistrust of the neighboring countries. For a more detailed discussion of this issue, see ch. 4 of this study.

2. "Their Monstrous Past"

1. See the images reproduced in ch. 1, "To Make Them See," in Barnouw, *Germany 1945,* 1–41.

2. On this predicament, see Barnouw, *Germany 1945,* 6–33. Heinrich Böll, "Befehl und Verantwortung. Gedanken zum Eichmann-Prozeß" (1961), in Böll, *Essayistische Schriften und Reden I. 1952–1963,* ed. Bernd Balzer (Cologne: Kiepenheuer und Witsch, 1978, 451–54); Martin Walser, "Auschwitz und kein Ende" (1979), in Walser, *Über Deutschland reden* (Frankfurt/M: Suhrkamp, 1989), 24–31.

3. See Barnouw, *Germany 1945,* 136–49.

4. See Charles S. Maier, *The Unmasterable Past: History, Holocaust and German National Identity* (Cambridge, Mass.: Harvard University Press, 1988); Peter Baldwin, ed., *Reworking the Past: Hitler, the Holocaust and the Historians' Controversy* (Boston: Beacon Press, 1990).

5. For excerpts from Richard von Weizsäcker's speech, see "Facing the Mirror of German History," *New York Times,* Oct. 22, 1988, International section, p. 4. See also Gordon Craig, "Facing Up to the Nazis," *NYRB,* Feb. 2, 1989, p. 1.

6. Saul Friedlander, "'A Past That Refuses to Go Away': On Recent Historiographical Debates in the Federal Republic of Germany about National Socialism and the Final Solution," in *Wissenschaftskolleg-Jahrbuch* 1985/86, ed. Peter Wapnewski (Berlin, 1986), 105–15.

7. Saul Friedlander, *Memory, History, and the Extermination of the Jews of Europe* (Bloomington: Indiana University Press, 1993), ix.

8. Now in Baldwin, *Reworking the Past,* 77–87. Saul Friedlander, "Reflections on the Historicization of National Socialism" (1987) and "Martin Broszat and the Historicization of National Socialism" (1991), both now in *Memory, History,* 64–84 and 85–101.

9. "The Shoah in Present Historical Consciousness," in *Memory, History,* 42–63, 51. See here also White, "Historical Emplotment and the Problem of Truth," in *Probing the Limits of Representation,* 37–53; Dominick LaCapra, "Representing the Holocaust: Reflections on the Historians' Debate," ibid., 108–27.

10. For similar developments in the U.S., see Peter Novick's nicely skeptical, detailed study *The Holocaust in American Life.*

11. Namely *Die Blechtrommel* (1959; *The Tin Drum,* 1961), *Katz und Maus* (1961; *Cat and Mouse,* 1963), *Hundejahre* (1963; *Dog Years,* 1965). Grass himself has repeatedly emphasized the connections between the three texts, which share the setting and some characters. On the thematic integration of the three novels, see J. Reddick, *The "Danzig Trilogy" of Günter Grass* (London: Secker and Warburg, 1975). For secondary literature on the three novels, see Volker Neuhaus, *Günter Grass* (Stuttgart: Metzler, 1992), 219–32.

12. George Steiner, "The Nerve of Günter Grass," in *Critical Essays on Günter Grass,* ed. Patrick O'Neill (Boston, Mass.: G. K. Hall, 1987), 30–36 (30–31).

13. Heinrich Böll's *Wo warst du, Adam?* (1951; *And Where Were You, Adam,* 1974), one of the first successful novels after 1945, had sold 800,000 copies by the late 1970s (Manfred Durzak, *Der deutsche Roman der Gegenwart* [Stuttgart: W. Kohlhammer, 1979], 63). Less interested in forceful "confrontations with the past," Böll's novels were often close to sentimentality but also psychologically imaginative and shrewd.

14. Steiner, "The Nerve," 30.

15. Ibid., 35. This would be true of most of his work.

16. Ibid., 36; see also the more coherent, if bemused, critique of Grass's hyperactive verbosity in Stanley Edgar Hyman's review of *Cat and Mouse,* "An Inept Symbolist" (1963), in *Critical Essays on Günter Grass,* 27–30.

17. See the reviews collected in Gert Loschütz, *Von Buch zu Buch: Günter Grass in der Kritik* (Neuwied: Luchterhand, 1968), 8–26.

18. See Judith Ryan, *The Uncompleted Past: Postwar German Novels and the Third Reich* (Detroit: Wayne State University Press, 1983), 56–57; Hans Magnus Enzensberger, "Wilhelm Meister auf Blech getrommelt," in Loschütz, *Von Buch zu Buch,* 8–12.

19. For a summary of different interpretations of the Oskar figure, see Neuhaus, *Günter Grass,* 54–61.

20. Grass was apprenticed to a stonemason at about the same time and after an equally short period entered the academy of art.

21. See Erhard Friedrichsmeyer, "The Dogmatism of Pain: *Local Anaesthetic,*" in *A Günter Grass Symposium,* ed. A. Leslie Wilson (Austin: University of Texas Press, 1971), 32–45.

22. See Günter Franzen, "Vor den Müttern sterben die Söhne," *Kommune* 5/04 (Oct./Nov. 2004): 56–62.

23. The late sixties and early seventies, a period of opening up the Nazi past,

was promptly followed by the *Väterbücher* of the late seventies and early eighties, with the sons' increasingly sterile psychologizing about their "authoritarian" fathers who had burdened them with German collective guilt: see here Wolfgang Türkis's whining *Beschädigtes Leben Autobiographische Texte der Gegenwart* (Stuttgart: J. B. Metzler, 1990), 134–232 and the critical accounts in Reinhard Baumgart, "Das Leben—kein Traum? Vom Nutzen und Nachteil einer autobiographischen Literatur," in *Glücksgeist und Jammerseele: Über Leben und Schreiben, Vernunft und Literatur* (Munich: C. Hanser, 1986), 198–228, and Marcel Reich-Ranicki, "Anmerkungen zur deutschen Literatur der siebziger Jahre," in *Entgegnung: Zur deutschen Literatur der siebziger Jahre* (Stuttgart: Deutsche Verlags-Anstalt, 1981), 17–35.

24. Wolfgang Preisendanz, "Zum Vorrang des Komischen bei der Darstellung von Geschichtserfahrung in deutschen Romanen unserer Zeit," in *Das Komische,* ed. W. Preisendanz and R. Warning, Poetik und Hermeneutik 7 (Munich: Fink, 1976), 153–64, argues that in these novels, including Grass's, the past is not represented "historically" but as it was lived, thereby complementing history. However, in Grass's or Lenz's narration, the grotesque, highly stylized aspects of that "lived" past tend to mask and obscure rather than illuminate the meanings of the historical experience.

25. See here Koeppen's laudatory review, "Hitler, der bleibt uns," of Horst Krüger's 1966 essay collection *Das zerbrochene Haus (A Crack in the Wall: Growing Up under Hitler* [New York: Fromm, 1982]). Koeppen's title is part of the concluding sentence of Krüger's essay on the Auschwitz trial, "Gerichtstag" (Day of Judgment): "This Hitler, I thought, will remain with us—all the days of our lives."

26. Notoriously reticent, Koeppen once described himself as "a spectator, a quiet watcher, a silent man, an observer": see Richard Salis, ed., *Motive: Deutsche Autoren zur Frage: Warum schreiben Sie?* (Tübingen: Horst Erdmann Verlag, 1971), 191.

27. Wolfgang Koeppen, "Rede zur Verleihung des Georg-Büchner-Preises 1962," in *Jahrbuch der deutschen Akademie für Sprache und Dichtung,* 1962, 103–10.

28. See Horst Bienek, *Werkstattgespräche mit Schriftstellern* (Munich: C. Hanser, 1965), 55–67, 65; Christian Linder, "Im Übergang zum Untergang. Über das Schweigen Wolfgang Koeppens," *Akzente* 19 (1972): 41–63. In 1971 and 1972 Linder published nine interview articles in newspapers, journals, and radio programs on the meaning of Koeppen's silence: see bibliography in Eckart Öhlenschläger, ed., *Wolfgang Koeppen* (Frankfurt/M: Suhrkamp, 1987), 440–41.

29. See Karl Korn's thoughtful 1951 review of *Tauben im Gras,* now in *Über Wolfgang Koeppen,* ed. Ulrich Greiner (Frankfurt/M: Suhrkamp, 1976), 25–29, 26: a "real novel" with a multitude of milieus, characters, events, levels of consciousness, it managed to be highly informative about the political situation of the Federal Republic. Alfred Andersch, "Choreographie des politischen Augenblicks" (1955), in ibid., 72–79; Lothar Baier, "Ein nichtgeschriebener Roman Zu *Der Tod in Rom,*" in ibid., 223–29; Peter Demetz, *Postwar German Literature* (New York: Pegasus, 1970), 168–72; Marcel Reich-Ranicki, "Der Fall Wolfgang Koeppen. Ein Lehrbeispiel dafür, wie man in Deutschland mit Talenten umgeht," in *Literarisches Leben in Deutschland. Kommentare und Pamphlete* (Munich: Piper, 1965), 26–35;

"Der gierige Zeuge Über Wolfgang Koeppen," in *Deutsche Literatur in Ost und West. Prosa seit 1945* (Stuttgart: Europäischer Buchklub, 1963), 34–54; "In einer deutschen Angelegenheit," in *Wer schreibt, provoziert Kommentare und Pamphlete* (Munich: Deutscher Taschenbuch, 1966), 109–12.

30. Now in Greiner, ed., *Über Wolfgang Koeppen,* 30–32.

31. Ibid., 11–13.

32. See the titles of reviews in the bibliographies in Greiner, ed., *Über Wolfgang Koeppen,* 283–94, Thomas Richer, *Der Tod in Rom. Eine existential-psychologische Analyse von Wolfgang Koeppens Roman* (Zurich: Artemis, 1982), 149–53, and Öhlenschläger, *Wolfgang Koeppen,* 444–70. Peter Demetz, *After the Fires: Recent Writing in the Germanies, Austria, and Switzerland* (San Diego: Harcourt Brace Jovanovich, 1986), links Koeppen's silence to his being "exhausted by these explosive novels" (316).

33. Walter Jens, "Melancholie und Moral Rede auf Wolfgang Koeppen," in *Jahrbuch der Deutschen Akademie für Sprache und Dichtung 1962* (Darmstadt: Deutshce Akademie für Sprache und Dichtung, 1963), 93–102.

34. J. R. Blanchard, *Library Journal* 86 (1961): 1620.

35. Ryan, *Uncompleted Past,* 15, 117–27. Her examples of such inability are, of course, found in other critics' readings, since the opinions of a general readership are not available to her. She herself is an intelligent critic who approaches the text with her own agenda—the well-known and inevitable hermeneutic circle. The issue is not that circle itself but the relative plausibility of the agenda that keeps it moving.

36. Hermann Vinke, ed., *Akteneinsicht Christa Wolf. Zerrspiegel und Dialog* (Hamburg: Luchterhand, 1993); see also the essays collected in Michael Geyer, ed., *The Power of the Intellectuals in Contemporary Germany* (Chicago: University of Chicago Press, 2001).

37. See my "'Partei wir danken dir': auf der Universität in Utopia," *Merkur* 37 (1983): 16–28.

38. This made her more successful and visible, particularly on U.S. college campuses, where newly established programs in women's studies created great interest in women writers, and a large number of largely uncritical doctoral dissertations were written on her work.

39. Some of these reflections are cut in the American edition (*A Model Childhood;* New York: Farrar, Straus and Giroux, 1980) for the benefit of the "common reader": see *Kindheitsmuster* (Darmstadt: Luchterhand, 1979), 530: "Es geht zu Ende, indem diese dritte Person, Nelly, und die 'Du'-Person, die darin ist, zusammenlaufen und eine sind, die 'ich' ist, von der dann auf andere Weise berichtet werden müsste: anders und auf andere Weise."

40. For a summary of critics' reactions, see Sonya Hilzinger, *Christa Wolf* (Stuttgart: Metzler, 1986), 94–105.

41. For an instructively simplistic and successful example of such "critical" expectations, see Ernestine Schlant, *The Language of Silence: West German Literature and the Holocaust* (New York: Routledge, 1999). Schlant's study conforms nicely to the current cultural-political orthodoxy regarding German collective inability to mourn and lack of remorse. She is unusually—and, if the situation were less serious, comically—rigorous in her emotional rejection of West German authors, among them prominently Grass, who have not met the expected mourning

and remorse quota. Since she argues from the assumption that all writers exhibit a literature-specific "seismographic" sensitivity to the movements of the (German) collective psyche, she simply declares the writers she finds insufficiently mournful and remorseful to be representative of all German writers and then all Germans: all of them have been silent, and their silence has meant immoral anti-Semitism. Since the issue is the Holocaust, there will be no critical questions. The study's lack of historical information and methodological intelligence is astonishing, and so is its publication by Routledge. Less astonishing and more disquieting is its very positive reception in the American elite media (and by some academic critics): Schlant is the German-born wife of Bill Bradley, who was at the time of the book's publication ahead of Al Gore in the Democratic presidential primaries. His handlers, apprehensive about the political implications of his father-in-law's membership in the all-volunteer *Luftwaffe*, must have thought his wife's book a healthy antidote to suspicions of possible association with Nazi Evil, be it ever so faint. On the power of Nazi Evil in American political strategies and rhetoric, see ch. 5 of this study.

42. Christa Wolf, *Voraussetzungen einer Erzählung: Kassandra* (Darmstadt: Luchterhand, 1983).

43. Wolf, *Voraussetzungen*, 27: "Ich will Zeugin bleiben, auch wenn es keinen einzigen Menschen mehr geben wird, der mir mein Zeugnis abverlangt."

44. See here my *Visible Spaces*, ch. 5, "Visible Spaces: Good Men and Good Citizens."

45. Robert Graves, *The Greek Myths* (Baltimore: Penguin, 1955), vol. 2, 332–33: Cassandra warns that the horse contains armed men, and she is supported in this by the seer Laocoon, who warns never to trust a Greek gift, hurling his spear at the horse and thereby causing the sound of clashing metal inside—the perceptible sign (indication) of concealed weapons. Other Trojans then want to hurl the horse over the wall, but Priamus's supporters argue not to violate a gift of Athene.

46. In an intelligent appraisal of the controversy, Frank Schirrmacher explicitly made this connection: he defends the continuing "political and intellectual" critique of Wolf's writing in *FAZ* (mainly by Marcel Reich-Ranicki, who also, and in this case justly, had consistently complained about Wolf's distinctly unimpressive writerly skills) but rejects the personal attacks on her: writers should not speak nor should they be seen as speaking from the position of higher authority; the "monströse" (pompous) belief that a writer is eo ipso morally privileged is illusionary: "Fälle. Wolf und Müller," *FAZ* 22 (Jan. 1993), now in *Akteneinsicht*, 170, 148–49.

47. Wolf made this claim in a controversial television interview from Santa Monica, California, on Jan. 24, 1993: *Akteneinsicht*, 170.

48. Her thoughtless remarks here and Fritz Raddatz's immediate, stunningly self-centered response were supported by their shared belief in the writer's a priori higher moral status. Raddatz and intellectuals like him had over the years reaffirmed Wolf and her East German male counterpart Heiner Müller in this belief: Fritz Raddatz, "Von der Beschädigung der Literatur durch ihre Urheber," *Die Zeit* 28 (Jan. 1993), now in *Akteneinsicht*, 168–71.

49. Walter Jens, "Christa Wolf bekümmert mich" (1993), now in *Akteneinsicht*, 233–35. Raddatz's tearful pleas to Müller and Wolf to stop prevaricating and "be true to the dignity of your work. Explain to us. Relieve me and your readers of the burden of our sadness," came out of his profound disappointment that Wolf,

his own construct of a morally pure writer, had been sullied. As he stated with remarkable emphasis, none of the other Communists who had been important to him had been "ein shake-hands man der Henker" (a man who shakes the hand of the henchman)—a very strange statement in any circumstance, indicating his belief that they had remained pure so as not to disappoint him (*Akteneinsicht*, 171).

3. Censored Memories

1. Now in Baldwin, *Reworking the Past*, 77–87. Friedlander, *Memory, History, and the Extermination of the Jews of Europe*, 64–84 and 85–101. See my *Germany 1945*, ch. 5, "Views of the Past: Memory and Historical Evidence."

2. For excerpts of his speech, see "Facing the Mirror of German History," *New York Times*, Oct. 22, 1988. See also Gordon Craig, "Facing Up to the Nazis," *New York Review of Books*, Feb. 2, 1989, p. 1. In a critical essay on the German reception of Daniel Goldhagen's *Hitler's Willing Executioners* (1996), Andreas Helle refers to Goldhagen's 1996 thesis of a specifically German "annihilationist" anti-Semitism as a "distorted echo of the bizarre debate of the late 1980s on the uniqueness of the mass murder of European Jews" ("Kein ganz gewöhnlicher Streit: Zur Zeitgebundenheit der Goldhagen-Debatte," *Leviathan. Zeitschrift für Sozialwissenschaft* 25 [1997]: 251–70, 268). But the issue of the "uniqueness of Auschwitz" has proved tenacious and has reemerged in full force in the current bizarre debates of reemerging German anti-Semitism: see below, this chapter.

3. See Charles S. Maier, *The Unmasterable Past*, and the essays collected in Baldwin, *Reworking the Past*.

4. For images of returning POWs, see my *Germany 1945*, 174–80.

5. On the disagreement among historians about the time and the nature of these changes and their implications for arguing a uniqueness of the Holocaust, see ch. 5 of this study.

6. See also the much discussed *Spiegel-Serie* on *Hitler und die Deutschen* in the summer of 2001, with more differentiating perspectives on the Nazi past and German memory, among them Bernhard Schlink, "Auf dem Eis Von der Notwendigkeit und der Gefahr der Beschäftigung mit dem Dritten Reich und dem Holocaust" (*Der Spiegel* 19/2001; May 7, 2001); *Spiegel-Gespräch* mit Joachim Fest "über seine Jugend unter dem Hakenkreuz und Hitler als Inbegriff der Unmenschlichkeit" (*Der Spiegel* 19/2001; May 7, 2001); *Spiegel-Gespräch* mit Lord Ralf Dahrendorf "über seine Jugendjahre im Nationalsozialismus, über Freiheit als Zentrum seines Denkens und seinen Widerwillen gegenüber Historikerdebatten (*Der Spiegel* 23/2001; June 5, 2001): for a discussion of these positions, see below, this chapter. See also *Spiegel-Serie über die Vertreibung der Deutschen aus dem Osten, Die Flucht* (*Der Spiegel* 13/2002; March 25, 2002).

7. Fritz Stern, *Gold and Iron: Bismarck, Bleichröder, and the Building of the German Empire* (New York: Vintage, 1979). Barnouw, *Visible Spaces*, ch. 3, "The Silence of Exile."

8. See Dagmar Barnouw, "Einzigartig. Rahel Varnhagen und die deutsch-jüdische Identität um 1800," in *Rahel Levin Varnhagen: Studien zu ihrem Werk im zeitgenössischen Kontext*, ed. Sabina Becker (St. Ingbert: Röhrig Universitätsverlag, 2001), 81–117.

9. See Dan Diner, "Mit östlichem Blick. Trotz der Anschläge muss Amerika durchhalten—in Bagdad und in Palästina," *Die Zeit* Online, 46/2003. For more on this argument, see ch. 5 of this study.

10. Hannah Arendt to Karl Jaspers, Aug. 17, 1946.

11. For Arendt's critique of political Zionism, see my *Visible Spaces*, ch. 3.

12. See Deborah Lipstadt, *Denying the Holocaust: The Growing Assault on Truth and Memory* (New York: Free Press, 1993), and Peter Novick's critical remarks about the uses of Holocaust denial in his *The Holocaust in American Life*, 270–72.

13. *Spiegel* Online, 19/2001, May 7, 2001. See also Tony Judt on the social usefulness of Evil (ch. 1 n. 5, of this study); Fest (see n. 6 above), much more rational, does not advocate but explain. See here also the arguments in ch. 5 of this study.

14. For instructive connections, see Manfred Henningsen, "Politische Religion versus Zivilgesellschaft," in *Politische Religion? Politik, Religion und Anthropologie im Werk von Eric Vögelin*, ed. Michael Ley, Heinrich Neisser, and Gilbert Weiss (Munich: Wilhelm Fink Verlag, 2003), 101–13. See here also Hannah Arendt's analysis of Eichmann and my discussion of her concept of "the political" as the counterprojection to the (misnamed) "banality of evil" that springs up more easily in situations where there is no civil society (*Visible Spaces,* ch. 6, "The Obscurities of Evil"). See also Helmuth Plessner, *Grenzen der Gemeinschaft* (Bonn: Friedrich Cohen, 1924) and my "The Limits of Utopia: Plessner and Arendt on the Phenomenon of 'the Political,'" in *Helmuth Plessner,* ed. Joachim Fischer (Frankfurt/M: Suhrkamp, 2005).

15. Peter Schneider, "In Their Side of World War II, the Germans Also Suffered," *New York Times,* Jan. 18, 2003, online.

16. Helke Sander's film about the rapes was criticized as "revisionist"; for the problem of rape under Soviet occupation, see Norman Naimark, *The Russians in Germany: The History of Soviet Occupation in Germany 1945–1949* (Cambridge, Mass.: Harvard University Press, 1995).

17. Roger Angell, *New Yorker,* Jan. 19, 2004, pp. 31–32.

18. Interview with Errol Morris, "Fresh Air," NPR, Jan. 5, 2004.

19. For Morris's concept and realization of documentary (visual) objectivity, see my "Seeing and Believing: The Thin Blue Line of Documentary Objectivity," *Common Knowledge* 4 (Spring 1995): 129–43 and "Thought-Images: A Brief History of Time," *Arcadia International Journal of Literary Studies* 38, no. 2 (2003): 239–42.

20. Angell, *New Yorker,* 31.

21. See above, this chapter, note 13; for a discussion of the book and its reception in the United States and in Germany, see ch. 5 of this study.

22. See "Punkt, Ende, Aus," interview with Volkhard Knigge, director of the KZ Buchenwald Memorial, *TAZ,* March 23, 2000. Knigge is skeptical about the historiographical relevance of most "eyewitness" stories of Holocaust survivors and highly critical of the methodological sloppiness of Spielberg's *Shoah-Foundation,* an enterprise that he thinks counterproductive to historical research.

23. See the flurry of articles in *Die Zeit* in the fall of 2003 linking increasing attention to German wartime experiences to decreasing attention to the suffering of Holocaust victims and to (allegedly) reemerging German anti-Semitism.

24. Peter Laufer, in his *Exodus into Berlin* (Chicago: Ivan R. Dee, 2003) credits the German government attempts at making amends to Jews, in this case the steadily increasing international Jewish population in Berlin, which he sees as gestures of generous good will rather than enduring moral obligation.

25. See Times Mager, "Überbietung," *FR* Online, Nov. 28, 2002. In the context of another anti-Semitism debate one year earlier that ended with the forced resignation of another MP (see below, this chapter, nn. 44 and 51), Mager argues against using the concept of "anti-anti-Semitism" because it could be misused by anti-anti-anti-Semitism. He advises to "develop a method to distinguish latent anti-Semitism from legitimate critique." But precisely the paranoia about "latent anti-Semitism" lurking everywhere has been responsible for the ever increasing automatic rejection of any critique, no matter how legitimate.

26. *FR* Online, Dec. 12, 2003, dossier, "Die Hohmann Affäre."

27. Aleida Assmann, currently correct German Remembrance incarnate, laments in her article "Die Flut der Erinnerung" a return of "German nationalism" and condemns the "scandalous ease" with which Germans now substitute their own memories for Holocaust memories and thus, "in the sense of a regained 'normality,' can freely indulge their 'anti-Semitic habits'" (*Tagesspiegel,* Nov. 8, 2003). A dismaying moralistic arrogance and thinly veiled threat of speech and thought control.

28. See the exhaustive dossier "Die Hohmann Affäre" in the *Dossiere* part of *FR* Online Erscheinungsdatum, Nov. 27, 2003 (continuously updated). Of the two reports in the *New York Times,* one was a seriously distorting piece by Richard Bernstein, "German General Fired for Backing Slur on Jews" (Nov. 5), the other an informative and reasonably balanced account by the Associated Press, "German Opposition Seeks Lawmaker's Ouster" (Nov. 10). Bernstein took quotes from Hohmann's speech out of context and mistranslated them to make them a "slur," which (although they were pretty stupid) they were not: "In his speech, made in early October to local constituents, Mr. Hohmann called Jews 'a race of perpetrators.' Mr. Hohmann was making the argument that Germans still labor under the burden of responsibility for the crimes of the Nazis, while other people who have committed atrocities present themselves as 'innocent lambs.'" If Hohmann had said that, the excitement would have been justified, but he had not. For about a week after the story broke, the *FR* included the full text of the speech in its *Hohmann Dossier,* from which I copied it, as national and international reporters could have done. Instead they produced thousands of pages of attacks on Hohmann suggesting truly incredible statements. Bernstein, too, did not check the speech and just passed on the distortions, since normal journalistic ethics apparently do not apply where it concerns what is hoped to be a juicy anti-Semite.

29. Axel Vornbäumen, "Hat der Antisemitismus die Mitte erreicht?" *FR* Online, Dec. 12, 2003.

30. *FAZ,* Feb. 6, 2004, front page, and *Rhein-Main-Zeitung,* p. 65. Does that mean that questioning the uniqueness of Nazi persecutions of Jews is a felony?

31. Vornbäumen quotes from the preliminary selected results of a ten-year study, "Deutsche Zustände" by Wilhelm Heitmeyer, director of the *Institut für interdisziplinäre Konflikt- und Gewaltforschung der Universität Bielefeld*: 14.6% with an anti-Semitic attitude vs. 12.7% in 2002; 69.9% with "sekundärer Antisemitismus" because they said "yes" to the statement: "Ich ärgere mich darüber

(am annoyed), dass den Deutschen auch heute noch die Verbrechen (crimes) an den Juden vorgehalten werden (blamed)." This response suggests to both men a "frightening" "attitude that, no longer popular only on the radical right, has reached the middle." Heitmeyer concedes that the study is not conclusive since 65.4% (2002: 67.7%) of the polled liked the fact that there are now again more Jews living in Germany.

32. Moshe Zuckermann, "Von Erinnerungsnot und Ideologie," in *Gedenken und Kulturindustrie: Ein Essay zur neuen deutschen Normalität* (Bodenheim: Philo, 1999), 9–32, 27 (hereafter in the text GK). On the 1998 Walser-Bubis controversy, see also ch. 1 of this study.

33. See Bubis's speech on the sixtieth anniversary of *Kristallnacht*, excerpted in *Süddeutsche Zeitung*, Nov. 10, 1998. The frequent use of the adjective "unspeakable" when denouncing yet another offense regarding alleged German laxness vis-à-vis the established hierarchy of suffering underlines nicely the power of taboos that have for many decades prevented rational speech about these issues.

34. Martin Walser, "Unser Auschwitz," in *Was zu bezweifeln war. Aufsätze und Reden 1958–1975* (Berlin and Weimar: Aufbau-Verlag, 1976), 7–21.

35. Dohnanyi had asked this question during the Walser-Bubis affair, and Bubis answered with the accusation of anti-Semitism. This, under more "normal" circumstances most obviously relevant, question has been absolutely "taboo" as the worst kind of "apologeticism." In December 1998, mopping up after the affair, Dohnanyi and Bubis met to affirm their basic agreement on many important issues regarding German-Jewish relations. Dohnanyi had suggested to Bubis that as chair of the influential *Zentralrat* he might treat his non-Jewish fellow citizens more gently since they too had feelings. ("Gemeinsamkeit bedeutsamer," *St. Gallener Tagblatt*, Dec. 9, 1998.)

36. Richard Herzinger: "Das Kalkül des Schuldumkehrers," *Die Zeit* Online, 43/2003. See also his *Kommentar* "Lehrstück Hohmann Der Antisemitismus frisst sich in die politische Mitte" three weeks later in *Die Zeit* Online, 46/2003. Untranslatable because of its onomatopoetic connotations, the word "dumpf," a combination of dumb and torpid, is used frequently in accusations of anti-Semitism.

37. *Der Spiegel* Online, 46/2003, Nov. 10, 2003: "Lieber Täter als Opfer: Der Fall Martin Hohmann und das vergebliche Bemühen, Antisemitismus durch Aufklärung bekämpfen zu wollen."

38. Hohmann's alleged references to Jews as *Tätervolk* are seen as representative for the "Furor der Antisemiten."

39. Herzinger's *Kommentar* "Offene Briefschlacht," (*Die Zeit* Online, April 5, 2004) is a rare acknowledgment of open Jewish-German disagreement: he reports that the liberal *Union progressiver Juden in Deutschland* is threatening to sue the *Bundesregierung* because the *Zentralrat der Juden in Deutschland* has not kept its obligation, according to its agreement with the *Bundesregierung* of Jan. 27, 2003, to share the state financial support for Jewish congregations regardless of the different groups' political or religious positions. Jewish infighting about privileges does not go so well with the nobility of their *Opfer* status, but the underlying acknowledgment of a plurality of Jewish life in Germany may be a start. See the letter of April 4 from the chair of *Union*, Jan Mühlstein, to the chair of the *Zentralrat*, Paul Spiegel, included in Herzinger's commentary complaining about the *Zentralrat*'s politics of *Zahlenspiele* (playing with numbers) to conceal the fact that it does not speak for all Jews.

40. Ulrich Speck, "Bekenntnis. Eine Frankfurter Debatte," Dossier "Antisemitismus," *FR* Online, Nov. 28, 2002. The institutes were das Fritz-Bauer-Institut für Jüdische Geschichte, das Frankfurter Psychoanalytische Institut, das Institut für Sozialforschung, das Sigmund-Freud-Institut. The controversy was important because it redirected the *FAZ* position towards more Holocaust piety.

41. Jürgen Möllemann, deputy chairman of the Free Democratic Party (FDP), was forced to resign in November 2002 because of allegedly anti-Semitic remarks; he had on the whole not shown sufficient piety in the matter of German-Jewish relations. Soon after his ouster he met with a fatal accident under somewhat mysterious circumstances. For more on his case see below, this chapter.

42. Like anti-Semitism, Holocaust denial has become a confusingly stretchable concept, partly because the two positions are often referred to as interdependent. Novick, 271–72, also points out the vicissitudes of polls where it concerns issues both highly emotional and fuzzy. Made public on the evening of the opening of the Washington Holocaust Museum, the results of a poll (commissioned by the American Jewish Committee) claiming that 22% of Americans were Holocaust doubters created great excitement, which, given the politics of the Holocaust Museum, may have been quite welcome, also in that it gave a nice lift to Deborah Lipstadt's just published *Denying the Holocaust*. The problem was the framing of the pollster's question: "Does it seem possible or does it seem impossible to you that the Nazi extermination of the Jews never happened?" When a rival polling firm posed the reformulated question (without the double negative), the result was between 1% and 2% of doubters.

43. Wolfgang Benz, "Ausgrenzung und Zuwendung. Antisemitismus und das Verhältnis der Deutschen zu Israel," *FR* Online, Jan. 1, 2002; Achatz von Müller, "Volk der Täter, Volk der Opfer. Deutschland auf dem Weg der Selbstversöhnung," *Die Zeit* 44/2003; Bernd Ulrich, "Deutschland Alle Deutschen werden Brüder: Notwendig oder heikel?" *Die Zeit* Online, 45/2003, Oct. 30, 2003; Nicolas Berg, "Eine deutsche Sehnsucht. Die Entlastungsstrategie (exculpation) ist nicht neu," and Dan Diner, "Mit östlichem Blick: Trotz der Anschläge muss Amerika durchhalten—in Bagdad und in Palästina," *Die Zeit* Online, 46/2003. All these texts work with generalizing, rejecting, and threatening judgments concerning the attempts of ordinary non-Jewish Germans to deal with their relations with Jewish Germans. With the exception of Benz's text, they were all written in the context of the Hohmann affair, relying on the anti-Semitism czar Benz (whose influence on *Die Zeit* is widely known) for the orthodoxy of their arguments.

44. "Ausgrenzung und Zuwendung. Antisemitismus und das Verhältnis der Deutschen zu Israel," *FR* Online, Jan. 1, 2002. Later that year, Benz's research institute would lament that huge "wave of anti-Semitism sweeping across Europe" without mentioning Israel's highly objectionable political and military conduct.

45. On the bizarre and troubling "Jenninger affair," see Jan Buruma, *The Wages of Guilt: Memories of War in Germany and Japan* (New York: Farrar, Straus, and Giroux, 1994), 244–45.

46. See Marion Pietrzok and Salomon Korn, "Es gilt gegen die Herrschaft dumpfer Gefühle anzukämpfen," *Nationaler Totenkult: Die Neue Wache* (Berlin: Karin Kramer, 1995), 101–103.

47. Joe Klein, "How Germany Was Suffocated," *Guardian Weekly,* June 27–July 3, 2002.

48. In a statement of October 1, 2004, the Bush administration admonished

Ariel Sharon to limit his bloody raids into Gaza to "proportional damage" in the civilian population since so many children had been killed on previous days: Orwell would have admired their verbal agility and moral obtuseness.

49. Born in Breslau in 1927, Bubis survived the war in Poland, where his family had gone in 1935 to escape the worsening situation in Germany. Having moved to Germany in 1945, he became a successful businessman in Frankfurt, joined the FDP in 1969, was made the chair of Frankfurt's "Jüdische Gemeinde" (congregation) in 1983, and the chair of the influential "Zentralrat der Juden in Deutschland" in 1992, a prestigious and powerful office he held until his death in 1999.

50. See her letter to Karl Jaspers, Aug. 17, 1946.

51. "Konferenz der Gutwilligen," *Die Zeit* Online, 09/2004.

52. For a reaction of the EU to Bush's acceptance on April 14, 2003, of Sharon's new plan circumventing the requirements of the Roadmap to Peace, see Martin Winter, "EU ruft 'Nahost-Quartett' zusammen," *FR* Online, April 16, 2004.

53. *Der Spiegel* Online, 06/2002.

54. Daniel Broessler, "Ein nationales Projekt verstört die Nachbarn," *SZ,* July 15, 2003.

55. Gustav Seibt, "Heimat und Totengedenken," *SZ,* July 18, 2003.

56. *Die Zeit,* June 20, 2002. See also the exchange between Michnik and Habermas about Polish problems with the combined perpetrator/victim status, Michnik proposing a more differentiating perspective on the Polish and German pasts and Habermas insisting on a uniqueness of Nazi criminality: "More Humility, Fewer Illusions," *NYRB,* March 24, 1994.

57. For instance a monument erected last year for twenty-six German civilians, killed by Czech soldiers in August 1946, in a Czech village close to the Polish border. The woman mayor who instigated the monument said that none of the expelled *Sudetendeutschen* who on occasion visit the village they had to leave have ever indicated that they wanted their property back, but they helped the village to restore the cemetery where Czechs have been lying next to Germans for many centuries.

58. See ch. 1 n. 30, of this study. The German social-democratic government had previously approved of the *Zentrum.* The number of Germans forced to leave their homes varies according to the situation in which it is used. The German government is here subtracting from the end sum of about 16.5 million deportees and refugees the number of refugees, though the conditions under which millions of German women and children left East Prussia as refugees were so harsh and dangerous that the distinction does not seem to make much sense: all of them were forced to leave.

59. See Mihran Dabag, "Über die Suche nach Erinnerung im universalen Europa. Ein Zentrum gegen Vertreibungen könnte die Unterschiede zwischen Massaker und Völkermord zum Verschwinden bringen," *FR* Online, Aug. 30, 2003. The most important issue for Dabag in this meandering essay is to keep a sharp line of distinction between *Opfer* and *Täter,* genocide and massacre—a line that may not always be possible and, more important, useful.

60. Herfried Münkler, "Vom Bombenkrieg bis zur Vertreibung: Seit einigen Jahren experimentiert Deutschland mit einer Politik des Opfers," *FR* Online, Sept. 24, 2003. He remarks in this context that even the armed conflict between Palestin-

ians and Israelis turns on the question of which side can lay greater claim to the status of victim.

61. See Adam Krzeminski, "Die schwierige deutsch-polnische Vergangenheits-politik," *Aus Politik und Zeitgeschichte,* B 40–41/2003, Oct. 2003: with its rapid juxtapositions, contradictions, hesitations, and lacunae, this wordy commentary mimics rather than analyzes the indeed difficult politics of the German-Polish past. For a more balanced, nuanced, and coherent account of the *Vertriebenen* issue, see Helga Hirsch, "Kollektive Erinnerung im Wandel," *Aus Politik und Zeitgeschichte,* B 40–41/2003. Hirsch's perspective has benefited from the fact that she lived in Germany and in Poland as a journalist writing for *Die Zeit* and, without sharing them, has been familiar with Polish concerns about their victim status in their relations to Germany.

62. See *Germany 1945,* chs. 1 and 2.

63. Denounced by the *Zentralrat der Juden in Deutschland,* Hohmann was found not guilty of denying the "Holocaust and its uniqueness" by the Fulda prose-cutor's office.

64. "Auf dem Eis. Von der Notwendigkeit und der Gefahr der Beschäftigung mit dem Holocaust," *Der Spiegel* Online, 19/2001, May 7, 2001, pp. 1–6, 3. See also the passage about Peter Schneider, above, this chapter. See the conversation with Ralf Dahrendorf in the same series: *Der Spiegel* Online, 23/2001, June 5, pp. 1–8, 4. In answer to the observation that he had not participated in German mem-ory debates, Dahrendorf said that he disliked the "German style of discussion: much too much (schrecklich viel) *Betroffenheit*" (ibid.).

65. Schlink, 4; Dahrendorf, 4.

66. "Unter Generalverdacht," *Der Spiegel* 15/2002, 178–81. An intelligent critique of the suspicion with regard to more differentiating perspectives on the bad German past in German literature as it is habitually expressed in the elite media, especially *SZ, Die Zeit,* and more recently also *FAZ.*

67. On female KZ guards, see *Germany 1945,* 80–83.

68. Dagmar Barnouw, *Critical Realism: History, Photography, and the Work of Siegfried Kracauer* (Baltimore: Johns Hopkins University Press, 1994), ch. 6, "Image, Imagination, and Historical Evidence."

4. The War in the Empty Air

1. *New Yorker,* Nov. 4, 2002, pp. 66–77. The essay is an excerption from "Air War and Literature," in *On the Natural History of Destruction* (New York: Random House, 2003), 1–104. The letters were published in the *New Yorker,* Dec. 2, 2002.

2. See Howard Nemorov, "The War in the Air," quoted above, preface.

3. Christopher Hitchens, "The Wartime Toll on Germany," *Atlantic Monthly,* Jan./Feb. 2003, pp. 182–89, 185.

4. W. G. Sebald, *Luftkrieg und Literatur* (Munich: Hanser, 1999). By the time of the American publication, Sebald had been killed in a car accident.

5. *Natural History of Destruction,* 10: "The darkest aspects of the final act of destruction, as experienced by the great majority of the German population, remained under a kind of taboo like a shameful family secret, a secret that perhaps could not even be privately acknowledged."

6. Corrections of Sebald's account in this matter have mostly just pointed out another author or text; the situation was slightly different in the former GDR because censoring memories of air raids for reasons of "apologeticism" was not an issue, though the evocation of the terror of air raids was in some cases controlled by "we started it." See Renatus Deckert, "Auf eine im Feuer versunkene Stadt. Heinz Czechowski und die Debatte über den Luftkrieg," *Merkur* 659 (March 2004): 255–59.

7. Klaus Harpprecht, "Stille, schicksalslose," in *Deutsche Literatur 1998,* ed. Volker Hage (Stuttgart: Reclam 1999), 269.

8. *Natural History of Destruction,* 25f.

9. Ibid., 26–28.

10. *New Yorker,* Nov. 4, 2002, pp. 66–77, 70.

11. One hundred ten thousand German soldiers were taken prisoner in the battle of Stalingrad; fewer than six thousand were to return from the SU. A poignant reminder: during the Warshaw uprising in 1944, both Russian and Allied forces waited on opposite sides of the Wisla (Weichsel) for the Germans to put it down.

12. *Natural History of Destruction,* vii–x, 12–14 .

13. *Natural History of Destruction,* vii: "born in a village in the Allgäu Alps in May 1944, I am one of those who remained almost untouched by the catastrophe then unfolding in the German Reich."

14. Jean Améry, *Jenseits von Schuld und Sühne* (1966); *Über das Altern* (1968); *Unmeisterliche Wanderjahre* (1971); *Hand an sich legen* (1976).

15. "Against the Irreversible," in *Natural History of Destruction,* 143–67. Améry's friend Elias Canetti thought this adamant stance of not forgetting problematic: in the end, talking so much about suicide, he almost had to commit it. But, then, Canetti had spent the war years in England in relative safety, and his reaction to the "killing years" was to explore death as a general social problem. As to Hitchens's reservations about Sebald's sympathies for air raid victims: if not "Air War and Literature," then certainly "Against the Irreversible" should have calmed his fears (probably Sebald's and his publisher's motivation to put these two texts together) if had he read the book.

16. Heinz Schuhmacher, "Wildes Denken," *Profil,* no. 16 (April 19, 1993): 60. See also Heinz Schuhmacher, "Aufklärung, Auschwitz, Auslöschung," in *Mitteilungen über Max Marginalien zu W.G. Sebald,* ed. Gerhard Köpf (Oberhausen: Verlag Karl Maria Laufen, 1998), 58–84. See Cynthia Ozick's gushy review of the *Emigrants,* "The Posthumous Sublime," *New Republic,* Dec. 16, 1997.

17. W. G. Sebald, *The Emigrants* (New York: New Directions, 1996), 29.

18. *Natural History of Destruction,* 70–71.

19. Hitchens, "The Wartime Toll," 183.

20. See Gunther Nickel, "Zuckmayer und Brecht," *Jahrbuch der deutschen Schillergesellschaft* 41 (1997): 428–59, on Brecht's and Zuckmayer's arguments in 1944 against the thesis of a German collective guilt claimed by, among others, Thomas and Erika Mann. Both wanted a "*Züchtigung*" (corporal punishment like flogging) of all Germans by the Allies to last at least ten years (445–47). Carl Zuckmayer, much better informed about the situation in Germany during the last years of the war, answered Erika Mann's collective condemnation "Eine Ablehnung" (*Aufbau,* April 21, 1944, p. 8) with an open letter (*Aufbau,* May 12, 1944, pp. 7–8) in which he argued that not much good would come for either Germany or the

world from fighting the "Wahnwitz (insanity) des Pangermanismus" with an equally "krassen Antigermanismus," which in Zuckmayer's view was in many ways not unlike anti-Semitism (446).

21. See my *Weimar Intellectuals and the Threat of Modernity* (Bloomington: Indiana University Press, 1988). See also ch. 6 of this study.

22. Hitchens, "The Wartime Toll," 183–85; see above, this chapter, and ch. 1 n. 26.

23. See my *Germany 1945*, ch. 3, "What They Saw: Germany 1945 and Allied Photographers."

24. *Germany 1945*, 108–21.

25. *Natural History of Destruction*, 30.

26. Ibid., 31; black clothes indicated mourning—there was death in almost all families; for images of the omnipresent bundles, see *Germany 1945*, 103–109.

27. *From Apes to Warlords* (London: Hamilton, 1978), 352; quoted in *Natural History of Destruction*, 19–20.

28. Zuckerman, *Apes*, 322.

29. *Natural History of Destruction*, 31–32.

30. Peter Schneider, "Deutsche als Opfer? Über ein Tabu der Nachkriegsgeneration," in *Ein Volk von Opfern? Die neue Debatte um den Bombenkrieg 1940–45*, ed. Lothar Kettenacker (Berlin: Rowohlt, 2003), 158–65, 161, 165.

31. Behnke papers, Hoover Institution Archive, Stanford; for images, see *Germany 1945*, 128–35.

32. *Natural History of Destruction*, ch. 2.

33. Volker Ullrich, "Weltuntergang kann nicht schlimmer sein," now in Kettenacker, *Ein Volk von Opfern?*, 110–15. Hitchins might even have read Ullrich's essay, which was first published in *Die Zeit* Nov. 28, 2002; but the two texts were also obvious choices.

34. "Weltuntergang," 114–15.

35. Ibid., 115.

36. Ibid., 114–15.

37. Goldhagen's book tour quickly took on rock-star energies: huge numbers of students spellbound by his dramatic performances of absolute German Evil for which they, as he would always assure them, had no responsibility; like young Americans, they were free to think and do what they liked. And so they adopted their bad past as an interesting, prefabricated identity, to be worn for a while and discarded when it no longer suited them. The real problem was their teachers, the history professors, who had not dared to insist on the historicization of the Nazi period and now decided that it was not in their interest to control what had become a nasty circus, of which the crowning event was awarding Goldhagen the Democracy Prize of the Republic at a ceremony in the Beethoven Halle by the social philosopher Jürgen Habermas—not a proud moment for German intellectuals, but a fitting allegory for the loss of historical memory in postwar Germany: see also ch. 5 of this study.

38. The book was so sloppily researched and argued that it would not have passed peer reviews, and no university press would publish it, despite its highly marketable topic; it was published by Knopf for its sensationalism, which promised high sales—approximately 70,000; the German publisher Siedler, a respectable publisher, happily sold approximately 275,000 copies.

39. Hitchens, "The Wartime Toll," 182.

40. *Natural History of Destruction,* 25.
41. Hitchens, "The Wartime Toll," 184–85.
42. Richard Overy, "Die alliierte Bombenstrategie als Ausdruck des 'totalen Krieges,'" a lecture given at the conference "A World at Total War" (Hamburg, 2001), now in Kettenacker, *Ein Volk,* 27–47, 28–29. See also Richard Overy, *Why the Allies Won* (New York: W. W. Norton, 1996). For more on the strategic circumstances, including the need to keep Russia in the war, see below, this chapter.
43. Overy, "Die alliierte Bombenstrategie," 30–31.
44. Ibid., 32–34.
45. Ibid., 40–41.
46. See *Germany 1945,* 66–67.
47. Friedrich is a respected, award-winning expert on the history of the Nazi regime, WWII, and its aftermath. See *Das Gesetz des Krieges: das deutsche Heer in Russland 1941 bis 1945: der Prozess gegen das Oberkommando der Wehrmacht* (1993); *Die kalte Amnestie: NS-Täter in der Bundesrepublik* (1984); *Freispruch für die Nazi-Justiz: die Urteile gegen NS-Richter seit 1948: eine Dokumentation* (1983); he also contributed to the *Enzyklopädie des Holocaust.*
48. Günter Grass said at the time that there was no evidence to support the reproach of anti-Semitism and that the Jewish German literary critic Marcel Reich-Ranicki satirized in Walser's novel *Tod eines Kritikers* had been very aggressive in his attacks on many writers over many decades (DPA, *FR Online,* Nov. 28, 2002). Grass thought that Walser should have written an essay instead of a novel, but Walser is preeminently a storyteller. Besides, the hurriedly and badly written novel made him a lot of money.
49. *Economist,* Nov. 23, 2002, p. 26.
50. Among the newspapers notably the *Times* (Nov. 19, 2002), with a good summary of Friedrich's arguments, in contrast to the *Daily Telegraph* (Nov. 19, 2002) and *Daily Mail* (Nov. 20, 2002), where almost nothing is said about the book's arguments and Friedrich's Churchill critique sharply rejected. Correlli Barnett's *Daily Mail* article, "Bombing of Germany Not a War Crime," denounced Friedrich's arguments as complete nonsense. Admitting that he had not read the book, Barnett, Keeper of the Churchill Archives Center and Fellow of Churchill College, Cambridge, thought its critique of Churchill an unforgivable offense and claimed wrongly that Friedrich had equated Churchill's area bombing with the "unspeakable atrocities" of Nazi war criminals, which could only be damaging in the current European situation (a "fear" also expressed by the *Daily Telegraph*). Interesting is Mark Connelly, "The British People, the Press, and the Strategic Air Campaign against Germany, 1939–45," *Contemporary British History* 16, no. 2 (Summer 2002): 39–58. On the basis of press reports, Connelly documents an explicit general informed British approval of the increasingly destructive all-out air war against Germany. The lead article in the *Daily Mirror* of Sept. 12, 1940, had already called for limitless air attacks, arguing that the distinction between combatants and civilians was no longer valid in modern warfare and thereby anticipating Churchill's stated position two years later. Starting with overly optimistic reports of the RAF's initial attack on the German fleet in Wilhelmshaven on Sept. 5, 1939 (meant to immediately impress Nazi Germany with British power in the air), the British press would enthusiastically celebrate the military and moral power of the air war, the more so the more limitless it appeared. See also Mark Connelly,

Reaching for the Stars: A New Interpretation of Bomber Command in the Second World War (London: J. B. Tauris, 2001). Richard Overy's critical review of *Der Brand*, in *Stern*, Dec. 18, 2002, "Barbarisch aber Sinnvoll," calls Friedrich's "assumptions" about the military effectiveness of area bombing "simply wrong" despite the ongoing historical debate of this issue.

51. See n. 36 above.

52. Kettenacker, "Churchill's Dilemma," *Ein Volk von Opfern?*, 48–55, 55.

53. Ibid., 53.

54. Ibid., 51.

55. Ibid., 50. *Bekanntlich* extends to German historians at German and U.S. universities, not to speak of German politicians and public intellectuals, but they rarely remind their readers of this very important fact. Kettenacker has taught in England for many years, perhaps one of the reasons for his fairness in this matter. William Shirer notes in his *Berlin Diary* on August 31, 1939, that the German population is against the war, that many complain about lack of information, and that the *Sicherheitsdienst* of the SS has informed the *Reichskanzlei* repeatedly about "*mangelnde Kriegsbereitschaft.*"

56. Hans Mommsen, "Moralisch, strategisch, zerstörerisch," in Kettenacker, *Ein Volk,* 145–51, 145 and 147.

57. Ibid., 147. Mommsen also argues in this context that Friedrich is not interested here in a mutual *Aufrechnung* of war crimes, and that his earlier work, especially his study of the crimes of the Wehrmacht in Russia (see above, n. 47) would in general hardly put him into the camp of those who want to engage in such *Aufrechnung.*

58. Ibid., 148.

59. Quoted Friedrich, *Der Brand,* 109.

60. See *Germany 1945,* 126: the eerie photograph of the shadows of allied planes flying very low over a farm house.

61. Friedrich, *Der Brand,* 108–109.

62. Ibid., 109.

63. Ibid., 112.

64. Ibid., 358. This approximate figure does not include all the fatalities of February 13–14. David Irving, *The Destruction of Dresden* (New York: Holt, Rinehart and Winston, 1964), the early classic account of that "poster child" air raid, describes the "double-blow" attack of 1,400 British planes as "the most successful night raid in the history of Bomber Command" (158). Only six of the planes were lost, since there was no defense on the ground. In the early morning, after the RAF was done, 1,350 American Flying Fortresses and Liberators moved in on Dresden for a day raid, the third heavy attack in fourteen hours. In Irving's account, the combined attacks came at the cost of 135,000 lives: "For the first time in the history of the war, an air raid had wrecked a target so disastrously that there were not enough able-bodied survivors left to bury the dead" (158). Respected for his archive research but also, more recently, tainted by his problematic relations with the radical right, Irving has tended toward higher approximations of German losses. Survivors of this horrendous triple attack, myself included, have remembered bodies lying around for days. Like many other women, my mother walked long distances and queued up for hours to get food for us and, above all, less-contaminated water. I remember much anxious talk about the rapidly growing typhoid and polio epidemics.

65. Friedrich, *Der Brand,* 362–63.

66. Irving, *Destruction,* 154, quotes from the German High Command's secret situation report: "For the first time a daylight attack was delivered by all available American heavies in the West on Dresden; firestorms were caused by this attack and those of the previous night. . . . Only 146 of our dayfighters [took off] in Dresden's defense; they were savagely beaten down by 700 American fighters. We shot down two bombers, but 20 of our bombers are missing."

67. Friedrich, *Der Brand,* 358.

68. Quoted, Irving, *Destruction,* 142.

69. Brockhaus Encyclopedia 2001: "Casablanca Conference."

70. *Der Brand,* 475; see also the photo of young people cheerfully cleaning up after an air raid, moving furniture, books, etc.: *Germany 1945,* 35.

71. *Der Brand,* 483–84, 487. The status of *Ostarbeiter* was more complicated than recent debates of reparations for forced laborers, *Zwangsarbeiter,* may suggest, especially where claims in their name are made by American Jewish lawyers such as the notorious Edward Fagan (whose latest pursuit is organizing American blacks to sue for reparations for slavery). On his unscrupulous, exploitative strategies, see a rare critical assessment in "An Avenger's Path," *New York Times,* Sept. 8, 2000.

72. *Der Brand,* 490.

73. See the images of individual reburial of Nazi victims thrown into mass graves in *Germany 1945,* 16 and 21–25.

74. *Der Brand,* 432.

75. Ibid., 489.

76. Irving, *The Destruction of Dresden,* 141. Contributing factors were jamming of German radio communication during every major night attack since the introduction of Radio Counter Measures in November 1943 and the interruption of telephone communication (the lines to Berlin passed through burning Dresden) so that no calls could be made to authorize the use of the few available anti-aircraft planes. One of the German pilots waiting in their cockpits and helplessly watching the burning of Dresden wrote in his diary: "Result: a major attack on Dresden; the city was smashed to pieces. We had to stand by and look on. How could such a thing have been possible? People are hinting more and more at sabotage, or at least an irresponsible defeatism among the 'gentlemen' in the command Staff. Have a feeling that things are marching to their end with giant strides. What then? Wretched *Vaterland*!" (quoted ibid., 145). Some Lancaster crews felt "almost ashamed" at the lack of opposition, circling the burning city several times, "unworried by any kind of defenses." One of them took a 400-foot-film for the R.A.F. film unit, now in the film archives of the Imperial War Museum, which provides the "final, conclusive evidence that Dresden was undefended: no searchlight, no flak appears on the film throughout its length" (ibid., 146).

77. Ullrich, "Weltuntergang," 114.

78. *Der Brand,* 491.

79. Ibid., 495.

80. Ibid., 504–505. See also the descriptions (505–14) of the physical effects of fire, gas, mines, of being buried alive under collapsed buildings, etc., on human bodies, which are more detailed and more precise than those of Sebald, who might even have found them sufficiently "authentic." In the last paragraph of this chapter Friedrich describes a dead young woman looking like a bad sculpture, "a creature

that does not express any feeling but its creator. It is the sculpture of *Brandkrieg"* (514).

81. *Der Brand,* 524.

82. *Der Brand,* 524–25.

83. *Critical Realism: History, Photography, and the Work of Siegfried Kra-cauer* (Baltimore, Md.: Johns Hopkins University Press, 1994); *Germany 1945.*

84. *FAZ* Online, English Version, Sept. 25, 2003. See Herbert Ammon, "Politisch-psychologisch brisant. Beim Thema Vertreibung weist die deutsche Zeitgeschichtsschreibung grosse Defizite auf," *FAZ,* Aug. 24, 1998, on the gaps in the historiography of *Vertreibung,* and Balduin Winter, "Europäischer 'Geschichtsdialog,'" *Kommune* 5 (2003): 26–27, both of them well-balanced accounts. For predictably moralizing commentaries, see ch. 3 nn. 55, 56, of this study. The numbers are huge and "soft," like all other numbers of mass destruction during WWII and the immediate postwar years: the "deportations" concerned approximately 12 million, 9 million from Poland and the rest mostly from Czechoslovakia; over 4 million became refugees from the eastern provinces, mainly East Prussia, because of the brutalities of the advancing Russian army and the attacks of non-German populations in these areas on all remaining Germans, with whom they had coexisted for centuries. For contemporary photographic and verbal reports on the chaotic migrations of millions of women, children, and old people, see *Germany 1945,* 88–108, 185–94.

85. The Hansestadt Danzig's rich and complex history reflects the frequent shifting of populations and political power in this area. The extensive, mostly German medieval and Renaissance part of the city was almost totally destroyed in 1945—most of the almost forty churches and the patrician houses of the sixteenth to eighteenth centuries.

86. The *Motorpassagierschiff* commissioned by *Deutsche Arbeitsfront,* launched 1937, was named after Wilhelm Gustloff, who had organized a branch of the NSDAP in Switzerland and was killed by a Jewish assassin, David Frankfurter, in Davos in 1936. The ship belonged to the fleet of the organization *Kraft durch Freude* (KdF), in the eyes of many working-class and lower-middle-class Germans one of the most successful Nazi organizations during the prewar stage of the Third Reich, which enabled large populations to see and enjoy parts of the world heretofore reserved for the upper classes. The ship was planned for a crew of 417 and approximately 1,465 passengers and took its first trip in March 1938; during the war it was used as a hospital ship anchored in Gotenhafen. Of the approximately 10,600 people onboard only 1,252 could be rescued by other ships.

87. Fridtjof Küchemann, "Aufzeichnungen eines Einsiedlerkrebses," *FAZ,* Feb. 5, 2002.

88. *Der Spiegel* Online, 2002/6.

89. Carol J. Williams, "We, the Victims Too," *LA Times,* Mar. 18, 2002, online, quotes Reich-Ranicki, who has mostly been critical of Grass's writing, as having been "moved to tears" by the *Gustloff* story and thinks that his "effusive praise is likely a major catalyst for the soaring book sales" (3). But this seems to me only part of the explanation, a more likely one being the release of an important and gripping wartime historical memory that would not be Reich-Ranicki's concern. Almost all the reviews mention that this is the best-written novel Grass has published in a long time. See also Jeremy Adler's admiring "'Crabwalk': Ship of State," *New York Times,* April 27, 2003, online. Some of his claims for the liter-

ary—and, by extension, moral—achievement of the novel are too grandiose; he rightly mentions the very capable (readable) translation by Krishna Winston.

90. "Guenter Grass Worries about the Effects of War, Then and Now," *New York Times,* April 8, 2003, online. Grass states in this interview that he does not agree with some of Sebald's theses in "Air War and Literature."

91. See his family novel *Die Bertinis,* 1982, made into a film in 1988: *Die zweite Schuld oder Von der Last ein Deutscher zu sein* (The Second Guilt, or On the Burden of Being a German, 1987).

92. Ralph Giordano, "Ein Volk von Opfern?," *Jüdische Allgemeine,* Jan. 15, 2003, now in Kettenacker, 166–68. See his approving reference (168) to the review of *Der Brand* by Hans-Ulrich Wehler, "Der Weltuntergang kann nicht schlimmer sein," *SZ,* Dec. 14–15, now in Kettenacker, *Ein* Volk, 140–44 (titled "Wer Wind sät, wird Sturm ernten"). In the *SZ* publication used by Giordano, the essay has subtitles such as "Aus Leidenschaft für die Opfer" (Passionate involvement with the victims), and "Rückzug ins Selbstmitleid" (Withdrawal into self-pity): in both cases misleading since Friedrich's representational narrative is in a very literal sense "objective," object-focused. Depending on their experiences and temperaments, his readers reacted in a variety of ways, and Wehler's essay is notoriously lacking in interest in such variety because he knows "his" Germans and a priori mistrusts them.

93. Hans Michael Kloth, "Vertriebenenverband: Giordano bekennt sich zu Steinbachs Politik," *Der Spiegel* Online, July 20, 2004.

94. As Giordano noted, in the eyes of many Poles Erika Steinbach had become an "icon of the enemy," yet her public demonization contrasted sharply with his own experiences of her conduct as president of the BdV.

95. Brockhaus Encyclopedia 2001. The summarizing article also mentions the "opferreiche Vertreibung" of millions of Germans, in contrast to the victors' self-deluding or simply callous admonitions that the expulsions should be carried out in a "humane and orderly" fashion.

96. Nazi Evil is still a powerful argument for a large majority of American Jews to blindly underwrite the politics of Israel, knowing nothing or nearly nothing about the wartime experiences of ordinary Germans. This is a politically important fact in the age of globalization and ought to have some influence on official German pieties regarding Holocaust and anti-Semitism, precisely because they are expected in the United States.

97. See the articles collected in the *FR* dossier on anti-Semitism over the last several years; for a critical discussion of their semantic strategies, see ch. 3 of this study.

98. *Life,* May 7, 1945, p. 83. These American faces are interchangeable with the faces of young German women contributing to the Nazi war effort as they appear on propaganda photographs: see the image reproduced in *Germany 1945,* 37.

99. Reproduced in *Germany 1945,* 184, 242.

100. Interview Feb. 29, 2004, *Weekend All Things Considered.*

5. No End to "Auschwitz"

1. For images of that scene, see my *Germany 1945,* 8–9.
2. See Elon, "The Politics of Memory," 3–5.

3. See *Germany 1945*, ch. 2 on the Signal Corps Photography Album; ch. 3 on the reflections of the politics of Allied victory in the editorial politics of *Life*.

4. Images of these piles of skeletal corpses would later be central to Holocaust iconography. For images of such "confrontations," see *Germany 1945*, 28–34: they clearly show the fear of the mothers, who had been ordered to bring their children, even younger than ten. A huge typhoid epidemic was sweeping over large parts of Germany at that time without access to hospitals, physicians, medications.

5. See Martin Broszat's "Plea for a Historicization of National Socialism," namely a historiographical approach that would focus on the entire Nazi period as experienced by Germans at the time, a perspective more differentiating than that of the "final solution" (*Merkur,* May 1985). Against the historian Broszat, the Holocaust scholar Saul Friedlander upheld the supra-historical uniqueness of the Holocaust requiring poetic rather than historiographic representation, arguments that are still made today: see ch. 1 n. 17, and ch. 2 nn. 4, 6, 7, 8, and 9, of this study.

6. Peter Novick, *The Holocaust in American Life* (Boston: Houghton Mifflin, 1999), 7–8 (hereafter in the text *HAL*).

7. "Moralisierung allein reicht nicht," interview with Ute Frevert, *TAZ*, Sept. 14, 2004. See also Aleida Assmann und Ute Frevert, *Geschichtsvergessenheit— Geschichtsversessenheit: Vom Umgang mit deutschen Vergangenheiten nach 1945* (Stuttgart: DVA, 1999), a study that affirms the uniqueness of Auschwitz and an indefinitely enduring German moral and political obligation to "never forget."

8. Robert Woodward, *Plan of Attack* (New York: Simon and Schuster, 2004), 320–21.

9. The usefulness of association with the Holocaust in politically trying situations such as scandals or elections also calls for its documentation: photo opportunities at Holocaust memorials have become a "must" for traveling politicians who want to stress the gravitas of their agenda. When Vice President Bush went to Israel, he took along a film crew to document his visit at Yad Vashem; the "most imaginative and subtle photo op," in Novick's view, came up in 1996 when Elie Wiesel lent his highly visible moral-political support to the beleaguered Hillary Clinton by appearing with her in the gallery of the House during the president's much televised State of the Union Address.

10. Novick, *Holocaust,* 249, nn. 39 and 40.

11. *New Yorker,* June 16 and 23, 2003, pp. 69–70.

12. See the ambivalent analysis in Michael Ignatieff, "Balkan Physics: Behind the Lines of Europe's Worst Conflict since 1945," *New Yorker,* May 10, 1999, pp. 68–80. For the German critique of the intervention and of the political uses of the Holocaust in this context, see Günther Jacob, "Die Metaphern des Holocaust während des Kosovo-Kriegs," *1999* 15 (2000): 1, 160–83.

13. This was clearly Tony Blair's motivation for speaking of a "racial genocide" in Kosovo: Interview with Lehrer, PBS, *NewsHour with Jim Lehrer,* April 23, 1999.

14. See Novick, ch. 3, "The Abandonment of the Jews," on the political uses of the alleged lack of American intervention on behalf of Jews during WWII. On stripping the German civilian population of its civilian status, see ch. 4 of this study.

15. Where the Kosovo conflict was based on an ideology of the territorial, Nazi ideology was supra-territorial: the perceived enemies of the *utopian* construct, the Third Reich, notably Jews and Communists, were international and had to be pursued everywhere to be excluded and finally annihilated.

16. See Novick's balanced and rational account of the uses to which remembrance of Jewish victimization as "lessons" for U.S. policies of intervention in foreign crisis situations, including Bosnia, has been put in the last decades: *Holocaust,* ch. 11, "Never Again the Slaughter of the Albigensians" (esp. 251–55). He quotes "offended" Jewish reactions to this use of "the Holocaust" as "trivializing" its extreme nature and its "uniquenes" but also strong sentiments supporting the analogy as long as it helped the decision for intervention (252–53).

17. See the staging of Reagan's visit to Omaha Beach and Utah Beach on June 6, 1984, on the fortieth anniversary of D-Day as part of a symbolic reconstruction of the Good War, not in historical terms but in the terms of a "total verinnerlichte Bilderwelt des Zweiten Weltkriegs"—a staging for which Reagan was the perfect actor: Manfred Henningsen, "Zur Symbolik des Zweiten Weltkriegs heute," *Merkur,* May 1985, pp. 444–51, 448.

18. See the explanation for the decision to go to Bitburg in Lily Gardner Feldman, "The Jewish Role in German-American Relations," in *The German-American Encounter Conflict and Cooperation between Two Cultures 1800–2000,* ed. F. Trommler and E. Shore (New York: Berghahn, 2001), 182: the wreath-laying ceremony was Reagan's "thank you" to Kohl for accepting Pershing missiles on German territory.

19. For a discussion of the Historians' Dispute, see ch. 2 of this study and *Germany 1945,* ch. 5, "Views of the Past."

20. See Norbert Frei, "Die Invasion," *FR,* June 2, 2004. There were protests coming from British veterans but Frei notes a "schwindende Zeitgenossenschaft": changes of attitude and belief as time passes. However, the history professor Frei still insists on the transhistorical uniqueness of "Auschwitz," which he wants to be accepted as historical "truth": see his article in *SZ,* Sept. 9 and 10, 2000.

21. Quoted Novick, 227 (339, n. 83).

22. Novick, 227; he also reports on the answers to another question in the committee poll: do we need to be reminded of the Holocaust annually, or should Jews stop focusing on the Holocaust after forty years? Forty-six percent wanted annual reminders of the Holocaust; 40% thought it was time to let up on it. Novick adds: "My guess is that some part of the 40% reflected resentment at the embarrassment recently visited on a popular president" (339, n. 85).

23. *Droste Geschichtskalendarium. Chronik deutscher Zeitgeschichte,* 3.1: *Das besetzte Deutschland 1945–1947,* 25.

24. Directive Joint Chiefs of Staff, April 26, 1945. For Eisenhower's strict if unsuccessful rules against "fraternization," see my *Germany 1945,* 59–63. In the fall of 1945 Eisenhower told the Germans that they were on their own regarding food, shelter, heating, and medical services, with the result that the bitter winters of 1945–46 and 1946–47 produced very high death rates, especially among older people and children. Chaotic and extremely difficult living conditions continued for several years after the war.

25. See a reproduction of that poster in Christoph Klessmann, *Die doppelte Staatsgründung. Deutsche Geschichte 1945–1955,* Schriftenreihe der Bundeszentrale für politische Bildung, vol. 193, (Bonn: 1982), 308; see reproductions of photos of Germans looking at photos and movies of the "atrocities" in *Germany 1945,* 8–10.

26. The French prosecution, "alone among the four victorious powers, made

no distinction between the Nazis and the rest of the nation (Eugene Davidson, *The Trial of the Germans* [New York: Macmillan, 1966], 7). France also did not comply with the rules of the Geneva Convention regarding the treatment of POWs but kept German POWs as forced laborers for several years after the end of the war, if under tolerable conditions. Russia kept back about 2.5 million POWs for the same purpose, of whom only about 5% survived to return many years later, when they were no longer fit for work: see the images in my *Germany 1945,* 178, 180.

27. See here Barnouw, *Visible Spaces,* ch. 4, "The Quality of Guilt: The Trial of the Germans."

28. See my *Germany 1945,* ch. 1, "To Make Them See: Photography, Identification, and Identity," and ch. 3, "What They Saw: Germany 1945 and Allied Photographers." The term "atrocities," as distinguished from war crimes, was introduced by Telford Taylor: see his *The Anatomy of the Nuremberg Trials: A Personal Memoir* (New York: Knopf, 1992), chs. 1 and 2.

29. See Jürgen Steinle, *Nationales Selbstverständnis nach dem Nationalsozialismus Die Kriegsschuld-Debatte in West-Deutschland* (Bochum: Universitätsverlag Dr. N. Brockmeyer, 1995), "Anklage der Alliierten," 40–42. Steinle has the most comprehensive documentation and discussion of the intense and extensive German debate of collective guilt, especially during the years 1946–1948: see his list of primary sources, 178–92.

30. Willy Brandt, *Erinnerungen* (Frankfurt/M: Suhrkamp, 1989), 13; see also Hans Mayer, *Ein Deutscher auf Widerruf. Erinnerungen,* vol. 1 (Frankfurt/M: Suhrkamp, 1982), 322. Mayer, in 1945–46 a stateless communist working as an editor for the American occupation forces, later a well-known literary critic in East and West Germany, was negatively impressed by the overbearing anti-fraternization regulations: "Dachte man nach über diese Anordnung der Sieger, so glich sie in bedenklicher Weise den Doktrinen und Praktiken deutscher Eroberer gegenüber den besiegten Untermenschen." See also the useful notes of Karl Jering, *Überleben und Neubeginn. Aus dem Tagebuch eines Deutschen 1945/46* (Munich: Olzog, 1979), 161: "In der Zugehörigkeit zu einer Nation liegt weder ein Verdienst noch eine Diskriminierung; dass hier verwerfliche Kategorien der Nazis von den Siegern weiter geführt werden, hängt mit der traurigen Erfahrung zusammen, dass die Sieger nur allzu willig die Laster der Besiegten annehmen" (April 18, 1946).

31. It appears also in the captions of Army Signal Corps photographs of anybody wearing a KZ jacket, a very desirable property: *Germany 1945,* ch. 2, "The Quality of Victory and the 'German Question.'"

32. Robert Haerdter, "Kollektivschuld," *Die Gegenwart,* Dec. 24, 1945, p. 10.

33. Ian Buruma, "The Destruction of Germany," *NYRB,* Oct. 21, 2004, pp. 8–12, 8 (hereafter in the text BU).

34. Alfred Grosser, *Deutschlandbilanz. Geschichte Deutschlands seit 1945,* 4th ed. (Munich: C. Hanser, 1972), 70.

35. See the wealth of documentation in Steinle, *Nationales Selbstverständnis,* 40–73 and passim. Steinle approaches the *Schuldfrage* from different angles, which makes for a good deal of (if clarifying) redundancy. But for the patient reader it is an intelligently argued documentation of the intellectual climate of these fascinating and difficult years.

36. Eugen Kogon, "Gericht und Gewissen," *Frankfurter Hefte,* April 1946, pp. 25–37, 36. Searching for explanations of the catastrophic Nazi persecutions,

this essay has a great many clichés about "the Germans," their idealizing of *Gemeinschaft*, their inability to take risks (like resistance to the Nazis) as individuals, their dreaming rather than doing, etc. One year later, Kogon's essay "Das Recht auf den politischen Irrtum" (*Frankfurter Hefte*, July 1947, pp. 641–55) explored the *Schuldfrage* in much more differentiating and realistic terms, including a nicely factual account of the confusions, corruption, and hypocrisy of denazification (645–49).

37. On the comments of former KZ inmates at a November 1945 test showing of *Die Todesmühlen*, the first film about the camps shown to Germans in the public space of a movie house, see *Germany 1945*, 148.

38. Steinle, 57. On the argument of Germany's conduct in WWI as "(almost) singular" in the context of Allied attempts at legitimatizing the (in this case) not unproblematic German war guilt thesis, see ibid., n. 124.

39. Quoted in Theodor Eschenburg, *Jahre der Besatzung 1945–1949* (Stuttgart und Wiesbaden: Deutsche Verlags-Anstalt, 1983), 58. See also Jering, *Überleben*, 166: "Wie ständen die Sowjets da, wenn der Prozess in Moskau geführt werden würde?" and ibid., 158: "Peinlich nur, dass die Befreier der Welt von Bluttat und Willkür als ihren wichtigsten Verbündeten Josef Stalin benötigten, der zur ideologischen Festigung seines Regimes u.a. 12, 000 000 Bauern umbringen liess."

40. "A Letter on Germany," *NYRB*, Dec. 3, 1998, pp. 19–21.

41. Reifenberg quoted in Steinle, *Nationales Selbstverständnis*, 58. In the beginning of the Nürnberg Trials press reports were positive and hopeful that they might initiate a learning process. The interest and hope waned as the trials dragged on and it became more and more obvious that this was in fact largely the victors' (not always sufficiently informed) justice.

42. See my "Inländische Differenzierungen: Kästner und die *Neue Zeitung*," in *Die Zeit fährt Auto—Erich Kästner zum hundertsten Geburtstag*, Katalog Beitrag Exhibition Deutsches Historisches Museum, Berlin, 1999, 143–52.

43. Harold Hurwitz, *Die Stunde Null der deutschen Presse Die amerikanische Pressepolitik in Deutschland 1945–49* (Cologne: Verlag Wissenschaft und Politik, 1972), 64–76.

44. *Geschichte als Bildungsmacht* (1946), quoted Steinle, *Nationales Selbstverständnis*, 59.

45. See the influence of this cultural Nationalism on National-socialist cultural politics, ch. 6 of this study.

46. For documentation of this perspective, see Steinle, *Nationales Selbstverständnis*, 174–75.

47. For excerpts of his speech, see "Facing the Mirror of German History," *New York Times*, Oct. 22, 1988, International, p. 4. See also Gordon Craig, "Facing Up to the Nazis," *NYRB*, Feb. 2, 1989, p. 1. In a critical essay on the German reception of Daniel Goldhagen's *Hitler's Willing Executioners*, Andreas Helle refers to Goldhagen's 1996 thesis of a specifically German "annihilationist" anti-Semitism as a "distorted echo of the bizarre debate of the late 1980s on the uniqueness of the mass murder of European Jews." ("Kein ganz gewöhnlicher Streit: Zur Zeitgebundenheit der Goldhagen-Debatte," *Leviathan. Zeitschrift für Sozialwissenschaft* 25 [1997]: 251–70, 268). But the issue of the "uniqueness of Auschwitz" has proved tenacious and has reemerged in full force in the current bizarre debates of allegedly reemerging German anti-Semitism: see ch. 3 of this study.

See also the new ironical twist to arguments along this line that now berate the Germans for having been too preoccupied with their bad past to notice the rapid growth of an increasingly aggressive Muslim *Parallelkultur* in Germany, with its own institutions of religious education and law (Shariah). Financed by the German government to avoid the familiar accusations of *Fremdenfeindlichkeit*, racism, and anti-Semitism, these premodern institutions are now seen as a profound threat to multiculturalism by anti-anti-Semitic public intellectuals such as Ulrich Beck ("Globalisierung des Hasses. Parallelgesellschaften und Multi-Kulti-Träume)" and Y. Michael Bodemann ("Unter Verdacht. Parallelgesellschaften und Anti-Islamismus," both in *SZ*, Nov. 20–21, 2004). Bodemann equates anti-Semitism and anti-Islamism in order to accuse "the Germans" of both; Beck blames the still somehow collectively anti-Semitic Germans for not having been sufficiently anti-Islamic. The absurdity of this argumentation after years of sermonizing about the bad German past is familiarly lost on both of them and was echoed abundantly in the German elite press in late 2004 after the spectacular murder by Muslims of the Dutch documentarist Theo van Gogh because of his sharp critique of their culture of aggression.

48. This is the theme of Bernhard Schlink's *The Reader* (New York: Vintage, 1998).

49. See the arguments in ch. 2 of this study.

50. Steinle, *Nationales Selbstverständnis*, 55. Drawing on the papers of politicians who were active in the immediate postwar years, Steinle (42–53) documents the different approaches to the *Schuldfrage* in day-to-day political discussions of policies and strategies, and the political-intellectual discussions concerned with the moral implications of German collective guilt. Social-democrats speaking for the working classes rejected in toto the thesis of collective guilt since the German *Arbeiterklasse* had paid their dues by suffering persecution, and thus moral questions were less important. See also ibid., 64–68, on ordinary Germans' reactions to arguments of collective guilt and shame.

51. "Eine der wichtigsten Aufgaben der Therapie, *die* Deutschen zur Anerkennung dieser Schuld zu bringen" (quoted in *"Als der Krieg zu Ende war": Literarisch-politische Publizistik 1945–50,* Ausstellung des Deutschen Literaturarchivs im Schiller-Nationalmuseum Marbach, ed. Bernhard Zeller [Munich: E. Klett, 1973]); on reeducation see Steinle, *Nationales Selbstverständnis*, 68–73.

52. Carl Gustav Jung, "Nach der Katastrophe," *Neue Schweizer Rundschau,* NF 13/1945 (June 1945). Despite his warnings, his widely read essay was used to argue that collective guilt was a moral judgment. Alexander Mitscherlich, "Geschichtsschreibung und Psychoanalyse," *Schweizer Annalen* (1945): 604–13.

53. See here the arguments in ch. 2 of this study.

54. The hugely successful representation of Jewish persecution during the fifties, the play and the movie based on the diary of Anne Frank, shared in and contributed to this universalism. Later the Hacketts' much praised adaptations of the diary for the stage would be attacked as "de-Judaizing," "stealing our Holocaust"—to the point where Cynthia Ozick could still argue in 1997 that given the damage done by the universalizing of Anne's story, it might have been better if her diary had been "burned, vanished, lost" ("Who Owns Anne Frank?" *New Yorker,* Oct. 6, 1997, p. 117).

55. Annette Wieviorka, "Die Entstehung des Zeugen" (hereafter in text EZ),

in *Hannah Arendt Revisited: "Eichmann in Jerusalem" und die Folgen,* ed. Gary Smith (Frankfurt/M: Suhrkamp, 2000), 136–59, 146–47.

56. See here Arno J. Mayer's argument in the introduction to his *Why Did the Heavens Not Darken: The "Final Solution" in History,* and my *Germany 1945,* 204–205. See also Novick, *Holocaust,* quoting Primo Levi: "The greater part of the witnesses . . . have ever more blurred and stylized memories, often, unbeknownst to them, influenced by information gained from later readings or the stories of others. . . . A memory evoked too often, and expressed in the form of a story, tends to become fixed in a stereotype . . . crystallized, perfected, adorned, installing itself in the place of the raw memory and growing at its expense" (275).

57. Tony Judt, "The Morbid Truth: In Defense of Holocaust Obsession," *New Republic,* July 19 and 26, 1999.

58. *LA Times* Book Review, Sept. 5, 1999.

59. Novick, *Holocaust,* 1. The first chapter, "We Knew in a General Way," looks at the historical events of Jewish persecution by the Nazi regime in ways that defy the scenario of "the Holocaust itself": there are the various policies, shifting over time, and perceived differently at different times, of a criminal regime regarding its perceived enemies, and those groups' various experiences. There are also problems with the usefulness of survivors' memories as a historical source: "some may be [useful], but we don't know which ones," Novick writes, quoting the director of the Yad Vashem archive about the unreliability of most of the twenty thousand testimonies collected: "Many were never in the places where they claim to have witnessed atrocities, while others relied on secondhand information given them by friends or passing strangers" (275).

60. This "denial" was the most fervently rejected issue, to be expected from conservative journals such as *Commentary;* but all three reviews of the book in the *New York Times* and a (stunningly hostile) review in the *Boston Globe* were critical of Novick's arguments in general, and of his position on that issue in particular.

61. See *Germany 1945,* 210–12.

62. Jon Wiener, "Holocaust Creationism," *Nation,* July 12, 1999.

63. *Holocaust,* 10. Novick sees a clear connection between an increasing Jewish preoccupation with drawing on Holocaust memory-discourses for group identity and an "inward and rightward turn of American Jewry in recent decades," citing Cynthia Ozick's notorious complaint in 1974 that "all the world wants the Jews dead" and its implications that Jews should focus exclusively on their own persecution and survival (10).

64. David Van Biema in his *Time* magazine review, "Spinning the Holocaust: Has the Century's Signature Horror Been Misused?" quotes James Young, a Holocaust expert, who told him that Novick is "a very good historian, and he wants to close the gap between the knowledge of historians and the public. And to that I say 'Great. But good luck.'"

65. "All about Abish," *New Yorker,* Feb. 16 and 23, 2004, pp. 188–91.

66. Jan-Holger Kirsch, *Nationaler Mythos oder historische Trauer? Der Streit um ein zentrales "Holocaust-Mahnmal" für die Berliner Republik* (Cologne: Böhlau, 2003), 85 (hereafter in text *NM*). Kirsch's study is an instructive and relatively even-handed documentation of the *Mahnmal* debate.

67. Though her closest associate, Eberhard Jäckel, is a respected mild-mannered professor of history: see his "Die Einzigartigkeit des Mordes an den euro-

päischen Juden," in *"Die Juden, das sind doch die anderen." Der Streit um ein deutsches Denkmal,* ed. Lea Rosh (Berlin: Philo, 1999), 153–70. Michel Friedman (see ch. 1 of this study), whose calculated journalistic aggressiveness is shared by Rosh, wrote the preface to this collection.

68. See Rudolf Augstein, "Dampfwalze Lea," *Der Spiegel,* July 10, 1995, p. 35. The Berlin magazine *Tip* ranked her as the "peinlichste [most embarrassing] Berlinerin" of 2003.

69. "Vom Mahnmal zum Wahnmal," *Der Spiegel,* Aug. 24, 1998, pp. 170–78, 173.

70. For a list of public activities and discussions 1999–2004, see Kirsch, *Nationaler Mythos,* 333–38.

71. Christian Jostmann, "Die neue Opfertümelei" (infatuation with the victim status), *SZ,* Dec. 13, 2004.

72. "Abhanden gekommen" (lost), *SZ,* Jan. 12, 2005.

73. *New York Times,* Jan. 27, 2005, and Jan. 25, 2005.

6. This Side of Good and Evil

1. See Joachim Lerchenmüller and Gerd Simon, *Masken-Wechsel: Wie der SS-Hauptsturmführer Schneider zum BRD-Hochschulrektor Schwerte wurde und andere Geschichten über die Wendigkeit deutscher Wissenschaft im 20. Jahrhundert* (Tübingen: Verlag der Gesellschaft für interdisziplinäre Forschung, 1999), 281–84. I have drawn on their research, so far the most extensive, for the discussion of Schneider's career in SS institutions: hereafter in text *MW.*

2. Hans Schwerte, *Faust und das Faustische. Ein Kapitel deutscher Ideologie* (Stuttgart: Ernst Klett Verlag, 1962).

3. Barnouw, *Visible Spaces,* ch. 5, "Visible Spaces: Good Men and Good Citizens."

4. See the arguments in Barnouw, *Weimar Intellectuals,* and *Critical Realism.*

5. *Hannah Arendt, Karl Jaspers Briefwechsel 1926–1969,* ed. Lotte Koehler and Hans Saner (Munich: Piper, 1985), no. 22. In later editions the title was changed to *Max Weber: Politiker-Forscher-Philosoph.* The Italian mystic Joachim of Floris (1145–1202) based his chiliastic concept of history on the assumption of a "third age" or *empirium:* after the age of the Father, and the age of the Son, the age of the Holy Spirit would complete the redemption of mankind. There were many variations of this seductive triad over the centuries, among them Hegel's and Marx's dialectics, and also Möller van den Bruck's conservative projection *Das Dritte Reich* (1923) as the last, redemptive stage after the medieval Holy Roman Empire of the German Nation and the modern German Empire founded by Bismarck. The suggestive term was used for propaganda purposes by National-socialism before WWII, but during the war its use as a name for the National-socialist state was forbidden on Hitler's orders.

6. *Ahnenerbe* (heritage of the ancestors) was founded by the Reichsführer SS Heinrich Himmler and the Reichsbauernführer Richard Walther Darré as a cultural-political center for Nazi *Schulung,* teaching and propaganda of Nazi ideology. SA is the abbreviation for *Sturmabteilung,* which, together (and later in competition) with the SS (*Schutzstaffel*), was the armed political combat unit of the

NSDAP (National-Sozialistische Deutsche Arbeiter Partei), first under the leadership of Hermann Göring (1923).

7. See Barnouw, *Visible Spaces,* 37.

8. He had not yet finished the second doctoral degree, the *Habilitation,* required for an academic career.

9. See here *MW,* 69–70; the old Schwerte told the interviewer Claus Leggewie that the young Schneider's "Königliches Gespräch" (1936), a fictitious conversation during the Seven Years' War between the Prussian king Friedrich der Grosse and the Königsberg scholar and poet Gottsched on the importance of literature for warfare, had made a positive impression on an official of *Rasse- und Siedlungshauptamt,* who then became his mentor and helped Schneider to join the SS when he got into difficulties with the SA over some article he had written for an East Prussian paper: Claus Leggewie, *Von Schneider zu Schwerte Das ungewöhnliche Leben eines Mannes, der aus der Geschichte lernen wollte* (Munich: Hanser, 1998), 54–55.

10. See my *Critical Realism,* ch. 4, "The Shapes of Objectivity."

11. Jan Kershaw, *Hitler 1889–1936: Hubris* (New York: Norton, 1998); *Hitler 1936–45: Nemesis* (2000). Kershaw's voluminous biography is in most part realistic and useful, but there is an overemphasis on Hitler's nonperson as the basis of an all-pervasive Hitler cult that gets in the way of making more understandable the initial appeal of National-socialist rule to many Germans even though they never gave it a majority vote.

12. This tendency has been supported by a generational change in the self-perception of scholars in the field of contemporary history, *Zeitgeschichte:* the generation of young historians, the grandchildren of the *Täter,* are invoking the superior authority of moral concerns when attacking historians of the older generation, the children of the *Täter,* for not having established this distance more rigorously and not having been more receptive to the historiographical work of Holocaust survivors that for them has carried automatic authority: see here the heated debates at *zeitgeschichtliche* conferences of Nicolas Berg's *Der Holocaust und die westdeutschen Historiker. Erforschung und Erinnerung* (Göttingen: Wallstein Verlag, 2003); see also the in parts critical review of the book by Norbert Frei, "Mitläufergeschichten," *SZ,* May 8, 2003.

13. See the argument in Benjamin Alpers, *Dictators, Democracy, and American Culture* (Chapel Hill: University of North Carolina Press, 2003).

14. On the photographic representation of German POWs by U.S. Signal Corps photographers, see my *Germany 1945,* 48–50.

15. On Schwerte's development during these years, see Leggewie, *Von Schneider zu Schwerte,* 40–46.

16. Ibid., 363.

17. See Mechthild Küpper, "Stiefel behalten, Vergangenheit verleugnen," *SZ,* no. 230, Beilage "Das politische Buch": Leggewie "is duped by Schwerte intellectually and stylistically"; see also Ulrich Greiner, "Der Mann mit allzu vielen Eigenschaften," *Die Zeit,* no. 39 (Sept. 17, 1998): Leggewie's book has "made visible the grey zones between opportunism and competence, stupidity and intelligence, mediocrity and individuality" and thereby made it more difficult to sentence Schwerte: "he is our brother or could be"—the ambiguous conclusion to an on the whole judgmental and condescending account.

18. On the intellectual Right during the Weimar period, see my *Weimar Intellectuals and the Threat of Modernity,* ch. 5, "The Magic Spaces of Terror," and the epilogue, "That Certain Grey Veil of Westgerman Boredom."

19. See here the "classic" but not sufficiently heeded analysis of this desire in Helmuth Plessner's 1924 *Grenzen der Gemeinschaft Eine Kritik des sozialen Radikalismus* (Frankfurt: M. Suhrkamp, 2002). See also *The Weather Underground* (2004), an academy-nominated documentary film by Sam Green and Bill Siegel on the student revolution at Columbia University in the late sixties, from the perspective of almost half a century later.

20. Quoted Leggewie, *Von Schneider zu Schwerte,* 13.

21. Schwerte has always denied publicly and in private conversations that he had anything to do with the human experiments concerning extreme cold, and the legal proceedings against him in this matter were closed for lack of evidence: see the arguments and documents below.

22. Ulrich Greiner, "Mein Name sei Schwerte," *Die Zeit,* May 20, 1995.

23. Schneider finished the dissertation in 1935, though there have been questions whether he really was awarded the Ph.D. in the summer of 1935 because of the loss of the dissertation and Hankamer's political difficulties with the Nazis. Hankamer lost the *venia examinandi* in 1936 but not the *venia legendi* (Marita Keilson to Schwerte, Oct. 29, 1998).

24. The model for *Arbeitsdienst* was the *Vaterländischer Hilfsdienst* during WWI, reactivated during the economic crisis in 1931 as voluntary *Arbeitsdienstlager* (work camp) for unemployed youth (18–25 years). The NSDAP introduced the *Reichsarbeitsdienst* in 1935.

25. The untranslatable *Volkstum* was the central concept of Nazi cultural politics: *Volk* as national identity. The organization *Kraft durch Freude* (KdF; strength through enjoyment) was an important aspect of the Nazi utopia of the good life "here and now," in contrast to the Communist utopia of deferred (eschatological) fulfillment. It organized events for workers' leisure time, including trips and cruises with stays in nice hotels in places to which they had never had access before. It gave many lower-middle-class people the illusion—much treasured, as most illusions are—of participating in a larger world, leading more interesting lives.

26. "Gau" was one of the many neologist archaisms invoking Germanic territorial and military power, e.g., the terms for military ranks. They seem silly to us now and seemed silly to many Germans then, but they were an important part of Nazi self-invention in the new-old utopia of the Third Reich. The information regarding Schneider's Königsberg promotion remains sketchy: *MW,* 24–25. Schneider used the title in 1936, before he joined the SS.

27. Intellectual Communism during the Weimar period produced highly speculative erratic arguments: reading Georg Lukacs's essays collected in *History and Class-Consciousness,* the nonbeliever can easily be depressed by their irrationalism: see my "Postmodernism and Weimar Culture," *Arcadia* 38, no. 1 (2003): 23–38.

28. The form, if not the content, of these self-affirming and -motivating pep talks shares certain qualities with the warrior business "culture" of twenty-first-century America with its emphasis on the new and innovative, the combative, competitive, constructive energy, the semi-religious belief in the elite group, the role of the new men and women in their shared effort of building the organization.

29. Listed in *Börsen-Zeitung,* Nov. 5, 1936 (*MW,* 55).

30. Weimar cultural individualism was strengthened rather than neutralized by the many individual messianisms invoking redemptive community in abstract terms.

31. Race and population agency (*MW*, 53–55). See *MW*, 69–71, on the difficulties of establishing Schneider's professional movements in 1937 on the basis of archival materials and information obtained from Schwerte. On the history of the *Rasse- und Siedlungshauptamt*, see *MW*, 71–78. The *Rassenamt der SS* was established by the order of Himmler in January 1932 (headed by Richard Walter Darré); was reorganized in June 1932 as *SS-Rasse- und Siedlungsamt* after the prohibition of SA and SS by the Brüning administration on April 1, 1932, which was revoked on June 16, 1932, by the succeeding Papen administration; and was renamed *Rasse und Siedlungshauptamt* in January 1935.

32. Leggewie, 62–64, does not explicitly blame Schwerte for remembering these years in these terms; but his perspective on lower-middle-class ambitions is typically contemptuous—they "profit" from, "exploit" the revolution from the Right—and his portrait of the young Schneider emphasizes the restrictions of his lower-middle-class (*kleinbürgerlich*) background and at best average talents; Schwerte, a member of the elite, is given much more respect, and the difference is not the criminal involvement of his former self but the class difference. It is important to keep in mind the rigid German class stratification that survived into the postwar era: it partly explains the original success of National-socialism as (illusionary) equalizer and the intellectuals' curious hatred for anything *kleinbürgerlich*, partly because many of them have risen out of this class—which would be very common but also something to be proud of in the United States.

33. At one point Schneider had unsuccessfully applied for a position in art history in the *Rasse- und Siedlungshauptamt*.

34. Leggewie, 64, thinks that precisely this concept of a new elite would have been particularly attractive to a person like Schneider.

35. At the end of the war, Sievers was sentenced to death for getting involved with Himmler's notorious *Unterkühlungsexperimente*, experiments with human subjects, testing the effects of extreme cold. Later they would be of great interest to the U.S. Army, causing international concern about the ethics of using the German data.

36. Lerchenmüller and Simon point out that the authors of the articles were frequently *Germanisten* in high positions at NSDAP institutions: *MW*, 163.

37. "Arbeitsplan für die Mitarbeiter des Ahnenerbes in dem Sektor Holland des Reichsministeriums für Volksaufklärung und Propaganda" (Oct. 1939): details in *MW*, 177.

38. Another good example for the structural link between *Ahnenerbe* and the universities, Plassmann, a Ph.D. in Germanic philology (dissertation on a Dutch mystic) was badly wounded in WWI and after the war was denied the career of research librarian because his wounds, though no impediment to his work, excluded him from the status of civil servant held by all German academics—a nice example of administrative "logic" that left him unemployable. He made connections to Dutch groups sympathetic to National-socialism in 1937, became head of the section "Germanische Kulturwissenschaft" in *Ahnenerbe* in 1938, finished his *Habilitation* with the respected Hermann Schneider (the first rector of Tübingen University after WWII) in 1943, and began his university career.

39. A "Stosstrupp" "leidenschaftlich und kämpferisch einsatzbereit" (quoted in *MW,* 164).

40. See the protocol of this meeting: "Der eigentliche kulturpolitische Zweck der Tagung soll durch möglichst wissenschaftliche Themengebung getarnt werden." We do not know who made this statement, which also could have been the summary of a group discussion of this issue (quoted in *MW,* 220).

41. The lecture was summarized in the minutes as an argument for an "Umwertung von Germanenkunde zum Erziehungswerk, ein sinnvoller Kriegseinsatz der deutschen Geisteswissenschaften": *MW,* 219–21.

42. See Joachim Lerchenmüller, "Hans Ernst Schneiders/Hans Schwertes Niederlande-Arbeit in den 1930er bis 1950er Jahren," in *Griff nach dem Westen. Die "Westforschung" der völkisch-nationalen Wissenschaften zum nordwesteuropäischen Raum (1919–1960),* ed. Burkhard Dietz, Helmut Gabel, and Ulrich Tiedau (New York and Berlin: Waxmann, 2003), 1111–40, 1131–32.

43. *Griff nach dem Westen,* 1132.

44. Hans Ernst Schneider, *Königliches Gepräch* (Braunschweig, Berlin, and Hamburg: Georg Westermann, 1936), 52–53.

45. Quoted *MW,* 242–43 and *Griff nach dem Westen,* 1133–34.

46. See *Germany 1945,* 181–85.

47. Leggewie, 54–55: this is Schwerte's explanation tentatively corroborated in *MW,* 69–70; Leggewie speculates that Schneider may have been connected at that time with *Sicherheitsdienst,* the office for security; Simon and Lerchenmüller think this unlikely on the basis of Schneider's correspondences and other archival documents. His difficulties with the SA had to do with his freelance journalism for East Prussian papers.

48. See *MW,* 70: *Rasse- und Siedlungshauptamt* appears to have been a transition to either the SS elite institution *Ahnenerbe* or *Sicherheitsdienst.*

49. Leggewie, 80–84. Among other things, Schneider was prevented from going to Poland at that time by a serious case of paradontosis (Leggewie, 82). The prosecution's preliminary proceedings in the question of Schneider's "Beihilfe zum Mord" at the Landesgericht München were suspended because of lack of evidence on Oct. 10, 1996 (see *MW,* 372, and correspondence with Marita Keilson, below).

50. More testimonies of former students in Aachen, Leggewie, 28.

51. Theo Buck, "Ein Leben mit Maske oder 'Tat und Trug' des Hans Ernst Schneider," *Sprache und Literatur* 77 (1996): 48–81.

52. See *MW,* 285: "Ich wollte Lehrer werden, welcher Art immer."

53. I am grateful to Marita Keilson for granting me access to her correspondence with Hans Schwerte, 1995–99; it includes many letters that complicate matters—a good thing in this case.

54. She had stated in a lecture at Erlangen University (one in a 1996 series of lectures on the Schwerte affair) her intellectual indebtedness to Schwerte, who had brought to the study of literature broader social and political questions, learning experiences mentioned by many other Schwerte students at Erlangen University in the years 1958–65 ("Hans Schwerte—Irrtum und Neuversuch," *Ein Germanist und seine Wissenschaft, Erlanger Universitästreden* 53 [1996]: 75–81, 75; see also Leggewie, 236–37).

55. Hans Keilson made these remarks in a lecture on his experience of exile, one of a series of lectures on this topic at the Berlin *Technische Hochschule* in

1996. His remarks are quoted in "Zweifache Überwindung," *Berliner Tagesspiegel,* Nov. 8, 1996.

56. Hans Keilson to Schwerte, early Oct. 1997.

57. See his letter to Hans Keilson, May 15, 1998, in answer to his organizational suggestions regarding their planned *Erfahrungsaustausch* (exchange of experiences).

58. See also the "persecution" by the media of Hans Robert Jauss, a distinguished professor of romance languages who had been a young officer in the *Waffen-SS,* a fact he kept secret when applying for graduate study at Bonn University in October 1945. It was discovered, he spent three years in France as a POW, and then he began his studies. In the late nineties, after his retirement from Konstanz University, the Getty Research Center in Los Angeles asked him to build up a research program for hermeneutics, but the highly public offer to a star scholar provoked the objections of the Wiesenthal Center, persuading the Getty Center to withdraw the offer. It was a typically fearful reaction to the fact that their professional interest in an internationally known scholar who half a century earlier had been fully rehabilitated might be "misunderstood"—a curious, if very common, lack of civil courage. Like Schwerte, Jauss had achieved much professionally, contributed much to postwar German culture, but unlike Schwerte, Jauss had paid his dues in 1945, then in his early twenties. A highly ambitious man, used to success and unable to cope emotionally with this, as he saw it, undeserved "fall," Jauss died soon after the media feeding frenzy over "the Jauss affair."

59. "Hans Schwerte—Irrtum und Neuversuch," 80; Marita Keilson here also draws attention to the fact that the protagonist in this mid-fifties story is neither a victim nor a perpetrator.

60. "Ein Leben und zwei 'Identitäten'? Oder: Gelegenheit macht Demokraten. Überlegungen zum Fall Schwerte-Schneider," *Merkur,* no. 562 (Jan. 1996): 73–80, 77–79.

61. Bernhard Schlink, "Auf dem Eis" (*Spiegel* Serie *Hitler und die Deutschen: Hitler's langer Schatten* May 7, 2001; online version, pp. 1–6).

62. "Ein Leben und zwei 'Identitäten'?" 80.

63. Marita Keilson to Anke Brunn, Dec. 3, 1995, and Mar. 27, 1996; Anke Brunn to Marita Keilson, Jan. 1996.

64. See Dagmar Barnouw, "Gespenster statt Geschichte: Kollektivschuld und Erinnerung," *Zuckmayer-Jahrbuch 5,* no. 1 (2002): 1–45.

65. *MW,* 254–58: at issue is a list of instruments for the cold experiment. Simon and Lerchenmüeller point out that one could not tell from the list of requested instruments what they would be used for; that it would have been difficult to get the information; that Schneider did not participate in medical conferences, being extremely busy with his *Germanischer Wissenschaftseinsatz;* that there is no evidence that he took part in staff meetings of *Ahnenerbe.* Hans Ernst Schneider's indictment as an accessory to murder, instigated by some of Schwerte's former colleagues at Aachen, was withdrawn by the prosecutor's office in October of 1996 for lack of evidence. See, however, Ludwig Jäger, *Seitenwechsel. Der Fall Schneider/ Schwerte und die Diskretion der Germanistik* (Munich: Fink, 1998), 132–50. Jäger's account is uncommonly suspicious and speculative, as pointed out in great and useful detail in Klaus Weimar, "Schneider/Schwerte und die Germanistik und Ludwig Jäger," *Merkur* 601 (May 1999): 445–53.

66. See however Jäger, *Seitenwechsel*, 7–26, who insists on "völkische Spuren" (traces) in most of Schwerte's postwar work.

67. *Faust und das Faustische*, 10.

68. *Das Nürnberger Gespräch Haltungen und Fehlhaltungen in Deutschland*, ed. Hermann Glaser (Freiburg: Rombach, 1965), 110–11.

69. See Leggewie, 233. He also points out here that in Schwerte's last radio lecture in early 1995, a highly critical review of Botho Strauss's *Spiegel* essay "Anschwellender Bocksgesang," he drew a line between his arguments in the *Faust* book and Strauss's regress to the mythical-tragic, neo-Romantic tradition of *konservative Revolution* (233). Like many French but few postwar German intellectuals, Botho Strauss accused "the West" of having no sense for *Verhängnis* (doomed, catastrophic destiny) and of "Westextremismus."

70. Greiner, "Der Mann mit allzu vielen Eigenschaften" (see n. 17 above).

71. Buck, "Ein Leben mit Maske," 57. Buck also refers to Eberhard Jäckel, "Der SS-Intellektuelle" (*Die Zeit*, March 29, 1996), presenting Schneider as one of the young intellectuals in the "Kerntruppe (core) der Genocidpolitik."

72. See the statement in Gjalt R. Zondergel, "Hans Ernst Schneider und seine Bedeutung für das SS Ahnenerbe," in *Vertuschte Vergangenheit*, ed. Helmut König, Wolfgang Kuhlmann, and Klaus Schwebe (Munich: H. Beck, 1997), 22: "deutlich antisemitische Äusserungen nur selten" (clearly anti-Semitic remarks were rare). Schneider seems to have been part of the not uncommon phenomenon that working with ideological political anti-Semitism did not mean anti-Semitic feelings. This does not make that work less problematic but helps to explain the transformation in the postwar era.

73. Leggewie, 247 and 238–41. Schwerte himself linked the older man's responses to changes and new beginnings to Schneider's responses in the mid-thirties.

74. "'Ich bin doch immun': Spiegel-Reporter Walter Mayr über das zweite Leben des SS-Mannes Hans Schneider," *Der Spiegel*, May 8, 1995, pp. 94–97.

75. Klaus Weimar, "Der Germanist Hans Schwerte," *Vertuschte Vergangenheit*, 46–59, 59. See here also Weimar's assessment that "Schwerte's position in his literary-historical work is not National-socialist, nor are his interpretative writings in any way influenced by an interest in dominance" (ibid.).

INDEX

Adler, H. G., 252
Al Qaeda, 5
Allied, 31, 102; air war (total), x–xii, 8, 26–28, 53, 102–43 passim, 146, 181; and "austerity" politics, 188; and conversion (rebirth) to democracy, 179, 257–58; denazification, 10, 185, 191 (*see also* Nazi); firebombing, 103–42 passim, 167; and German civilians, 107, 126–28, 130–42 passim, 151; German reeducation, 191; as (invading) liberators, 122–23, 172, 177–79; mass destruction of German cities, 111, 113, 123, 130–42 passim, 151, 183; mass expulsions (deportations) of German civilians, 53, 127, 150, 154, 181; and media control, 188; "moral bombing," 110, 114, 122, 135, 137, 148; occupation, 168, 178, 185; political and military ethics of, 184; *Tiefflieger,* 134, 137, 153; total warfare, 114, 121, 126–32, 135–42 passim, 148, 181, 184; as (innocent, omnipotent) victors, 65, 112–13, 122–23, 136, 138, 141–42, 174, 177–82, 188; war of annihilation, 122, 137, 139; war of extermination, 131. *See also* Churchill, Sir Winston
American Jewish Committee, 178
American-German relations: friendship, 28; special relationship, 9
Améry, Jean, 108
Ammon, Herbert, 281n84
Angell, Roger, 63
Arab, 12; anti-Semitism, 90; conflict with the US and Israel, 52, 72, 82, 90, 196. *See also* Muslim
Arendt, Hannah, 16, 57, 71, 78, 89, 174, 194, 198–200, 209, 211–12, 262n15; *Eichmann in Jerusalem,* 56, 194; *The Human Condition,* 209; *The Jew as*

Pariah, 262n15; on Zionist identity politics, 20
Assmann, Aleida, 271n27
Augstein, Rudolf, 289n68
Augustine: on memory, 167–68
Auschwitz, xi, xiii, 8, 19, 59, 78, 89, 150, 170–72; aftermath, 85; collective remembrance of, 33–34, 165–207 passim; commemoration ceremonies, 206–207; cultural centrality of, 7, 19, 33, 176, 206–207; Frankfurt Auschwitz trial, 252–53; historicization of, 33, 76–77, 190, 193–200; politics of, xiii; relativization of, 76–77, 198–99; and ritualization of, 165–207 passim; supra-historical status of, xiii, 3, 7, 24, 69, 176, 186, 190; uniqueness of, 7, 32–34, 45, 52, 64–67, 75–76, 98, 176–77, 186, 190–207 passim. *See also* Nazi: persecution of Jews

Baghdad, 8, 125, 172
Barnett, Correlli, 278n50
Barringer, Felicity, 262n10
Bauer, Fritz, 252–53
Behnke, Albert Richard, 115–16
Bellamy, Edward, 216; *Looking Backward,* 216
Benz, Wolfgang, 70, 82–89
Berg, Nicolas, 290n12
Berlin firebombing, 134
Berlin Holocaust *Mahnmal,* 58, 167, 201–205
Berliner Republik, 59, 68, 75, 202, 210
Berliner Zentrum für Antisemitismus-Forschung, 69, 85
Bismarck, Otto von, 289n5
Bitburg cemetery, 175–77
Blair, Tony, 5, 173
Böll, Heinrich, 112, 255
Bomber Command, 114, 120, 131, 133–34,

DAGMAR BARNOUW is Professor of German and Comparative Literature, University of Southern California, and author of *Weimar Intellectuals and the Threat of Modernity* (Indiana University Press, 1988); *Visible Spaces: Hannah Arendt and the German-Jewish Experience; Critical Realism: History, Photography, and the Work of Siegfried Kracauer; Germany 1945: Views of War and Violence* (Indiana University Press, 1997); *Naipaul's Strangers* (Indiana University Press, 2003), and other books of cultural criticism.